The Transfer of the Sudeten Germans

The Transfer
of the Sudeten Germans

A STUDY OF CZECH-GERMAN
RELATIONS, 1933-1962

Radomír Luža

 NEW YORK UNIVERSITY PRESS · 1964

To the Memory of My Father

PREFACE

THIS STUDY was prompted by a desire to understand the reasons for such a far-reaching historic measure as the transfer of the German minority from Czechoslovakia after World War II. Since one cannot fully understand the transfer without tracing the history of its antecedents, this study is an attempt to summarize the significance of three decades of German-Czech relations. In the Introduction I have outlined the elementary geoeconomic and social factors which underlie the heart of the story. This essential frame of reference shows its usefulness in the unfolding narrative. In Part I, I deliberately returned to the pre-1914 period and selected the rise of pan-Germanism as a first possible point of reference. It was in the Austrian part of the Habsburg Empire that the main tenets of National Socialism were elaborated prior to World War I. The Nazi use of German minorities as the spearhead of a drive for hegemony was a brutal variation of an old theme.

The major topics which run throughout Parts II and III of the study are the consolidation of Nazism in Czechoslovakia, the fall of the Czechoslovak Republic, and the rise of Czech resistance against the process of Germanization. The facts indicate that the decision to transfer the Sudeten Germans from the Republic in 1945–46 arose from the policies of Konrad Henlein, Adolf Hitler, and Karl H. Frank. Thus, the period 1933–45 forms a single bloc whose elements cannot be considered apart from the actual historical context. In this sense, the transfer represents only the final stage which German-Czech relations had reached by 1946. I have thus focused my attention on the basic problems and on the nature of the causes of the transfer. The actual removal of the Sudeten Germans and the present policies of their leaders are described in Part IV.

Except for the introductory chapters, I have arranged the evidence, in the main, in chronological form, so that the many-faceted story of German-Czech relations might emerge, and its various phases might more readily be seen, in proper perspective. Inevitably all the aspects of the story could not receive equal treatment. The narrative has therefore concentrated on what seemed most relevant, at least to this writer. In some parts of the work I have sought to bring the story up to date as much as possible. Thus, I have elaborated upon the Czech resistance movement at some length, because it seems to me that its activities and importance need reemphasis, in view of some current notions about it prevailing in German, Czechoslovak, American, and English literature.

The main problem confronting the historian of the transfer is a lack of primary sources. The present political position of Czechoslovakia and the Soviet Union and the policies of the Western Powers in the classifying of their records prevented the gathering of certain documentary data, some of which are available only in a very incomplete form in secondary sources. Moreover, since some of the issues are still very much alive today, a certain degree of caution is necessary in handling the evidence. Although in some areas the dearth of data presents a major obstacle in assembling and evaluating material, other parts of the story are obscured by a jungle of documents. I have selected for presentation only the evidence pertinent to the narrative. The fact that almost all the data concerning the transfer had to be regarded as conjectural created another fundamental difficulty. I hope I have presented fairly reliable, albeit rough, estimates. Some statistics appeared to be sound, others ill-founded. On the whole, because of the fragmentary nature of many of the statistical data, no one can claim to arrive at strictly accurate figures. A few sections are of a more technical or complex nature. Here the aim was to offer some permanent reference rather than completeness.

The study is a part of all that I have been and known. Therefore my debts are as numerous as the number of people who have helped me to understand the Czech-German problem. My sincere appreciation goes to the late former Czechoslovak Minister František Němec, who generously opened his private papers for my use. I am grateful to former Minister Dr. Ladislav Feierabend, who permitted me to use his unpublished "Memoirs"; to Prof. Eduard Táborský for permis-

sion to quote from his personal papers; and to Dr. Theodor Procházka, who put his unpublished account of the Second Czechoslovak
Republic at my disposal. I am indebted for informative letters to
Mr. G. Bernard Noble, chief of the Historical Division of the Depart-
ment of State, and to Mr. Herman Kahn, director of the Franklin D.
Roosevelt Library. I give particular thanks to the late former Minister
Dr. Hubert Ripka, to former Deputy Premier Dr. Petr Zenkl, to the
late former minister Gen. Antonín Hasal, to Mr. Blažej Vilím,
former secretary general of the Czechoslovak Social Democratic
Party, to Prof. Vladimír Krajina, former secretary general of the
Czech Socialist Party, to Arnošt Heidrich, former secretary general
of the Czechoslovak Ministry of Foreign Affairs, to Gen. František
Dastich, to Dr. František Ševčík, to Dr. Pavel Korbel, and to Col.
Ferdinand Monzer, who gave aid and advice. I should like to thank
the former members of the central political committee of the Sudeten
German Party, Dr. Walter Brand and Dr. Hans Neuwirth, for giving
me valuable information.

Grateful acknowledgment is made to the Bundesministerium für
Vertriebene, Flüchtlinge und Kriegsgeschädigte in Bonn, which was
helpful in providing me with background material. I am much
obliged to Dr. Heinrich Kuhn, director of the Sudetendeutsches
Archiv in Munich, for his friendly help. I should like also to record
my very real gratitude for the patience and courtesy of those who
helped me in the Library of Congress, particularly to Dr. Fritz T.
Epstein; to Dr. Bernard Ziffer of the research section of the Library
of Free Europe Committee, Inc., in New York; to the staffs of the
New York Public Library, of New York University Library, of the
National Archives in Washington, D. C., of the YIVO Institute for
Jewish Research in New York, of the Bibliothèque Nationale and the
Centre de documentation juive contemporaine in Paris, of the In-
stitut für die Zeitgeschichte in Munich, of the J. G. Herder-Institut
in Marburg/Lahn, of the Sudetendeutsches Archiv in Munich, of the
Collegium Carolinum in Munich, particularly to Dr. Karl Wild, of
the Nationalbibliothek in Vienna, of the Institut für osteuropäische
Geschichte und Südostforschung of Vienna University, and of the
Yad Washem in Jerusalem.

I am profoundly grateful to Prof. A. William Salomone for his
constructive criticism of the manuscript. With unstinted sacrifice of
his time he has brought his criticism to bear on the entire manuscript. Needless to say, for whatever errors may be evident I alone
am responsible.

A fellowship from the Samuel S. Fels Fund and a grant from the

M. L. Annenberg Foundation allowed the research and writing to be accomplished in a time of freedom from material responsibility. I warmly thank Mr. Frederick P. Gruenberg, Mr. Dale Phalen, and Mr. Harry C. Coles, Jr., for their sensitive and generous administration of their grants. I wish to acknowledge especially the generosity of Operations and Policy Research, Inc., Washington 16, D. C., in providing help and assistance. Mrs. Ellen Lynn MacKenzie was of invaluable assistance in the preparation of the final version of the manuscript. My wife, who typed the whole manuscript with inexhaustible patience, deserves special thanks.

NOTE

The Czech names of places in Czechoslovakia have been used as a general rule. Wherever an English term exists (Prague, Carlsbad, etc.), it has been used.

Up to 1938, the Czechoslovak crown (koruna, plural koruny, both abbreviated Kč) was equal to one thirty-fourth of a United States dollar. The monetary unit during the Protectorate was the Protectorate crown (K). The post-1945 crown was again the Czechoslovak crown (Kčs).

The hectare (abbreviated ha) is used as the common unit of land measure. It is equivalent to 2.471 acres.

FOREWORD

THE WRITING of contemporary history is a difficult and controversial art. Those who attempt it can afford to harbor no illusions concerning the risks they run in producing works which may be visibly more than ephemeral and still considerably less than definitive. And yet, despite the dangers involved, great masters of the historical craft as well chroniclers of lesser talents have at some time during their careers tried their hand at the recording and interpretation of the history of their own age. In a sense, Thucydides spoke for them all when he wrote, at the beginning of his history of the "great war" between the Peloponnesians and the Athenians, while that epoch-making conflict was still in course, that he believed it to be "more worthy of relation than any other that had preceded it." Each of the great historians who, from the era of the Renaissance to the twentieth century, wrote of his own times offered some implicit or explicit variant of Thucydides' own motivation. Whether they penned accounts of the tragedy or of the splendor of their ages, of great wars and civil conflicts, of a political system at its height or of a civilization in decay, master-historians of the stature of Guicciardini, Clarendon, Voltaire, Ranke, Burckhardt, Meinecke, and Croce have left unique evidences that they could not escape *their* present. When Benedetto Croce came to reflect directly upon this universal, historiographical phenomenon, he arrived at the philosophical conclusion that, in a larger sense, all history is contemporary, not only because great historians had written of their own times but chiefly because even when they had turned their gaze upon the past they had really been impelled by some deep psychological urge deriving from the compulsion of a present problem which secretly stirred them toward historical inquiry. Whatever dangers may lie in the uncritical acceptance and application of Crocean presentism, there is hardly any question that the Italian philosopher had come upon a profound truth which illuminates one of the most powerful, motivating forces behind the intellectual activity of the historian.

Paradoxically, the Crocean distinction between objective spheres upon which the subjective, historical intelligence must necessarily operate has tended to become superfluous in our time. During the half century since 1914, European and world history has become "explosive," not only through the rise and fall of great States and Empires, global wars and continental upheavals transforming traditional systems of world power, and intellectual, cultural, and scientific revolutions shaking the foundations of classic orders of civilization, but also because the quickening of the historical process has centered on an organic metamorphosis, an almost total conquest of the past, with godlike powers of life and death over the future of mankind. In East and West, the past has suddenly come "alive" and has almost literally exploded against the present. Some of the most fundamental problems which men had believed were "resolved" once and for all, as during the "progress" and "evolution" of the pre-1914 liberal era, have engaged again the greatest human efforts. Thus, in our time, millions upon millions of men have had to face the elemental problems of survival or mass death, and the ancient questions of war and peace, of tyranny and social justice, of racial persecution and civil existence. When brave new worlds appeared to be looming on the bright horizons of men's hopes some parts of humanity discovered again and again that in the realm of history the dead do not always bury the dead.

Dr. Radomír Luža's study of the Czech-German problem during the Hitlerian and the post-Nazi periods traces the history of an awesome time past in Central Europe that, in a real sense, refused to "die." Dr. Luža's book is the history of how a freedom-loving people recently attempted to conquer a past during which its lethal German antagonist had brought it to the brink of civil death and to peer over the darkest abysses of national and cultural annihilation.

The author of this important book belongs to a generation of Europeans destined to witness helplessly the eternal recurrence of historic problems and to watch nations and peoples torn by the oscillation between brief historic idylls and stupendous catastrophes. Like the rest of us born during or immediately after the end of the

Great War of 1914–18, Dr. Luža lived the greater part of his
adolescence and youth in an era of almost constant tension between
expectation and frustration, fulfillment and disenchantment. As ado-
lescents we would have looked in vain for the word "totalitarian" in
the classic dictionaries of the West European languages; we had
quickly become men by the time the strange new science of "geo-
politics" was being applied, through the National Socialist conquest
of the bastion of Bohemia. Munich was a geo-cultural expression
when we were children; it was a byword for one of the lowest points
in the demoralization of European politics by the time we were
reaching manhood. We had been stirred to read in our school books
of the deeds of valor of the young patriots and libertarians of the
nineteenth century and we had childishly grown wrathful of the
persecutions against them by "evil," illiberal governments and Met-
ternichian "despots." When the nightmare of the Hitler era began to
subside, we found ourselves stunned before the testimony of evil
in our fellow human beings, of the genocidal beast in the breast of
"civilized" men. We had been taught that the new State of Czechoslovakia was a unique, luminous experiment in multinational democracy. We grew up to see it sacrificed, with many other ideal experiments, in the name of a spurious peace in our time, by the self-
appointed custodians of European law and international security, to
the insatiable German lust for *Lebensraum* and demonic power. And
we watched a new war come just the same.

This was the history which Dr. Luža's generation lived. This is the
contemporary history on which he now writes, not as a participant
but rather as a sensitive chronicler and observer for whom the suffering has become transmuted into a serene, historical reconstruction
of a "great war" and its outcome between Germans and Czechs which
he believes to be "more worthy of relation than any other that had
preceded it."

Dr. Luža's own modesty prevents us from offering here more than
a schematic summary of the exceptional prerequisites he possesses
for his undertaking. Born in Prague, Dr. Luža was sixteen when, together with other members of his generation, he learned that Munich was no longer only the name of the capital of the former German
kingdom of Bavaria. The decade that went from the conquest of
Czechoslovakia to the usurpation of the restored democratic Republic in 1948 saw this young man, whose father was a General in
the Czech Republican Army and later Commanding Officer of the
Home Resistance Army, engaged in a democratic fight for the freedom and independence of his country. In 1939 young Radomír

joined in the underground war against the Nazis. Jailed in 1941, conditionally released, and then hounded again by the Gestapo from September, 1942 to the end of the German rule over Czechoslovakia, he was made Deputy Commander of a Partisan Brigade by the eve of the Liberation in May, 1945. His father had been killed in the underground Resistance against the Nazis; an uncle, former member of the Beneš party in the Czech National Assembly, had been captured by the Germans and perished at Buchenwald. Nazi terrorism, the unspeakable crime of Lidice, the iron clutches of the Gestapo, prison, the Czech Resistance to the German oppressor—these were the first "universities" young Luža attended between the ages of 17 and 23. With the Liberation, he quickly returned to the peaceful pursuits of the intellect and registered in the Faculty of Law at Masaryk University in Brno where, during that fateful month of February, 1948, he was awarded the doctorate "with distinction."

The second fall of the democratic Czech Republic, this time under Communism, saw Radomír Luža, who had become a militant in the young Czech Socialist movement and Acting Chairman of the Social Democratic Youth of Czechoslovakia, once again active in "the Opposition." In the elections during the spring of 1948, Dr. Luža was to be a candidate, with almost absolute chances of winning as a representative from the region of Brno to the Czech National Assembly. The new Communist masters of Czechoslovakia decided otherwise: Dr. Luža suddenly found himself a dangerous *persona non grata* to the regime. In quick succession he was stripped of his Young Social Democratic Party's leadership and then membership in the Czech Socialist movement itself. Stalin's war against an Eastern European Social Democracy, that had greeted Soviet troops in the closing days of the common struggle against the German-Nazi enemy and helped to open the gates of power to the Moscovite activists in Prague, had to be carried to its bitter end. The suicide of Jan Masaryk on March 10, 1948 proved only the last act of moral protest against a fate which had taken his name and the freedom of his country. The incredible pretexts of "ideological deviation" and "political incompatibility" soon covered Dr. Luža and other resisters in a pseudo-legalistic mantle of Machiavellian deceits spun by the new victors in Czechoslovakia. Almost overnight the young Resistance fighter changed from a participant in the Czech War of Liberation against the Nazis to an enemy of the Communist "People's Republic" of Czechoslovakia. There was no chance of victory for underground activity at home—at least not yet, nor in the manner of the recent struggle against the Germans. In March, 1948, Dr. Luža took the

road to exile, via Austria, to Paris and spent five dreary years in
work, waiting, and hope, relieved only by attendance of classes at
the Sorbonne and sustained by the love of his Libuše.

In 1953, Dr. Luža was allowed to emigrate to the United States
where he became an outstanding member of the Council of Free
Czechoslovakia and was appointed to the Executive Committee of the
Socialist International Youth with its headquarters in Vienna. In
New York he became editor of the review of politics and culture,
Svědectví (*Witness*). Through his contribution to this intellectual
and courageous organ of Czech political exile, Dr. Luža sought to
bridge the Manichean approaches of the "two-worlds concept"
which held West and East in the glacial grip of the Cold War. He
emphasized constructive possibilities intrinsic to the pursuit of a
policy of gradual liberalization and humanization vis-à-vis with the
Communist societies of Central and Eastern Europe. Dr. Luža attended the Graduate School of Arts and Sciences of New York University between 1954 and 1959 and was awarded the second doctoral
degree of his career "with distinction," in modern European history.
Though he claims that he has for some time now "made peace with
politics," those of us who know him well wonder how a libertarian
of Dr. Luža's intellectual temper can keep that "peace" as long as
his native country keeps its gates shut against such free sons of
Czechoslovakia.

The political map of Central Europe at the time Dr. Luža was
born appeared to be a splash of new states to the Western observer.
German revanchists and Soviet Communists were of a different persuasion as to what that crisscross of new frontiers signified. The
map represented, in fact, the result of a long historical process by
which Central and Eastern Europe had at long last succeeded in
disengaging from four sprawling Continental Empires, during the
crisis 1917–18. A new complex of nationalities thus emerged. Soon
they were insisting that their demand, in the name of historic tradition, ancient frontiers, and economic and geostrategic necessity, be
fully legalized as their right to constitute self-determining political
communities. For where were the great European Empires of yester-
year—Hapsburg, Hohenzollern, Romanov, and Ottoman—when the
Great War drew to a close? Now the question was: Who were these
claimants from the fragments of the shattered Imperial estates and
how effectively and to what ends would the older members of the
European "family of Nations" grant them the privilege of occupying
ancient places of power? Had those Imperial fixtures disintegrated
into their component "national" parts merely to have these "upstarts"

arrayed one against the other and thus threaten the peace of the world?

Partly in answer to such questions, spokesmen for the suppressed nationalities at least of the Austro-Hungarian Empire, acting under the Wilsonian peace programme of January 8, 1918, on April 10 of that year entered into "The Pact of Rome." The spirit of this compact conjured up again the lines of the grand design for freedom and unity of European peoples which men had thought long ago torn to shreds on the barricades of 1848. In blood-drenched trenches and at home a European humanity, sickened and dying of nationalistic rivalries, glimpsed the possibility that the new multiplicity could be disciplined through limitations imposed upon the principle of self-determination. They were made to hope that both the principle and its necessary limitation would be equally applied in such a way that the "chemistry of history" which had dissolved the old Imperial mixtures might recompose the national elements into sturdier stuff, toward that "Commonwealth of Central European Peoples" which might join as one in the "great experiment" toward a "United States of Europe." For this was the legacy of the "grand design" which had not seemed chimerical in June, 1848, nor alien to the German democrats at the Frankfurt Assembly of St. Paul's Church in 1848–49, before the first experiment at the conciliation of the peoples of Central Europe.

Now, what else can Dr. Luža be telling us in this book but that such hopes inspired the founders and sustained the restorers of freed Czechoslovakia in 1918 and 1945, when he writes of Thomas G. Masaryk's democratic humanism and of Eduard Beneš' liberal Europeanism? Dr. Luža's book is an historical study not of the fulfillment of a great European dream but of a unique European tragedy. Dr. Luža dissects the culminating phase of peaceful coexistence between the Slavic people and the Sudeten German enclaves.

The reconstruction of that "experiment" at Czech-German coexistence given in this book amounts to one of the most lucid and penetrating historical analyses we now have. Dr. Luža is too historically-minded to suggest that a bio-ethnic element makes for the absolute incompatibility between Czech and German. Any such suggestion could justly be interpreted as a delayed contagion by the madness of Nazi racism. As a matter of fact, nothing could be more repellent to Dr. Luža's personal and cultural make-up. As the attentive reader sees for himself, there is too evident a fusion of Western, German, and Slavic cultural elements in Dr. Luža's work to suggest anything short of a secular, ecumenical spirit behind the writing of these chapters on Czech-German relations. There is no doubt that for Dr. Luža the German-Czech conflict and its tragic denouement were the creatures of historic contingency. After the creation of the free Czechoslovak State, the negative elements in that historic contingency, were not attenuated by the blunders of omission committed by the Czech political classes. But none of those political blunders would have been irreparable had they not smashed against their alienation from the new Czechoslovak nation, and then a conspiracy against the very survival of the Czech State by the leaders and the large majority of the Sudeten Germans.

Again and again Dr. Luža reminds us of Masaryk's illusions on the capacity of Czechoslovakia to resist all forces of internal disintegration, and of Eduard Benes' optimistic faith in the West-European system of collective, Continental security. Apparently this security pivoted upon the French chain of alliances and the League of Nations, constituting a built-in protective shield against external attack. To the eve of Munich in September, 1938, no other Central European state appeared to possess sturdier guarantees of its territorial integrity and national sovereignty than democratic Czechoslovakia. But, alas! those guarantees were mere scraps of paper that ultimately secured the Czech Nation and people against every dangerous contingency except the one that then arose to overwhelm them.

Beneš had apparently foreseen all elements which might threaten the unity, indeed the very existence, of the Czech State: the ramifications of the Sudeten German subversion by ideological warfare; the exploitation of "self-determination" as an appeal to the democratic conscience of the West by totalitarians within the Czechoslovak State; responses to such appeals by liberal opinion in England, France, and National Socialist blood-brotherhood on the frontier of the Reich; the fear and need of Soviet Russia for active resistance against German aggression; the ghostly structure of Geneva; the Nazi-Fascist solidarity of the Duce with the Fuehrer; the "neutralist" disengagement of Washington; and, withal, a European humanity fearful of war, eager for a peace whose price it was made to ignore practically until September, 1939. Some time after 1933, Beneš espied these forces at work against the security of Czechoslovakia. He seems to have been unable or unwilling to face, until Munich confronted him with disaster, and to act upon the possibility that those forces might suddenly fuse and that the collective whirlwind could lead to the dissolution of Czechoslovakia. The judgment on Benes by one of the keenest students of his diplomacy, Dr. Paul E. Zinner, seems implicitly harsh but is essentially correct: "In sharp

contrast with the beginning of his career, when he had managed to
secure representation in high international councils without having a
state behind him, Beneš now [at Munich] had to suffer the humiliating experience of having his country's destiny decided without
benefit of consultation with him. It was an ignominious end to a
diplomatic career that had begun so brilliantly."* But Munich was
in fact a tragedy which transcended the private destiny of any
individual.

Dr. Luža's discussion of the Munich tragedy should make it clear
that both the executioners and executors of the Czechoslovak State
and, therefore, the agents and abettors of the dissolution of the first
experiment at democracy in Central Europe bear an historic responsibility before which the errors and defections of the leaders of
the Czech political and social classes, not to speak of the Czech
people, pale into practical insignificance. Whatever political, diplomatic, or military differences separated Masaryk and Hindenburg,
Beneš and Hitler, no one can deny that they belonged to different
breeds of contemporary humanity.

In September, 1938, the Western engineers of Munich had clearly
betrayed their trust in Czechoslovak democracy through the imple-
mentation of an appeasement policy ostensibly designed to placate
Nazism in Germany, to keep the peace of Europe, and to contain
Communism at the frontiers of the Soviet Union. Within six months
Germany had dismembered Czechoslovakia; within a year the
Soviet-Nazi pact signaled the beginning of Hitler's war against the
West; within less than a decade Communist regimes ruled Central
Europe. *Never again Munich!* This, Dr. Luža tells us, became the
foundation of a new moral consensus among the Czech people and it
sustained them through six long years of Nazi tyranny. *Never again
Munich!* After the "satisfaction of the Polish claims" of October,
1938, after the "Vienna Award" to Hungary of November, 1938, after
Hitler's "millennial proclamation" of March, 1939, after the razing of
Lidice in June, 1942, after three years of the Nazi "liquidation policy"
throughout Czechoslovakia, after the Liberation, there could be no
return to the past. In Czechoslovakia, as in Israel, the living felt
called upon to lift the dead hand of the past. The survivors of
Auschwitz, Dachau, Buchenwald, Mauthausen, Ravensbrück, Tre-
blinka, Sachsenhausen, *Landesgericht* I, Berlin-Plötzensee, and
Lidice asserted their right to a life without fear. *Never again Mu-*

---

* Paul E. Zinner, "Czechoslovakia: The Diplomacy of Eduard Benes," in
Gordon A. Craig and Felix Gilbert, eds., *The Diplomats, 1919–1939* (Princeton:
Princeton University Press, 1953), p. 122.

nich! This desperate Czech cry to the Sudeten Germans sounded in some of our Western ears as nothing but a variant of the magnificent apostrophe of Risorgimento patriots to the Austrians: *"Passate l'Alpi e tornerem fratelli!* ("Go back across the mountains and we shall be brothers again!").

At first sight, as one follows Dr. Luža's historical inquiry into the reasons for failure at civil coexistence between two Central European peoples, it might seem superficially plausible that he is engaged in a political activity whose purpose is erecting a moral justification for the post-War transfer policy adopted by Czechoslovakia. Nothing could be further from the truth. Again and again throughout his study Dr. Luža emphasizes that the removal by the Czechs of millions of their fellow citizens was a profoundly painful but necessary action, arrived at after the collapse of all alternatives and then undertaken with the separate and collective consent of all the Great Powers, West and East, who had engaged in struggle with Nazi Germany.

> What for the one [the Sudeten Germans] was a struggle for a greater living space and a hegemonic position, was for the other [the Czechs] a matter of life and death. . . . The dismemberment of the Republic in 1939 stripped bare the true issues of power politics. . . . [The] abuse of democratic freedoms annihilated what remained of the possibilities of German-Czech cooperation and left unbridged a no-man's-land between the two peoples. Henceforward a reconciliation became almost impossible. . . . The idea of a transfer of the disloyal majority of the German group to Germany [was] a necessary measure of protection, not of punishment. . . .

Notice in this passage how, almost imperceptibly, Dr. Luža reiterates conclusions on "practical policy" which derive from the very logic of his historical analysis of German-Czech relations before and after the creation of the Czechoslovak Republic in 1918, the rise of Hitler in Germany in 1933, Munich in 1938, and the dismemberment in 1939.

For Dr. Luža the problem of the Sudeten Germans, like that of the Germans in all Central and Eastern Europe after the Bismarckian era, is clearly a function of the larger question of the power of the German State in Europe. The more than two and a half million Sudeten Germans involved in the transfer from Czechoslovakia after 1945 were not simply passive victims of a wanton political act by a victorious enemy. As Dr. Luža documents, the majority of them had

consistently refused every shred of moral consensus, every show of
political commitment, practically every elementary effort at democratic solidarity at least for the real survival of the Republic. Many
of them had been active in a colossal process through which, in
cooperation with their "brothers" in Germany, they had sought,
through the debauchment of the principle of "self-determination,"
to "go home to the Reich"—a Reich whose hegemonic, geopolitical,
and racial aims had been the living denial of coexistence between
the Germans and practically all other political, cultural, and ethnic
communities in Central Europe. Willingly they had acquiesced in
what Konrad Henlein and his superiors in Germany had told them
of the National Socialist master-plan for victory over the despised
Czech State—and, after March, 1939, that plan was clear for all the
world to see: a policy of annihilation aimed at the Slavic and
Jewish communities of Central Europe, a perverse "grand design"
for a genocide through "assimilation, deportation, colonization, and
extermination."

The "iron policy" of the transfer adopted by the Czechs after 1945,
as Dr. Luža traces its implementation, represented not a contradic-
tion but a coherent sequel to an historical choice made by the bulk of
the Germans of Central Europe, in unison with Germany herself
during her experiment at totalitarian hegemony over Europe. "In
the final historical analysis," says Dr. Luža, "the issue between two
contending groups cannot be reduced to the simple question of moral
values." We cannot but agree. We know of no scales upon which
Nazi genocidal terrorism and the Czech iron policy of the transfer
can be balanced. Certainly the fate of millions of men, women, and
the guiltless young, torn from their homes, can never be a matter of
indifference for anyone who has the most elementary notion of the
limits of retributive justice and of the potentialities of human compassion. And yet, until such time as Immanuel Kant's anti-Machiavel-
lian dream of "perpetual peace" has become a reality for all Nations,
men will be forced to remember the tragic vicissitudes of which
they are guilty and not guilty.

No one has more poignantly caught this tragic sense of the
demons of folly and death than the Czech revolutionary writer,
Julius Fuchik. In the very shadow of the Nazi gallows, only a few
months before he was beheaded by the Gestapo at Berlin-Plötzensee
on September 8, 1943, Fuchik jotted this entry in his secret prison
diary: "Man is not diminished even if he is shortened by a head.
. . . I have never felt rancor toward the Germans." But he further
on exhorted his Czech fellow citizens, all men, "not to forget":

I ask only one thing of you: if you survive this epoch, do not forget. Do not forget either the good men or the evil ones. Gather up patiently the testimony of all those who have fallen for them and for you. Some fine day, today will be the past and people will speak of a great epoch and of the anonymous heroes who have made history. I would want everyone to know that there are no anonymous heroes. They were all persons, with a name, a face, desires and hopes, and the anguish of the least among them was not less great than that of the first whose name will survive. I would like them all to be always close to you like persons whom you once knew, like members of your own family, like yourselves.

These are the words of a free spirit, not of a partisan of the political struggle, for whom men of conscience, are the true actors and victims of human history. With this book, Dr. Luža has courageously fulfilled the exhortation of his martyred compatriot and of all freedom-loving men and women of the European Resistance who fought or fell under the axe of Nazi-Fascism. Not abstract justice but the love of historical truth has inspired Dr. Luža's work. And thus he has indeed patiently gathered here the testimony of good men and evil ones, of the victims and victors in a fearful conflict. This is the document of an immense historic tragedy. It closes a chapter on days of wrath and opens another on future days of fruitful concord between two peoples. It is for all men to see to it that no part of humanity is ever again faced with the terrifying dilemma which confronted the Czech people after their long season in the inferno of pan-Germanic imperialism and Nazi nihilism.

A. William Salomone

University of Rochester
Easter, 1964

CONTENTS

The Transfer of the Sudeten Germans

INTRODUCTION

Economic and Social Foundations
of the German-Czech Problem

The Czechoslovakia[1] which arose in 1918 as an independent state after three hundred years of foreign domination formed an essential part of Central Europe. It stretched across the Bohemian basin and the Carpathian Mountains and guarded the access to the Danube basin, blocking any hostile thrust into Southeastern Europe. Hanging like a dividing curtain between the cultures of the industrial West and the agricultural East, it presented an obstacle to the limitless Eurasian plain spreading from the Caucasus and the Urals across Poland and East Germany. Whoever possessed the Bohemian barrier manned the boundary between East and West, South and North. This focal area could serve either as a channel for the mutual exchange of Western and Eastern influences or as a fortress against invaders from whatever direction they approached.[2] The vital Bohemian control

1. The Czechoslovak Republic had an area of 140,493 sq km (87,299 sq mi). Its frontiers extended for 4,098 km, of which the German boundary totaled 1,539 km. The census of Dec. 1, 1930, listed 14,729,536 inhabitants (of whom 3,231,688 were Germans), including 7,109,376 (2,270,943 Germans) in the province of Bohemia; 3,565,010 (799,995) in Moravia-Silesia; 3,329,793 (147,501) in Slovakia; and 725,357 (13,249) in Sub-Carpathian Ruthenia ([Czechoslovak State Statistical Office], *Annuaire statistique de la république tchécoslovaque*, Prague, 1934).

2. For a survey of geopolitical factors, see Hans Hummel, *Südosteuropa und das Erbe der Donaumonarchie;* David Mitrany, "Evolution of the Middle Zone," the *Annals of the American Academy of Political and Social Sciences*, v. 271 (September, 1950); Johannes Kuhn, "Böhmen in Mitteleuropa—Böhmen in der Welt," *Aussenpolitik*, III (December 1953). A good geographical survey is given by Harriet Wanklyn in *Czechoslovakia* and by E. Meynen, ed., *Sudetendeutscher Atlas* (hereafter to be cited as *Atlas*).

point could become either the basis for a German advance eastward and southward or the narrow western salient of an immense Russian hinterland.[3]

The Czechoslovak Republic was a long narrow country, hard to tie together. Its western part (Bohemia and Moravia-Silesia), a promontory surrounded on three sides by Germany, possessed strong mountain frontiers providing natural barriers and forming a geographical unit that cut across national frontiers. In the past, it had divided the Germans when they advanced eastward along the Danube and crossed over the Elbe. The interior of this western Czech land consisted of rolling country and plains, plateaus and hills.

The natural boundaries did not correspond to the ethnic borders.[4] Within this natural fortress there was a long history of competition between the Czechs and the Germans who had settled there later. The Germans formed ethnic islands in many areas with different cultural backgrounds. Ethnically, they had been related originally to the central and northern Bavarian, east Franconian, upper Saxon, and Silesian tribes.[5] Their present inclusion within a single state, separated from Germany by belts of mountains, drew various German groups together.[6]

3. Bismarck stated: "Whoever is master of Bohemia is master of Europe. Europe must therefore never allow any nation except the Czechs to rule over it, since the Czech nation does not lust for domination. The natural boundaries of Bohemia are the safeguard of European security; and whoever tries to move them, will plunge Europe into misery" (Jaroslav Císař, *The Role of Czechoslovakia*, p. 9).

4. The Committee on Czechoslovak Questions at the peace conference stated in 1919: "Bohemia forms a natural region, clearly defined by its fringe of mountains. The mere fact that a German population has established itself in the outlying districts at a relatively recent date did not appear to the committee a sufficient reason for depriving Bohemia of its natural frontiers." The reasons of natural security "depend on geographical considerations. The chain of mountains which surrounds Bohemia constitutes a line of defence for the country. To take away this line of mountains would be to place Bohemia at the mercy of Germany" (E. L. Woodward and Rohan Butler, eds., *Documents on British Foreign Policy 1919–1939*. Third Series [London, 1949], I, 302; hereafter to be cited as *DBFP*). The term "Bohemia" describes the provinces of Bohemia and Moravia-Silesia which formed the core of the old Bohemian kingdom. They are sometimes called the "Historic Provinces."

5. *Atlas*, pp. 27–28. Another German study speaks of 12 different ethnic types of Bohemian Germans (The Göttinger Arbeitskreis, ed., *Sudetenland*, p. 19; hereafter referred to as *Sudetenland*).

6. During the Nazi era the term "Sudeten Germans" was used frequently to designate the German inhabitants of Bohemia and Moravia-Silesia. It was coined in 1902 by Franz Jesser in an article in the Prague weekly *Deutscher Volksbote* (Wilhelm Pleyer, ed., *Wir Sudetendeutschen*, p. 203). For more information, see J. W. Brügel, "Die Aussiedlung der Deutschen aus der Tschechoslowakei," *Vierteljahrshefte für Zeitgeschichte*, VIII (April 1960), 134–35; Hubert Ripka, *Likvidace Mnichova*, p. 32.

Their lack of geographical compactness split the Germans into eight separate and isolated units.[7] As the leading German Social Democrat, Josef Seliger, who became vice governor of the province of German Bohemia in 1918, stated in a Viennese review in October 1918:

The eight territorial fragments in which Germans are settled are separated from each other by broad belts of territories in which the Czech tongue is spoken, and they therefore cannot form a State or even a united administrative area, for such a thing must be, above all, an economic entity. . . . The formation of such a State would be without parallel in the world, and, as a political State, it would be completely nonsensical.[8]

Moreover, it was impossible to draw an ethnographical line between Czechs and Germans because many of them lived in mixed German or Czech regions, in linguistic enclaves, or as dispersed individuals. The Germans had no center of their own, and hence Prague and Brno became their natural capitals; their zones, divided into several districts, were linked by the Czech central area. Thus, the province of Bohemia provided a natural unity.[9] When in 1918 the Germans desired to separate from the newly founded Czechoslovak Republic, they had to form several unconnected provinces which still contained many Czechs. Deutschböhmen and Sudetenland were united

7. According to the census of Feb. 15, 1921, Germans in Czechoslovakia numbered 3,123,634 persons (23.36 percent of the population); according to the 1930 census, 3,231,688 (22.32 percent). In addition, there were 691,923 Hungarians and 81,737 Poles (Annuaire statistique, 1934).
   Many authors followed the division of the Germans into eight units: (1) northwestern Bohemia, (2) southeastern Bohemia, (3) northern Bohemia, (4) northeastern Bohemia, (5) northern Moravia, (6) the enclave of Svitavy, (7) the enclave of Jihlava, and (8) southern Moravia (R. W. Seton-Watson, "The German Minority in Czechoslovakia," Foreign Affairs, XVI [July 1938], 655–56). Pierre George of the Sorbonne University selected different fragments in his Le problème allemand en Tchécoslovaquie, pp. 12–13. Bohemicus [E. Sobota], Czechoslovakia and the Sudeten Germans, p. 17, indicated that in the eight unconnected areas 2,495,633 Germans and 440,561 Czechoslovaks lived together. Josef Chmelař in his very informative study, The German Problem in Czechoslovakia (p. 12), pointed out six large self-contained German entities.
8. Der Kampf, October, 1918 (Franz Koegler, Oppressed Minority?, p. 22). See also Vojta Beneš, The Vanguard of the "Drang nach Osten," p. 76. In 3,213 communities with absolute or relative German majorities, there were 2,609,110 Germans (Sudetenland, p. 20). See also F. W. Essler, Twenty Years of Sudeten-German Losses 1918–1938, p. 1.
9. Franz Jesser, a popular German nationalist leader, stated this fact in a treatise written in 1914. Extracts were reprinted by the Prague daily Deutsche Landpost on July 8, 1936 (Kamil Krofta, The Germans in the Czechoslovak Republic, pp. 30–31).

with German Austria;[10] Böhmerwald joined Upper Austria;[11] and Südmähren proclaimed itself an independent area, while the district of Nová Bystřice as well as the German enclave of Jihlava were attached to Lower Austria.[12] Similar developments followed the agreement of Munich in 1938. While the German area of settlement extended along the frontiers, most of the 7,406,493 Czechs[13] occupied the heart of the Historic Provinces. They formed a continuous area of settlement, with belts of their districts driving a wedge between the zones inhabited by the Germans; and, having a higher rate of natural increase, they expanded faster.

In the nineteenth century the growth of capitalism had furthered German predominance in the Habsburg Empire, since German capital was chiefly responsible for its industrial development. The similar industrialization of the predominantly German region of northwest Bohemia led the Czechs to abandon the poor rural districts of the Bohemian interior for the German section, where higher wages, a shortage of German labor, the increasing growth rate of industry, and development of the lignite area acted as stimuli to Czech immigration and provided a natural outlet for the abundant and cheap Czech labor. In 1880 the Czech minority in this region amounted to 8.03 percent. By 1930 it had grown to 35 percent.[14] This migration was also

10. Deutschböhmen (German Bohemia), with an area of 14,496 sq km, had 2,070,438 Germans and 116,275 Czechs. Dr. Lodgman von Auen became its Landeshauptmann and Josef Seliger his deputy. Sudetenland, with an area of 6,435 sq km, had 643,804 Germans and 25,028 Czechs (Hermann Raschhofer, *Die Sudetenfrage. Ihre völkerrechtliche Entwicklung vom ersten Weltkrieg bis zur Gegenwart*, pp. 114, 117; hereafter cited as *Sudetenfrage*). Professor Raschhofer became one of the scholarly spokesmen of the Hitlerite new Europe. The above data were based on the Austrian census of 1910, which determined nationality through the colloquial language used in daily life. In German-dominated Austria this worked to the detriment of the Czechs. For example, Wickham Steed, Viennese correspondent of the London *Times*, was counted as German (London *Times*, Oct. 10, 1938). Prof. R. W. Seton-Watson voiced a critical opinion on the 1910 census in *A History of the Peace Conference of Paris* (H. W. V. Temperley, ed.; London, 1920–24), IV, 269.
11. Böhmerwald had an area of 3,281 sq km, with 176,237 Germans and 6,131 Czechs (*Sudetenfrage*, p. 117).
12. Südmähren had an area of 2,225 sq km, with 180,449 Germans and 12,477 Czechs (*ibid.*). The basis for these data was the unreliable census of 1910.
13. Alfred Bohmann, *Das Sudetendeutschtum in Zahlen*, p. 13; hereafter cited as *Sudetendeutschtum*. There were 2,282,277 Slovaks in the Republic.
14. Figures and conclusions from a competent study by Franz Sigl (*Die soziale Struktur des Sudetendeutschtums, ihre Entwicklung und volkspolitische Bedeutung*, pp. 69 ff.). For a survey, see also André G. Whiteside, "Industrial Transformation, Population Movement and German Nationalism in Bohemia," *Zeitschrift für Ostforschung*, X (No. 2, 1961), 261–71.

facilitated by the fact that the Germans were abandoning inferior posts in their own area for better paid positions in Austria. The Czechs took over the manual tasks left by the Germans.[15] Moreover, by 1900 the decline in the German birth rate had already manifested itself in the German cities, although until 1910 it was more than balanced by a corresponding decline in the death rate. After 1910 the natural increase started to drop.[16]

After 1918, the new Republic furthered Czech migration into the cities and industrial centers,[17] until the principal Bohemian cities with a German majority showed a drop in the number of Germans.[18] Many Germans imputed their declining birth rate to Czech nationalist policies. Yet in the province of Bohemia, where the bulk of the Germans lived, there was a practical equilibrium between Czechs and Germans. According to Minister of Health Dr. Ludwig Czech, a German Social Democrat (Nov. 20, 1936), in the past decade there had been an average excess of births over deaths of 3.71 per 1,000 population for the Czechs, and 3.07 per 1,000 for the Germans in

15. Sigl, p. 151.
16. *Ibid.*, p. 161. Koegler (p. 64) pointed out the declining rate of the Germans in Bohemia per 1,000 inhabitants: 1900: 36; 1910: 26; 1936: 13.9. The correspondingly low birth rate of the Czechs in Bohemia was counterbalanced by higher rates in Moravia-Silesia. As in many European countries there was a decline in birth and death rates after 1910. The natural increase continued to fall until 1938 (Waller Wynne, Jr., *The Population of Czechoslovakia*, p. 44).
17. In successive censuses the ratio between Germans and Czechs in the Historic Provinces was as follows:

	Czechs (percent)	Germans (percent)
1880	62.95	36.04
1900	62.93	35.39
1910	63.41	34.95
1921	68.54	30.28
1930	69.50	29.19

(Kurt Vorbach, *200,000 Sudetendeutsche zuviel !*, p. 371.) This is a propaganda book but it contains helpful data. See also *Sudetendeutschtum*, pp. 24–28.
18. Compare the number of Germans in several principal German cities in Bohemia:

	1930 (percent)	1921 (percent)
Liberec	81.9	84.6
Ústí nad Labem	78.5	81.2
Jablonec nad Nisou	82.5	84.5
Cheb	87.4	94.1
Carlsbad	92.3	94.3
Duchcov	50.7	51.2

(Vorbach, pp. 64–65.)

Bohemia.[19] The inability of the Germans to evaluate the natural forces lying behind the population move aroused a feeling of national frustration, making the Czech expansion seem an intentional design of the new state.[20] They complained that the migration was managed from Prague and had the character of a Czech administrative measure. Although the state did evince preference for Czechs in state positions in the German-speaking areas, this endeavor to make up for decades of neglect of Czech interests did not involve any significant control of the natural demographic trend.

The progressive industrialization of the Historic Provinces during the second half of the nineteenth century brought changes in the social structure of the population. Since the Czech lands were a part of Western Europe, their economic, political, and social institutions resembled those of the West. Well-balanced industry, agriculture, commerce, and administrative machinery operated effectively in this now predominantly industrial country. Independent peasants and a rising middle class, recruited mainly from the peasantry, formed the backbone of society. The establishment of a modern factory system created a strong working class. Consequently, the new economic conditions were reflected in the changing composition of populations, with the Germans having a higher percentage of population working in industry and trade.[21]

The early impetus of the German industrial development was favored by the natural conditions of the German-settled mountainous borderland, rich in minerals and forests but containing far less fertile land—and consequently less propitious to farming—than the Czech-settled territory which comprised most of the good cereal land. This predominance of thickly wooded highlands and plains with their

19. Czechoslovak Sources and Documents, *Czechoslovak Cabinet Ministers on the Complaints of the Sudete* (sic) *German Party in the Czechoslovak Parliament*, p. 32; hereafter cited as *Czechoslovak Cabinet Ministers*.
20. Essler, pp. 8–12; Vorbach, pp. 64 ff. But, see *Atlas* (p. 31), which states that with the exception of the lignite districts and "the large towns, which as a result of the transfer of Czechoslovak officials since 1918 showed an unimportant percentage of Czechs," the German area of settlement preserved "its entirely German character up to 1945."
21. In 1930 the numbers of Germans and Czechs working in the respective branches of the economy were: agriculture, forestry, and fisheries—Germans, 23.03 percent, Czechs, 27.33; industry and trade—Germans, 45.48, Czechs, 39.43 (Sigl, p. 97; *Atlas*, p. 29). Albin Oberschall, a German authority on the subject, compared the respective industrial and agricultural developments of Germans and Czechs: agriculture and forestry—1920 (Germans, 27.3 percent; Czechs, 34.1); 1930 (Germans, 23.0; Czechs, 26.9); industry and trade—1920 (Germans, 43.1; Czechs, 37.3); 1930 (Germans, 45.5; Czechs, 39.1). (*Berufliche Gliederung und soziale Schichtung der Deutschen in der Tschechoslowakei*, p. 42.)

abundant meadows and pasture lands forced the Germans to concentrate on stock-breeding and on restricted production of rye, potatoes, oats, barley, hemp, and flax.[22] It also made demands upon the productive capacity of the Germans who achieved remarkable results in the development of a new industrial era, laying the foundations of an economy which brought them as artisans and workers into shops and factories while the Czechs, still attracted by their rich cereal and turnip lands, continued to give preference to agriculture. When industrialization came of age for the Czechs, however, their advances led to an astonishing industrial expansion which saw the creation of new industries and the raising of old industries to new levels of productive achievements. Despite their earlier uneven rate of industrial growth and dissimilar geographical conditions, the professional distribution of Czechs and Germans differed only slightly in the years preceding the Munich crisis.

After the disintegration of the Habsburg Empire, Czechoslovakia, with 26.4 percent of the population, inherited 70 percent of the total production of the Dual Monarchy.[23] The former domestic market of 54 million people was now restricted to 13.5 million.[24] Therefore, in view of the size of her industry, Czechoslovakia emerged as a first-class economic power. The Historic Provinces became the center of powerful metal and machine industries. The massive achievements of her agricultural production also created a flourishing food industry. While heavy industry was located mainly in the Czech region, the preponderance of raw materials in the German areas encouraged the existence of a vast consumer industry. In the Czech area the pervasive influence of new methods and products made itself felt in new industries like hardware, engineering, automobiles, and electrical supplies; while the German consumer industries, which still bore witness to earlier technical achievements, displayed an excessive dependence on such unstable industries as chinaware, glass, or textiles, which were susceptible to any change in world economic conditions. In particular, the textile industry—noted for quality and workmanship—which was the most important German industry, became to a great extent

22. *Sudetenland*, p. 150.
23. Rudolf Olšovský et al., *Přehled hospodářského vývoje Československa v letech 1918–1945*, p. 24. The Czechoslovak share in Austria-Hungary's industrial production was estimated as follows: chinaware, 100 percent; glass, 92; sugar, 92; malt, 87; wool, 80; shoes, 75; chemicals, 75; cotton, 75; leather, 70; paper, 65; metals, 60; and beer, 57 (*Sudetenland*, p. 151).
24. Robert Polzer, *Die sudetendeutsche Wirtschaft in der Tschechoslowakei*, p. 30. The book is a competent study written from the German point of view.

an index of the standard of living of the German people.[25] The entire production of the textile industry, two thirds of which was exported, was valued at about 12 milliard Czechoslovak crowns (Kč) in the 1920's. With a drop in exports from 7 milliard Kč to 1.6 milliard, mass unemployment resulted during the great depression,[26] since the high degree of industrial concentration aggravated the economic difficulties.

Most of the German industries were located in western, northern, and northeastern Bohemia, where more than 50 percent of the inhabitants drew their living from industry and trade, while in southern Moravia and southern Bohemia more than 50 percent of the inhabitants worked in agriculture and forestry.[27] The high productive capacity of the main branches of German consumer industries made them heavily dependent on exports.[28] As a result, the economic slump of the thirties changed their progress radically. On the other hand, Czech industry demonstrated an abounding resilience in the same period, despite the enduring effects of the great crisis which had unsettled the economy.

The early predominance of German industrial capital[29] in the Czechoslovak economy had been viewed by the Czechs with distrust and apprehension. Because of the policy of German shareholders,

25. Deutsche Bank, *Das Sudetenland im deutschen Wirtschaftsraum*, p. 30; Polzer, p. 20. More than 80 percent of the textile industry was reportedly owned by the Germans. According to Polzer (p. 21), in 1930 out of a total of about 206,000 employees some 191,600 worked in the predominantly German areas, among them obviously many Czech workers. Oberschall (p. 33) put the share of German employees in the textile industry at 53.6 percent in 1920, and 55.3 in 1930. But Sigl (p. 129), using new unpublished statistical material, put the numbers at 185,818 German and 141,954 Czech workers. The discrepancies among these three serious writers indicate the difficulty of arriving at accurate figures. Sigl's estimate appears the most reliable, because it is based on primary statistical data. For our purpose it is enough to present fairly reliable rough estimates to indicate the main tendencies.

26. Polzer, p. 22.

27. Deutsche Bank, p. 11.

28. *Deutscher Hauptverband der Industrie* indicated the dependence of the following industrial branches on export in 1930: Gablonz (Jablonec) glassware and costume jewelry, 95 percent; chinaware, 85; window and plate glass, 79.2; bottle glass, 77.3; silk, 67.6; woolens, 61.7; cottons, 54.2; and sugar, 52.1 (*Sudetenland*, p. 152).

29. According to estimates of Czech economist Jiří Hejda published in the Prague weekly *Přítomnost* (*Presence*) in 1927, the German share in the Czechoslovak industry was: silk, 100 percent; chinaware, 90; textiles, 89; glass, 86; wool, 85; paper, 80; lignite, 80; cement, 80; electrical industry, 70; iron foundries, 70; coal, 66; malt, 64; chemicals, 60; fertilizers, 60; sugar refineries, 58; locomotives, rolling stock, 40; and metallurgical industry, 29 (*Sudetenland*, p. 151; Koegler, p. 18).

German entrepreneurs had secured preeminence among the administrative forces in heavy industry.[30] The Czech endeavor to make up for its late arrival in the economic field was matched by the increased wealth and economic and political maturity of the Czech people. This intensified public awareness of the inequalities in the distribution of industrial capital accounted for the new state policy of preference for Czechs in the civil service. Rudolf Schlesinger argued rightly that "an otherwise unalterable distribution of social importance between the nationalities" could be modified only through the use of state machinery. Civil service became the field "where the Czechs could try to restore the balance against what private ownership was doing to preserve the social distinctions."[31]

However, the inequality in industrial ownership was more than balanced by the remarkable development of the Czech banking system. By 1918, the balances of the Czech banks were two and a half times higher than those of the German banks.[32] In 1929 the proportion of Czech and German banking capital was estimated at 75 percent and 25 percent respectively.[33] Before 1918, manufacture in the Czech areas had been controlled largely by Viennese capital owned by Germans and German-speaking Jews. Under the driving stimulus of the new Republic, Czech banks took over a large part of the Viennese capital and, in conformity with the tendency in Germany and elsewhere, continued to rise to a dominating position in economic life, thus helping Czech capital to win control of the chief branches of industry. In the first decade of the Republic a few leading banks and savings institutions controlled much of the economy,[34] supplying 80 percent of corporate capital.[35]

Before the depression of 1929, both Czech and German industries had benefited from this stabilization of capitalism. Prague had replaced Vienna as the financial center, and German industries and

30. Sigl, p. 118. According to Sigl (p. 116), the Czech share in the mining industries was 56.7 percent of the workers, but a mere 38.8 percent of salaried officials.
31. *Federalism in Central and Eastern Europe*, p. 298, a competent and stimulating study.
32. Jan Hajda, ed., *A Study of Contemporary Czechoslovakia*, p. 560.
33. Olšovský et al., pp. 249–50. However, one has to take into consideration that joint stock ownership was largely anonymous. A part of the banking capital was estimated as being nationally mixed (*ibid.*, p. 238).
34. Anatol Dobrý, *Materiály ke studiu dějin československého hospodářství v letech 1918–1945*, p. 27. These are scripts of lectures given at the University of Prague.
35. *Ibid.*, pp. 29–32; Jaromír Hořec, *Cesty, ktoré viedli k Mníchovu*, pp. 350–53. The latter book contains a list of industrial enterprises under the control of the big banks.

banks had adjusted to the new political situation. The German business community developed better relations with the government, and in 1926 German bourgeois parties entered the coalition government. The financial exigency of 1931 was accentuated by speculative investments in the Reich by many German businessmen.

The German and Austrian financial collapse in 1931 froze the assets of the majority of the Czechoslovak German banks, which were forced to turn to the more prudent Czech banks for help. State subsidies to the German banks amounted to one milliard Kč (out of a total aid of 3,500 million Kč). When the Central Bank of German Savings Banks collapsed in 1932, it received 44 million Kč in aid. This financial rescue resulted in some limitations of German economic independence and a more strict control of the banks by the state. The Czech banks, by their willingness to assist their German countrymen, played an even more important role in relation to German businessmen.[36]

Conditions in land ownership made redistribution a matter of necessity. Under the Austro-Hungarian Empire about one third of the land in the Czech territories had belonged to large estates,[37] especially those of the German high aristocracy who had come into the country after the end of Bohemian independence (1620). Now, urgent social and democratic developments called for rapid and profound changes in farm ownership.[38] For the new state, land reform presented a paramount issue that clamored for immediate action. After passage of the Land Reform Law of April 16, 1919, a land office was created to administer the reform. However, far-reaching as the achievements of the land reform were to be, they were slow in being carried out. Up to the end of 1936, only 4,066,221 hectares (ha) were requisitioned, of which 1,309,536 were arable land. The former owners were permitted to retain farms up to 250 ha, and were compensated at prewar value for the remainder. However, 1,795,227 ha of the requisitioned land were returned to their previous owners for

36. The address of Minister of Finance Dr. Josef Kalfus to Parliament, Dec. 5, 1936, in *Czechoslovak Cabinet Ministers*, pp. 50–52. For a good survey, see Elizabeth Wiskemann, *Czechs and Germans. A Study of the Struggle in the Historic Provinces of Bohemia and Moravia*, pp. 166–67, 292. This volume is the best available account of Czech-German relations and will hereafter be cited as *Czechs and Germans*.

37. Vorbach, p. 160, stated that prior to land reform 36.99 percent of land in Bohemia and Moravia-Silesia belonged to big estates (2,688,403 ha).

38. In the National Assembly on April 17, 1919, Czech Social Democratic Deputy František Modráček called the reform "not only a social reform, but also a republican reform and . . . a national reform" (Essler, p. 15).

disposition. Some 1,786,129 ha were distributed to a total of 638,994 new proprietors; of this acreage, 867,160 ha were in arable land. The state administered 506,586 ha, and the 2,296 remainders from the large estates (the so-called Restgüter), constituting 227,186 ha, were allotted according to political interests.[39] A lengthy controversy ensued between Germans and Czechs, the former complaining that some 400,000 ha had been taken from the German aristocracy in the predominantly German area,[40] mainly forest land near the frontier.[41]

The Czechoslovak Ministry of Agriculture stressed that 198,909 more ha were requisitioned in the Czech areas of Bohemia and Moravia-Silesia than in the mixed or German districts, and that some 48,820 German families had been allotted 57,270 ha (4.5 percent of the allotted land) up to Jan. 1, 1937. Elizabeth Wiskemann, who gathered these figures on the spot in Czechoslovakia, pointed out that she had never heard any thoughtful Sudeten German deny "that the German tenants working on expropriated land were quite justly treated in being allowed to become its owners."[42] One had also to take into consideration the fact that it was inevitable that the Czech peasants should be given preference, because the German population was chiefly industrial and centered in the cities, and the landless Czech or Slovak population was larger.[43] After the Nazi occupation of Czechoslovakia in 1939, the Germans attempted to prove the validity of their

39. *Annuaire statistique 1938*, pp. 55–56; Eduard Kučera and Zdeňka Kučerová, *O agrárnický stát*, p. 139; *Czechs and Germans*, pp. 147–60. For the German point of view, see Essler, pp. 15–19; Vorbach, 160 ff; K. H. Frank, *Sudetendeutschtum in Kampf und Not*, pp. 38–39.

40. In the bulletin, *Communications of the Association of German Landed Proprietors* (May 31, 1938), it was stated that the entire land taken from the Germans during the reform amounted to about 600,000 ha, of which some 400,000 ha were in the German area. Essler (p. 17) and Vorbach (p. 177) put the figure at 750,000 ha in the German districts. This is only one example of exaggerations so freely indulged in by German nationalists. The German daily, *Sozialdemokrat* (Feb. 14, 1937), wrote that German applicants were given about 14 percent (189,000 acres) of the total acreage already distributed. Of this, 16,200 acres of woodland were given to German parishes and districts, and about 2,700 acres were handed over to the Germans in the form of remainders from the former large estates. About 164,700 acres were parceled out in small holdings (Hans Richter, *No Oppression of the Sudeten Germans in Czechoslovakia?*, p. 52).

41. Forest land was partitioned into 2,487 estates, each over 30 ha. These were allotted 772,790 ha, of which only 33,019 ha were arable. (Kučera, p. 139).

42. *Czechs and Germans*, pp. 151–52. Miss Wiskemann cited the German review *Land-und Forstarbeiter* for Feb. 20, 1926, which stated that 31.8 percent of the land distributed to the tenants went to Germans.

43. *Czechs and Germans*, p. 151. Through the reform many German foresters of south Bohemia and the Bohemian Forest "have been changed from serfs into men" (*ibid.*, p. 152).

complaints,[44] but the results of their investigations showed that, on the whole, land reform had been a successful measure. The reform suggested the application of a more democratic and just scale of value to the rural strata of modern society. It helped to liquidate remaining segments of the feudal system and to break up social castes. It made possible a shift from large farms to small holdings. It furthered the penetration of capitalist methods into agricultural production; provided an opportunity for the consolidation of the agrarian bourgeoisie (the Agrarian Party became the strongest party in the Republic); slowed the rise of rural discontent; and did away with the rural predominance of the German feudal conservatives.

The majority of agricultural units were of small or medium size. The structure of German and Czech agriculture was almost identical: 68.3 percent of the German holdings and 74.2 percent of the Czech formed farms up to 5 ha.[45] These small holdings were characteristic units in general farming.[46]

The relative stability and well-being of the independent peasantry were derived from progressive methods, wide adoption of cooperatives, and the rising rate of state support that limited the risks of commercialized enterprise and helped to create a peculiarly favorable environment characteristic of Czechoslovakia. In addition, the influence of the Agrarian Party enabled it to sway the economic policy of the state in favor of the agrarian segment of the population. However, there was also a darker side to rural Czechoslovakia: the cottagers and rural workers formed an underprivileged class, pointing up the social and economic limitations of the relatively well-adjusted Czechoslovak agricultural economy.

The comparative prosperity of agriculture did not prevent the development of a fierce struggle for land between Czechs and Germans along the national frontiers. They fought over even the smallest parcel of land, over every building lot and home property. The Germans were mostly on the defensive, with German landed property often passing without governmental interference into Czech ownership.[47] Both sides used their national societies for the protection of

---

44. See below, p. 59. *K. H. Frank* (pp. 38–39) indicated that out of the 520,000 ha of German land confiscated, some 96 percent were distributed to the Czechs, the Germans receiving 31,320 ha as tenants and only 10,000 ha in ownership. Some 2,828 holdings with 38,319 ha were allotted to the Czech colonists. All figures were strongly biased.

45. Bohemicus, p. 22.

46. *Ibid.*

47. The German-Czech national frontier was still flexible. In the decade 1920–30 the Czech area of settlement increased by 96 communities (1,010 sq km) because of the more rapid natural increase of the Czech population (Dr.

their interests. For the Czechs the struggle was simply a continuation of their earlier defensive fight against the German colonists. On the German side was the memory of the time, not too long ago, when they had been masters of the country and bearers of an advanced culture.[48] For many of them their relationship with the Czechs had been that between master and servant, and they could not yet believe that their former "servants" had reached full political, economic, social, and cultural maturity.

The economic crisis which descended on the Republic in 1931, and reached its height in the spring of 1933, confronted the government with a period of industrial depression. The cataclysm fell upon a country dependent on extensive export and a large foreign trade. Exports declined rapidly.[49] Foreign trade failed to recover, despite some notable achievements.[50] In 1937 the index of industrial production rose to 96.3 percent (1929 = 100), while the index of export reached a modest 40 percent.[51] There was also a structural change in the commodity composition of exports: a relative decline in the importance of textile exports—from 34.5 percent of total exports in 1929 to 21.5 percent in 1937—was accompanied by a rise in the export share of the metal industries, from 15.4 percent to 24.9 percent.[52] Thus the less pronounced revival of light industry[53] redounded unfavorably against the German areas, which had already suffered

Vladimír Šlamínka in the frontier dwellers' periodical *Stráž Moravy* [Guard of Moravia], XVIII, 1936, No. 2, and in *Národnostní obzor* [Nationalities Review], VII, December 1936, 148).

48. Some 160,000 Czechs lived in the German areas in 1880; in 1930 their number rose to 382,490. The German population in the predominantly Czech territories steadily declined to 424,454 persons in 1930 (*Národnostní obzor*, VII–VIII, June and December 1937).

49. Compare the indexes of world and Czechoslovak export trade (1928 = 100): 1934: world, 33; Czech, 29. 1937: world, 46; Czech, 40 (Ústav dějin KSČ, *Na obranu republiky proti fašizmu a vojně. Sborník dokumentov k dějinám KSČ v rokov 1934–1938 a k VI., VII. a VIII. sväzku spisov Klementa Gottwalda*, p. 587; hereafter cited as *Na obranu republiky*). The volume presents an excellent treatment of the economic history of the Republic during the pre-1938 years from the Communist point of view. The export trade of Czechoslovakia in Kč was as follows: 1929, 20,458 million; 1933, 5,842 million; 1937, 11,935 million (*Sudetenland*, p. 182).

50. Antonin Basch, *The Danube Basin and the German Economic Sphere*, passim.

51. 1928 = 100 (*Na obranu republiky*, p. 586).

52. *Ibid.*, pp. 590–91.

53. The index of industrial production fell to 60.2 percent in 1933 (1929 = 100). Light industry suffered more severely. In 1937 the increase in the volume of production of light industry was 41.4 percent; that of heavy industry, 86.1 percent; the total increase of production was 60.0 percent (*ibid.*, p. 524).

heavily. The most seriously hurt were the regions of Jablonec and the Ore Mountains with their preponderance of home industries. In the district of Jablonec alone, there were more than 1,500 foreclosures by March 1931.[54] Recovery in heavy industry, located chiefly in the Czech areas, favored the Czechs, while in the export industries —glass, china, textiles, etc.—in which the Germans had a conspicuous share, recovery failed to develop despite valiant efforts of the state. Most of the German industrial region became a distressed area. In the textile industry alone, 166 mills employing 30,000 workers were closed from 1929.[55]

The standard of living naturally reflected the conditions of depression. The annual average of the unemployment had risen from 41,600 in 1929 to an unprecedented high of 738,300 by 1933. Prices evinced an upward tendency while wages and purchasing power in various sectors of the economy declined and by 1937 were about 10 percent lower than in 1929.[56] The factor which seemed to concern the German man in the street was that the distress was most evident in those industrial areas which happened to be German. The Czechoslovak liberal capitalistic regime was unable to take radical measures which would speedily eliminate the distress and could not direct the wealth of the state into channels that would be constructive in terms of common welfare. While all branches of administration exhibited full understanding of the necessity of relief measures, they were necessarily affected by the state's liberal economic doctrine. The effects of the relief measures on employment and business were therefore indirect. The average German, however, failed to understand that it was not accurate to speak about German and Czech districts but rather about industrial and agricultural districts, and that those areas with German majorities most seriously hit were industrial districts, while those with a Czech or Slovak majority were of a more

54. Jiří Kořalka, "Jak se stal německý lid v Československu kořistí fašismu," *Československý časopis historický*, III (1955, No. 1), 59. This is a competent study. See also Anatol Dobrý, *Hospodářská krize československého průmyslu ve vztahu k Mnichovu*, pp. 81 ff.

55. SB Sudeten-German *Newsletters*, Prague, Aug. 20, 1938. Another reason for the grave state of German light industry was its structural weakness resulting from its many small firms distant from markets, antiquated machinery, and obsolete business methods. The German daily, *Prager Presse*, for Sept. 2, 1938, stated several reasons for the decline of German industry: (1) backward technical equipment, (2) obsolete calculation methods, (3) speculation in raw materials and foreign exchange, and (4) absenteeism by business executives.

56. *Na obranu republiky*, p. 635. The index of real wages fell from 100 in 1929 to 89.4 in 1935. The index of the nominal wage fell to 83.7 in the same period (*Sudetenland*, p. 157).

rural character.[57] As a result, the Germans blamed the Czechs for economic conditions over which they actually had no control.

In a broad sense, the main reason for high unemployment in the predominantly German areas was a decline in exports. In 1936, in the districts with a German minority of 10 to 20 percent, there were 70 unemployed among each group of 1,000 normally employed people. In those with a German majority of 50 to 80 percent, the ratio was 146 : 1,000; and in those of 80 to 100 percent, the ratio was 153 : 1,000.[58] Since the Germans were dependent to a great extent on those branches of industry concerned with exports, their prosperity was determined by trade relations with foreign countries.[59] In addition, there were declining economic opportunities in the lumber industry and forest production which prevailed in wooded mountainous zones inhabited mainly by the Germans.[60] Moreover, the German regions contained many well-known spas and health and recreation resorts which had severely suffered from a decline in the number of permanent guests, including many from abroad.[61]

When the economy started to recover, it was primarily heavy industry that profited from the vast scale of investment. The armament race which sparked the recovery injected purchasing power into the income stream chiefly in the Czech and Slovak areas where the armament industry was located,[62] although there was also a partial recovery in the German districts which provided the basis for a grad-

57. This was the thesis of the minister of Social Welfare, Jaromír Nečas. He stated that the same situation existed in Germany, where in agricultural East Prussia the index of unemployment was 0.2, while in the city of Cologne it amounted to 35 and in Dresden to 28 (*Nationality Policy in Czechoslovakia. Speeches by Dr. Hodža, Franke, Nečas, and Dérer in the Czechoslovak Parliament*, pp. 63–69).
58. *Na obranu republiky*, p. 640.
59. Jaroslav Kšíkal, "Závislost na vývozu—příčina vysoké nezaměstnanosti v pohraničí" (Dependence on Export—the Cause of the High Unemployment Rate in the Frontier Districts), *Národnostní obzor*, VIII (September 1937), 29–38.
60. Kšíkal, pp. 29–30.
61. *Ibid.*, p. 31. The decline in the number of guests in the spas and resorts was as follows (1929 = 100): 1933, 26.3 percent; 1936, 31.4.
62. The state expenditure for defense rose constantly from 1934:

Year	Amount in Millions of Kč	Percent of State Expenditure
1934	1,485.0	15.5
1935	2,384.8	23.6
1937	5,274.5	37.9

(*Na obranu republiky*, pp. 600–601.)

ual rise in incomes.[63] The economic upheaval, however, tended to break ground for the recrudescent nationalism of German Nazism, since most Germans interpreted the economic depression in terms of national struggle.

The growth of both extremes among the Germans, the Communists, and the Nazis, at the communal elections in 1931 was a sign of a reversion to a more radical mood.[64] As the catastrophic slump of the years 1930–33 assumed greater proportions, the social and political structure of the German borderland underwent changes that made the people respond more easily to radical programs which promised early and easy improvement.

The German democratic press voiced serious complaints against economic plagues which encouraged extremism. According to the *Sozialdemokrat*,[65] once flourishing districts lay impoverished, with factories idle and machinery rusted away. Another daily[66] called for more public works to create employment because Nazism was gaining ground chiefly as a result of the all-prevailing misery. In 1936 the Carlsbad Social Democrat daily[67] stated that the frontier areas remained unaffected by the economic recovery,[68] and that the difference between the German and Czech areas had become more marked as the Germans had derived no benefit from the armament industry and had not received any commissions for public undertakings. Yet, despite some bad spots in industrial areas, impoverishment had remained static, and the inhabitants of Czechoslovakia

63. Kšíkal, p. 36, indicated the drop in the rate of unemployment between June 1936 and June 1937: engineering, 67 percent; mining, 41.4; metal industries, 41.5; glass industry, 40.5.
64. In the parliamentary elections of 1929 the greatest increase in Communist votes was in districts with a German population of 90 percent. In the elections of 1931, the Communist Party reported considerable gains in the German districts of northwestern and northern Bohemia. In the predominantly German territory spreading from Aš to Děčín, the membership of the party increased by 70 percent during the period between the fifth and sixth congresses of the party. D. S. Manuilskij hailed its success at the ninth plenary meeting of the executive committee of the Communist International at Moscow (Kořalka, p. 60).
65. For Feb. 2, 1935, as cited in Richter, p. 7.
66. *Nordböhmischer Volksbote*, Oct. 23, 1935, as cited in Richter, p. 10.
67. Carlsbad *Volkswille*, Sept. 25, 1936, in Richter, p. 21.
68. The German Social Democrat leader, Wenzel Jaksch, stated in the *Sozialdemokrat* (Dec. 1, 1936) that in October 1935, some 62 percent and, a year later, some 69 percent, of all the unemployed in Czechoslovakia lived in German-speaking districts. As compared with October 1935, the average unemployment rate decreased by 28.2 percent in the entire area of Czechoslovakia, while the decrease was only 14.9 in the German districts of Bohemia (Richter, p. 23). Jaksch, however, failed to point out that there were many Czech workingmen in the mining districts of northern Bohemia and elsewhere in German areas.

were no worse off than those of Western Europe. There was, to be sure, a drop in tax yields and state undertakings, with a corresponding increase in state expenditures because of relief measures. A rise in tax rates[69] was paralleled by salary cuts for all civil and public officials.[70] However, the traditional deflationary measures to reduce the deficit, combined with the necessity for growing relief payments, had little effect on the rate of economic activity in the country, since, in accordance with classic economic theory, fiscal policy aimed at economy rather than increased employment.

Czechoslovakia enjoyed a highly advanced policy of social legislation.[71] In 1925 she introduced a system of unemployment insurance, the so-called Ghent system,[72] based on trade unions. During the depression, about one third of the unemployed benefited from the system, and the remainder took advantage of state relief.[73] During 1930–35 state assistance to unemployment insurance totaled 1,900,-000,000 Kč, of which Czechoslovak labor received 958,976,752, German labor 704,940,948, and nationally mixed trade unions 135,073,-293.[74] German workers, consequently, received more than their national share.[75] The government rightly affirmed that there was a "totally different social and economic distribution of the population in the districts" with German and Czech populations, and that the districts with a German majority, being industrial, "have suffered more from unemployment than the agricultural regions."[76]

Prague strove assiduously, within the framework of the existing private enterprise system, to improve the economic and social status of the working class during this period of acute social and economic misery. Its policy, which was cautiously progressive, never con-

69. The increase involved the income tax and the turnover tax.
70. Dr. Josef Kalfus in the London *Financial Times* of June 15, 1936.
71. The working day was limited to 8 hours, employment of children under 14 years was prohibited, health insurance was compulsory, and old-age pensions and permanent disability allowances were introduced.
72. Under the Ghent system, trade unions allocated benefits to their members and the state contributed directly to the trade unions.
73. Between one half and one third of the unemployed benefited under the Ghent system, which concerned only the members of the trade unions. Benefits varied between 60 and 150 Kč a week (Edgar P. Young, *Czechoslovakia: Keystone of Peace and Democracy*, pp. 150–51). In 1936 there were 2,216,000 trade unionists, 391,000 of whom were members of German unions and 1,825,000 belonged to the nationally mixed and Czechoslovak unions. Vincent Urban's *Hitler's Spearhead*, p. 59, is an informative propaganda pamphlet.
74. *Czechoslovak Cabinet Ministers*, pp. 67–68. The figures were included in a speech of Minister Nečas on Dec. 3, 1936, and are considered reliable.
75. *Ibid.*, p. 69.
76. *Ibid.*, p. 65.

templated a complete overhaul of the economic system itself.[77] Besides the unemployment benefit which was distributed adequately without regard to the nationality of the workingman, the state contributed benefits in kind. Those who might be ineligible for relief based on the Ghent system received weekly state relief in goods with an additional 10 Kč if they were single, or 20 Kč if they were married. The government was determined to support "according to need only and not according to nationality."[78] The state, moreover, contributed large sums to alleviate distress among needy children, distributing aid to each province in proportion to its total population. The scheme was set up on a national autonomous basis,[79] the state allotting funds, according to the respective share of the population, to provincial child-relief centers created separately for German and Czech children.[80] This arrangement aimed at avoiding any inequality in national distribution and made certain that all benefits were enjoyed equally by children of all nationalities.

On the German side, however, there developed not only a misunderstanding of the measures of relief[81] but also a tendency to

77. At the beginning of the crisis the minister of Social Welfare was the German Socialist, Dr. Ludwig Czech. He was succeeded by Jaromír Nečas, a member of the Czechoslovak Social Democratic Party, whose national impartiality was recognized by the Germans themselves. For detailed data on Dr. Czech, see J. W. Brügel, *Ludwig Czech. Arbeiterführer und Staatsmann*. This excellent study gives much information on the Czechoslovak nationalities policy. Brügel's interpretation of the period 1918–38 differs sharply from that of Wenzel Jaksch.

78. Urban, p. 60. Minister Nečas gave the following figures on the amount of benefits distributed in kind during the years 1930–35: state expenditure on food, gifts, etc., in Czech districts, 507,702,570 Kč, and in predominantly German districts, 520,729,280 Kč. In Czech districts were distributed 6,576,000 gallons of milk and 39,946 metric tons of flour, sugar, fat, rolled barley, etc.; 36,860 metric tons of coal; 1,355,760 loaves of bread, and 14,240 metric tons of potatoes. In predominantly German districts these amounts were 6,074,000 gallons of milk and 37,522 tons of flour, fat, sugar, etc.; 30,175 tons of coal, 1,379,050 loaves of bread, and 13,560 metric tons of potatoes (*Czechoslovak Cabinet Ministers*, pp. 69–70). The figures are close approximations.

79. Urban (p. 57) based his arguments on the figures of J. Nečas.

80. Minister Nečas on Dec. 3 and 17, 1936 (*Czechoslovak Cabinet Ministers*, pp. 64–78; also Urban, pp. 57–58). For example, in Bohemia the Czech Provincial Center for Child Relief in Prague and the Deutsche Landes Kommission für Kinderschutz und Jugendfürsorge in Liberec were set up as the directing bodies for the district child-relief societies. The autonomous centers made their proposals directly to the ministry, taking into consideration the funds secured from the local authorities and from charity.

81. The central organ of the Henlein Party, *Die Zeit*, stated on Dec. 2, 1936, that "the relief schemes conducted by the State authorities for the starving Sudeten Germans are pretty much a farce." A deputy of the same party, Dr. T. Jilly, asserted in the House of Deputies on Nov. 4, 1936, that "the manner in which German child relief is neglected in connection with the distribution of

question the whole government policy. Mutual relations were not strengthened by German allegations of an unjust distribution of unemployment benefits or of neglect of needy German children. Nevertheless, whatever mistakes may have been committed on the Czech side in other fields, it appears evident that national justice and equity were applied by the government to its relief measures.[82]

The coming of the depression transformed the political situation of all of Europe. The inherent issues and problems involved were too difficult to be solved by any country alone. As a result, the economic crisis coupled with the rise of Nazism changed the state of affairs in Central Europe. It reawakened a more belligerent, less understanding, and more rigid way of setting forth policies and ideas in Germany. In Czechoslovakia—in the appalling wake of the crisis—the government was subjected to strong criticism from German national parties within the country, which found a favorable breeding ground among many Germans who insisted that the reasons for the economic hardship had to be sought in Czech policy. This animosity toward Czechoslovakia did not mellow with the improvement of the economy, because emphasis on the crisis served many German leaders as a channel for the promotion of their nationalist aspirations and designs. They strove to arouse the public against the alleged chief "malefactors"—the Czechs—and their unimaginative bureaucratic officialdom.[83]

food by the State to needy children is absolutely amazing" (*Czechoslovak Cabinet Ministers*, p. 58). These affirmations proved to be wrong.

82. It was alleged by the Germans (an anonymous member of the Henlein Party stated it in his article "The German Minority in Czechoslovakia," *The Slavonic and East European Review*, XI, January 1936) that during the years 1920–30 some 20,000 Germans committed suicide in Czechoslovakia. A leading Czech expert undertook a close scrutiny of this accusation and concluded that the German allegations were nonsensical. According to his study, the figure for the province of Bohemia amounted to about 7,777 Germans for the period (more than two thirds of the Germans lived in Bohemia). In the years 1929–33, suicides in the German districts of Bohemia were 43.4 per 100,000 inhabitants, while there were 42.9 in Saxony and 48.1 in Hamburg and Berlin. This proves that Germans everywhere had a very high percentage of suicides. It is interesting to note that the percentage of suicides of the Czechs living in the German districts equaled that of the Germans (Dr. Jaromír Korčák in *Národnostní obzor*, VI [March 1936], 203–207).

83. Conspicuous examples of this attitude were the volumes of Frank, Essler, Vorbach, Richter; also Karl von Galéra, *Sudetendeutschlands Heimkehr ins Deutsche Reich;* Josef Pfitzner, *Das Sudetendeutschtum;* Rudolf Jung, *Die Tschechen. Tausend Jahre deutsch-tschechischer Kampf;* Hans Krebs and Emil Lehmann, *Wir Sudetendeutsche !* The volume of Hugo Hassinger, *Die Tschechoslowakei. Ein geographisches und wirtschaftliches Handbuch,* also showed an anti-Czech bias, but there was less sacrifice to propaganda.

The Czechs felt that some of their less imaginative measures destined to preserve and stabilize German economic life had been taken
out of context and warped. They admitted their clumsy presentation,
but claimed that the matter was more of style than of content. If only
the Germans would recognize that the Republic was also their
state,[84] the Czechs gave the impression of intending to be more
cooperative and less arbitrary than they had been when they assumed leadership of the new Republic. The favorable ground that
was held by moderate groups on the German side was, however,
eroding under the impact of economic and political circumstances.

The relationship between Czechs and Germans was a vast and
complex subject, with the economic factor representing only one aspect. Needless to say, an analysis of the economic factors in Czechoslovakia indicated that the majority of Czechs and Germans were
mutually dependent. A real desire for understanding and cooperation in the interests of both nationalities required recognition of the
view which was exemplified by the statement of the Versailles
Committee on Czechoslovak Questions in 1919:

> The whole of the region occupied by the Germans of Bohemia is
> industrially and economically dependent upon Bohemia rather
> than upon Germany. The Germans of Bohemia cannot exist with-
> out the economic cooperation of the Czechs, nor the Czechs with-
> out the economic cooperation of the Germans. There is between
> them a complete interdependence in this respect.[85]

It may be said that the undertakings for economic and social better-
ment, if motivated and conditioned by economic principles alone,
and if viewed by both sides as a basic approach to the solution of
national problems, would have served the well-being and long-range
interests of all the peoples of Czechoslovakia. Yet this alluring path
could not be followed because of other elements in the Czech-
German pattern.

84. Dr. Kamil Krofta, the successor of Dr. Eduard Beneš as minister of Foreign
Affairs, asked the Germans to display a sincere "mental attachment" to the state.
See his address delivered at Carlsbad on Dec. 3, 1936 (in *The Germans*, p.
37).
85. *DBFP*, I, 301. The views of the Peace Conference of Versailles were discussed
in the report of the British minister in Prague, Basil Newton, to Viscount Halifax
(May 16, 1938).

Part I

HISTORICAL BACKGROUND

CHAPTER I

Czechoslovakia and Her Germans

Central Europe has always been a traditional ground of national conflicts, and one of the perennial features in the history of this area has been the rivalry between Czechs and Germans. The Germans began to settle in the Bohemian kingdom in the middle of the twelfth century, with the peak of the first wave of colonization coming in the thirteenth century. The Hussite wars caused a temporary retreat of the Germans, but after 1526 under the Habsburg rule the influx of settlers rose again. In the wake of the Battle of the White Mountain in 1620, which marked the end of Czech independence, German became the second official language. The forced emigration of a part of the Czech Protestant middle class and aristocracy, the enormous confiscations covering some three quarters of the land, the immigration of many German-speaking aristocrats who took over the confiscated estates, and the new wave of German colonization accounted for the fact that by the eighteenth century German had become almost exclusively the official language. From 1848 on most of the Germans inhabiting Bohemia and Moravia-Silesia thought themselves to be members of the German nation,[1] and their century-long competition

1. In my use of the word "nation," I have followed both the literary and the customary use of the concept by Germans and Czechs. While among Anglo-Saxons the term is used in the sense of "political state," in Central Europe it connotes a group of people characterized by a common language, culture, territory, history, character, and will. For the German view of the development,

with the Czechs gave further impetus to the rise of German nationalism.

After the defeat of Austria in 1866, the Austrian Germans were restricted to the Habsburg Empire. The Compromise of 1867 inaugurated dualism in Austria-Hungary, the Magyars winning recognition of their supremacy in the territories included in the kingdom of Hungary, and the Germans strengthening their predominance in the western half of the monarchy. When Austrian Prime Minister Count Kasimir Felix Badeni attempted to secure equality for the Czech language with German and introduced a bilingual administration in Bohemia in 1897, he met with violent resistance from the Germans. Badeni's struggle for linguistic equality, however, indicated that there were two main tendencies among the Germans. The Germans from the Danubian and Alpine provinces, inhabiting the territories of present Austria, manifested more comprehension and restraint because of their loyalty to the monarchy and empire. On the other hand, many Germans from the historic lands of the Bohemian crown, separated by the Czechs from the Austrian core of the empire, failed to realize the approaching end of their supremacy and rallied under the nationalist colors, some of them advocating an all-German program to preserve their dominant position.[2] The rapprochement and alliance of the empire with Germany tended to strengthen the German tendency against the Austrian, and during the 1914–18 war the first clearly dominated, strongly assisted by the policy of the Berlin government, which considered the maintenance of German supremacy in Austria a vital necessity for Germany.[3]

---

see Hans Krebs, *Kampf in Böhmen,* pp. 34–35. Krebs was one of the founders of the Nazi Party in the Czech lands. After his flight from Czechoslovakia to the Reich in 1933 he became a member of the Reichstag. After 1939 Krebs was one of the heads of administration of the Sudeten province. In 1947 he was sentenced to death in Prague. His informative book is Nazi-oriented.

2. In 1910, Germans formed 35.5 percent of the population of the Austrian half of the empire; Czechs, 23.0 percent; Poles, 17.8; Ukrainians, 12.6; Slovenes, 4.5; Serbo-Croatians, 2.8; Italians, 2.7; Rumanians, 1.0 (Jurij Křížek, "Příspěvek k dějinám rozpadu Rakouska-Uherska a vzniku Československa," *Příspěvky k dějinám KSČ,* September 1958, p. 79). M. K. Kašpar (*Why without the Sudeten Germans?,* pp. 8–9) extracted some nationalist utterances from German sources. Writing about the Sudeten German movement for unity, Josef Pfitzner, then professor of history at the German University in Prague, affirmed: "Until 1918 the Sudeten Germans had lived in a State in which Germandom had occupied a leading position as the preservers of the Empire and the cement of the State" (*Sudetendeutsche Einheitsbewegung,* p. 33).

3. Kamil Krofta, *Les nouveaux états dans l'Europe centrale,* p. 66. For the steady support by Berlin of the German hegemony in Austria, see the excellent study by Prof. Fritz Fischer, *Griff nach der Weltmacht,* pp. 253 ff.

Between 1770 and 1848 a seeming miracle occurred.[4] The fusion of the ideals of the French Revolution, Romanticism, and the arrival of the Industrial Revolution helped to save the Czech nation from extinction. Its national awakening is not readily classifiable, having been a cultural, economic, political, demographic, and social phenomenon. With this proviso, however, it may be affirmed that one factor stood out: the Czech language as the unique instrument by which the Czechs were able to achieve cultural and political maturity.[5]

The Czechs strove valiantly for national equity. They knew that in a multinational empire ruled by the Germans they could not gain political and economic equality by radical actions or through a coup d'état. Conquest could be achieved only as the result of long hard work on the part of all political, social, cultural, and economic organizations. As the Czech middle class became relatively prosperous, it pushed back the tide of the German thrust, slowly but relentlessly.[6] The progress of democratic and progressive ideals in Western Europe found a strong echo among the Czech intelligentsia, creating a common cultural and political background for the promotion of national aspirations.

The furthering of a reasonable democratic policy was in the best Czech interests, and the Czech élite intentionally strove to tie Czech culture with the more liberal and democratic forces of Europe. It exposed Austrian imperialism in the Balkans, promoted efforts to gain universal franchise, and protested against any evidence of national oppression, injustice, or intolerance. Czech political leaders became spokesmen for the democratization of the empire as opposed to the absolutist state and its militarist policy. They pleaded for equal rights of small nations. They asserted their amity toward France and their big Slav brother, Russia. Many Czechs sided—partly, it is true, for

4. In 1810 the famous Czech scholar Josef Dobrovský stated: *"Causa gentis nostrae, nisi Deus adjuvet, plane desperata est"* ("Without the support of God, the fate of our nation is utterly desperate"). In 1827, Josef Jungmann, another prominent figure of the Czech revival, affirmed: "Our tragic fate has been to be witnesses and accomplices in the definitive annihilation of our maternal language."

5. The Czech political leader František Rieger complained in the Viennese Reichsrat: "How many times have we had to hear that only German could be the language of civilization and of science for us, and that science could be pursued only in German! This is the peril that threatens the Czechs. We demand that our language be used in schools, in administration, in public life, in the debates of the Diet" (M. Mercier, *La formation de l'état tchécoslovaque*, p. 49).

6. For the development of the Czech bourgeoisie, see Wiskemann, *Czechs and Germans*, pp. 28–30; Křížek, pp. 20 ff.

their own sake—with those dynamic democratic forces that had sprung up prior to World War I. The Czech leaders excelled in combining their national self-interest with more universal tendencies and their nationalism with liberal humanism. Both presidents Tomáš G. Masaryk and Eduard Beneš continued in this tradition when they deliberately ranged the Czech and Slovak peoples in the camp of liberal and democratic Europe.

The German national leaders never seriously attempted to put their national ideology at the service of a universalist ideal. As the real rulers of the monarchy, they had never succeeded in developing any political program other than an outworn nationalist terminology justifying their racial predominance. They refused to consider members of a Slav nationality as worthy of equal rights. Their program had no appeal to the non-German nationalities because the principle of national superiority, in whatever terms it might be couched, could not attract any of them. The ensuing split between the ideologies of the two nations emphasized the general climate of uneasiness and tension. The language struggle for every German and Czech soul was waged in a true crusading spirit on both sides.

When Czech workers moved to German Bohemian areas, where they were offered jobs by German employers, they were threatened with Germanization. Consequently along the Czech-German national frontier a number of Czech national defense societies[7] appeared with the aim of building Czech schools and maintaining Czech teachers. In 1884–85 special national unions came into being for the purpose of securing material aid for Czech traders and workingmen. The Germans on their part founded the Deutscher Schulverein (German School League) in 1880 to foster their schools in South Tyrol and Austria.[8] In the 1880's also, other protective societies were set up to bar Czechs from German regions by forcing them to send their children to German schools.[9]

7. V. Beneš, p. 37. The Czech Central School Society was founded in 1880.
8. It changed its name to the Verein für das Deutschtum im Ausland (VDA) in 1908. In 1933 the Volksbund replaced the Verein, in accordance with the new emphasis on the *völkische*. The Volksbund für das Deutschtum im Ausland (VDA; League for Germanism Abroad) continued the activities of the Verein. In 1924 the VDA united 1,914 local and 1,172 school organizations extending to the Alps and Sudeten lands. It took care of the schools, libraries, and newspapers of Germans abroad. (See Raymond E. Murphy, ed., *National Socialism, Basic Principles, Their Application by the Nazi Party's Foreign Organizations, and the Use of Germans Abroad for Nazi Aims*, U.S. Department of State Publication No. 1864, pp. 111, 113; and Ralph F. Bischoff, *Nazi Conquest Through German Culture*, pp. 83, 85. Murphy's able study will hereafter be cited as *National Socialism*.)
9. All of them were private associations aiming to protect the German language and German schools (Bischoff, p. 80).

The long German rule of the country had paved the way for a continuing process of Germanization.[10] The political revival of the Czechs therefore concentrated on a defense of the Czech language, since they could not allow themselves to be submerged by the German wave again. Linguistic equality gave the Czechs a protective safeguard for their national community. It was natural, therefore, that there were clashes, quarrels, and disputes between the two nationalities.

The Russian revolution and the Wilson program of self-determination broke ground for a favorable reception of the efforts of smaller nations for independence.[11] In this new climate of freedom, the Czechoslovak exile movement was able to crown its endeavors by obtaining recognition as an ally,[12] and during the last days of Austria-Hungary, Czechoslovakia was proclaimed independent, uniting Czechs with Slovaks.[13] The political objective of Czechoslovak resistance at home and abroad was achieved.

The Czechoslovak Republic did not wish to become an instrument to be used by or against Germany.[14] As a new state it intended to pursue a policy of natural alliance with those powers who were able to guarantee its legitimate international position and its independence. The appeal of France, as the largest continental power which had assisted Czechoslovakia during the war and helped her in her first steps toward nationhood, was strongest among the Czechoslovak political leaders, and an alliance with France was considered the surest means of preserving the new status. Only thus could a permanent agreement with Germany[15] and the stabilization of a

10. Krofta, *Les nouveaux états*, p. 35.
11. Wenzel Jaksch in his anti-Beneš polemical book, *Europas Weg nach Potsdam* (p. 175), belittled the provisional figures given by T. G. Masaryk in 1925 as the total amount of the Czechoslovak Army fighting for Czechoslovak independence in exile: in Russia there were 92,000 soldiers; in France, 12,000; in Italy, 24,000. In addition, after the armistice there were about 54,000 Czechoslovaks organized in Italy. Some 45,000 men fought within the ranks of the British, Canadian, Serbian, and American armies.
12. On Oct. 15, 1918, France recognized the Czechoslovak provisional government with T. G. Masaryk as its head, M. R. Štefánik as secretary of war, and E. Beneš as foreign minister (F. Lee Benns, *European History Since 1870* [New York, 1950], p. 384). The government proclaimed that the Czechoslovak people accepted the principles of American democracy as their own in the Declaration of Independence in Washington on Oct. 18, 1918. The declaration stated that the rights of minorities would be preserved by proportional representation. (See Koegler, p. 5.)
13. On Oct. 28, 1918.
14. An Active and Responsible Czechoslovak Statesman [E. Beneš], *Germany and Czechoslovakia*, II, 21.
15. I follow the views set forth by Eduard Beneš in his succinct survey of Czechoslovak foreign policy (*ibid.*, I, 12–45).

reconstructed Central Europe be envisaged. These main tenets of Czechoslovak foreign policy were based on what the Czechs considered to be the self-interest of the Western Powers and the fundamental facts of Central European geography, economy, politics, and strategy.[16]

In contrast to the West- and Slav-oriented policies of the Czechoslovaks, the Sudeten Germans consistently demonstrated their full support and solidarity with the increasing dependence of Austrian policy upon Germany.[17] Although there was a moderate faction among the Austrian Germans, power rested with those who regarded themselves as the Herrenvolk and thought of the war and the coming German victory as a means toward national domination of the "inferior" Slavs. During the war there were attempts to introduce German as the only official language,[18] and punitive measures[19] against the Czechs, who were sympathetic to Russia and the Western

16. At the peace conference in 1919, the Czechoslovaks were ready to accede to some territorial concessions and compensations, but the conference stressed the integrity of the historic frontier line. Slight rectifications in favor of Czechoslovakia were made in the region of Hlučín in Silesia and in southern Bohemia and Moravia. In Slovakia there was a short war with the Béla Kun regime for the new Slovak-Hungarian boundaries. For a concise analysis, see J. Borovička, *Ten Years of Czechoslovak Politics*, pp. 18–20. For a German account, see Kurt Rabl, *Das Ringen um das sudetendeutsche Selbstbestimmungsrecht 1918/19*.

17. Krebs (p. 47) noted that "neither in the German nor in the Slav or Magyar camp was there anyone in doubt that this was to be a decisive war one way or the other." The leaders of the German Austrian bourgeois parties, under the influence of the German successes in the war, asked for German to be the state language and stressed German expansion toward South and Southeastern Europe in their "Easter demands" in 1916. There were, moreover, many anti-Czech utterances by German nationalist leaders from the Historic Provinces, such as the speech by Karl Hermann Wolf of September 1917, or the interventions by Rafael Pacher, Hermann Ullmann, etc. (Wiskemann, *Czechs and Germans, passim;* Jaroslav César-Bohumil Černý, *Politika německých buržoazních stran v Československu v letech 1918–1938,* I, 43–49; hereafter to be cited as *Politika*). For the German point of view emphasizing the defensive character of German reactions, see Jaksch, *Europas Weg*, pp. 165–69. Henry Cord Meyer, in *Mitteleuropa in German Thought and Action 1815–1945*, pp. 303 ff., surveys the German Central European conception and points out that grossdeutsch sentiment flourished in the area of prewar Austria.

18. German was made the only official language on all railways in Bohemia in 1916 (Koegler, p. 48; Wiskemann, *Czechs and Germans*, p. 75).

19. Many Czechs were executed. The national leaders, Dr. Karel Kramář, Dr. Alois Rašín, and others, were arrested in 1915 and sentenced to death in 1916. The Czechs saw in these sentences—never carried out—the shadow of things to come. The gymnastic society, the *Sokol* (*the Falcon*), which was immensely popular and was regarded as a device to promote national education, was dissolved on Nov. 23, 1915. Under the rule of the new Emperor Charles the repressive measures were alleviated and Kramář and Rašín were released, but the pressure still continued strong (*ibid.*, pp. 74, 76–77).

Powers,[20] revealed the growing gap between German-dominated Austria and the national aspirations of the Czechs. The Czechs learned from nationalist Germans what might be in store for them after a German victory, and they worried openly about the pro-German trend in Austrian policy.[21]

In 1918 the Sudeten Germans were facing a test of common sense and statesmanship. It was an undeniable fact that the Germans could not hope to win the war alone, without allies, within an empire undermined by internal national subversion. For one thing they should have faced realities and stopped living in what might be called the grossdeutsch dream. It ought to have been obvious to their leaders that negative reactions without the balance of a constructive policy could not win friends among the oppressed non-German nationalities in their midst. However, they felt that they were defending Western culture against the drive of the "primitive" Slavs, and thought to establish a defense against what they regarded as encirclement by the Western Powers. They still wielded vast power, but they did not see that power alone could not influence people who were not disposed to subscribe to their own vassalage. As a result, the downfall of Austria-Hungary found the Sudeten Germans surprised at what the Czechs had accomplished. Defeated, mourning their high war losses,[22] they saw behind the Czech victory and the peace settlement a vicious combination of pan-Slavism and political greed, betrayal of promises of national self-determination, and a decline of courage, loyalty, and selflessness. Their world had disintegrated, and they looked for a new scale of values that would help them against what they believed to be national humiliation and injustice. Converted from masters into a minority, they became strangers in the new climate of postwar Europe.

20. Some units of the Czech regiments went over to the Russians. For instance, the desertions of the 28th Regiment of Prague and of the 36th Regiment in April and May 1915, respectively, were widely known. For an account, see Vladimír Konopka, ed., Živé tradice, pp. 25–50.

21. In May 1918, Emperor Charles agreed to the establishment of an autonomous Deutschböhmen (Wiskemann, pp. 79–80). One of the war aims of the German Reich was to achieve the closest possible union with Austria-Hungary (the so-called Mitteleuropa) as the basis for German hegemony in Europe (Fischer, Griff, pp. 252, 256–57, 564–69, 693, 698–99). For the pro-German course of the Habsburg Empire, see the able study by Z. A. B. Zeman, The Break-up of the Habsburg Empire 1914–1918, pp. 86–87, 148–50, 160–61.

22. The war losses of the Sudeten Germans were among the highest in Austria; German Moravia-Silesia had 44.4 dead per 1,000, and German Bohemia 34.5 (A. Ciller, Deutscher Sozialismus, p. 139). The losses of all Austrian Germans amounted to 35.2; of the Reich, 27.8 till the end of 1917 (Bohmann, Sudetendeutschtum, p. 38).

The Czechoslovak Germans were the most powerful German minority[23] in the Central and Eastern European states. They were a highly developed, vigorous, competent, and wealthy group. Sober, hard-working, self-righteous, and endowed with a strong sense of duty toward their national group, the Sudeten German bourgeois classes lived in a private world, populated with the princes and countesses who remained the real symbols of success and prestige. The gloomy mood of apprehension and sense of national anxiety brought on by the German defeat provided the framework for their irrational return to a mythical past. Frustrated by the abrupt fading of the hopes of a victorious German nation, they sought a way out by rejecting compromises and by glorifying the national virtues of virility and discipline. Their sentimentalism and romanticism repudiated the more pragmatic values of contemporary life, degraded—they felt—by egotism and opportunism. Estranged from the outside world, they enjoyed a strange form of escapism based on the ideal existence of a national community (Volksgemeinschaft) endowed with all the heroic virtues. Various conceptions of post-1918 Europe offered the embittered German bourgeoisie a refuge where it could contemplate its own sufferings, humiliations, and degradation. There is not, of course, a single simple portrait of the Sudeten German mind. But most of the German political leaders epitomized the latent nationalism which was always a part of any political movement among the Germans from the Czech lands. It was this emotional, aggressive nationalism of a somewhat provincial provenance, stimulated by sublimated memories of past glories, which fanned Czech fears.

October 1918 was a month of decision for the Sudeten Germans. The right of self-determination—which they consistently denied to all Slav nationalities—became the keystone of their leaders' policy. On Oct. 21, 1918, the German deputies of former Austria convened their national committee in Vienna. They demanded the right of self-determination for the Germans also, providing a basis for the immediate annexation of two larger German provinces by German Austria. On Oct. 29, 1918, the province of German Bohemia was formed, with its capital at Liberec. The next day the new province of the Sudetenland was established. Later, the districts of the Bohemian Forest and a zone in southern Moravia joined Upper and Lower

23. There were 513,000 Germans in Yugoslavia in 1921, 700,000 in Rumania in 1918, and 551,000 in Hungary in 1920 (Krofta, *Les nouveaux états,* pp. 112–13, 117). J. César and B. Černý rightly stressed local patriotism and provincialism in the Sudeten Germans' split into many groups and national islands. This heterogeneity also explained their economic, political, linguistic, and psychological differences (*Politika,* I, 482–85).

Austria. German Austria demanded, in addition, other German districts.[24] These provinces were separate entities geographically, and the larger part of them was not even linked territorially with the state of which they claimed to be members. The mood of the German people, struck by their unexpected defeat in the war, was, however, sullen and indifferent. Some of them favored settlement with the Czechs; a small nationalist faction strove for occupation by the Reich;[25] and the largest part called for union with German Austria. The eventual occupation of the German areas by Czechoslovak troops[26] (consisting of a mere three regiments) started in November and continued almost without bloodshed. The Germans restricted themselves to vocal protests.[27] They failed, however, in their goal of blocking the formation of the Czechoslovak Republic within its historic borders. Their efforts to arouse world public opinion came to nothing and the Allies ignored their appeals.

Against this background, the Czechoslovak leaders faced a test of their political maturity. They were sincere in their efforts to ease national pressures, applying pragmatic efficiency as their guiding principle in dealing with the Germans. They were aware that the German question presented one of the main issues that challenged the new state. Tomáš Garrigue Masaryk, the scholarly philosopher and humanist who became the first president and the highest moral authority of the Republic, stated in October 1918 that the Czechs should negotiate with the Germans over their acceptance of a Czechoslovakia which would become "a modern progressive and

24. See above, pp. 3–4. See also Jan Opočenský, *The Collapse of the Austro-Hungarian Monarchy and the Rise of the Czechoslovak State*, pp. 174–79. In his detailed treatment, Opočenský (p. 181) rightly stated that "the German pretensions could not have been greater" even in the case of a German victory. The seized territory had an area of 26,911 sq km and included 3,109,825 Germans and 169,680 Czechs, according to the census of 1910 (Raschhofer, *Sudetenfrage*, p. 117).

25. On Oct. 22, 1918, three radical German deputies, two of them from Bohemia, came to the headquarters of the German Army in Berlin and negotiated with the high command and some nationalist circles for the occupation of the Bohemian frontier area by the German Army (Opočenský, *The Collapse*, pp. 175–76).

26. The juridical basis for the occupation was the Armistice agreement. On Dec. 21, 1918, the French government promised to uphold the frontiers of the Historic Provinces. Great Britain agreed on Jan. 7, 1919, and Italy on Jan. 8, 1919 (*ibid.*, pp. 191–92).

27. The Austrian government lodged a protest against the occupation, which for all practical purposes had the character of an administrative measure. The Germans offered no organized armed resistance. The capital of German Bohemia, Liberec, fell on Dec. 16, 1918 (Jaroslav César-Bohumil Černý, *Od sudetoněmeckého separatismu k plánům odvety*, p. 135. The study is useful but Communist-biased).

democratic State."[28] Czech policy proceeded on the assumption that
the Germans had to be won over to cooperation and that just means
should be developed which would enable the government to deal
with the sources of disagreement. Even the pronationalist first
Czechoslovak prime minister, Karel Kramář, appeared to share the
feeling of the liberal Czech politicians when he declared on Nov. 14,
1918, that

> faithful to our past and our democratic traditions, we have no
> desire to hinder in any way our German fellow countrymen in the
> development of their culture and language. It is our desire and
> pride that no one among us who is not a Czech should feel
> oppressed or unfree. . . . We do not wish to imitate the old
> Austrian system. . . . We want all parts of our Republic to have
> equal and just shares in our new economic and social progress.[29]

The strong impulse to avoid conflicts created an atmosphere of
tolerance among the Czech leaders despite the open rebellion of the
German deputies in the Austrian Assembly. The Germans refused to
take part in the Czechoslovak Provisional National Assembly, still
hoping that at the Paris peace conference they would enjoy the
advantages of being, as Austrians, a party to the negotiations.

The negative attitude of the Germans could not help them to gain
the confidence of the Czechs who sought to restore governmental
authority and to calm things down. In his message to Parliament on
Dec. 22, 1918, President Masaryk discussed the German question at
greater length. He noted that the Republic had been created by the
Czechs and that the Germans had come into the country as colonists.
It was difficult to forget, he said, that the Germans had furnished the
most violent supporters of pan-Germanism. Like the United States of
America, Czechoslovakia would never accept any secession of her
mixed Bohemian districts. The Germans could be assured, however,
that they would be free to enjoy complete national rights and civil
equality.[30]

Not the threatening but futile German gestures, but the existing
balance of power and a stimulating breeze of freedom and social and
national justice determined international recognition and acceptance
of the Republic. This liberal tide was still vigorous enough to act as
a powerful rationale at the peace conference, and within this frame of

28. Masaryk in a dispatch to Eduard Beneš. (See Vojta Beneš, p. 57.)
29. Vincent Urban, p. 8. Urban used the wrong date, November 16. See also the
relevant chapter in Brügel's *Ludwig Czech*, pp. 57 ff.
30. The message was quoted in the able survey by Jaromír Smutný, *Němci v
Československu a jich odsun z republiky* (pp. 31–32).

mind a critical approach was maintained as the experts searched for the best solution before making concrete decisions.[31] It was only after an examination of all the factors involved that the Czechoslovak frontiers were fixed and the Germans left within Czechoslovakia.[32] Both sides—the Czechoslovaks and the Germans[33]—had presented memoranda with their respective claims.[34] The German cause encountered hostility, however, because it was recognized generally that geographical, strategic, political, and economic reasons required that the predominantly German area remain within Czechoslovakia.[35] It was agreed that without retaining its historic frontiers the Republic could not exist as an independent state. The conference, however,

31. For the Czechoslovak settlement at the peace conference, see the relevant chapter in the sound study by Piotr Wandycz, *France and Her Eastern Allies, 1919–1925*, pp. 49–74. Before any decision was taken, the Allied experts studied all the facts. For example, the American delegates, C. Seymour, G. Johnson, J. Kerner, and A. Dulles, as well as the British and Italian experts, had visited the Republic and examined the situation on the spot (*Germany and Czechoslovakia*, II, 24–25). Beneš expressly stated that "before a decision was arrived at on any territorial or minority question, there was a whole flood of discussion, criticism, and oral and written elucidations in commissions and in personal interviews" (*ibid.*, p. 26).

32. Harold Nicholson, *Peacemaking 1919*, pp. 25, 252.

33. The delegates of the Sudeten Germans—Dr. Lodgman von Auen, Josef Seliger, Dr. Robert Freissler, Anton Klement, and Hieronymus Oldofredi—formed part of the Austrian delegation as its experts. Their memorandum presented to the conference was based on the principle of self-determination and advocated the annexation of the Germans by Austria. (Raschhofer, *Sudetenfrage*, pp. 114–120). The leaders of the Czechoslovak delegation were Karel Kramář, the prime minister, and Eduard Beneš, the foreign minister.

34. Dr. Beneš submitted to the conference 11 memoranda and proposals dealing with Czech internal affairs and territorial claims on the basis of the preservation of the historic frontier. In 1937, Hermann Raschhofer published the memoranda (*Die tschechoslowakischen Denkschriften für die Friedenskonferenz von Paris 1919/1920*) wherein he pointed out that the Czechoslovak delegation had used false data. Beneš replied in a series of articles in the *Prager Presse*, which were reprinted as a book in 1937 (*Germany and Czechoslovakia*, II. *Czechoslovakia at the Peace Conference and the Present German-Czechoslovak Discussion*). He defended himself against the campaign of reproach that Czechoslovakia had not kept her promise, as stated in her note of May 20, 1919, to the Paris conference, "to make of the Czechoslovak Republic a sort of Switzerland" (*ibid.*, pp. 45 ff.). The somewhat unfortunate mention of Switzerland, when viewed in the context of the note, meant clearly the engagement to the effect that the new state would adopt some of the liberal principles of the Swiss system. All the points of the note calling for national and individual equality were carried through. The note also made clear that "a special position will be reserved for the Czechoslovak language" and that the privileges "which the Germans previously enjoyed will be reduced to their due proportions." As a result, the reproaches of deceit were groundless. (See also Rabl, *passim.*)

35. The separation of the German areas and their annexation by Austria was regarded as unfeasible. The final outcome, it was felt, would be their incorporation into Germany (*Germany and Czechoslovakia*, II, 69).

inserted into the peace treaty safeguards for the rights of minorities, and Czechoslovakia accepted these obligations by her signature of the St. Germain Treaty on Sept. 10, 1919.[36] All the provisions of the minority protections were inserted into the Czechoslovak statutes, which, in some cases, even went beyond the international obligations.[37]

The breakdown of the Habsburg Empire and its defeat at the Paris conference intensified German nationalism. German resentment was also inflamed by the frustration at Paris and the humiliation of being subject to the Czechs. The consequent German attacks on Czechoslovak Army barracks and the mass demonstrations held on March 4, 1919, in many German cities as a protest against the government's decision to bar the Germans from the elections to the Austrian Parliament, brought the first real bloodshed. Fifty-four Germans were shot by the Czechoslovak Army.[38] Naturally, the German reaction was one of anger. This unfortunate development left deep emotional scars within the psychological and historical context in which German-Czech relations were conducted. Yet even more important was the lack of communication between the political leaders of both nations. The Germans absented themselves from the Czechoslovak Provisional National Assembly. As a result, they were unable to influence the Parliament in its promulgation of the constitutional basis of the state.

The Czech and Slovak people were elated over their newly won freedom. Czechoslovak propaganda never ceased pointing to World War I as an instance of the German drive to the East, and it was inevitable that many German utterances conjured up in the Czech mind recollections of the evil days of German hegemony. There were, indeed, instances of unfair humiliation of the Germans which harmed the Czech image, but the transfer of power and the subsequent consolidation of the state was effected with a minimum of violence. The Czechs were still too absorbed with their success in fulfilling their maximum goals and with their efforts to build up the new Republic. They felt no need to press their victory any further.

Czechoslovakia established a democratic parliamentary regime built on humanitarian and liberal traditions which made it unique

36. Jacob Robinson et al., *Were the Minorities Treaties a Failure?*, p. 154. The study presents a fair survey of minority protection after 1918.
37. *Ibid.*, p. 210.
38. Ernst Frank, *Sudetenland—Deutsches Land*, pp. 90–92. This book describes the German attacks on the Czech Army barracks in a western Bohemian town. The army began to shoot only when it was directly assaulted. The greatest death toll (25 dead) was suffered at Kadaň. See also César-Černý, *Politika*, I, 140–45.

among the states of Central and Eastern Europe.[39] The Republic
tended to reflect the flexibility of the Czechs, their practical imagination, working abilities, political prudence, and shrewd sense of the
possible. These practical and utilitarian qualities were coupled with a
strong propensity to self-flagellation and masochism among their
intelligentsia. The more the Czechs advanced, the more their intellectuals admired foreign—particularly French—culture. Where the fighting spirit and the relentless drive of a Masaryk strove to open the
Czech cultural world to the purifying breeze of European culture, his
followers hardly enhanced Masaryk's reputation by the facile elo-
quence with which they expressed their naïve theories of the eternal
goodness of man, and raised these beliefs to a political credo.

It was perhaps unavoidable, in view of the differing political ideals
of Germans and Czechs, that while the Czech leaders strove to erect a
perfect house for individual inhabitants, many Germans viewed in
these endeavors a device to prevent their national community from
arriving at an autonomous status.

The Republic was declared to be a national state composed of the
Czechoslovak nation and national minorities.[40] The Czechoslovak
political leaders felt that the election of German representatives to
municipal bodies would prove to all the minorities that the Republic
deserved the respect of all of its citizens. The Provisional National
Assembly therefore passed a local government franchise law on the
basis of equal rights and proportional representation. When the
municipal election was held on June 16, 1919, it placed the local
administration of all towns and parishes with a German majority into
German hands.[41] Much of the local administrative power was also
transferred to the Germans. The School Act of April 3, 1919, provided

39. The National Assembly was divided into two houses elected by direct, equal,
and universal suffrage based on proportional representation. The president of the
Republic was elected by the Assembly for seven years. He appointed a cabinet
of ministers responsible to the Assembly. In practice, the Republic developed
into a regime of political parties. See Eduard Táborský, *Czechoslovak
Democracy at Work*. Táborský called pre-Munich Czechoslovakia "a state
of political parties" (p. 94). Emil Franzel regarded her as "a clear State of
parties" (in Helmut Preidel, ed., *Die Deutschen in Böhmen und Mähren*, p.
342). Preidel's book is an interesting collection of articles surveying the history
of the Germans in the Czech lands. It is, however, strongly biased.
40. Dr. E. Beneš at the National Assembly on Sept. 30 and Oct. 1, 1919 (Smutný,
p. 25).
41. The German politicians were still absent from the Assembly when it passed
these laws. Even the German nationalists recognized that the principles of
proportionality and universal suffrage were progressive and nationally just. See
the speech of Dr. Anton Kreissl at the Carlsbad Congress of the Henlein Party in
1938 in *Der Lebenswille des Sudetendeutschtums* (Carlsbad-Leipzig, 1938), p.
9. J. W. Brügel called the elections "the first really democratic elections" taking
place in the Historic Provinces (*Ludwig Czech*, p. 64).

for the establishment of German elementary schools whenever there was an attendance of at least 40 German children. The Public Libraries Act of July 22 assured all parishes with more than 400 members of a minority group the right to set up public libraries. In addition, the rights of national, racial, and religious minorities were incorporated into the Constitution of Feb. 29, 1920, with section VI ensuring full equality for all citizens and prohibiting forced denationalization. National minorities were guaranteed a due proportion of public funds for educational, religious, and charitable purposes. The Language Law allowed a minority language to be used as an official language in districts in which more than two thirds of the inhabitants spoke that language. (According to the census of 1921, about 2,225,000 Germans lived in districts affected by this legislation.)[42] In any district where any language was the mother tongue of at least 20 percent of the population, it was permitted to be used in public instruction and in official communications. (About 753,000 Germans, forming from 20 to 66 percent of the total population, lived in such districts.[43] Only about 130,000 Germans lived in districts where they formed a minority under 20 percent.) However, the law displayed a certain preference for the Czechoslovak language by declaring it the official language to be used on state notes, on banknotes, and in the Army. All public corporations were also bound to accept and deal with applications in the Czechoslovak language,[44] and every commune was required to have a Czech or Slovak official name. With this minor display of sovereignty, Czechoslovakia fulfilled her pledges of minority protection. She kept all the obligations faithfully, and there is general agreement that she was most generous in her minority legislation.[45]

42. Emil Sobota, *Das tschechoslowakische Nationalitätenrecht*, p. 122. This is an authoritative survey of Czechoslovak minority legislation.
43. *Ibid.*
44. The government instruction of Feb. 3, 1926, implemented the language law in courts, offices, public corporations, etc. All state employees had to know Czech. Language examinations were made very difficult, and many dispensable German officials were retired or dismissed (Harry Kelpetář, *Seit 1918. . . . Eine Geschichte der tschechoslowakischen Republik*, p. 223. This book gives an excellent political survey of the history of Czechoslovakia.). There are useful sections on the minority problems in Chmelař (pp. 35 ff.) and Bohemicus (pp. 36 ff.).
45. According to Beneš, in his declaration at the Sixth Committee of the League of Nations (1934), "the policy of the Czechoslovak Government has preceeded on the following lines" when a complaint was lodged with the League: "(a) When a petition was well founded, we raised no questions of prestige. . . . The Government simply put matters in order. . . . (b) When the petition was not justified . . . we gave . . . a definite, clear . . . reply" (Robinson, p. 183).

After amnesty had been extended to them by the president on Oct. 10, 1919, the leading members of the German separatist movement returned from Vienna.[46] In the meantime, the German bourgeois parties had formed an Arbeitsblock (Working Bloc) in June 1919, and the German Social Democratic Party had held a congress (August 30 to September 3). Although both groups defended German self-determination, the Social Democrats were more receptive to the Republic, and its democratic system found in them sincere supporters. Because of international recognition of the Czechoslovak state, the Germans bowed before the inevitable, and 72 German deputies, representing the traditional German parties from the old empire, were elected in the first Czechoslovak parliamentary elections in April 1920,[47] although they still opposed the existence of the Republic. In the name of the German parliamentary union, Dr. Rudolf Lodgman von Auen[48] made a solemn declaration in the House of Deputies on June 1, 1920:

46. Klepetář, p. 98; César-Černý, *Politika*, I, 190.

47. The following list of the German parties with the results of all the Czechoslovak parliamentary elections was taken from Táborský (*Czechoslovak Democracy*, p. 85):

Elections	April 1920	November 1925	October 1929	May 1935
Social Democrats	31	17	21	11
Christian Socialists	9	13	14	6
Agrarians (BdL)	13	24	16	5
National Party (DNP)	12	10	7	0
National Socialists (DNSAP)	5	7	8	0
Democrats	2	0	0	0
Retailers	0	0	3	0
Henlein Party (SdP)	0	0	0	44

Bohmann gives different figures for the elections of 1920 and 1925 (*Sudetendeutschtum*, pp. 84–85). On the Czech side the strongest parties were the Agrarians, the Social Democrats, the left-center Czech Socialists, the Catholic People's Party, and the bourgeois National Democrat Party. The Communist Party combined Czechs and Germans. The Social Democrats were the strongest party up to 1920, but a split within the party and the formation of the Communist Party in 1921 weakened their ranks so that from 1925 the Agrarians held first place as the strongest Czech party.

48. The union was founded on May 13–14, 1920, as an assembling body of all non-Socialist members of the National Assembly (César-Černý, *Politika*, I, 211 ff.). After his return to Czechoslovakia on Oct. 1, 1919, Dr. Lodgman became the leader of the radical National Party and was the spokesman of German radical nationalism. On Oct. 27, 1922, he declared in the Assembly: "He who does not think that the supreme duty of a German Deputy is to commit high treason in this State, makes a mistake" (Klepetář, p. 175). His eclipse came with his defeat at the election of 1925, and he retired from public life. Only after 1945 did he become again the leader of radical nationalism in West Germany. For his pan-German ideas, see *Pátá kolona v severních Čechách*, pp. 75–104.

We, representatives of the German people in the Czechoslovak
State, declare that the ideas and principles which had guided the
Allied Powers in drawing up the Peace Treaties were fallacious,
that this State has developed at the expense of historical truth. . . .
The Germans of Bohemia, Moravia and Silesia, and the Germans of
Slovakia never desired to unite with the Czechs. . . . On the
contrary, the Deputies of the Austrian Reich's Council elected in
the Sudeten German districts in 1911 . . . expressly declared their
wish . . . to join German-Austria. . . . We . . . shall never recognize the Czechs as masters. We proclaim with solemnity that we
shall never cease in our demands for the self-determination of our
people. We do not regard ourselves to be bound by the Laws
passed by the Revolutionary National Assembly.[49]

This radical proclamation expressed the frustrations of a proud
national group. Its very radicalism rendered futile the German efforts
at unity and condemned them to a policy of parliamentary obstruc-
tion. They did not exert much practical influence in the Parliament,
where the Czechs held a clear majority. However, the return to
economic prosperity, the visible initial successes of the consolidation
of the Republic, and the gradual recognition of the futility of a
negative approach worked for a relaxation of tensions. More Germans
followed those leaders who were prepared to recognize Czechoslovakia as their state.

The first split occurred in the bourgeois camp on June 26, 1922,
between those who rallied under the banner of implacable nationalism—the German National Party (the DNP) and the National
Socialist Party (the DNSAP)—and the more moderate groups represented by the German Agrarians (Bund der Landwirte: BdL), the
Christian Socialists, and the German Democratic bloc,[50] who rejected
the policy of secession. The Activist parties gained the election of
1925 over the Negativists. When the Czechoslovak Socialist-Agrarian
governmental coalition parted over the question of the high agrarian
protective tariff, the German Agrarians and Christian Socialists
entered the cabinet. Berlin viewed the new approach with sympathy
and threw its weight on the side of those urging mutual accommodation. It favored exploration of a compromise and advocated acceptance of the Czechoslovak state as a permanent factor. The German

49. Koegler, p. 21; Klepetář, p. 125.
50. *Ibid.*, p. 178. The uncompromising negativists were called the "fighting
community" (Kampfgemeinschaft). The term for the moderates was the
"working community" (Arbeitsgemeinschaft). The Social Democrats did not
form a part of either front but favored the Activist trend politically.

Foreign Ministry fully endorsed the Activist policy and opposed the unyielding stand of Dr. Lodgman.[51] Harry Klepetář rightly pointed out[52] that not national sentiment but economic motives united Czechs and Germans. It was a marriage of reason, not of love, favored by the climate of the Locarno pact. The Germans therefore tried to win advantages by working within the government coalition.

The worldwide stabilization of capitalism in the boom conditions of the middle 1920's and the easing of international pressure by the policy of Gustav Stresemann drew Czech and German bourgeois leaders together. The German Agrarian leader, Dr. Franz Spina, propounded his conception of the social symbiosis of Czechs and Germans, conceding that German-Czech coexistence was mutually fruitful and presented a challenge as well as an opportunity to both peoples. Alfred Rosche, heading a group of German industrialists, formed a splinter group[53] of the German National Party and moved toward activism in 1928.

The policy of activism was predicated on the belief that the economic welfare of the Germans called for more than sitting back and permitting the Czechs to run the show. Mutual economic dependence tended to favor the opinion of those who held that the problems should be thought out jointly instead of fought out by both sides in terms of their individual interests. In 1929 the German Social Democrats entered the coalition government.[54] The leading Czechoslovak politicians regarded their entry as the happy beginning of a

---

51. Dr. Franz Spina, professor of Slav philosophy at the German University of Prague and chairman of the Agrarian deputies' club at the National Assembly, became minister of Public Works. The Christian Socialist, Dr. Robert Mayr-Harting, became minister of Justice. The German minister in Prague, Dr. Walter Koch, considered the presence of the Germans in the government as "immense progress." The policy of Stresemann had been strongly in favor of the Activists. (See Dr. Koch's correspondence with Berlin in Brügel, *Ludwig Czech*, pp. 84 ff.). Dr. Koch was appointed to Prague on Oct. 29, 1921 and stayed until June 1935.
52. Page 219. See also César-Černý, *Politika*, I, 376–80.
53. The group was called the German Working and Economic Communion (DAWG). The political brain of the group was Dr. Gustav Peters. In 1935 the majority of the DAWG joined the Henlein Party (Franzel, as cited in Preidel, p. 360).
54. Until the joint Prague Congress of German and Czech Social Democrats met on Jan. 28–29, 1928, there was a series of disputes between the parties. The German Socialists lodged complaints against the Czech party, charging it with the abandonment of the right of self-determination at the congresses of the Socialist International at Hamburg (1923), Marseilles (1925), and Brussels (1928) (František Soukup, *Revoluce práce. Dějinný vývoj socialismu a čs. sociálně demokratické strany dělnické*, Prague, 1938, II, 1355–76). The new German Social Democrat minister, Dr. Ludwig Czech, succeeded the Socialist leader Josef Seliger as head of the party in 1920.

definitive agreement, and were encouraged in their conviction that it was one of their principal tasks, as the leaders of a majority, to win over this largest ethnic group for the Republic.[55] They gave credit for the accord to the mechanisms of the democratic system. It was felt that democratic procedure, and the way it had worked out compromises, presented the surest means to allay German fears and to help them to endorse freely the Czechoslovak Republic and to emulate its democratic ideology. Through freedom and democracy the Germans would learn to look upon Czechoslovakia with more confidence and goodwill and less apprehension. Both sides, however, were aware that grave tensions were present which might erupt as a result either of domestic political actions or of factors beyond their control. Nationalist actions and reactions were permanent realities in this difficult area. Given the psychological, political, and social and economic differences which existed in the historical tradition and ethnic setup, any issue developed a distinctive national tinge.

Despite the enlightened objectives of Czech policy, the program for a democratic national settlement lay more in individual convictions than in a well-prepared government plan. Moreover, although the treatment of the German minority in Czechoslovakia was second to none in Europe in its fairness, the very fact that the Germans did not regard themselves as a minority but as an independent collective entity[56] made it evident that the simple discharging of obligations to a minority would not satisfy the majority of Germans. That the Czechs committed blunders, they were first to admit; some of the German grievances were justified. Yet the democratic system offered the Germans traditional democratic means of redress for their legitimate complaints. The Czechoslovak nationality policy granted the minorities a proportional share in the legislative and administrative bodies.[57] Ac-

55. See the speech of President Masaryk on the anniversary of Independence Day, Oct. 28, 1928 (Klepetář, p. 266). J. W. Brügel rightly points out that "belated abolition of old privileges is never immediately followed by an era of the rule of pure justice and right" (*Ludwig Czech*, p. 81).

56. Dr. Gustav Peters stated at the Congress of European Minorities in 1931: "We are de jure . . . a minority . . . but we must state that we do not believe that we can . . . manage with the stinting provisions of the minorities protection" (Robinson, p. 256). Peters' book, *Der neue Herr von Böhmen*, is one of the few good studies dealing with the German-Czech problem from the German point of view.

57. In the provincial councils, where two thirds of the members were elected and one third appointed, the national proportion was as follows: Bohemia, 37 German and 83 Czech members; Moravia-Silesia, 14 German and 44 Czech. (See the Czechoslovak Memorandum on the Nationality Policy, April 1938, in *DBFP*, I, 190.)

cording to nationality statistics, there were 72 Germans in the House of Deputies in 1920, 75 in 1925, 73 in 1929, and 72 in 1935. Thus, of the 300 members of the House, some 24 percent were Germans.[58] The same policy on the local level enabled the Germans to control 3,362 parishes and 46 districts.[59]

The Germans were provided with a higher percentage of national schools than they were entitled to proportionately.[60] They had 3,311 elementary schools, 455 higher elementary schools, 90 secondary schools, 198 specialist schools, two technological institutes, and one university.[61] The new state also created a German school system in Slovakia.[62] In all, some 96.2 percent of German schoolchildren attended schools controlled by German school councils.[63] On the whole, the Czechoslovak Germans were better equipped with schools than the Germans, Poles, and Magyars in Germany, Poland, and Hungary. While there was one German elementary school for every 862 German inhabitants in Czechoslovakia, there was only one German school per 1,112 inhabitants in Prussia.[64] In view of the large number of German public libraries, theaters, newspapers, and

58. Joseph S. Rouček as quoted in Robert Kerner, ed., *Czechoslovakia*, p. 175.

59. The Czechoslovak Memorandum of April 1938 (*DBFP*, I, 190). There is a discrepancy in the figures. Bohemicus (p. 23) put the number at 3,466 out of 15,734 communes and parishes in the state and at 50 districts out of 239. *Sudetenland* (p. 22) set 3,397 communes with a German majority.

60. It was understandable that the Republic attempted to remove all the inequalities which the dominant German minority had created during the Austro-Hungarian regime. For comparison, one should note that in the school year 1913–14 the Czechs, who amounted to 62.54 percent of the total population of Bohemia and Moravia-Silesia, were provided with 60.1 percent of elementary schools, 58.1 percent of higher elementary schools, and 52.68 percent of secondary and normal schools, while the proportion of German schools (the Germans amounted to 34.92 percent of the total population) was, respectively, 37.8, 41.5, and 46.3 percent (The Rectors of the Czechoslovak Universities, etc., *Czech School Facilities under Austrian Government and German School Facilities under Czechoslovak Government*, pp. 9–10).

61. In the Czechoslovak Memorandum (*DBFP*, I, 190). The date of the statistics was Oct. 31, 1936. (See also Vincent Urban, pp. 54–57.) Both Essler (pp. 36 ff.) and Walter Wannemacher (*Sudetendeutscher Schicksalskampf*, pp. 5–6) gave exaggerated figures. (See also E. Winkler, *Die Tschechoslowakei im Spiegel der Statistik*, p. 76; Chmelař, pp. 75–76. Winkler's book was used as an almost official German reference book. Slight differences in figures are due mostly to different dates for the collection of the statistical data.)

62. While the Germans in Slovakia and Ruthenia had only 22 elementary schools before 1918, their schools numbered 116 elementary, 6 higher elementary, 3 secondary, and 26 other in 1935–36 (*Czech School Facilities*, p. 21).

63. Bracket Lewis, *Democracy in Czechoslovakia*, p. 39.

64. In Poland the proportion was one school per 952 population, and in Hungary, 1 per 1,191. According to Koegler (p. 34), one million Germans in Poland had only 490 elementary and 20 secondary schools.

books—in addition to the educational system—one could assert that the Germans were provided with ample means to maintain and develop their national existence.[65] The eventual reduction in the number of German schools resulted from the change from their privileged position in the past and from the decline in the number of German children born during the war.

The Germans complained of the existence of new Czech minority schools in the predominantly German areas, although this was simply the outcome of the legislation providing for schools for any minority, irrespective of nationality, from which they themselves benefited.[66] Education is perhaps the most important part of national culture, and there is ample evidence that the German educational system in the Republic was one of the most liberal and advanced in Europe and ensured the Germans free cultural development.

German criticism was justified in the matter of its share in state service. The government itself admitted that German representation in public services was inadequate.[67] This was due partly to the fact that the Germans had boycotted state service for many years, preferring better paid private employment. There was, therefore, a shortage of loyal qualified German candidates when the advent of the depression aroused German interest in public services. By 1918, the number of German state officials and employees was high, but most of them were considered unfriendly to the new state. Some were ousted, some retired, and thousands, unable to pass the Czech language tests made expressly too difficult for them, were dismissed. Their places were taken by Czechs who moved to the German areas.

According to the Henlein Party's figures,[68] the number of German

65. The Germans were provided with 3,357 public libraries (DBFP, I, 190). From the declaration of Minister of Education Dr. Emil Franke (Dec. 10, 1936), one can follow the growth during the existence of the Republic: 1920—458 German local public libraries with 282,255 volumes; 1935—3,570 with 2,020,893 volumes (Czechoslovak Cabinet Ministers, p. 37). The difference in the total number of public libraries between the two official statements indicates that nationality statistics were not conducive to strict accuracy.

66. According to Essler (p. 39), on Oct. 1, 1937 there were 15,382 German children in Czech schools, 5,454 of whom attended Czech minority and private elementary schools and 3,053 Czech minority and high elementary schools. The Czech minority schools in Bohemia numbered 428 in 1921 and 850 in 1936. There were 23 German minority schools in the predominantly Czech area in 1930 (Bohmann, Sudetendeutschtum, p. 69).

67. Dr. Milan Hodža, the premier, on Nov. 17, 1937 (Nationality Policy in Czechoslovakia, p. 29).

68. Essler, p. 33. The figures were used at the Carlsbad congress of the Henlein Party on April 24, 1938. (See Wilhelm Sebekowsky, The Expansion of the Czechs—Its Psychology, History, Methods, and Results.)

public servants declined by 41.2 percent in the postal service, by 48.5 percent in the railways service, by 49 percent in the state and provincial service, and by 70.4 percent in the army during the years 1921–1930. The quota of Germans in other branches was adequate, however: 21.11 percent of all teachers and professors were German, as were 33.69 percent of the staff in the tobacco monopoly and 22.6 percent of the judges and public prosecutors.[69] The government of Dr. Milan Hodža deplored the insufficient German representation in state service, and in the wake of its Declaration of Feb. 20, 1937, a special committee was set up to remedy the justified German grievance.[70] Although the Czechs were fully within their rights in seeking to replace unreliable public servants, they neglected to examine realistically the probable consequences of such an action and to look more carefully for trustworthy German candidates. This costly blunder resulted in a shortage of an able German bureaucracy and serious embarrassment when Nazi propaganda broadcast news unfavorable to Czechoslovakia in order to conceal German gains from constructive programs. There is little doubt that the Czechoslovak official lack of diligence in preserving and expanding the number of German public servants exacerbated the annoyances which accompanied the government's dealings in this extremely sensitive matter.

A similar political blunder was committed when contracts for public works and supplies in the predominantly German areas were placed with Czech contractors because their bids were lower than those of the Germans.[71] When Czech workers came along with the Czech firms, the resident Germans regarded this influx of Czechs as a sign of discrimination, and local labor felt cheated by the loss of an opportunity for employment. With the national problem inextricably interwoven with almost any question, what was actually in this case a policy of purely economic and technical efficiency became a source of constant irritation for the Germans. Thus, the absence of psychological insight and a wholly unimaginative and purely economically motivated approach proved detrimental to the interests of the state. It was not until 1937 that the government established the principle that a 22-percent quota of government tenders should be earmarked for

69. Dr. Milan Hodža at the National Assembly on Nov. 17, 1937 (*Nationality Policy*, p. 30).
70. *Ibid.*, p. 32. See Dr. Ivan Dérer, minister of Justice, Nov. 17, 1937 (*ibid.*, pp. 92–93).
71. Essler, pp. 25–28. In the German-speaking areas, state contracts for public works and supplies were placed in the period from March 1, 1937 to Jan. 20, 1938, as follows: 23.3 percent of the contracts went to German firms, 69.2 percent to Czech firms, and 7.5 percent to nationally mixed firms.

German firms, without regard for the economic aspect of the tender.

The Czechoslovak nationality policy cannot be understood entirely from glosses on legislation or from printed records. It was affected by the whole atmosphere of the country, by the attitude of its citizens, and by the spirit of its intelligentsia. It is difficult to exaggerate the influence exerted by the humanistic democratic ideas of President Masaryk. They pervaded all strata of public life and were incorporated in the official ideology of the Republic. Masaryk's argument for democracy in action was his belief in man himself, his spirituality and his immortal soul.[72] Through her democratic institutions Czechoslovakia regarded herself as linked to a historical secular democratic movement that was bound to spread throughout the world. Democracy gave to the Republic its very reason for existence. For Masaryk the meaning of Czech history was to serve God, not Caesar; the mission of Czechoslovakia was to promote democracy in its march forward. This ideological climate established the individual German as a free citizen of equal rights, it gave to all minorities an opportunity of developing any political ideas they might desire to hold, and it made forced denationalization impossible.

The profession of high moral principles did not prevent the development of a struggle for power. Basic and complex national tensions precipitated repeated ups and downs throughout the postwar era, for the historic dispute had produced a deep-seated malaise which made a cohesive German-Czech policy difficult. Past German predominance and the effects of the war had left deep psychological and political scars, so that feelings on both sides were translated into bitterness which exploded repeatedly.

In the years 1920–21 and in 1930 there were national mass demonstrations and outbursts of mob violence in several cities which evidenced the intensity of the undercurrent of national hostility.[73] The ill-considered deflationary policy of 1919–23 had raised the value of the Czechoslovak koruna and thus weakened the position of the predominantly German export industries, causing economic losses to the German bourgeoisie. Moreover, the problem of payment of the war loans of the Habsburg Empire exacerbated the early postwar atmosphere. The loans had been enthusiastically subscribed to by the Germans during the years 1914–18. After the disintegration of the

72. Karel Čapek, *Hovory s T. G. Masarykem*, pp. 300–301. This is a Czech reprint of the famous book published in Czechoslovakia in 1935.
73. Klepetář, pp. 149, 153, 154, 172, 307–308.

empire, its war bonds became worthless. Nevertheless, in July 1920, Czechoslovakia offered to honor the loans at a reduced rate.[74] The German bourgeois classes, which had put their savings into the war bonds, resented both the loss of their unfortunate investment and the Czechoslovak solution. The financial collapse of Germany in 1923, in which many Germans of Czechoslovakia lost large sums deposited in the Reich (because of their lack of confidence in Czechoslovakia) further increased their discontent.

National divisions, however, could not efface the strong social, economic, cultural, and geographical bonds formed during centuries past. The history-long sentimental ties of the Germans with the cultural centers of the country, such as Prague, Brno, and Olomouc, and their affection for the common homeland, were among the strongest bonds linking the nationalities. Whatever their tensions and idiosyncrasies, however exasperating their national moods, however unpredictable their political course, both peoples could have looked upon the democratic regime as their unique chance for bringing about a more permanent settlement of national problems.

The Czech political leaders were willing to achieve an equitable solution of the German demands. They had no desire to dominate the Germans, who had become part of Czechoslovakia mainly because of historical, geographical, economic, and political circumstances.[75] The paradox was that *the very existence and independence of Czechoslovakia involved the presence of the Germans within her frontiers.* To resolve the problem within the present framework seemed like trying to square a circle. The gradual easing of tensions brought some favorable results, but from the outset it encountered disagreements. What many Germans really wanted was autonomy, a reality which could hardly be accepted by the Czechs, who feared that it would ultimately lead to the separation of the German areas from the Republic and to the dismemberment of Czechoslovakia. The national haughtiness which animated a large part of the Sudeten German middle classes, who regarded themselves as missionaries of a higher culture and a German salient thrust at the Slav-German border, prevented their reconciling themselves unconditionally to the existence of the democratic Republic. The initial negative attitude of most Germans to the state itself had affected much of Czech policy toward them. Actually, many Czechs were sincere in their efforts to create a

74. *Ibid.*, p. 127; Dobrý, *Hospodářská krize*, pp. 23–28; Olšovský et al., pp. 103–22.
75. *DBFP*, I, 188.

better understanding with the Germans. But they considered it essential that the Germans accept obligations of loyalty and good citizenship.

At the end of the 1920's, Czechoslovakia seemed prosperous, calm, and stable. Yet there were rumbles of disquiet under the surface. With the coming of the great depression and the rise of National Socialism in adjacent Germany, another historic phase was opened.[76]

76. Czechoslovak Communist historians focus their attention on contemporary history. There has been an interesting discussion concerning the periodization of modern Czechoslovak history. Some historians put the turning point at 1934 or 1934–35 (*Československý časopis historický*, II, 1954, 566). Jiří Kořalka (*ibid.*, III, 1955, 61) and the Soviet historian S. I. Prasolov regarded the first half of 1933 as the watershed because of the victory of Nazism in Germany. I consider this date the real dividing line of the history of the Czechoslovak Republic.

CHAPTER 2

Forces of German Nationalism

Partly as a result of the rapid industrialization of the Habsburg Empire of the 1880's, a more intense German nationalism voicing the resentment of the German middle classes over the growing strength of non-German nationalities in the Austrian segment, brought new and disturbing elements into Austrian politics. Industrial expansion caused increasing national and social protest. There was widespread awareness of the necessity for social reforms, with the nationalist parties concentrating on meeting workers' needs. The Linz program of 1882, setting forth a platform for a modern form of German nationalism, warmly endorsed a reform of factory legislation and expressed sympathy for the working classes. However, it challenged the venerable all-German ideology (hitherto serving the Habsburg aspirations in Germany) with a new emphasis on the all-German character of the Austrian half of the empire. The atmosphere of rising tensions hardened under the pressures of the German demand for the establishment of a separate German territory within Bohemia. Such a territorial division would have entailed the Germanization of all Czechs included within the German area, and had been repeatedly rebuffed by the Czechs.[1]

1. In 1880, 1918, and 1938. For a discussion of German nationalism in Austria, see *Historický ústav ČSAV, Přehled československých dějin,* II, 616–18, 633, 664, 937. This survey presents a Communist reinterpretation of Czechoslovak history. See also an interesting account by Eberhard Wolfgramm, " 'Grenzlandkämpfer.' Zur Ideologie, den historischen Wurzeln und den Hintergründen des sudetendeutschen Revanchismus," *Jahrbuch für Geschichte der UdSSR und der volksdemokratischen Länder Europas,* IV, 9–39.

Political wrangling took on a bitter, vituperative tone. The new pan-German feeling was summed up by the Georg von Schönerer movement. The movement bitterly denounced Jews, Slavs, Socialists, and Liberals as enemies of the German race, adopted the idea of a classless national community (Volksgemeinschaft), and espoused the pan-German national objectives.[2] What was really new was the emotional violence which pervaded the atmosphere and bred racial hatred and intolerance. When the movement disintegrated at the opening of the twentieth century, its anti-Jewish and anti-Czech ideology was taken up by new parties. The renewed program of invective affected particularly the delicate political climate of the Bohemian territory, where the expansion of industry and finance had brought increased Czech economic and political prominence. The fierce and increasingly nationalist approach also gained ground among the German workers, stirred by the growing competition of cheap immigrant Czech labor.

The pan-German Radical Party of Karl Hermann Wolf[3] and the Deutsche Arbeiterpartei in Oesterreich (DAP; German Workers' Party in Austria), founded in Ústí nad Labem in November 1903,[4] reiterated the basic motives of German nationalism contained in the Linz program — particularly the concept of a Volksgemeinschaft made popular by Schönerer — and the demand for union with the German Reich. In 1911 the DAP entered the Reichsrat in Vienna with three deputies.[5] The party favored German self-administration of the predominantly German territories in the Historic Provinces, and assumed that in the Czech areas German would be equal to the Czech language. Rudolf Jung, Hans Krebs, and Hans Knirsch became leaders of the DAP which, at its congress in Vienna in 1918, changed its name to the Deutsche nationalsozialistische Arbeiterpartei (DNSAP; The German National Socialist Workers Party).[6] Its

2. Hans Krebs, *Kampf in Böhmen*, pp. 34–35. Schönerer gained 17 deputies in the elections of 1891 but only 4 in 1907 (Koegler, p. 73; H. W. Seton-Watson, *Munich and the Dictators*, p. 30). Wiskemann (*Czechs and Germans*, p. 41) stressed that the Schönerer movement "had much more significance than the votes he ever polled would suggest. For one thing he formulated the expansionist views of a great many Germans."

3. Wolf declared in his famous speech in the Reichsrat (on Sept. 27, 1917) to the Czechs: "In a menagerie one does not work with promises and caresses, but with the whip" (*ibid.*, p. 77). See also Jaksch, *Europas Weg*, p. 169.

4. Krebs, p. 39. For a useful account, see Andrew G. Whiteside, "Nationaler Sozialismus in Österreich vor 1918," *Vierteljahrshefte für Zeitgeschichte*, IX (October 1961), 333–59.

5. Krebs, p. 40.

6. *Ibid.*, p. 83. The congress was held from May 2 to May 4, 1918.

Czechoslovak branch was constituted as the DNSAP in Czechoslovakia on Nov. 15, 1918.[7]

In 1920 National Socialist leaders from Germany, Austria, and Czechoslovakia met at Salzburg, Austria, to discuss the political situation.[8] As a result, Czechoslovakia inherited a National Socialist Party which was mostly Sudeten German in origin and character. It was set up chiefly in the industrial areas around Most in northern Bohemia and Moravská Ostrava at the Polish-Moravian border.[9] The DNSAP became the main bearer of German negativism in the Republic.

When the National Socialist movement started in Germany, it absorbed many elements from its Austrian roots. According to Henry Cord Meyer, National Socialism derived the essence of its spirit of intolerance, hatred, and arrogant racial and cultural superiority from the prewar frictions on the German-Slav frontier. Adolf Hitler's and Alfred Rosenberg's political views and motivations were rooted solidly in the tensions and frustrations of the German borderlands in Austria and the Baltic.[10] In addition, the Austrian background of Hitler accounted for much of his irrational hatred of Czechs, whom he regarded as the gravediggers of German Austria.[11] The first article

7. [Czechoslovak] Ministry of Information, *Český národ soudí K. H. Franka*, p. 170; hereafter cited as *K. H. Frank*. This is an indispensable volume containing the record of the trial of K. H. Frank.
8. Krebs, p. 83. The meeting was held on July 7–8, 1920. Hitler, Drexler, Knirsch, Jung, and others took part (*ibid.*). Munich became the center also for German Nazis from Czechoslovakia. They often visited Munich to confer with Hitler, Hess, Frick, Bormann, and Rosenberg.
9. Jaksch doubts that the German Nazis from Czechoslovakia generated National Socialism in the Reich. He thinks that, on the contrary, they took over some of the theories of Gottfried Feder. Only after the coming of Mussolini to power did the totalitarian wing around Jung and Krebs appear to win a dominant position in the party (*Europas Weg*, pp. 236, 482–83). The pan-German program of the DNSAP had preceded, however, the draft of the 25 points of the NSDAP stressing the all-German objectives of the movement. This would point toward the Austrian and Sudeten German roots of Nazism.
10. Meyer, *Mitteleuropa*, p. 315.
11. See Alan Bullock, *Hitler. A Study in Tyranny*, p. 402. Bullock indicated that Hitler saw in the Czech "the very type of those Slav Untermenschen." Hermann Rauschning noted Hitler's opinions in his conversations with the latter in 1932. "The Bohemian-Moravian basin . . . will be colonized with German peasants. The Czechs . . . we shall transplant to Siberia or the Volhynian regions. . . . The Czechs must get out of Central Europe. As long as they remain, they will always be a center of Hussite-Bolshevik disintegration. . . . But at this price I shall not hesitate for a moment to take the deaths of 2 or 3 million Germans on my conscience" (*The Voice of Destruction*, p. 38). In his conversations during the war Hitler referred frequently to his Viennese experiences and recollections. On Jan. 23, 1942, he stated: "Every Czech is a born nationalist who naturally relates everything to his own point of view. One must make no mistake about

of the NSDAP (National Socialist German Workers Party) program
of Feb. 24, 1920, demanded "the union of all Germans to form a Great
Germany on the basis of the right of self-determination."[12] Its spiritual
father, Gottfried Feder, added: "We will not relinquish our claim to
any German in Sudeten Germany, Alsace-Lorraine, Poland, Austria."[13]
The National Socialist principle, "the German people form a closed
community which recognizes no national borders,"[14] promoted the
basic idea of the German Volks- und Kulturgemeinschaft, the all-
permeating community of German race, which had been elaborated
in the German part of Austria in the second half of the nineteenth
century. Prof. Gerhard Ritter noted correctly that

> . . . the most dangerous element [of Nazism], its inflamed, antago-
> nistic nationalism, came not from Potsdam, but rather from
> Bohemia-Moravia and the other Austrian-German borderlands
> with their [Austrian] Pan-German movement, unbridled anti-
> Semitism, and notions of Raumpolitik. . . . Through Hitler this
> aggressive nationalism took possession of the Prussian sword.[15]

The pan-German program of the union of the German nation
developed a new pattern of the ethnic group law. It aimed at the
exclusive recognition of the national group as opposed to the isolated
individual, who now became a member of a wider national community. The protection of the group would be guaranteed by the

---

him: the more he curbs himself, the more dangerous he is . . . I don't despise
them, I have no resentment against them. It's destiny that wishes us to be adversaries. To put it briefly, the Czechs are a foreign body in the midst of the
German community. There is no room both for them and for us. One of us
must give way" (*Hitler's Secret Conversations, 1941–44*, p. 192). Erich Kordt
noted that Hitler, as an Austrian, regarded himself as competent in all questions
of Southeast Europe (*Nicht aus den Akten*, p. 224). Paul Schmidt (*Hitler's Interpreter*, pp. 122, 124) recalled that Hitler was unable to speak quietly about
the Czechs. Schmidt ascribed the fact to Hitler's Austrian past.

12. Alfred Rosenberg, ed., *Das Parteiprogramm. Wesen, Grundsätze
und Ziele der NSDAP*, p. 15.

13. *Das Programm der NSDAP und seine weltanschaulichen Grundgedanken*
(Munich, 1933), p. 42 (as quoted in *National Socialism*, p. 68).

14. Ernst Rudolf Huber, *Verfassungsrecht des grossdeutschen Reiches* (Hamburg, 1939), p. 158 (as quoted in *National Socialism*, p. 24).

15. *Deutsche Rundschau* (April 1947, pp. 11–12), as cited in Meyer, p. 334.
Professor R. W. Seton-Watson remarked in his introduction to Vincent Urban's
book (p. vi) that "It is still not properly understood how many of the ideas
to-day condemned by us as Nazi and 'Prussian' did in fact originate among the
Sudeten Germans, and that the latter—in contrast to the less intransigent
'Alpenländer' . . . —were a natural spearhead of the German *Drang nach
Osten,* and never ceased to regard the Germanization of Bohemia as the ultimate
goal of their endeavour."

mother country.[16] These fundamental ideas of German nationalism clearly infringed upon the sovereignty of any state with a German minority, and the destructive aspects of the theory played a major role in dissolving Czechoslovakia, especially when the pan-German ideas became an avowed policy of the majority of her German inhabitants. The late Franz Neumann rightly pointed out in his distinguished study that recognition of the German ethnic group as a public entity would create "a state within a state" and would exempt "the German group from the sovereignty of the state."

> Acceptance of the principle that the mother country is the political guardian of the minorities means not only the rejection of rational international relations but also the end of internal unity in every state having sizable minorities. It makes the mother people the arbiter of disputes between the state and the minority living therein. . . . The National Socialists demand the arbitrary intervention of the mother state. . . . Racial Germans throughout the world remain Germans, members of the folk group, subject to its law. The fifth column is elevated to an institution.[17]

The National Socialists reawakened the latent forces of German nationalism, since there was undoubtedly considerable sentiment among the Germans for a closer relationship with their brethren abroad.[18] There had always been an emotional and patriotic justification among the Germans for the existence of protective national societies embracing Germans around the world. Some organizations epitomized that part of German nationalism which dreamed of an all-embracing national German community. For example, the League for Germanism Abroad (Volksbund für das Deutschtum im Ausland; VDA) was originally founded as a protective school society,[19, 20] with

16. Franz Neumann, *Behemoth. The Structure and Practice of National Socialism*, p. 162.
17. *Ibid.*, p. 163.
18. The Germans abroad totaled some 33 million, according to the estimate of the VDA, including 60,000 in Denmark, 150,000 in Belgium, 250,000 in Luxemburg, 80,000 in Holland, 1,600,000 in Alsace-Lorraine, 300,000 in Italy, 1,350,000 in Poland, 360,000 in Danzig, 30,000 in Estonia, 75,000 in Latvia, 130,000 in Lithuania and Memel, 1,000,000 in Russia, 6,300,000 in Austria, 3,500,000 in Czechoslovakia, 700,000 in Yugoslavia, 600,000 in Hungary, 800,000 in Rumania, 2,860,000 in Switzerland, 10,000,000 in the United States, 300,000 in Canada, 800,000 in South and Central America, 160,000 in Australia, 197,000 in Asia, and 125,000 in Africa (Otto Schäfer, *Sinn und Wesen des VDA* [Frankfurt, 1933], p. 5, as quoted in *National Socialism*, p. 399). The somewhat exaggerated figures are instructive of the nature of the German claims.
19. See above, p. 26.
20. In 1908 the following protective German societies (Schutzvereine) were in

the slogan "Germans of all countries unite."[21] It advocated the recognition and protection of Germans in all countries of the world,[22] and spent about 2.5 million Reichsmark (RM) per year on its program.[23] The Weimar Republic discretely subsidized German institutions abroad[24] and selected the VDA to assist Germans in Czechoslovakia.[25]

Hitler's rise to power led to an increase in assistance to the VDA. On Oct. 27, 1933, a new directive by Reich Minister Rudolf Hess entrusted "all questions regarding the German element beyond the borders" to his supreme jurisdiction and secretly created a new Volksdeutsch council as his central executive organ with Prof. Karl Haushofer as its head and Dr. Hans Steinacher, the VDA leader, as its secretary. To coordinate the assistance given to the Germans in Czechoslovakia, another directive by Rudolf Hess instructed (March 13, 1934) "that sole responsibility for handling Sudeten German questions lay with the Volksdeutsch Council." Under the guidance of the council the VDA continued to operate in Czechoslovakia through "specially trained and prudent persons" to strengthen the political, cultural, and social ties of the Sudeten Germans. The VDA maintained close ties with the Henlein movement, which it helped financially. It served as Henlein's intermediary in his contacts with the Berlin authorities.[26]

---

the Czech territories: Deutscher Böhmerwaldbund with 399 local groups and 37,740 members; Bund der Deutschen Nordmährens, 534 groups and 44,200 members; Bund der Deutschen in Böhmen, with 765 groups and 65,419 members; Bund der Deutschen in Ostböhmen, with 74 groups and 4,531 members; Bund der Deutschen Südmährens, with 146 groups and 8,128 members; Bund der Deutschen der Iglauer Sprachinsel, with 2,977 members (Bischoff, p. 185). The figures are approximate.

21. *National Socialism,* p. 433.

22. *Ibid.,* p. 30.

23. Louis de Jong, *The German Fifth Column in the Second World War,* p. 274. An informative study.

24. *Ibid.,* p. 282. One of the official channels was the Deutsche Stiftung. It was "a confidential agency of the Reich and Prussian Governments whose tasks lay in the social and cultural spheres." Its executive committee was composed of one representative of each of the governmental coalition parties in 1930 (*Documents on German Foreign Policy 1918–1945, from the Archives of the German Foreign Ministry.* Series C (1933–1937). *The Third Reich: First Phase,* IV, 613; hereafter referred to as *DGFP,* Series C).

25. Bischoff p. 111. (See Kořalka in the *Československý časopis historický,* 1955, p. 76.) The activities of the VDA spread over the Historic Provinces. The VDA regarded its work there as strictly defensive. For an account, see *National Socialism,* p. 25.

26. *DGFP,* Series C, IV, 229–30, 614–15, 679; [Czechoslovak] Ministry of Information, *Zpověd K. H. Franka. Podle vlastních výpovědí v době vazby u krajského soudu trestního na Pankráci,* pp. 27, 35; hereafter cited as *Zpověd.*

The purpose of the new policy formulated jointly by the Nazi Party and the Ministry of Foreign Affairs was to elaborate a new method of assistance to the Sudeten Germans in place of the previous somewhat crude approach by a number of separate groups engaging in uncoordinated activities. The new setup aimed at coordinating hitherto disparate undertakings from a center in Berlin. It planned to operate in a clandestine manner in Czechoslovakia so "that the new national movement that now was slowly taking shape among the Sudeten Germans . . . must develop independently, without any noticeable intervention by Reich German organization."[27] In the process of further Nazification, the Volksdeutsch council was dissolved in 1935 and replaced by the so-called von Kursell Bureau. Consequently the VDA lost much of its former influence.[28] The Volksdeutsche Mittelstelle (the VoMi, or Liaison Office for Ethnic Germans) replaced the bureau as the supreme coordinating agency in 1937.[29]

The second most important channel of German propaganda abroad was the Deutsches Auslands-Institut (DAI; German Foreign Institute), founded in Stuttgart in 1917, and entrusted with the maintaining of contacts with Germans abroad by way of publications, books, etc. As a private institution, it was financed by German export trade leaders and industries. After the Nazis came to power, it was supported by the Reich government.[30] A kindred organization was the Deutscher Schutzbund (German Protection League) headed by Dr. Karl von Loesch, which furthered German culture abroad and

---

This confession contains important information. See also J. W. Brügel, "Henlein a čeští agrárníci," *Tribuna*, XII, (No. 2, 1960), 5–6; Alexander Henderson, *Eyewitness in Czecho-Slovakia*, p. 110 (an informative report by a British correspondent); Josef Fischer, Vaclav Patzak, Vincenc Perth, *Ihr Kampf. Die wahren Ziele der Sudeten deutschen Partei*, p. 98 (the volume contains valuable data; it is hereafter cited as Fischer et al.). Wiskemann (*Czechs and Germans*, p. 247) notes that "it appears to have been mostly through the VDA or Stuttgart [DAI] that Reich German money was transmitted to Germans in Czechoslovakia."

27. *DGFP*, Series C, II, 43–44, 49, 617–18, 681–82, IV, 721, 1115; Helmuth K. G. Rönnefarth, *Die Sudetenkrise in der internationalen Politik. Entstehung–Verlaug–Auswirkung*, I, 183–87; hereafter cited as *Sudetenkrise;* Hans von Rimscha, "Zur Gleichschaltung der deutschen Volksgruppen durch das Dritte Reich," *Historische Zeitschrift*, 182 (1956), 32–39.

28. *DGFP*, Series C, IV, 721, 1115.

29. Robert L. Koehl, *RKFDV: German Resettlement and Population Policy 1939–1945. A History of the Reich Commission for the Strengthening of Germandom*, p. 37, a very good study based on primary sources. For an interesting summary, see MacAlister Brown, "The Third Reich's Mobilization of the German Fifth Column in Eastern Europe," *Journal of Central European Affairs*, XIX (July 1959), 128–48. See below, p. 101.

30. *National Socialism*, pp. 122, 127.

became a center for all protective societies working among Germans abroad.[31] Even more controversial were the organizations focusing their activities exclusively on the Sudeten Germans. The Sudeten-deutscher Heimatbund (Sudeten German Home League), established after the war in Dresden, Berlin, and elsewhere, was the largest Reich group organizing the Sudeten Germans in Germany. It gathered many extremist German refugees.[32] After the conclusion of the pact with Poland in 1934, the Bund Deutscher Osten also directed its attention to Czechoslovakia. Its branch was a secret Sudeten-deutscher Kampfring. Der Sudetendeutsche Kulturverband dealt with cultural questions.[33]

The existence of organizations indulging in nationalist propaganda which virtually disregarded frontiers was perhaps inevitable in the curious ambiguity surrounding the development of pre-Hitler Germany. The Nazis merely assimilated them and used them to channel their orders.[34]

Granted Czechoslovakia's proximity to Germany; the close economic, cultural, and spiritual association of the Sudeten Germans with the Reich; and the apprehension centering on the Czech thrust toward the area of German settlement, there was every indication that the highly developed German inhabitants of Czechoslovakia would attempt to expand their network of national societies inherited from the empire. In 1919 the old German School League was replaced by the Deutscher Kulturverband, which in 1935 embraced some 400,000 members in more than 3,050 groups and aimed at maintaining and promoting German schools and national consciousness.[35]

31. Bischoff, p. 98.
32. Fischer et al., p. 103; Henderson, p. 110. For an account of Sudeten irredentism, see J. César–B. Černý, "Iredentistické hnutí německých buržoazních nacionalistů z ČSR v letech 1918–1929," *Československý časopis historický*, IX (No. 6, 1961), 795 ff.; *Německý imperialismus proti ČSR (1918–1939), passim;* hereafter cited as *Německý imperialismus*. This is a collection of documents published by a special commission of the Prague Foreign Office.
33. Fischer et al., pp. 101, 103; Wiskemann, *Czechs and Germans*, p. 129.
34. In his survey, *Weltmächte und Weltkriege. Die Geschichte unserer Epoche 1890–1945* (p. 320), Hans Herzfeld noted that "National Socialism has not only found a considerable part of its leaders among the ethnic Germans abroad but has also always exhibited a special, often very unfortunate, liking for them."
35. The Library of Congress Manuscript Division, "The Rehse Collection" (Container 463). The assistance of the Kulturverband to German schools had amounted to 75 million Kč since 1919. Among other items, it took care of 105 kindergartens and 31 elementary schools (*Národnostní obzor*, V [September 1934], 29). Prior to 1933, the VDA clandestinely supported the Kulturverband, granting a minimum annual subsidy of 800,000 Kč in 1930 and 1931 (*Německý*

All of the national protective societies, with almost 600,000 members in 1926, were loosely concentrated in the Hauptstelle für deutsche Schutzarbeit in Teplice-Šanov[36] and subordinated to the Berlin central agency, the Deutscher Schutzbund. In 1934, under the impact of Nazism, the protective societies in Czechoslovakia joined to form one organization, the Bund der Deutschen.[37] After 1935 the Bund—with many other German organizations—followed the instructions of the Henlein Party.[38] The apparent goals and activities of these societies were legitimate—they even received Czechoslovak financial aid[39]—and many Czech protective societies engaged in similar activities.[40] It was only when the German societies secretly endorsed pan-German aims that they were criticized.

Although scores of Germans seemed at times to be unaware of their ultimate objectives, the societies provided a network for the activities of the Henlein Party. They formed a mass basis for nationalist propaganda embracing almost every German family.[41] The minutes of the Society of Jesters (Gesellschaft der Juxer) at Jablonec nad Nisou give some indication of the German mood. (Some of the last minutes in its record book were devoted to the thanksgiving meeting on the occasion of the union of the Sudeten borderland with Germany in 1938. The speaker recalled with satisfaction the activities of the society and emphasized that it had fostered hatred of the Czechs in

imperialismus, pp. 196–97). In 1936–37 some differences arose between the Bund and the Kulturverband, which included many German Jews. The Kulturverband defended itself against becoming a mere subsidiary of the Henlein Party (César-Černý, *Politika,* II, 379–80).

36. Dr. A. Frank in his review *Nové Čechy* (New Bohemia), 1928, No. 1, 18–19, as cited in Kořalka, p. 77.
37. Fischer et al., p. 47; Vlastimil Louda, *Politika soustavné zrady. Studie o německé politice na území ČSR,* p. 69.
38. *Zpověď,* p. 36; César-Černý, *Politika,* II, 377–79.
39. For example, the Kulturverband received a state subsidy of 742,000 Kč in 1932 (D. Rusý, "Německý kulturní svaz v Československu," *Národnostní obzor,* V (September 1934), 30.
40. For example, National Czech Council, National Union for northern Moravia, National Union of the Bohemian Forest, National Union of northern Bohemia, National Union of southwestern Moravia, Central School Society, etc. (See *Národnostní obzor, passim.*)
41. For a useful summary, see César-Černý, *Politika,* I, 472–80. When the Henlein Party protested in a letter (by K. H. Frank, Nov. 21, 1935) against the separate actions of the Bund in the economic field, it was agreed, after a discussion between K. H. Frank and the representative of the Bund, that the two should lay out joint plans and apportion their activities. A list of barristers, notaries, and physicians, all "German Aryans," was prepared. These would be assisted in case they needed employment. Another register would establish the nationality and trustworthiness of owners of homesteads over 5 hectares in order to defend the German character of the soil (Louda, p. 70).

the expectation of the final liberation by Great Germany.)[42] Many such societies offered a responsive state of mind and ideological weapons to Nazism to make it congenial to the German audience. While democracy came to the average Sudeten German in Czech guise and was therefore under suspicion, Nazism echoed many well-known traditional motives of German nationalism. As a result, German nationalism and its widespread distrust of parliamentary democracy helped to make Nazism respectable to the masses of the German people.

Until 1933, however, the Czech-German struggle had all the aspects of a long game of chess where the principal players clamored for victory but charged the other side with no crime. The rules were kept, on the whole, and the battle lines were clearly drawn. Both nationalities were assured of the righteousness of their causes. The framework of democracy made it almost certain that one side would never be able to impose its will. The existence of national societies provided an outlet for both Czech and German nationalism during a time when the Locarno spirit ruled supreme, and presented outlets for legitimate anxiety. At the same time they were battle outposts, if what was regarded as peace turned out to be only a truce.

Czechoslovak democracy prided itself on being able to avoid national conflicts. Yet no indulgence in semantics could prevent the flow of events. Nationalism was still a dynamic force, even if for the time being it was overshadowed by economic issues or was presented under democratic disguise, as the Czechs preferred. Favored by the international situation, Czechoslovak democracy succeeded, however, in tenuously balancing all the existing social forces. It was in need of a peaceful international atmosphere to thrive on.

42. The Regional Archives of the Region of Liberec in Jablonec nad Nisou. *Stillhaltekommissar für Organisationen*—Dissolved organizations in Jablonec nad Nisou; Society of Jesters: Minutes of Meetings (Kořalka, *Československý časopis historický*, 1955, p. 77).

Part II

THE RISE OF NAZISM IN CZECHOSLOVAKIA

Prologue

The date was Nov. 19, 1937.

By that date the Sudeten German Party, which at the elections of May 19, 1935, had won more than 60 percent of the German vote,[1] was confident of future progress, but its leaders felt an urgent need for a thoroughgoing discussion of their policy with the highest authorities of the Reich. The time had finally arrived, they thought, to solve the Sudeten German question, which had now become a vital political issue. They had been in contact with competent German authorities in the Reich, and had been receiving financial assistance on a regular basis, but now the whole outlook changed. Amid the present quiet reigning in Czechoslovakia, the leaders of the Sudeten German Party secretly proposed to Hitler that their mutual policies be reviewed. Their sense of grievance against and hatred for the Czechs had reached a combustion point, and they looked forward to the moment, for which they had been working so hard, when they might destroy the Czechoslovak Republic. The party, supported by a large majority of its countrymen, was determined to make the necessary national effort against its enemies at home. Its success presupposed that all Sudeten Germans would be grouped around the man who had rebuilt national unity, the leader of the German Reich, Adolf Hitler. The party called for his assistance.

On Nov. 19, 1937, Henlein submitted a secret report to the Führer

1. The Sudeten German Party (SdP), led by Konrad Henlein, gained 1,200,000 votes and 44 deputies at the 1935 elections.

and Reich chancellor[2] and asked for consultations involving German objectives and aims. In his report, Henlein briefed Hitler on the situation of the Germans in Czechoslovakia:

> The Sudeten Germans are today imbued with National Socialist principles and organized in a comprehensive, unitary National Socialist Party, based on the Führer concept. . . . The Sudeten German Party . . . has imbued the racial group and their sphere of life with National Socialist principles. In the face of "democratic" world opinion the Sudeten German Party has given proof that the National Socialist order of leadership and following corresponds with the law of the inner life of the German people, for not only has it been called into existence among the Sudeten Germans by their own free will, but in the face of pressure by the Czech State. . . . The Sudeten German Party must camouflage its profession of National Socialism as an ideology of life and as a political principle. As a party in the democratic parliamentary system of Czechoslovakia, it must, outwardly, alike in writing and by word of mouth, in its manifestoes and in the press, in Parliament, in its own structure, and in the organization of the Sudeten German element, employ democratic terminology and democratic parliamentary methods. In consequence, it may appear to uninitiated German circles of the Reich to be disunited and unreliable. This disunion, however, cannot be avoided so long as there still exists the necessity of a legal party, and the existence of such a party in Czechoslovakia presupposes the profession of democratic principles. The apparent lack of unity of the Sudeten German Party is intensified by the circumstance that at heart it desires nothing more ardently than the incorporation of Sudeten German territory, nay of the whole Bohemian, Moravian, and Silesian area, within the Reich.[3]

As the years passed, the bitterness between Germans and Czechs had mounted, and with it the German sense of injustice and frustration. The Sudeten Party's goal was to recreate national unity under Hitler's leadership. Would the coming contest be just another phase of the long national dispute or a decisive climax to what was

2. For a copy of the report to Hitler (sent to German Foreign Minister von Neurath on Nov. 19, 1937), see *Documents on German Foreign Policy 1918–1945, from the Archives of the German Foreign Ministry. Series D* (1937–45), II, 49–62; this indispensable collection will hereafter be cited as *DGFP.*

3. *Ibid.*, pp. 56–57. By stressing his loyalty to National Socialism, Henlein also attempted to dispose of the charges of the SS and Martin Bormann that the SdP was too close to Austro-Fascism.

viewed by some Germans as years of chagrin, indecision, and persecution? Was it to be simply a struggle for political influence or a matter of life or death? Would the German passionate determination unleash violence, revolt, and bloodshed?

How could it be possible that the largest German party in democratic Czechoslovakia sought the joint action and direct sponsorship of a foreign totalitarian power? How had such a situation been created? Could not the necessary reforms or changes be carried through in a state of legality and mutual respect within the framework of the Republic? Was the Czechoslovak regime, after all, a bankrupt political system, intent on pursuing an anti-German policy in order to annihilate the Germans? Or, perhaps, were the forces generating the present crisis beyond the personal control of the participants —the outcome of an irrepressible conflict between two nations? Such were the questions which, if they were not already in the minds of contemporary observers, really arose as Konrad Henlein surveyed the policy of his party in what was still independent Czechoslovakia.

CHAPTER 3

The Foundation of the Henlein Party

Disappointment and frustration over the German defeat of 1918 and the peace settlement of 1919 marked the union of the Germans with the Czechoslovak state. There had been an element of hopelessness and bewilderment among soldiers coming home after more than four interminable years of unsuccessful warfare. Having been barred from victory for reasons beyond their control, they found themselves under a new state and saw no hopeful prospects of their participation in the new political order.

In contrast to the firmness, discipline, and decision demanded daily at the front, the compromises and indecisiveness of a democratic regime appeared unworthy of their attention. The young men, especially, who could have expected to find a successful career under the empire, did not see any likelihood of national or personal advancement in the Republic. They tended naturally to vent their bitterness on the democratic system. The political divisions of the postwar period could not efface the emotional bonds formed during the war. Passively subjected to Czechoslovak reality, many young Germans strove to find a honorable way out of the dilemma between insurrection and submission. They grouped in the Wandervögel (Wandering Birds) and gathered around camp fires to forget the exasperating present in recollections of the days of glory. They felt themselves members of an ever-living but deeply hurt national community, to which they pledged secret and strict obedience. Their romantic, quasi-mystical reactions had something of the ideals of medieval knighthood. Deeply affected by the decline and misfortunes of their nation, desirous of authority, they looked for a savior.[1]

German activism was too practical, pragmatic, and utilitarian and too drawn into everyday politics to be able to capture what was a tradition-bound, antiliberal, and nationalist movement. As a consequence, the German camp divided between those who favored a division in parties and those who wanted to put an end to party confusion and to create a national rally.[2] The advocates of a German rally were not necessarily totalitarians. They envisaged it merely as a logical expression of the demands for national unity and one which would facilitate the implementation of national objectives.

Besides numerous groups of the Wandervögel (which had been formed before the war)[3] and other similar groupings of youths, the postwar atmosphere sparked the formation of a Böhmerland-bewegung in 1919.[4] This movement furthered the traditional tenets of German nationalism. Its principles called for a renovation of the national community represented by strong personalities. Later, the Henlein Party absorbed many of its ideas and members.

In the middle twenties some of the youths grew weary of impractical dreams, nature wandering, and oaths of secrecy and obedience by the blaze of a camp fire. They felt that their activities should become more efficient and practical, and embraced the idea of the Bündische (an organic grouping), which also found wide acceptance among former soldiers. The corporate ideas of the Viennese professor Othmar Spann[5] elaborated the Bündische into a theory which became the doctrine of a half-secret, closely bound group, the Comrades' Union (Kameradschaftsbund; KB), founded in 1926 by the students

1. For a description of the postwar German mood, see Fischer et al., pp. 9–13, and Josef Pfitzner, *Sudetendeutsche Einheitsbewegung*, pp. 33 ff. This survey is very instructive. (See also Franzel as cited in Preidel, ed., pp. 357 ff.)
2. Pfitzner, p. 62. Attempts to achieve a union of all German parties and forces ran like a red thread through the years 1918–33. In 1933 these attempts were revived. The constitution of the Heimatfront of Henlein was the final result of this long series of efforts.
3. In 1912 (Louda, p. 37).
4. Pfitzner, pp. 35–36. Among the members of the movement were Erich Gierach, Emil Lehmann, and K. H. Frank. The program was set forth in the so-called Schreckensteiner Principles (see Wolfgramm, "Grenzlandkämpfer," pp. 22–24).
5. The principal work of Othmar Spann is *Der wahre Staat* (Leipzig, 1929). For the links between Spann and the KB, see Fischer et al., p. 37; Franzel, p. 362. R. W. Seton-Watson, in *A History of the Czechs and Slovaks* (p. 351), characterized the neo-romantic influence of Spann as a reversion from liberalism toward the Middle Ages. (See also Anton Karlgren, *Henlein-Hitler and the Czechoslovak Tragedy*, p. 12.) For more information on the KB, see Rönnefarth, *Sudetenkrise*, I, 128–33, 148–50.

of Professor Spann (Dr. Walter Heinrich[6] and Heinrich Rutha[7]) to
implement his ideas.[8]

Spann advocated the formation of a corporate state to replace the
egalitarian democratic state. The state, strongly hierarchical, was to
be organized according to the professions, the highest being that of
political leaders, the Staatsstand. These leaders would form a caste,
specially educated and responsible to no one, whose task was to
administer and lead the state. In the same way as the corporate state
would create order out of a liberal chaos, the new German Reich
would organize its living space. "It is only in Eastern Europe that
Germany can find her natural mission. Today we understand clearly
why Poland, Bohemia, Hungary . . . were at one time German fiefs;
that is how it must be again."[9]

The KB—never amounting to more than 200 members—aimed at
forming such a directing Staatsstand, which would take over the
leadership of the Sudeten Germans. Disguising themselves under the
title "Working Group for the Social Sciences," they worked at
penetrating existing mass organizations.[10] In this way they gained
influence in many German national societies and groups, particularly
in the Gymnastic Union (the Turnverband), where KB members

6. Heinrich was a student of Spann and the ideologist of the KB. He became a
professor at the Hochschule für Welthandel in Vienna. (See also Franzel as
cited in Preidel, p. 362.)

7. Rutha, who seems to have been one of the ablest brains of the Sudeten
Germans, became chief advisor of Henlein on foreign affairs. After the war he
was a member of the Wandervögel. In October 1937 he was arrested with
Walter Rohn and others under suspicion of homosexuality and committed
suicide in prison (ibid., p. 366; Fischer et al., pp. 37, 80).

8. According to Louda (pp. 39–40), who used Czech official sources, a secret
meeting of the KB was held at Castle Heinrichsruhe as early as 1926.
Czechoslovak authorities learned about the secret activities of the KB in 1934. In
1930, the KB began publishing its periodical Die Junge Front. Its program
stated: "Die realpolitische Aufgabe der jungen Generation liegt in der
Heranbildung   eines   antiliberalen,   autorität-wünschenden . . . Menschen-
schlages durch planmässige Erziehung von Jugend auf mit dem Blicke auf die
Selbsterhaltung und spätere politische Einmütigkeit einer ganzen Generation"
(Pfitzner, pp. 71–72). The cradle of the KB was the city of Česká Lípa in
northern Bohemia, the home of both Heinrich and Rutha.

9. Richard Freund (Watch Czechoslovakia, p. 69) gives a lucid and fair account
of the pre-1939 development.

10. The Arbeitskreis für Gesellschaftswissenschaften was formed in 1926.
According to Fischer et al. (p. 38), the KB was composed of a narrower circle
(with some 50 members) and Jungmannschaft. The KB was supported later on
by German funds. At the end of June 1936, there were 64,300 RM in its
Berlin banking account (ibid., pp. 81, 84). See also Německý imperialismus, pp.
376–79. For the penetration of German organizations by KB members, see
Jaroslav César-Bohumil Černý, "The Nazi Fifth Column in Czechoslovakia,"
Historica, IV, 201–202.

Konrad Henlein, Walter Brand, and Heinrich Rutha occupied leading positions from which they launched the Sudeten German Home Front in 1933. The KB was the rallying point of able young Germans, most of whom gained prominence in the Sudeten German Party: Dr. Walter Brand,[11] Dr. Wilhelm Sebekowsky,[12] Ing. Friedrich Bürger,[13] and Dr. Ernst Kundt.[14] They distrusted parliamentarian democracy and liberalism, and sought a more stable authoritarian government, admiring the discipline of a strong leadership.

The KB stood closer to the Austrian semi-Fascist corporate regime than to Nazi Germany and regarded the Nazis as plebeians who did not grasp the value of a trained elite.[15] It entertained close contacts with Berlin, however, which supplied it with material support. The KB endorsed the expansionist aims of the Nazis but preferred to maintain a certain degree of autonomy vis-à-vis the Reich. Opposition between the exclusive KB and the more popular-minded Sudeten Nazis led to violent strife that ended in the defeat of the KB.[16] The KB

11. Dr. Brand was one of the founding fathers of the KB. He studied under Professor Spann in Vienna. With Rutha he greatly influenced the ideas of the German Turnverband, where he was put in charge of indoctrination and education. He was elected directing manager of the KB and later became head of the Henlein office and chief editor of the Henlein Party review, the *Rundschau,* and of its central organ *Die Zeit.* He led the KB in the interparty dispute against the Nazi group Der Aufbruch. The KB suffered its first major defeat when an honorary court brought some charges against Dr. Brand. On July 23, 1936, Brand withdrew from public life and acted ably as party representative in London and Paris. After the annexation of the Sudeten territories in 1938, the leadership of the KB was unjustly accused by the Nazis of homosexuality in the Dresden trial against Brand and Company. Dr. Brand was held in a concentration camp until April 1945. Today Dr. Brand is a leading member of the Witikobund, a national-minded society of expelled Sudeten Germans in West Germany (Franzel as cited in Preidel, pp. 364–66; Fischer et al., pp. 74–77; César-Černý, *Politika,* II, *passim;* Rönnefarth, *Sudetenkrise,* I, *passim*). For his present point of view, see Walter Brand, *Die sudetendeutsche Tragödie* and *Von der inneren Struktur der sudetendeutschen Volksgruppe.*

12. Dr. Sebekowsky was an important leader of the Henlein Party, the head of its press service and, after 1938, the Regierungspräsident at Carlsbad in the Sudetengau. Today he lives in West Germany and is a leading member of the Witikobund.

13. Representative of the Henlein Party in Berlin and the VDA Czechoslovak expert (Fischer et al., pp. 70, 100–109).

14. He succeeded K. H. Frank as chairman of the parliamentary club of the Henlein Party. After Munich Kundt became the head of the remaining German minority in the Czech part of the Republic. During the war he stayed at Cracow. For more information, see *Anklageschrift gegen die Abgeordneten und Senatoren der Sudetendeutschen Partei,* pp. 79 ff. This copy of the original text from 1946 was published in Munich in 1962; hereafter cited as *Anklageschrift.*

15. Franzel in Preidel, p. 362.

16. Fischer et al., pp. 42–43. The first phase of the long dispute between the KB and the Sudeten Nazis occurred in the years 1930–33 and was conducted by the pro-Nazi group Bereitschaft (Readiness). The second phase of the strife reached

kept its sectarian character for some time after 1933, when its leaders dominated the Sudeten German Party.[17]

The true basis of KB activities was the German Turnverband.[18] Konrad Henlein, a modest, calm, self-possessed, and placid-looking man,[19] was elected to one of the highest posts (Verbandsturnwart) of

its climax in the W. Brand article in the *Rundschau*, "Wir schlagen an," against the Nazi group around *Der Aufbruch* (Rudolf Kasper, Dr. Gustav Jonak) on May 29, 1936, and ended with the victory of the Nazis (*ibid.*, pp. 44–46).

17. Dr. Hans Neuwirth, a prominent lawyer and deputy of the Henlein Party, considers the influence of the KB overrated (Collegium Carolinum, *Die Sudetenfrage in europäischer Sicht*, p. 144).

18. For more data on the Turnverband, see the account of the Deutscher Turnverband in der Tschechoslowakei, *Die völkische Turnbewegung* (this third edition was published after 1934); Historický ústav Slovenskej akadémie vied, *Nemecká otázka a Československo* (1938–1961), pp. 70–76. The Turnverband embraced about 1,100 local groups with a membership of more than 180,000 people. The movement spread in Austria after 1848, splitting into liberal and nationalist wings. The Sudeten Turners, particularly those from the region around Cheb, were radical nationalists and introduced the Aryan paragraph barring entry to Jews. After the war, this intolerant racism linked the Austrian and Sudeten German groups. They faced opposition from the more liberal Reich German Turnerschaft. (Compare Rudolf Jahn, *Konrad Henlein. Leben und Werk des Turnführers*, pp. 73 ff.) Rutha and Brand seem to have had the merit of bringing about a spiritual revival of the movement; Henlein devoted himself to the organizational tasks.

19. Henlein was born on May 6, 1898, near Liberec. His grandmother, Helena Dvořáčková, was of Czech nationality. Henlein fought on the Italian front, where he was captured on Nov. 17, 1917. In the years 1919–25 he worked as a bank clerk, and in 1925 as a paid gymnastic instructor at the oldest Turnverband group in Aš. After 1933 he became leader of the Sudeten German Party, the SS-Gruppenführer, and the Reichsstatthalter of the Sudetengau. He was captured by the Americans and committed suicide on the night of May 9–10, 1945. (See Jaksch, *Europas Weg*, p. 503.) For more information, see Jahn; Karl August Deubner, *Der Politiker Konrad Henlein. Schöpfer der sudetendeutschen Einheit*; the pictorial book by Ernst Tscherne, ed., *Das ist Konrad Henlein*; Rönnefarth, *Sudetenkrise*, II, 103–104; Emil Franzel, *Sudetendeutsche Geschichte*, pp. 367–68, hereafter cited as *Geschichte*; and the short biographical sketches by Dr. Hans Neuwirth in the collections of articles published by the Collegium Carolinum, *Bohemia*, I, 247–49, and *Die Sudetenfrage in europäischer Sicht*, pp. 146 ff. (See also interesting notes on the conversations of the members of the Runciman mission with Henlein in *DBFP*, II, 656–60, 668–70.) The observations by Dr. Walter Brand given to the author (in an interview June 10, 1963) seem balanced. Henlein was described as a man who was ready to listen to the advice of his colleagues and experts. It was after weighing all arguments that Henlein made the final decision. On the other hand, Franzel (cited in Preidel, p. 363) regards Henlein as a typical subaltern bureaucrat, with little political talent and incapable of independent decision. It seems, however, that Henlein—a man of a somewhat colorless mediocrity—incorporated many of the vices and virtues of the average Sudeten German. He was surely more than just a puppet. Faithful to what he believed to be the good of his nation, he readily accepted the nationalist tenets of National Socialism although some of them hardly pleased his hardheaded, narrow-minded provincialism. It was the KB—Rutha and Brand—which taught Henlein to take cognizance of the

the movement in 1931. At this date it had become very clear that the Comrades' Union was striving to reanimate the Turnbewegung as the instrument of German national reawakening, since Henlein viewed the Germans as split among too many parties and without a responsible leader. He felt that the German decline was due to the impact of liberalism from the Western countries, which presented an egotistic, un-German conception of the world. The un-German liberal spirit, by preferring the individual to the collective, had poisoned the minds of the members of the Turnverband.[20] Henlein's ideal man desired to fight, to take risks, and to brave dangers. His foremost principle was service to the national community and voluntary subordination of the individual to the whole.[21] For their part, the comrades with Henlein went a long way toward committing themselves to an ideology which in many respects disregarded, with calculation, democratic ideas.[22]

The coming of the economic crisis coupled with the rise of National Socialism transformed the situation in Czechoslovakia. First, the great depression served as an explosive to blast apart the elements of the hitherto prosperous economy; then deepening economic and financial difficulties centering on the German areas awoke the latent forces of German nationalism. National rifts became more concentrated and apparent. As the gravity of the crisis intensified, the government attempted to master the situation. But as the slump was prolonged, bitterness overwhelmed the entire German middle class and a large part of the working class. In their opinion, the democratic regime in conjunction with the Czechoslovak majority had not done enough to

importance of international public opinion and made him undertake his much publicized visits to London in 1935–38. Berlin became fully aware of the usefulness of the activities of the KB members in Western Europe. Being no Nazis, they were used to cover the expansionist aims of Berlin.

20. Extracts from Henlein's utterances in Jahn, p. 123.

21. Henlein's speeches (*ibid.*, pp. 125, 129, 134). In his article in the organ of the KB in November 1930, Henlein stated: "Der Liberalismus in dessen Gefolge die grossen auflösenden Mächte der Gegenwart stehen (Demokratie, Parteizerklüftung, Kapitalismus, Klassenkampf) bedeutet eine Brechung des Lebenswillens des Volkes, das sich im Pazifismus, steigender Genusssucht und sinkender Geburetnziffer äussert." He declared "war to the death to liberalism. . . . Disciplined mass organizations rule the present: Fascism, the Heimwehr, the Hitler Movement; for men wish to be led in manly fashion" (Fischer et al., pp. 57–58; Seton-Watson, A History, p. 351).

22. For the views of a number of prominent members of the KB, see *Anklageschrift*, p. 52; *Německý imperialismus*, pp. 306–309. Another radical nationalist group was called Bereitschaft. Its leaders plotted against the integrity of the Republic and were sentenced to prison in 1936 (Wiskemann, *Czechs and Germans*, pp. 137–38). An important cultural center of German nationalism was the German University at Prague.

avert the impact of the distress.[23] The dismal days of the depression only intensified national conflicts and sharpened grievances.

The impressive victories of National Socialism in the crisis-stricken German Reich did nothing to smooth the social and national effects of the depression upon the Germans in Czechoslovakia. Although left-wing publications were warning of the peril of a Nazi dictatorship, the collapse of parliamentary government in adjacent Germany and the successes of Nazism did not fail to impress the majority of Germans. Vigorous measures taken by Hitler to fight the crisis aroused the approval of many Sudeten Germans and increased their contempt for the multiparty democratic system.[24]

On the other hand, the prevailing mood of the Czech people, suffering almost as deeply as the Germans, was one of critical realism and hope rather than exasperation. The apprehension that centered on the Nazi movement seemed to be concerned less with its exercise of power in Germany—although Czech sympathies were openly on the side of the Weimar Republic—than with the possibility that the ultimate reaction to it might be the rise of a radical nationalist front among the Sudeten Germans. The Czechs clearly did not relish a Nazi movement in their midst.

Meanwhile, the DNSAP was gaining ground.[25] Increasingly sympathetic response to its program was reflected among the youth in the creation of the Volkssportverband in 1929, a paramilitary replica of the SA stormtroopers who dressed, like the SA, in brown shirts and caps. Their jackboots, outstretched right arms, and swastika banner appealed to widening classes of Germans. As concern grew over their strength and military training, the Prague cabinet disbanded the Volkssport and the National Socialist Studentenbund on Feb. 29, 1932. The leaders were jailed and the wearing of the swastika was banned. In the trial of members of the Volkssport at Brno in 1932, its leaders were condemned for conspiracy against the Republic.[26]

23. Wenzel Jaksch noted that democracy had nothing to offer to its adherents in the Sudetenland except total economic insecurity (*Sudeten Labour and the Sudeten Problem*, p. 27). One can, however, reply that the same democracy offered nothing essentially different to the Czechs, who still did not espouse Nazism.

24. *Ibid.*, p. 28. Jaksch pointed out that the dark days of the depression created a mystical mood in the masses.

25. At the elections of 1925 the DNSAP gained 168,000 votes; in 1929, over 200,000 votes (Krebs, p. 183). At the congress at Děčín (May 29, 1932), the party claimed to have 1,024 local groups with 61,000 members (Pfitzner, *Sudetendeutsche Einheitsbewegung*, p. 55).

26. Klepetář, pp. 217, 314–15. The trial lasted from Aug. 8 to Sept. 24, 1932. On Feb. 8, 1933, Hitler denied to Vojtěch Mastný, Czechoslovak minister in

On Oct. 2, 1933, the final verdict of the Supreme Court was published. "It is patent that a political party must forfeit its existence when it develops a program threatening the territorial integrity of the State."[27] The following day the DNSAP forestalled prohibition through voluntary dissolution. On Oct. 4, 1933, the Czechoslovak authorities formally banned the DNSAP and the German National Party.[28] Thus Czechoslovak democracy unequivocally condemned National Socialism and disciplined the dissident extremists.

Having mastered this political problem, however, Prague did not solve the disquieting economic questions with equal dispatch. This period might have provided an excellent opportunity to launch a program of long-range economic assistance to poverty-stricken German industrial areas. Moreover, the Prague cabinet should have tried to meet other reasonable German grievances by giving freely what it was forced to concede later under the pressure of circumstances. But, still conforming to the tenets of liberal economic theory, the cabinet was reluctant to engage in a new deal for the Germans. In view of the ensuing events it was probable that the majority of the Germans would not have been reconciled to the Republic and its democratic regime even by far-reaching economic action, for the German-Czech issue was much more complex: economic measures alone could not solve it. Prague, however, ought to have seized the initiative in reviewing the issues at stake and in taking vigorous steps toward reconciliation between the two peoples. Such measures would have acted to strengthen the forces of democracy still in existence among the Germans in Czechoslovakia.

The old leaders of the German nationalist parties aroused little response among the German population, which sought something more inspiring. Many Germans, particularly among the young, dreamed of a resurgence of the Greater German Reich. This mood implied, at the very least, that not a few Germans sought the solution to their own problems outside the democratic framework. The year 1933 saw simultaneously the climax of the economic crisis and the victorious march of the Nazi revolution. Againt this background of

Berlin, that there were any contacts between the Volkssport and the Nazi Party (Friedrich Berber, ed., *Europäische Politik 1933–1938 im Spiegel der Prager Akten*, p. 20. This badly edited volume contains a few extracts from the archives of the Prague Foreign Office.)

27. Klepetář, p. 344. The Henlein Party retained the wording of the verdict and kept proclaiming its loyalty to the state and democracy for a long time.

28. Klepetář, pp. 345–46. The Nazi leaders fled to the Reich (B. Bílek, *Fifth Column at Work*, p. 26). This study contains many unpublished Czechoslovak official records and is extremely valuable.

emotional nationalism, Sudeten German discontent assumed an ultranationalist posture. During 1933 the tendency arose again to form a supreme organization uniting all Germans under the auspices of a national Sudeten Front. Particularly the DNSAP, menaced by dissolution, urged the German bourgeois parties to come to such an agreement. Despite this favorable climate, however, the Nazi bid fell through in September 1933.

In July the great festival of the Turnverband had taken place in Žatec under the guidance of Konrad Henlein. As a result, Henlein's name came to the forefront of attention. Henlein was approached separately by Nazi deputies Hans Krebs and Hans Knirsch and National Deputy Othmar Kallina, who urged him to act before the DNSAP was officially dissolved.[29] The Comrades Union did not favor the bid and preferred to wait.[30]

Henlein contacted other groups, parties, and personalities, but when they were not responsive to his proposition for a national ralliement, he decided to take the challenge alone. It was a difficult decision and a risky one. He had to fill the place left by the two dissolved nationalist parties. Through a public repudiation of ties with the extremists, he sought to win the confidence of the Czechoslovak authorities, which otherwise would suspect his movement of being a mere substitute for the disbanded parties. By restraint and careful speeches, Henlein professed loyalty toward the Republic and its democratic regime.[31] His decision was facilitated by the situation in

29. Krebs in the *Neueste Zeitung*, Innsbruck, Oct. 1, 1943, as quoted in Bílek, p. 26. (See also Franzel in Preidel, p. 363; Franzel, *Geschichte*, pp. 365–66.) Krebs stated that his conversations with Henlein were held on several occasions after he had learned at the beginning of September that the Supreme Court would confirm the verdict of the Volkssport trial. At the trial of Henleinist deputies in Prague in 1946, it was learned that in 1933 Knirsch and Krebs had looked for a leader who could found a new national movement. Krebs approached Dr. Marian San Nicoló, rector of the German University, who recommended Henlein (*Svobodné slovo*, Dec. 11, 1946; *Anklageschrift*, pp. 13–15).

30. Franzel, *Geschichte*, pp. 365–66. Dr. Walter Brand stated (conversation with the author, June 10, 1963) that he and H. Rutha had paid a visit to Henlein in Aš on Sept. 24–25, 1933. Dr. Sebekowsky arrived one day later. Henlein affirmed his decision to found a new movement even without the participation of his friends at the KB. He gave assurance that he had not entered into any secret agreement with the leaders of the DNSAP.

31. German writers agreed on the necessity of an open disavowal of the radical nationalist aims. Rudolf Jung noted: "Der Anschein musste vermieden werden, dass es sich um Fortsetzung der Tätigkeit einer verbotenen Partei handle" (Erich Kühne, ed., *Sudetendeutscher Schicksalskampf*, p. 50). K. H. Frank stressed: "Wollte Henlein in 1933 seine Bewegung vor der Auflösung bewahren musste er eine vorsichtige Formulierung des Programmes . . . und durch Loyalitätserklärung das Misstrauen der Staatsgewalt einzuschläfern. Dadurch

the German nationalist camp, in which there existed a virtual political vacuum. The strategy of his aides was to present a new political personality who would reinforce the move toward a concentration of national forces. As a man beyond and above parties he would call on everybody, without regard for origin, ideas, or feeling, to rally around him in the political renovation of the German group.

On Oct. 1, 1933, this young, little-known instructor of gymnastics offered himself as the leader who would restore the unity of all Czechoslovak Germans.

> I appeal above all parties and estates . . . to the Sudeten German people and place myself at the head of this movement.

He announced that the new movement would endeavor to rally all the Germans who were ready to accept the idea of a national community and the Christian concept of the world.[32] The Sudeten German Home Front (Sudetendeutsche Heimatfront; SHF), in which the KB members took over the key positions, was thus created.[33] A week later

---

wurde wieder die Gewinnung vieler Nationalsozialisten erschwert" (Friedrich Heiss, ed., *Das Böhmen und Mähren-Buch, Volkskampf und Reichsraum,* p. 212). Ernst Frank put it: "Dass Konrad Henlein in Oktobertagen . . . 1933 das Banner Adolf Hitlers ergriff, das ahnten oder wussten nur ganz, ganz wenige. . . . Für die Masse des Volkes war damals sein Tun weder das Fortsetzen der DNSAP . . . sondern wirklich etwas von Grund an Neues" (p. 135).

Konrad Henlein himself confessed, in a speech delivered in Vienna in 1941 and published in the *Mährisch-Schlesische Landeszeitung* on March 5, 1941, that "to start with, we had to deny our allegiance to National Socialism in order to escape the interference of the Czech authorities and the possibility of dissolution. That was the greatest mental trial to which I had to expose my followers" (Vincent Urban, p. 17). Franz Höller affirmed in 1939: "Hätte sich Konrad Henlein 1933 offen zum Nationalsozialismus bekannt, wäre das Schicksal seiner Partei besiegelt gewesen. . . . Aber dass der Geist des Nationalsozialismus in allen Versammlungen der Bewegung Konrad Henleins lebte, dass empfand jeder, der einmal selbst dabei gewesen war" (introduction to *Von der SdP zur NSDAP. Ein dokumentarischer Bildbericht*).

Dr. Hans Neuwirth (Collegium Carolinum, ed., *Die Sudetenfrage in europäischer Sicht, passim*) and Dr. Walter Brand (*Die sudetendeutsche Tragödie, passim*) defended the view that the Henlein movement strove sincerely to achieve a federalist solution of the Sudeten German problem within the framework of the Republic. Yet Dr. Brand had to recognize the far-reaching international and internal consequences of such a solution: "Wenn es auch klar war, dass eine solche staatsrechtliche Umgestaltung die Tschechoslo-wakei in einem gewissen Sinne in den Einflussbereich eines starken deutschen Reiches gebracht hätte" (*Die sudetendeutsche Tragödie,* p. 33).

32. The emphasis on the Christian conception was reportedly designed to suggest the Aryan character of the movement. Ernst Frank (p. 134) openly stated that the mention of the Christian basis was the only possible way to stress the fact that the Jews were "not welcomed."

33. For the text of the declaration, see *Sudetendeutschtum im Kampf* (published

(October 8) Henlein held his first press conference at Prague and explicitly endorsed the principles of democracy and the integrity of the Republic.

> Fate has placed us in this place which has become our home, bound to us by a thousand years of history; and it is in this place—and therefore in this State—that we shall have to shape our destiny. . . . Since we embrace the Czechoslovak State, we also embrace the principles of democracy, which guarantee the equal rights of nations. . . . We are and shall remain Germans, but we embrace with the most profound conviction the task which has been allotted to us Sudeten Germans within the framework of the Czechoslovak State.[34]

The movement set afoot by Henlein was a protest of the younger generation against the impotence and compromises of the regular German parties. The overall atmosphere, which hitherto had been relaxed and tranquil, now became suspicious and nervous. A growing bitterness at the accumulating economic and social grievances was combined with a mood of hope derived from both intense Sudeten German nationalism and the triumph of Nazism in the Reich. On the other hand, many Czechs strongly suspected that the SHF was merely a screen for the real objective, which was destruction of the Republic.[35]

Henlein limited his political commitments to mild expressions of national solidarity and declarations of loyalty to the democratic state. He maintained regular contacts with the Prague authorities, and had

by the Henlein Party), p. 174, and Paul Meier-Benneckenstein, ed., *Dokumente der deutschen Politik*, VI, part I, 274. The manifesto was written with the assistance of Dr. Walter Brand (see Dr. Neuwirth in *Die Sudetenfrage in europäischer Sicht*, p. 149). In his speech at the Carlsbad congress of the Henlein Party in 1938, Henlein explained his decision: "So wurde im Jahre 1933 die Deutsche Nationalsozialistische Arbeiterpartei der Tschechoslowakei aufgelöst und die Deutsche Nationalpartei eingestellt. Man wollte damit gleichzeitig die Widerstandskraft des Sudeten Deutschtums treffen und ihm die Möglichkeit nehmen, den Kampf um sein Recht im Rahmen völkischer Parteien zu führen. Dieser Zugriff kam aber bereits zu spät" (*Dokumente der deutschen Politik*, p. 273). In 1938, Henlein had already discarded his professions of loyalty to democracy. For the first reactions in Germany, see *Německý imperialismus*, p. 373.

34. Vincent Urban, pp. 14–15.

35. *Survey of International Affairs 1936*, p. 493. This volume, belonging to an extremely valuable series of surveys, was written by Arnold J. Toynbee; the series will hereafter be cited as *Survey*. It contains an excellent treatment of Czech-German relations during the years 1918–36 (pp. 469–501). Toynbee regarded the position of the Sudeten Germans as "almost up to the Swiss or Canadian standard" (*ibid.*, p. 197). For the Czech state of mind, see the Prague moderate center-left review *Naše doba*, XXXXI (1933), No. 1 and No. 4.

consulted the German Agrarians before founding the SHF.[36] Following his public appearance on October 1, Henlein reached an agreement with the German Small Traders' Party—which he gradually absorbed—and concluded a pact with the German Agrarians (BdL).[37] The role of Henlein's protectors was assumed by the German and Czech Agrarian parties, which sought to use the rightist SHF as a potential pawn against the socialist parties. German Agrarian Minister Dr. Franz Spina had already urged Henlein to specify his program publicly, to allay Czech fears of a new totalitarian movement, when some influential Prague circles advocated the dissolution of the SHF.[38] In 1933 and in the spring of 1934, Henlein conferred with the prominent leader of the right wing of the Czech Agrarian Party, Viktor Stoupal, who twice handed him large amounts of money.[39]

The SHF realized, however, that until it dispelled equivocation with regard to its aims, it was threatened with sharing the fate of the DNSAP. An address to this effect was prepared for Henlein to deliver at the manifestation in Česká Lípa on Oct. 21, 1934. In a stormy meeting, over the opposition of Karl Hermann Frank,[40] the cautious policy line of the KB group, led by Brand, Neuwirth, Kundt, and Sebekowsky, prevailed and a passage aiming to appease the Czechoslovak authorities was inserted:[41]

It accords . . . with our fundamental conviction, that both Fascism and National Socialism lose the natural conditions for their exist-

36. Kořalka (p. 67) used Dr. Spina's evidence as reported by Karl Kreibich in the Prague German weekly *Aufbau und Frieden* on Nov. 20, 1953.
37. Klepetář, p. 362; Bílek, p. 22.
38. Klepetář, p. 363.
39. Pavel Auersperg in Vladimír Soják, ed., *O čs. zahraniční politice 1918–1939*, p. 270; the volume contains a series of interesting, if biased, studies based on official records. (See also the Prague official review *Zahraniční politika*, 1935, p. 202.) According to the testimony of Henleinist Deputy Rudolf Sandner, Henlein mentioned that Stoupal had given him 20,000 and 50,000 Kč in 1933–34 (*Právo lidu*, March 8, 1947).
40. Frank was born Jan. 24, 1898, in Carlsbad. He entered the SHF in October 1933 and after the elections of 1935 became chairman of its parliamentary club. In January 1937 he became the deputy leader of the party. He was hanged in 1946 for his role during the war. He represented the radical anti-Czech wing of the SHF (K. H. Frank, p. 30; Rönnefarth, *Sudetenkrise*, II, 102–103; Neuwirth in *Bohemia*, I, 247). Frank was considered to be extremely ambitious, a kind of Renaissance condottiere. The arrest of Dr. Brand, Dr. Kundt, Dr. Sebekowsky, and Dr. Köllner in the winter of 1933–34 enabled Frank to gain influence in the SHF (Dr. Neuwirth in *Die Sudetenfrage in europäischer Sicht*, pp. 150–51). The removal of Dr. Brand in 1936 left the way open to the promotion of Frank. For a description of the struggles within the SdP in connection with the removal of Dr. Brand, see César-Černý, *Politika*, II, 362 ff.
41. Rönnefarth, I, 137–39; Franzel, *Geschichte*, p. 371. For the text of the declaration, see *Die Sudetenfrage in europäischer Sicht*, pp. 154–58.

ence at the frontiers of their respective States. . . . We shall never
abandon . . . the unconditional respect for individual rights.

The leaders of the SHF were anxious to move within the framework
of the given international situation which did not allow for any
adventure. They gave public recognition to the unity of the state and
its democratic form. The prevailing political situation made it
impossible for the SHF to make use of any other terms of reference.
The address met with disapproval among the former members of the
DNSAP.[42]

While mending its fences with the Czechs, the SHF kept in secret
close touch with Berlin. Its representative, Dr. Hans Neuwirth,
quietly negotiated a grant of financial support from the VDA.[43] Reich
Minister Rudolf Hess, Hitler's deputy, who had been in charge of
Sudeten German affairs since October 1933, and the German Foreign
Ministry gave their full support to the underhanded methods of the
Henlein movement. Hess's office even urged the Foreign Ministry to
forbid the German legation in Prague to work with the former leaders
of the DNSAP, who were too openly tied to the National Socialist
regime in the Reich. For the time being, Berlin sacrificed almost
completely the old Sudeten Nazis and threw its full support behind
the leadership of the SHF. Its most urgent task was to create a vast
nationalist movement which would unite all national German forces
and thus would be able to assist the Reich policy in Czechoslovakia.
On March 11, 1935, an order by Hess and his deputy, Joachim von
Ribbentrop, instructed the German press to "cease" all "attacks on
Henlein."[44] Before the Czechoslovak elections in May 1935, the VDA
asked the German Foreign Ministry for a financial grant for the

42. One has to keep constantly in mind that the double role of the SHF and
Henlein was suspected but not yet proved before the summer of 1938.

43. Dr. Hans Neuwirth stated to the author (June 14, 1963) that he had
discussed the financial problems of the SHF with the head of the VDA, Dr. H.
Steinacher, in October 1933. In January 1934 there was a meeting of Henlein,
Dr. Steinacher, F. Bürger, and Herrmann Ullmann on the Czech-German border
on the top of the Sněžka mountain. Henlein was promised a subsidy for social
and cultural purposes. Dr. Neuwirth also negotiated with the VDA in April 1935
on the grant of a subsidy of 800,000 Kč for the election. For other information,
see Anklageschrift, pp. 29 ff.; František Uhlíř, Prague and Berlin, p. 51; Bílek,
p. 28. Uhlíř's booklet is useful, although biased.

44. DGFP, Series C, III, 43–44; 994–95. The security service (SD) and some
circles around Himmler, Bormann, and Goebbels distrusted Henlein and the KB
and supported the group of K. H. Frank and the former National Socialist
faction working in the Henlein movement (MacAlister Brown, "The Third
Reich," pp. 141, 143). In May 1936, the Reichssicherheitshauptamt in Berlin
sent to Hitler a secret memorandum which was highly critical of the KB
(Rönnefarth, Sudetenkrise, I, 128–31).

Henlein movement. A subsidy in the amount of 331,711.30 RM
—approved by both the Reich Ministry of Finance and the Foreign Office—was sent to the Henlein Party to cover election expenses.
The VDA and the German legation in Prague secretly transmitted
the sum to the party.[45]

Henlein's main political decisions were made dependent upon "the
approval and support" of the Reich authorities as early as March
1935. His emissaries moved covertly between Prague and Berlin;[46]
relations with Nazi Germany were gradually enlarged; and the
Henlein Party even cooperated with the Reich Ministry of the Interior
and the Foreign Policy Office of the Nazi Party.[47] In the fall of 1936,
Henlein became the head of an association uniting all German
minorities in Europe, the Verband Deutscher Volksgruppen in
Europa. He subordinated it completely to the policy line of Berlin
and made strenuous efforts to give it a basic Nazi character.[48]

International tensions increased during 1935. The repudiation of
the Versailles Treaty by Hitler and the reintroduction of conscription
in Germany led to the conclusion of a security pact between Soviet
Russia and France, signed on May 2, and of the identical Soviet-
Czechoslovak Treaty of Mutual Assistance of May 16. Through a
special protocol, the treaty was made dependent on the Soviet-
French agreement and obligations of mutual assistance arose "in so
far as assistance may be rendered by France to the Party victim of
the aggression."[49]

In May, elections were to be held in Czechoslovakia. The Henlein
speech in Česká Lípa had drawn the SHF and the German Agrarians
(the BdL) closer, and in protracted negotiations they tried to prepare
a basis for a common electoral list. Finally, however, in March 1935,
the SHF refused any further negotiations, and each party entered
the elections separately. Henlein had achieved his objective: through
consultations and conferences with a governmental party he had
gained a name as a loyal patriot. However, he had not accepted the

45. *DGFP*, Series C, III, 908–909, 968–69; IV, 229–30, 679, 821. Henlein
   negotiated the subsidy with the president of the Reichsbank, Hjalmar Schacht
   (*ibid.*, IV, 679).
46. *Ibid.*, III, 995; IV, 679, 742. Henlein met Hess in June 1935 in Oberpfalz
   (report by Walter Schmidt, June 3, 1958, in the archives of the Collegium
   Carolinum, deposit No. 202, and César-Černý in *Historica*, IV, 226).
47. Uhlíř, p. 51. See also Jacques Delarue, *Histoire de la Gestapo*, pp.
   217–18.
48. Rimscha, pp. 42–43.
49. *Documents on International Affairs 1935*, p. 139. (Hereafter this useful
   reference collection will be cited as *Documents*.)

compromise that would have seriously curbed his freedom of action and made the SHF a prisoner of the Agrarians. It was evident that the latter, by conferring with Henlein, had helped not only to legalize the SHF but also to weaken their own position.

Meanwhile, the Henleinists flourished their ammunition. So far it consisted of propaganda slogans against the red menace, Marxism, and the Jews. Through emphasis on overall national support for their program, they strove to create a favorable psychological background. The popular mood was stimulated at mass rallies. The Germans gathered in the meeting halls in every locality where Henlein or his aides made their appearance, together with a special uniformed Ordner service in black jackboots and white shirts which attracted wide-eyed admiration. With bands blaring German martial airs and banners proclaiming slogans, crowds of Germans applauded the speeches reaffirming the invincibility of the movement and its determination that the Sudeten Germans[50] should remain forever united.

The German people answered Henlein's call with frenzied enthusiasm. The discipline of the masses, the methodically prepared electoral techniques, the impeccable organization—the whole pattern of the campaign resembled that of the Nazis. With Nazi techniques and national slogans, Henlein flooded the German areas of Czechoslovakia with the full force of German nationalism. German farmers, the upper bourgeoisie, the middle class, and a large segment of the workers accepted the leadership of the SHF. In an atmosphere of aggressive nationalism, indirect pressure was brought to bear upon the German population. The spirit of national radicalism brought threats and intimidations; non-Henleinists were ostracized from the national community, and many German employers favored those employees and workers who became members of the Henlein movement.[51]

To be sure, there was no lack of vigorous and resolute resistance, particularly by the German labor organizations. They mobilized labor support for the defense of the Republic. Yet the cohesive strength of German democratic forces was impaired by the fact that in all the activist parties there were groups responsive to nationalist appeals. In

50. It is interesting to note, however, that the German authors—although some of them otherwise displayed their anti-Semitism—included the German-speaking Jews in the German ethnic group whenever they blamed the Czechs for some anti-German measure and wanted to present favorable population data.

51. It was ascertained that at many factories in the district of Duchcov, Liberec, Varnsdorf, and Podmokly in northern Bohemia, employers hired only Henleinist workers (Kořalka, p. 70). For a description of the various methods of intimidation, see Jaroslav Koutek, *Nacistická pátá kolona v ČSR*, pp. 106 ff. This volume is Communist-biased.

fact, the solidarity of the German democratic camp was neither so massive, so cohesive, nor so durable as it seemed.

The policy of Prague combined the practice of liberal democracy with a use of expedients in a perplexing manner. On the one hand the Czechs backed German democratic forces, while on the other they allowed German newspapers to publish subversive propaganda. In the final analysis, this was bound to menace the security of the Republic and its liberties. The non-German part of the country remained calm, and but for reminders of an electoral campaign, all seemed to be normal. The Czechs mistrusted the campaigning methods of the SHF, however, and there was growing clamor for its dissolution.[52] Although the SHF had given no overt sign of disloyalty, most observers believed that such caution was due primarily to the fact that the SHF was not yet certain that the cabinet would not react unfavorably in the face of a direct espousal of pan-German aims.

Henlein's major asset was the trend of Czech right-wing opinion, which was looking for allies against the socialists.[53] Another potential asset was the conviction of the circle around President Masaryk that a recrudescence of the Nazi Party was impossible in Czechoslovakia. It also preferred to have national radicalism organized openly through legal channels rather than see it go underground. Masaryk, already a venerable old man, regarded Henlein as merely an honest German schoolmaster.[54]

When the issue of the dissolution of the SHF rose in the cabinet in April 1935, the political committee, by a four-vote majority, disallowed SHF participation in the election. It was agreed, however,

52. The Social Democratic minister, Rudolf Bechyně, characterized the SHF as disguised Nazis (*Zahraniční politika*, 1935, p. 143). Moreover, the year 1935 brought a big shift in Communist tactics. At the Seventh Congress of the Communist International (August 1935), the campaign for the Popular Front was launched. Even prior to the congress, the Prague central organ of the party, *Rudé právo* (Red Right), voiced a warning (April 28, 1935): "A new Fascist Henlein's Home Front will make a bid for the votes of the German people. . . . The German Fascists will declare . . . that the only way to save the German people consists in the annexation of the German areas of settlement to the Hitlerite Third Reich. . . . The road of German Fascism leads toward a terrible war. . . . The Czech nation is menaced . . . by a new national oppression" (Klement Gottwald, *Spisy*, VI, 123, 125).

53. The Czech socialist and national press called for the dissolution of the SHF (Klepetář, p. 367). For the plan of the right wing of the Czech Agrarian Party to bring the Henlein Party into the cabinet, see the daily *Lidové listy* (Prague), for Jan. 12, 1938, as cited in Jaromír Hořec, *Cesty, ktoré viedli k Mníchovu*, p. 397. It must be stated, however, that this Agrarian faction seemed unaware of the real intentions of the SHF.

54. For the official minute of the conversation of Masaryk with the chief of his office (Feb. 6, 1935), see *Dokumenty o protilidové a protinárodní politice T. G. Masaryka*, p. 254.

that the final decision would be left to President Masaryk. Foreign Minister Eduard Beneš—who favored the dissolution—and Agrarian Premier Jan Malypetr consulted Masaryk, who decided to give the SHF an opportunity to work within the Parliament.[55] The failure to take a firm stand against a movement which was jeopardizing democracy and spreading Nazi propaganda proved to be a fatal mistake. While firm toward the wearied and leaderless DNSAP, Prague allowed free play to the new subversive party. In this, the Republic ran the terrible risk of being divided, for a movement bearing many marks of a Fascist party could not be reconciled to the democratic form of the state.

When in the euphoria of victory Henlein was free to speak frankly, he stated his aims and former tactics vis-à-vis the Czechoslovak state:

> During the great wave of persecution in the autumn of 1933, when the leaders of the Party asked me to assume leadership of the Sudetens, I had to decide whether the National Socialist Party was to carry on illegally or whether we should camouflage the movement with a show of legality and fight in that way for our self-preservation as Sudeten Germans and our return to the Reich. Only the second way lay open to us because it was . . . a fight with embittered foreigners intent on our destruction. It would have been easier . . . to confess openly to National Socialism and go to prison, but it was doubtful whether by this method we should achieve the political task of smashing Czechoslovakia as the spearhead of the anti-Reich system of alliances. The fact is that the Sudeten Germans succeeded in a short time in endangering the internal stability of Czechoslovakia so thoroughly and creating such confusion that she was soon ripe for liquidation within the framework of the new continental order. We knew that we could only win if we succeeded in making three and a half million Sudeten Germans into National Socialists, but if we were to avoid Czech interference, we had to pretend to deny our allegiance to National Socialism. With admirable discipline and unshakable confidence my comrades realized what was at stake and behind our tactics saw our aim to return to Adolf Hitler's Germany. . . . Our fight was a part of Germany's National Socialist Revolution.[56]

55. Hořec, p. 397; Klepetář, p. 369; Deubner, p. 54; Václav Král, ed., *Politické strany a Mnichov*, pp. 20–21; César-Černý, *Politika*, II, 273 ff.

56. London *Central European Observer* fortnightly review, May 2, 1941. The *Observer* was published by the Czechoslovak government. The extract is taken from the Prague official German daily *Der neue Tag*, reporting on Henlein's visit

Surely, not everyone who invoked the leadership of Henlein and indicated willingness to accept the main tenets of his motley program, designed to please every section of the national community, was a Nazi. But National Socialism encompassed and expressed all the elements of the anti-Czech and anti-Slav aggressive nationalism that had existed long before Henlein rose to leadership. The chances of reversing the move toward Nazism appeared to depend on the ability of the parliamentary regime to take stern measures against the dissident forces (first among them those within the SHF), on its reassurance of the middle-of-the-road and democratic German elements through necessary reforms, and on the possibility of establishing an international democratic front against the Nazi threat. Only bold, vigorous measures, not declarations of high moral and humanitarian principles, could have been effective in a world of power realities.

Following the cabinet's suggestion that the SHF change its name in order to participate in the elections—the title Home Front appeared incompatible with the requirements of the democratic system—the SHF became the Sudeten German Party (Sudetendeutsche Partei; the SdP). Henlein did not become a candidate for Parliament. As the leader he chose to stand aloof from parliamentary disputes. From his point of view it was a clever decision which enhanced his emotional appeal as a trustee of national sovereignty and lifted him out of the confusion of party politics. In his speeches Henlein criticized the German parties for being unable to resolve the problems facing the German community. He limited himself to posing the problems and defining his party's ability to deal with them. He refused to get involved beyond his general statements appealing to all classes to help his party resurrect the German community. The singing, marching, shouting crowds reflecting the mood of popular excitement set the tone, although the outward surface of life in the country remained unaffected. German labor organized the riposte and many German democrats took part in electoral meetings calling for the defense of democracy. Yet the balance of forces—psychological, political, economic, and physical—appeared to be shifting toward the SdP.

The results of the elections of May 19, 1935, gave full evidence of a

---

to Vienna on March 4, 1941. Some extracts are in Vincent Urban, pp. 16–17; Vojta Beneš, pp. 171–72; *Survey 1938*, II, 49. Professor Raschhofer pointed out that the Vienna lecture should be viewed as an attempt by Henlein to prove his trustworthiness to Nazism *post festum* (Raschhofer, *Die Sudetenfrage*, pp. 162–63). However, available evidence and the relevant facts themselves deprive Raschhofer's argument of validity. It might be simply that Henlein and his aides intentionally somewhat exaggerated their achievements.

popular ground swell in favor of the Sudeten German Party, which polled 63.18 percent of the German vote in Bohemia and 56.12 percent in Moravia-Silesia.[57] Other German parties trailed far behind. The German Social Democratic Party polled 14.97 and 14.08 percent of the German vote, respectively; the German Agrarian Union, 7.25 and 6.84 percent; the German Christian Socialist Party, 6.21 and 13.47 percent. About 7.4 and 7.2 percent of Germans voted for the Communist Party.[58] The losses of the Activist parties were tremendous, the German Social Democrats losing 49.2 percent of their votes in Bohemia and 40.6 percent in Moravia-Silesia.[59] The Henleinists succeeded in carrying their strength even into the normally red strongholds of the northern Bohemian industrial centers. Not only the middle class but also the majority of the German working class rallied under the Fascist banner. There is no need to add any comment to Henlein's own confession:

> National Socialism quickly took hold of us Sudeten Germans as well. Though we were obliged to act differently when we appeared in public, we were of course intimately linked up with the National Socialist Revolution, so that we should be a part of the struggle for greater Germany which was also fought on Sudeten soil.[60]

If one analyzes the returns closely, it is evident that the SdP received far greater support than did the Reich German Nazis at the last relatively free German elections on March 5, 1933. The count gave Hitler, who was Reich chancellor, only 43.9 percent of the total tally, while *the results in Czechoslovakia indicated that more than 60 percent of the German voters cast their ballots for the Sudeten German Party at a free democratic election.*[61]

The flood of Henleinist votes came mainly from the city areas. The ballot count showed that the SdP received 69.74 percent of the German vote in Bohemia in places with more than 5,000 inhabitants, while gaining 60.14 percent in places with fewer than 5,000 residents.

57. The SdP received 918,434 votes in Bohemia and 302,006 in Moravia-Silesia (Vincent Urban, p. 28).

58. The tabulation gave the Social Democrats 217,570 votes in Bohemia and 75,791 in Moravia-Silesia; the Agrarian Union, 105,333 and 36,814; the Christian Socialists, 90,303 and 72,478. The Communist Party received both Czech (108,000) and German (38,500) votes (*ibid.*).

59. The figures are taken from Vincent Urban (p. 29), who used figures from the elections to the Chamber of Deputies, which comprised voters age 21 and upward. The Senate was elected by citizens over 25 years.

60. Vojta Beneš, pp. 171–72. It is an extract from Henlein's lecture in 1941.

61. The facts cited here and in the following paragraphs are taken from Vincent Urban, pp. 29–32.

The figures for Moravia-Silesia were 58.02 and 55.20 percent, respectively. The surge of Henleinist strength was greater in the medium- and large-sized cities than among the inhabitants of smaller towns. The compact German areas showed the greatest percentage of Henlein votes, while the Germans scattered among the Czech population displayed little enthusiasm for the SdP.[62]

Of the major political parties competing for the Czech vote, the Agrarian Party forged ahead, with the Social Democrats as the second strongest party. Nationalist parties did not receive any increased endorsement. The traditional parties once again attracted the majority of the voters who voiced approval of the coalition government policy pursued by the major Czechoslovak parties.

The vast popularity of the SdP, as evidenced by the voting, catapulted new German leaders into prominence, with a strong prospect of new developments of an unusually dangerous nature. A strange but disciplined alliance of mixed motives appeared to have developed in the German camp. The Germans had thrown impressive support behind a movement inimical to the present Republic. That movement, however, did not yet dare to challenge Prague's authority.

No grave incidents marred the still confident climate of the country. However, the massive SdP propaganda machine had been arousing nationalist passion for months. The call to power by the nationalists—if these were by no means all outright Nazis, they were at least more amenable to Hitler's expansionist policies—had tacitly been launched. The unclear international situation made it necessary for Henlein to proffer promises, both to Prague and to the West, that his deep involvement with the wave of German nationalism would not stand in the way of a Czech-German rapprochement. Nothing could have been, at that juncture, more dangerous for Henlein than confirmation of the beliefs of many Czech politicians and publicists who coupled the SdP with pan-Germanism. Henlein and his aides combined the evidently sincere desire to improve the lot of their own people with a burning ambition to be associated with the pan-German expansionist policy. To implement both aims they needed to have the whole German group firmly united around them as their recognized leaders.

62. For instance, from 302 Germans scattered in the district of Benešov, and 289 Germans in the district of Mělník, no one voted for the Henlein Party, although one could have expected that, according to the average percentage, 114 and 110 votes would have been cast by the two groups, respectively, for the SdP (*ibid.*, p. 31).

CHAPTER 4

Preparations

Czechoslovak foreign policy did not reflect the confusion and divisions that marked other countries. It was closely linked with the personality of Eduard Beneš, its foreign minister from 1918 until his promotion to the presidency on Dec. 18, 1935.[1] Hard-working, with an acute intellect, ready to compromise, cautious but obstinate in negotiations, and possessing political intelligence and diplomatic skill of the highest order, Beneš won an international reputation at the League of Nations in Geneva. In public, his style was restrained; his speeches were weighty and often tedious. With a rigid concept of public service, he had fought all his life for the principle that the public interest comes first. A democrat and humanist by nature and conviction, he was too often anxious to conciliate. Having mastered the game of political bargaining in a democratic system, he lacked the aggressiveness necessary to meet the challenge of modern totalitarian forces in two decisive moments. Beneš believed that a cause that

1. Dr. Beneš was born in Kožlany in 1884. He studied sociology in France and began his academic career in Prague. During the war he joined T. G. Masaryk and became one of the most distinguished leaders of the movement for an independent Czechoslovakia. For more information, see Edward B. Hitchcock, *I Built a Temple for Peace. The Life of Eduard Beneš;* Compton Mackenzie, *Dr. Beneš;* Jan Opočenský, ed., *Edward Beneš. Essays and Reflections Presented on the Occasion of His Sixtieth Birthday.* The chapter on the Beneš policy by Paul E. Zinner in *The Diplomats 1919–1939* (Gordon A. Craig, ed.), pp. 100–22, is competent. The brief portraits by Lewis Namier (*In the Nazi Era,* p. 135), P. Wandycz (*France,* pp. 383–86), and the Earl of Avon (*The Eden Memoirs. Facing the Dictators,* pp. 172–73) are lucid. Jan Křen gave an interesting—although biased—picture of Beneš (*Do emigrace,* pp. 242 ff.).

hewed to morality could exert more potency with the people than any rattling of sabers, and felt that one could find solutions through negotiation, no matter how much it might try one's patience.

This rational outlook appeared somewhat unreal in the era of Freud, Bergson, and Spengler, and the predominance of the irrational, emotional, and subconscious. However, as the leader of the Left-Center Party, Beneš displayed a surprisingly penetrating and discerning grasp of the great social forces abroad in the world. He keenly realized the implications of modern nationalism and democratic socialism, and energetically supported the demands of the working classes for a larger share of power and wealth, understanding that a political democracy had to be supplemented by a social and economic one.

The fate of the new state was bound intimately with the new European order built around the League of Nations and the predominance of Great Britain and France. Czechoslovakia formed an important link in the French system of alliances[2] designed to bar any attempt to revise the Versailles Treaty, and was a keystone of the postwar structure of Europe. Her policy sought to reflect this position, since Beneš believed that whenever there should be a threat to Czechoslovak independence, the very fundamental vital interests of the Great Powers would be at stake.[3]

For Beneš, "the permanence of the Czechoslovak State was dependent on the existence of a democratic, socially mature and steadily developing Europe."[4] However, Czechoslovakia could not escape the hard geographic facts that she was a neighbor of another Great Power and stood as a barrier to its thrust to the East.[5] As no state could base its independence solely upon the mutual trust of individual countries, Czechoslovakia was obliged to ensure her existence and integrity not

2. France and Czechoslovakia were linked by two treaties. Under the first (Treaty of Alliance and Friendship of Jan. 25, 1924), both parties undertook to proceed jointly in all matters of foreign policy which might put their security in danger and to agree on adequate measures for the protection of their common interests. In accordance with the second (Treaty of Mutual Guarantee, concluded Oct. 16, 1925) as a part of the Locarno treaties, both states undertook mutually to render immediate help and support in the event of an unprovoked attack by Germany (*DGFP*, II, 10). For French-Czechoslovak relations, see the account by Wandycz.
3. Beneš in his exposé of Nov. 5, 1935, as reported in Felix J. Vondráček, *The Foreign Policy of Czechoslovakia, 1918–1935*, pp. 416–17.
4. Dr. Eduard Beneš, *Memoirs of Dr. Eduard Beneš. From Munich to New War and New Victory*, p. 9; hereafter cited as Beneš, *Memoirs*.
5. Czechoslovak Information Service, *President Beneš on War and Peace* (New York, 1943), p. 154. In an address at a state dinner at Ottawa, June 4, 1943.

only through momentary good relations with the German Reich but also through a "balance of power in a system of collective security."[6] During the period of the Weimar Republic, Beneš pursued a correct and loyal policy toward Germany.[7] There were almost no direct disputes, serious conflicts, or difficulties between the two countries.[8]

Prague was aware of the impact of Hitler's coming to power. Beneš declared in the National Assembly on Oct. 31, 1933:

> The German National Socialist revolution has interrupted this gradual development. In my opinion, the final aims and ideals of Stresemann's policy were, broadly speaking, not much different from the final aims of the policy of present-day Germany.[9] The two differed only in their external manifestations and procedure and in the better understanding of the aims, efforts and needs of the rest of Europe, which exercised a passing influence on the tactics and methods of Stresemann's Germany. Ever since the unification of the German nation in modern times, especially after the Revolution of 1848, German policy has had a Pan-German basis. . . . But present-day Germany considered the pace and methods of Stresemann's Germany for the realization of German national aims, as too slow. It has therefore broken away from this line of development and begun to use more radical methods.[10]

For Masaryk and Beneš the rise of Nazism represented a challenge to the objectives and ideals of postwar European order — the opposition of two different worlds.[11] Their perilous position and historic experiences made the Czechs perceptive of any change of mood in their big German neighbor. Beneš warned the Czechoslovak General Staff as early as July 1932 that "a dreadful" crisis was approaching.[12]

6. Beneš, *Germany and Czechoslovakia*, I, 91.

7. *Ibid.*, pp. 60, 69–70. See the statements of Beneš before Parliament on Sept. 30, 1919 and Oct. 31, 1933. The study by Wandycz brings out the moderate features of the German policy of Beneš. See also the biased treatment by Koloman Gajan, *Německý imperialismus a československo—německé vztahy v letech 1918–1921*, pp. 160 ff., 199 ff.

8. *Germany and Czechoslovakia*, p. 71.

9. To support this contention, see *Gustav Stresemann: His Diaries, Letters and Papers*, II, 159, 216–18, and the sound, well-balanced account by Hans W. Gatzke, *Stresemann and the Rearmament of Germany*.

10. Beneš, *Memoirs*, pp. 4–5.

11. *Ibid.*, p. 6.

12. *Ibid.*, p. 22. Gen. Louis Faucher, head of the French military mission in Prague, confirmed this affirmation of Beneš but placed it in October 1932 (*Les événements survenus en France de 1933 à 1945. Témoignages et documents recueillis par la Commission d'enquête parlementaire*. Assemblée Nationale. Première Legislature. Session de 1947, V, 1195). This collection of French testimony is particularly important in view of the fact that almost all the French

After the signing of the Polish-German Treaty in 1934, Czecho-slovakia replaced Poland as the main target of German expansion toward the East. Prague immediately began to seek for collaboration between East and West to check the German advances, since Beneš was convinced that "without the participation of the Soviet Union in European . . . affairs, Germany would be again supreme in Europe and would endanger European peace."[13] However, he regarded Czechoslovakia as an indispensable part of Western Europe, and to allay fears that she would be bound to the Soviet Union, he initiated the insertion of a protocol in the Mutual Treaty with the Soviets in 1935, making its application contingent upon French assistance.[14] Thus, Beneš prevented the automatic application of the Soviet-Czechoslovak Treaty when it might have been most effective. More-over, he barred any direct military agreement between the Soviet and Czechoslovak general staffs and so deprived the treaty of its teeth.[15] This calculation failed to note that automation of the treaty and its military implementation were primarily advantageous to the Czecho-slovak Republic. Nevertheless, cooperation with the Soviet Union evolved satisfactorily in a series of regular contacts[16] that were equally fruitful for both countries.

Czechoslovakia followed a systematic policy of peace, collective security, and firm opposition to Fascist aggression. She opposed the Japanese invasion of Manchuria in 1932 and the Italian attack on Abyssinia in 1935, and insisted on the application of sanctions against any aggressor. The most fateful infringement of European security, the military occupation of the Rhineland on March 7, 1936, found her ready to go to war against Nazi Germany. She warned the Western Powers repeatedly of the danger involved in the possible destruction of Austrian independence. Again, to no avail.[17]

Hitler attempted to lure Beneš by promises to recognize the Czechoslovak borders. Beneš rejected Hitler's overtures on Nov. 13

official data from 1938 on were burned in 1940. The collection will hereafter be cited as Les événements.

13. Beneš, Memoirs, p. 24.

14. Alexander Ort in Soják, ed., p. 255.

15. Pavel Auersperg in Soják, ed., p. 284. When asked about Czechoslovak General Staff participation in the talks with the Soviet General Staff, Beneš replied (April 5, 1936): "I do not need agreements—do not enter into binding talks." Beneš feared that France and Great Britain regarded Czechoslovakia as a potential ally of Communism. Therefore he wanted to achieve military collaboration with Moscow via Paris, which remained lukewarm (see General Faucher in Les événements, V, 1199).

16. For their list, see Beneš, Memoirs, pp. 40–42; Hubert Ripka's article in Zahraniční politika, 1935, pp. 504–11.

17. Beneš, Memoirs, pp. 12–13; President Beneš on War, p. 103.

and Dec. 18, 1936, when two German emissaries, Albrecht Haushofer and Count Trauttmannsdorff, arrived in Prague to sound out Beneš on the possibility of mutual agreements. Germany would require—it was intimated by the emissaries—that in the case of war Czechoslovakia would not put her treaties into operation. In reply to this attempt to neutralize the Republic, Beneš sent his counterproposal to Berlin in January 1937.[18] It was based on the existing German-Czechoslovak arbitration clauses of the Locarno Treaty of Oct. 16, 1925, which stated that both parties should undertake to solve all disputes through diplomatic channels. Beneš' proposal was never answered.[19]

It should not be believed that starting with the foundation of the SdP all its leaders had decided on destroying the Republic and steadily followed this course. Their policy had to be fitted into the existing political situation and the international position of Berlin. The aim was to bring the Czechs, if necessary through the federalization of the state or its outright dismemberment, into the power sphere of the Reich. The present tactics called for a cautious policy line that would give no cause for a Czech intervention. After its electoral triumph, the SdP became the fulcrum of German nationalist forces. It prided itself on avoiding partisan politics, and still gave lip service to the Republic. Yet it maintained secret contact with Nazi Germany and received material support from Berlin. Its leaders stressed by every means at their disposal the nationalist and unitarian coloring of their movement. They proceeded, however, with infinite caution in the hope of preparing more suitable ground for their real objectives. They were aware that their electoral success attracted public interest in the West, and they contemplated the creation of the widest possible area of international support. They considered the achievement of their aims as dependent on assistance from abroad. An important role was assigned to England.[20]

Some time during 1935 Henlein entered into contact with the former British air attaché in Berlin, Col. Graham Christie. Colonel Christie made the necessary arrangements for Henlein's visit in London, where he gave a lecture on Dec. 9, 1935. Henlein pretended that his party was not in touch with the NSDAP. He proclaimed as his sole aim the achievement of an understanding between Czechoslovakia and her German minority. He affirmed that he had never spoken

18. The text of Beneš' draft treaty is in his *Memoirs* (pp. 46–47).
19. The best descriptions of this strange episode are in Beneš, *Memoirs* (pp. 15–20) and Gerhard L. Weinberg, "Secret Hitler-Beneš Negotiations in 1936–37," *Journal of Central European Affairs*, XIX (January 1960), 366–74.
20. W. Brand, *Die sudetendeutsche Tragödie*, pp. 34–35, 38.

against the Jews, and that there was no Aryan paragraph in the statutes of his party. To say that the Sudeten Germans were Nazis in the German sense was wrong. His party desired to maintain the unity of the Republic.[21]

Henlein's next visit took place in July 1936, when he arrived with Rutha to lecture at Chatham House. They described Czechoslovakia as a state "tainted" with Bolshevism, and pictured the SdP as striving to block the radicalism of the German minority.[22] In London Henlein gave the impression of an honest man genuinely striving toward a settlement of just German claims within the framework of Czechoslovak democracy.[23] Favorably impressed, the British cabinet took steps to draw the attention of the Czechoslovak authorities to the German problem. Foreign Secretary Anthony Eden urged the Czechoslovak ambassador in London, Jan Masaryk,[24] to support the steps necessary for improvement of Czech-German relations.[25] British Under-Secretary Sir Robert Vansittart also discussed Henlein's demands with Rudolf Hess and the representatives of the German Foreign Ministry during his visit to Berlin on Aug. 13, 1936, and Eden again stressed the importance of the Sudeten problem in his meeting with Kamil Krofta, the successor of Beneš, in Geneva in September

21. It is interesting to note that the NSDAP organ, the *Völkischer Beobachter*, disagreed with some of Henlein's remarks (Kamil Krofta, Z *dob naší první republiky*, pp. 185–86). For Henlein's lecture, see the *Central European Observer*, XVIII, June 27, 1941. The *Observer* was published in Prague until 1938; then it moved to London.
22. Auersperg in Soják, ed., p. 293; Krofta, Z *dob*, p. 190. *Německý imperialismus*, pp. 259–62, published the reports by the Czechoslovak minister in London. Henlein boasted in his report to Hitler (Nov. 19, 1937) that the SdP had succeeded in drawing attention to Czechoslovakia as a state tainted with Bolshevism (*DGFP*, II, 57).
23. Prof. R. W. Seton-Watson was at first favorably inclined toward the Henlein Party. He asserted in the Brno liberal daily *Lidové noviny (People's News)* on April 26, 1936: "I regret the criticism of Henlein on the part of some of my Czech friends, I consider it unjust and political." He had trusted Henlein. Therefore he judged him severely in 1943, when he put down his own experiences in dealing with Henlein: "The Sudeten German agitation, led by K. Henlein, was the Trojan Horse of the whole European tragedy. It was used with great skill to delude sentimental public opinion in the West, which imagined itself to be vindicating the principle of self-determination, when in reality it was playing into the hand of blatant Pan-Germanism." He wound up with the warning that "this tale of perfidy should be ever present in the minds of those who will have to deal with the Sudeten Germans after the war" (*History*, pp. 393–94). It was a candid reminder for all who trusted the Sudeten German leaders.
24. The son of President Masaryk. He was the Czechoslovak minister in London from July 23, 1925 on. He served as foreign minister from 1940 to March 10, 1948, when he either committed suicide or was slain.
25. Soják, ed., p. 294.

1936.[26] Eden did not regard "this to be just a minority problem." Unwilling to "play Hitler's game," Eden stated to the new British minister in Prague, Basil Newton, in March 1937, that the British government was "not prepared to take the responsibility for counselling Dr. Beneš to negotiate a settlement . . . which might, indeed, entail dangerous or humiliating concessions."[27]

The German question in Czechoslovakia became an international issue as the Henlein Party skillfully exploited complex political and economic grievances. The most disturbing feature was the popular espousal of the policies of Nazi Germany[28] and the satisfaction which the Henlein success gave to many radicals. The victory of the Henlein Party made many Czechs and Slovaks, from the president down, concerned over the fate of the Republic, and made the government ponder over its future policies toward the Germans.

Henlein turned the German question into Prague's gravest problem. It was a painful experience, but perhaps necessary to awaken the Republic to its deepest problems, its deficiencies, and its opportunities. However, another question had to be faced first: was the German problem an internal problem which should and could be solved on its own merits, or was it merely a disguised form of Nazi-German expansionism? Prague correctly assumed that the Czech-German question was inextricably woven into the political objectives of Hitler and that consequently its solution was contingent on factors transcending the Czech-German issue. Hence it started its great rearmament program.[29]

With the personality of the new premier, Dr. Milan Hodža,[30] who

26. *Ibid.*
27. The Earl of Avon, *The Eden Memoirs. Facing the Dictators,* p. 503.
28. Wenzel Jaksch, elected deputy chairman of the Sudeten German Social Democracy on June 23, 1936, declared in the National Assembly on June 25 to the SdP: "The great majority of your voters charged you with the mission to work for the annexation to Germany. You are giving yourself the best evidence of your connections with Hitler through your attitude toward the German political emigrés" (Klepetář, p. 389).
29. The new armament industry was set up in the eastern part of the state. Stocks of munitions were increased three times. As early as 1934, special pioneer groups were established to construct huge belts of fortifications. In March 1935, the Direction of the Fortification Works was formed and the first light machine-gun blockhouses were constructed. In September 1938 there were about 3,800 such blockhouses (General Faucher in *Les événements,* V, 1196; Oberkommando des Heeres, *Denkschrift über die tschechoslowakische Landesbefestigung,* pp. 22, 49. The latter is a competent study of the Czechoslovak fortification system). Two-year military service was introduced in 1934.
30. A member of the Slovak branch of the Agrarian Party, energetic, able, capricious, and easygoing. Hodža resigned on Sept. 22, 1938, went to Switzerland and the United States, and died in Florida in June 1944.

succeeded Jan Malypetr on Nov. 5, 1935, and the election of Dr. Beneš to the presidency of the republic,[31] Czechoslovak policy entered a new phase. On May 13, 1936, Parliament passed the Law for the Defense of the State which placed restrictions upon unreliable elements and made important provisions for the defense of the Republic. The law set up a frontier zone where special restrictions were to be applied: expropriations of land for defense purposes were to be carried out by the military, and construction of roads or buildings and other changes were to be subject to special permits. Simultaneously a law was passed extending the death penalty for military espionage.[32] Construction began on a belt of fortifications within the frontier zone. The army underwent radical reorganization[33] and started to outfit its units with the most modern weapons, so that by the summer of 1938 it ranked among the best equipped armies in the world.[34]

The Czech leaders also set to work for a gradual solution of the German issue which, according to Beneš, was not only a political but also a psychological problem which could be attacked and settled only by degrees.[35] To gain more confidence among the Germans, President Beneš set himself to define the preliminaries for mutual understanding:

> My relation to the Germans of our State is a human one; they are my compatriots, my fellow-workers, suffering with me in the days of need, and rejoicing with me in the days of prosperity. I have confidence in the Germans and Czechs. . . . I am convinced

31. The first president, T. G. Masaryk—four times reelected—resigned in December 1935 because of his advanced age. He died on Sept. 14, 1937. For a biased description of the presidential election in December 1935, see Alena Gajanova, *Dvojí tvář*, pp. 154–81.
32. *Survey 1936*, pp. 141–42. With the Defense Law the cabinet acquired the right to dismiss all unreliable persons in the basic defense industries. In June 1937, a new law made militiary training obligatory for all citizens (*DGFP*, II, 12).
33. As of Oct. 15, 1935, seven army corps were established with 17 infantry divisions and 4 rapid divisions. New special fortification regiments were created (Beneš, *Memoirs*, p. 28; *Les événements*, V, 1196). Gen. Ludvík Krejčí, chief of the general staff, submitted a new fortification program to the Supreme Defense Council on June 2, 1936. The center of the fortification system was to be a belt—with several groups of heavy forts—stretching for about 125 miles from Moravská Ostrava to Trutnov, between the Oder and the Giant mountains in northern Moravia-Silesia and east-northern Bohemia (*Denkschrift*, p. 21).
34. The former director of the Small Arms Works at Brno, Karel J. Staller, reported the statement of Hitler in 1941: "Only two states carried out their war preparations expertly and efficiently, Germany and Czechoslovakia" (Svaz československých důstojníků v exilu, *Generál Ingr*, p. 15).
35. *DGFP*, II, p. 122.

that . . . the Czechs and Germans will in the fairly near future
come to a definitive political understanding in the State. I am in
favor of the Germans in our Republic receiving all that they require
for their cultural and economic prosperity.[36]

In August 1936 Beneš toured the cities of northern Bohemia, where he
gave a series of speeches outlining his conception of the Czech-
German problem which were hailed by most of the Czechoslovak
press. He regarded nationality conflicts at all ethnographical frontiers
as natural and inevitable, and, in his most important address at
Liberec on August 19, Beneš gave every indication of a sincere desire
to bring about an understanding between Germans and Czechs:

> Our political philosophy and morality take the form of democracy,
> a democracy that provides us with the key to a solution of all our
> problems since it postulates in all political negotiations a respect of
> the human person and complete civic equality. . . . We stand for
> the principles of a reasonable decentralization combined with an
> expedient economic and administrative regionalism. . . . I know
> that our Germans have complaints, desires, and demands of a
> practical character. In the language and educational spheres . . .
> these are easy of disposal. . . . In economic matters . . . mistakes
> have been made . . . such as, for instance, that contractors and
> workmen have been called from Czech or from Czech-German
> districts into German districts where unemployment prevails. . . .
>
> The greatest difficulties arise in the questions of the State
> officials. A number of the German wishes are in this connection
> justified. Yet there is the question of confidence. A democratic State
> does not wish to entrust its administration to officials who profess
> Fascist, Totalitarian or Communist principles.

Then Beneš solemnly called on the Germans:

> You will not take it ill when I am candid enough to say that this
> work can only be successful if you follow in the footsteps of those
> classic figures of the German spirit which are great and classic for
> the Czechs too—in the footsteps of Herder, Lessing, Goethe,
> Schiller and their like—if we all do what we can to come closer
> together in our ideal conception of the world, and if neither the one
> nor the other of us allow ourselves to be bewildered by the chaos of
> ideas of post-War Europe, by temporary ideologies which separate

36. Czechoslovak Sources and Documents, No. 11, *The Problems of Czechoslovakia. Speeches of President Beneš in Northern Bohemia*, pp. 14–15.

peoples instead of drawing them together, and which ere long will be ousted by the genuine ideals of humanity and a sensible Europeanism.

Beneš concluded:

We have remained . . . a democracy which rejects all methods of violence in internal policy, the suppression of personal liberty and of the free expression of public opinion, a democracy which solves the problems of internal politics with the aid of evolutionary methods.[37]

The words of the Czechoslovak president presented an outstanding example of the spirit of the Czechoslovak policy which was attempting to clear up the conflicts and misunderstandings that had accumulated in the past atmosphere of distrust.

Central to the internal and external strains of Czechoslovakia was the constant effort of the SdP to confuse appearance with reality. The appearance intended, of course, was of a German bloc having a national and social program aimed at building a national community as a front against capitalism. The SdP claimed to be a democratic movement. It proposed that the Republic become a bridge between the German heart of Central Europe and Southeastern Europe. The party, contesting Marxism, class struggle, and capitalism, was evasive on concrete measures, however, and indulged in generalities appealing to all strata of German society. However, it took various steps toward the assistance of the unemployed and displayed some attention to social problems in order to win the support of many members of the working class. Seeking to win over many different elements, the party aimed to alienate no one and to conciliate everyone. The fear of disenchantment with his party among the Sudeten Germans no doubt prompted Henlein to cast the outlines of his program in cryptic terms and to invoke the nationalist aim as the *ultima ratio* of his movement.[38] Gradually, he shifted the tone of his appeal in the direction of pan-Germanism, although he still pretended to stand for the Republic. In his cultural address at Prague on Feb. 23, 1936, he emphasized his refusal of "abstract internationalism" and decadent literature, and stressed the virtues of the German community as the only source of the highest cultural achievement. In effect, the goal of German

37. *Ibid.*, pp. 15–19, 25.
38. Konstantin Höss, ed., *Die SdP im Parlament. Ein Jahresbericht 1935–36*, pp. 38, 39, 61, 99, 105, 109, 191, 204, 224. For the ideology, program, and propaganda of the SdP, see Koutek, *Nacistická pátá kolona*, pp. 69 ff.

politics was to be the implementation of national ideas in all branches of national life.[39] He stated proudly that

> as Germans of the Sudetenland we feel that we belong, in spite of our special political position, to the great cultural community of Germans throughout the world, and that, today as always, we have to fulfill the German cultural mission in this country in model fashion.[40]

Appearance, however, receded before reality. The verbal façade of Henlein's speeches began to crumble as the emptiness of Henlein's assurances of 1933 became more apparent. Nationalism became the only cultural creative force; culture was subordinated to political expediency. Henlein as the leader was entitled to fix the rules for German cultural life.[41] The SdP took slight pains to disguise its totalitarian aims. Once one looked beneath the surface of a delusive appearance, the Nazification of the SdP became evident.

A secret agreement was reached at Berlin, on May 27, 1936, between the Union of the German Homeland Organization (Bund der Binnendeutschen Heimatsverbände) and the press department of the SdP, which received the exclusive right to use the news from the Reich Propaganda Ministry. Henlein's headquarters at Berlin were recognized as the sole authoritative voice of the Sudeten problem. The Reichspressestelle (Reich Press Office) of the Nazi Party, Department C, promised to assist it to issue a fortnightly review of the Czechoslovak German press. The SdP Bureau was granted priority over all information dealing with Sudeten questions, and it was agreed that the newspapers of the Reich would support the bulletin in their editorials. The head of the bureau and the confidant of the VDA, Ing. Friedrich Bürger, a member of the KB, was made directly subordinate to Henlein. The agreement was signed secretly by Hans Krebs, Christian von Loesch, and the Reichspresseleiter of the NSDAP, Amman.[42] In the middle of June 1936, Bürger reported

39. For extracts from the February speech, see Emil Sobota in *Naše doba*, XXXXV (November 1937), 70–71. See also *ibid.*, March 1936, p. 360.
40. Vincent Urban, p. 16. For the text of the Prague cultural lecture, see Konrad Henlein, *Sudetendeutschtum und gesamtdeutsche Kultur.*
41. Sobota in *Naše doba* (November 1937), pp. 70–71. Henlein also complained that German paintings and sculpture were not national enough and that the German theater "am Werden der Volksgemeinschaft so gut wie keinen Anteil hat" (*ibid.*). Sobota quoted the statement of Professor Pfitzner, that Henlein widened "den Begriff des Politischen . . . und fühlte sich als verantwortlicher Politiker dazu berufen, vom Blickfelde des Gesamtdeutschtums her die Forderungen an das kulturelle Schaffen bekanntzugeben" (*ibid.*, p. 70).
42. I follow Bílek, p. 28; Uhlíř, p. 53. The first report on the secret agreement was published in 1937 (Fischer et al., p. 106).

from Berlin that the Berlin-protectors (the "Schutzherren") demanded from Henlein specific mention of his solidarity with Germany.[43] Henlein complied in his speech at Cheb on June 21, 1936:

> It is essential that Prague should create a new, decent relationship to the entire German race and particularly to the German Reich. . . . I prefer to be hated in company with Germany than to draw any advantages out of hatred of Germany.[44]

In the meantime, Josef Goebbels inaugurated a violent campaign against Bolshevism, in which Czechoslovakia was described as a country harboring Red Army airfields for an invasion of Germany and Europe.[45] The appointment of three Sudeten German Nazis to the Reichstag by Hitler on the recommendation of Reich Minister Wilhelm Frick[46] added to the deterioration of relations betweeen the Reich and Czechoslovakia. Henlein went to the Reich in the late summer of 1936 to attend the Olympic games. He held secret conferences with the top brass of the Reich: Hess, Rosenberg, Goebbels, Himmler, Ley, Funk, and Ribbentrop. He also conferred for forty-five minutes with Hitler. During his stay in Berlin, Henlein also consulted with Jung and Krebs and was awarded the highest German decoration which had been set up for the Olympic games.[47]

The concern of Prague and of Czech public opinion was heightened by the peculiar character of the SdP which, for all practical purposes, was increasingly taking the shape of a totalitarian party. The discussions between Prague and the SdP which had taken place after

43. *Ibid.*, p. 109.

44. Sobota in *Naše doba* (November 1937), p. 70. Dr. Hodža replied to Henlein on Nov. 10, 1936 (*Czechoslovak Cabinet Ministers*, p. 19).

45. *Documents 1936*, pp. 293–94. Dr. Goebbels' fierce anti-Czechoslovak speech was given on Sept. 10, 1936, and the Czechoslovak démenti was issued on Sept. 11.

46. The Reich minister of the Interior, Dr. Wilhelm Frick, recalled in a leader in the *Zeitung* (Sept. 21, 1941) how he had delivered Hitler's greetings to the DNSAP's rally at Teplice-Šanov on Oct. 18, 1928. Frick confessed to being "for several years in constant touch with the Sudeten members of the Party and deputies of the Prague Parliament, namely Hans Knirsch, Dr. Rudolf Jung, and Hans Krebs." He pointed out that "as early as 1936 Hitler acted on my suggestion and appointed three Sudeten Germans to be members of the Reichstag," i.e., H. Krebs, R. Jung, and Leo Schubert (Bílek, p. 202).

47. *Ibid.*, pp. 89–90. Prague watched carefully the strange series of Henlein's confidential visits. For Hitler's invitation to Henlein in the spring of 1936, see Rönnefarth, *Sudetenkrise*, I, 158. For a brief survey of the meetings between Hitler and Henlein, see the account by W. Schmidt in the archives of the Collegium Carolinum in Munich, deposit No. 202.

the elections had ended in failure, as it was difficult for a democratic regime to adjust itself to such a party.

The Sudeten German Party was rooted in the same soil that had generated the political and intellectual forces of German nationalism. Its consciousness of belonging to an organic national community transcended all political frontiers and represented the distinguishing sign of the true German. It firmly believed that the German community was linked to German soil and thus entitled to territorial autonomy.[48] Therefore, as representative of all that was truly German, the SdP asked to be recognized as the sole agent of the German group and refused to recognize other German parties. The will of all members of the national community was incarnated in the Führer (Leader). Thus, all the political representatives of the SdP swore obedience and allegiance to their Führer, Konrad Henlein,[49] who alone could make final decisions. The organizational structure was based on the so-called Führer-system, which stressed wide authority on the part of the heads of party organizations.[50]

This ideological and political content assumed sharp forms in the context of everyday activities of the party. The imitation of Nazi methods was striking: the sea of party banners, the uniformed Ordner storm troops, the outstretched right arms fixed in the German greeting, the pictures of the leader, the slogans and the fanatical masses chanting *Sieg Heil*—all these copies of the Nazi models

48. Chmelař, pp. 52–64; Bischoff, pp. 126–27; Sobota in *Naše doba* (November, 1937), 69–73; the *Central European Observer*, XIII (June 14, 1935). Rutha declared at the caucus of the leaders of the SdP in Prague (July 23, 1936) that for tactical reasons the demand for Sudeten German autonomy should still remain concealed (Bílek, pp. 88–89).

49. After the 1935 elections, 44 deputies, 23 senators, and 26 members of the provincial councils swore obedience and allegiance to Henlein at a solemn ceremony in Cheb on June 2, 1935 (Klepetář, p. 383). According to the German minister in Prague, Dr. W. Koch, the new SdP deputies formed a "conglomeration" consisting of "practically all shades . . . ranging from implicit loyalty to absolute rejection" with regard to the Czechoslovak state (Dr. Koch's report of May 22, 1935, *DGFP*, Series C, IV, 187).

50. Gustav Peters, deputy of the SdP, explained his party's point of view in *Naše doba*, XIV (June 1936), 538–40. The organizational structure of the SdP consisted of local groups, districts, and regions. The leader of the party was elected at a special meeting comprising the heads of the district and regional organizations, members of Parliament and provincial councils, members of the Hauptrat and all the Hauptleiter. The last two groups were nominated by the leader himself. The supreme directing body, the Hauptrat, was composed of the leader, the heads of the regional organizations, and the Hauptleiters. The Hauptleiters were officials in charge of special departments (Louda, p. 61). For the activities of the central secretariat of the SdP in Prague, see Oskar Ullrich, *Sie kamen aus aller Herren Länder*, pp. 67–68. The volume deals mainly with the year 1938 and is of little value. For a description of the organization of the SdP, see Koutek, *Nacistická pátá kolona*, pp. 95 ff.

presented a challenge to the democratic regime. The British news correspondent G. E. R. Gedye recorded his visit to Henlein's headquarters in Aš, where Henlein assigned an aide to accompany him on a tour of the distressed German areas. Gedye was introduced to "a series of the roughest Nazi leaders," who confirmed his opinion that the SdP was simply an outpost of Nazi Germany.

> There was naked Nazism, savage racial hatred of Czechs and Jews, adoration of Adolf Hitler and an unconcealed determination to bring the whole area under the rule of German Nazi dictatorship.[51]

Under these circumstances, the Czechs hardened their attitude; their distrust increased.[52] A keen sense of being threatened was "provoked to a large extent by the SdP with its Fascism, totalitarianism, and worship of material power."[53]

There was a general feeling in official circles in Prague that it was essential to sway German public opinion to a prodemocratic course. Prague particularly encouraged new, young leaders of those German parties which still clung to the democratic regime and indicated a willingness to accept the existence of the Czechoslovak state[54] and its democratic system as bases for the national development of the German group. The Czech feeling of urgency was translated by a tour

51. G. E. R. Gedye, *Betrayal in Central Europe*, p. 386.
52. The German Agrarian leader, Dr. Spina, who had attempted to make Henlein respectable, confessed on Dec. 1, 1935, that "the distrust felt by the Czechs has increased tremendously. . . . this tension has been chiefly caused by the doubtful method of the Henlein Party itself" (*Central European Observer*, XIII, Dec. 13, 1935).
53. *Ibid.* See also Henlein's statement on Aug. 10, 1936: "There are matters which cannot be discussed in public, just as in a front trench one does not speak of a coming offensive two days ahead" (Freund, *Watch Czechoslovakia!*, p. 74). Rönnefarth (*Sudetenkrise*, I, 163, 167, 173) sets the initial stage of the SdP contacts with Berlin and the NSDAP as late as 1936 and affirms that Henlein and his main aides remained loyal to the Republic up to November 1937. He makes K. H. Frank alone answerable for the pro-Nazi policy line of the SdP. Frank has been made out to be the sole bad spirit of the SdP and left to bear the entire brunt of the Sudeten German guilt. This thesis does not stand confrontation with available facts and documentary evidence.
54. The three main representatives of the younger generation, the Socialist Wenzel Jaksch, the Agrarian Gustav Hacker, and the Christian Socialist Hans Schütz, came out with their activist speeches on April 26, 1936. Hacker was elected chairman of the Agrarian Party in January 1936. He was still willing to come to an agreement with Henlein on Jan. 18 and 26, 1936, but Henlein refused any rapprochement. Hacker and Schütz dissolved their respective parties after the Anschluss in 1938 and went over to the SdP. Jaksch escaped to England in 1939 (*Naše doba* XXXXIII, February–March, 1936; César-Černý, *Politika*, II, *passim*).

of the German regions by President Beneš with the purpose of
conveying to the German and Czech public the realities of the
situation as they were seen from Prague.

After establishing a more favorable psychological atmosphere,
Beneš and Hodža quietly proceeded to carry out the necessary
improvements. They hoped that these efforts would result in a
restraint of the SdP extremists. They were only too aware of the
turbulent forces that had brought about the rise of Henlein. By
making concessions to the Activists, they sought to curb the radical
nationalists.[55] Hodža asked the German ministers[56] for their proposals
for achieving better understanding and solidarity between the two
peoples, and the German Activist parties outlined their program in a
memorandum on Jan. 27, 1937.[57] After negotiations the government
agreed (on Feb. 18, 1937) to a program that promised proportional
German participation in public services, distribution of public expenditures on a regional basis, allocation of a just share from public
funds for German welfare and cultural purposes, the placing of
government contracts with German contractors in German districts,
and the use of both languages in all official communications to
communities of under 3,000 inhabitants.[58] The February agreement
indicated Czech willingness to remedy an important part of the
German grievances.

Gratifying as this program was to the Activists, it presented a
serious menace to the SdP, for if the situation of the Germans
improved as a result of the program, then the SdP would be faced
with a grave problem, posed by the relaxation of tensions in the
German area. Consequently Konrad Henlein strove to weaken the impression of the agreement by stating on February 28 that what the
Germans were striving for was "self-determination and codetermina-
tion within the settlement area and also in all central State organizations." He called for the safeguarding of the national frontier and

55. The German grievances were set forth in articles by Deputies Jaksch, Hacker,
and Schütz in the Prague liberal review Přítomnost, Nov. 19, 1936.
56. The German parties disposed to cooperate within the cabinet were the
Christian Socialists, Social Democrats, and Agrarians. There were three German
ministers in the Hodža cabinet.
57. Naše doba, XXXXIV (February 1937), 298. The text of the memorandum is
in Young, pp. 211–12. All the demands were granted on February 18, except the
last two: a special parliamentary committee to deal with German issues and the
use of German in the presentation of draft laws (ibid., p. 212).
58. Survey 1937, I, 449–50. See also the Czechoslovak Consulate General at New
York, Agreement between the Czechoslovak Government and the Germans
Concerning Minority Policy.

demanded compensation for injustices done to the Germans during the existence of the Republic.

Henlein announced new draft laws which the SdP presented to the National Assembly on April 27.[59] The bills proposed to draw up special national registers which would list all members of respective nationalities over eighteen years of age. Once enrolled, citizens would not be able to change their nationality. Children would be placed automatically on the same national register as their fathers. Each nationality would be declared a national corporation. Such a corporation would be entrusted with the care of all economic, cultural, and social matters pertaining to its national group. The deputies and senators of each nationality would elect, by a mere majority, a speaker (Sprecher) who—invested with executive powers—would be the official representative of the nationality, although not necessarily a member of Parliament. Any attempts to denationalize—including any change of property—would be punishable.[60]

The bills, if implemented, would have split the state into several national fragments which would obstruct the functioning of the administrative machinery, since national considerations only would prevail. The SdP, having a majority in the German corporation, would have formed a totalitarian regime within a democratic state. The Sprecher would be for all practical purposes a national leader responsible to no one. Any closer contacts between the nationalities, such as marriage, would be rendered impossible. The Czech press unanimously rejected these proposals as impracticable and directed against the integrity of the state and its democratic system. Yet the SdP achieved its intended goal: the draft laws weakened the impact of the February agreements.

The resulting radicalization of the Germans, increasingly agitated by the inflammatory speeches of party leaders who could not offer any tangible success, led the masses to expect direct intervention by the Reich.[61] Against this background, the SdP realized that a settlement between Czechs and Germans was impossible on a German basis unless the Reich assisted the German cause in Czechoslovakia more efficiently and the SdP brought its aims and tactics

59. For an interesting analysis of Czechoslovak internal development as given by Ernst Eisenlohr, the German minister in Prague, on Feb. 4, 1938, see *DGFP*, II, 119–21.
60. *Survey 1937*, pp. 452–53. Also the Czechoslovak Consulate General at New York, *The Proposals of the Sudeten German Party in Czechoslovakia. Why They Are Put Forward* (New York, 1937).
61. *DGFP*, II, 119–121; Brand, *Die sudetendeutsche Tragödie*, p. 51.

"into harmony with the policy of the Reich."[62] The draft bills were aimed at putting the Czechs in the wrong before public opinion in Europe, above all in Great Britain.[63] Their announcement entailed, moreover, a strengthening of the German conviction that "a military liquidation of Czechoslovakia is only a question of months."[64] This radical tendency found ardent promoters within the former DNSAP wing of the party. Henlein seemed aware that the time was not yet ripe for any adventure, and that the radical tendencies "would again place the Government in a position to justify measures against the Sudeten Germans in the eyes of the outside world and of persons of moderate views."[65] Hence he needed Reich support "in the rear"[66] to maintain discipline in his party, when it came to the break between the extremist Nazi Aufbruch circle and the Henleinist majority.[67]

The German press campaigns in favor of the Sudeten Germans[68] and the clear interest evinced in the Czech-German problem in Great Britain, carefully fostered by Henlein's visits to London,[69] made the basically internal problem assume the proportions of an international

62. The report of Henlein to Hitler, Nov. 19, 1937 (*DGFP*, II, 55).
63. Henlein's statement in his report (*ibid.*, p. 58).
64. *Ibid.*, p. 59.
65. *Ibid.*, pp. 60–61.
66. Henlein to Eisenlohr (*ibid.*, p. 123).
67. Henlein intervened against the radical Aufbruch group at the VoMi and the German Foreign Office (*ibid.*, pp. 64–66). He felt that the radicals might imperil the existence of the SdP (*Anklageschrift*, pp. 30, 47, 52, 56). The "monopolistic tendency" of the KB was "a source of grievances to the rival group, the Aufbruch . . . composed of the members of the old, proscribed National Socialist Party. The leading member of the Aufbruch group, Kasper, was also leader of the more radical of the local German labour movement, discontented with the Party's attitude on labour questions" (*Survey 1937*, I, 454). Henlein expelled the leaders of the Aufbruch group, Rudolf Kasper and Ing. Rudolf Haider. It was alleged that this group denounced Architect Rutha to the police for homosexual practices. Rutha was arrested on Oct. 6, 1937, and was found hanged on Nov. 5, 1937 (*Zahraniční politika*, 1937, pp. 622, 705–708, 744; *Survey 1937*, I, 455). Kasper and some members of the Aufbruch group came back to the party in 1938. See also César-černý, *Politika*, II, *passim*.
68. For example, the Reich German press alleged in June 1937 that Reich citizen Bruno Weigel had been tortured. After Czechoslovak denials, the whole affair was suddenly dropped. In another outburst, indignation was voiced by the German press when the Czechoslovak authorities refused to give permission to send 6,000 German children for a holiday in the Reich (*Survey 1937*, I, 446).
69. Henlein was in London in October 1937. In his conversation with Sir Robert Vansittart, Henlein was reportedly assured that Britain would urge the granting of "the most far-reaching autonomy for the Sudeten Germans" (*DGFP*, II, 30–31). Henlein reported personally to Reich Foreign Minister von Neurath on his visit (*ibid.*, p. 31). (See also Auersperg in Soják, ed., pp. 316–17, and the report by Jan Masaryk as quoted in *Německý imperialismus*, pp. 268–70.) Henlein went to London again in May 1938 (Krofta, *Z dob*, p. 271).

issue. Henlein was aware that European opinion had to develop a more favorable frame of mind toward the strivings of the SdP, be these a wide autonomy, the abandonment of the Czechoslovak alliances with France and Russia, and the harmonizing of foreign policy with that of the Reich, or finally if possible, the incorporation of the German areas in Nazi Germany.[70] Therefore, the SdP had to follow a double policy: outwardly to stand for the integrity of the Czechoslovak state and advocate autonomy as the implementation of the right of self-determination as long as the international situation was not ripe enough to force the acceptance of its real aims; but secretly, in harmony with Berlin, to undermine the international position of the Republic and its internal order.[71] In effect, the assistance of the Reich was a precondition for the success of the policy of the SdP. This very fact brought an internal affair to the international forum. It also necessarily made the SdP and the masses behind it tools of Berlin's policies.

On the whole, Henlein and his aides foresaw the extraordinary happenings with clarity. They knew that events had to become sufficiently dramatic to enable the SdP to break up the democratic system. The SdP seemed to harbor no illusions that it alone could successfully challenge the regime. Yet what the Czechs called plots against democracy and the state had to be weighed against the intense patriotism of the German leaders, who of their own free will were organizing what they believed to be a national revival. They rallied to the Nazi cause, some with reluctance, because it advanced the pan-German objectives.

The SdP had been in intimate and systematic contact with the Reich authorities.[72] "The Sudeten German Party, since its election success in 1935, has been currently supported with funds from the Foreign Office [Berlin] for the purpose of strengthening and further developing the Party organizations," stated Dr. Günther Altenburg, head of Czechoslovak section IV(b) of the Political Department of the Wilhelmstrasse after Henlein's visit in January 1937. Henlein strongly urged the Foreign Office to continue its support for the next fiscal year. Dr. Altenburg, in a memorandum, regarded further subsidies as

70. *DGFP*, II, 55–57.
71. *Ibid.*, p. 60.
72. International Military Tribunal, *Trial of the Major War Criminals before the International Military Tribunal*, XXXII, 10, 3061-PS; this indispensable source will hereafter be cited as *IMT*. (See also J. César–B. Černý, "Německá iredenta a henleinovci v ČSR v letech 1930–1938" [German Irredentism and Henleinism in Czechoslovakia in 1930–1938], *Československý časopis historický*, X, 1962, 1–17.)

necessary, "judging by the insight gained into the local conditions through close cooperation with the Sudeten German Party." As a result, he recommended "to appropriate for use by the Sudeten German Party the total amount of 180,000 RM, of which 12,000 RM should be converted into Czechoslovak Crowns and paid out via the German legation, each month. The remaining amount of 3,000 RM per month would have to be paid as usual to the functionary of the Party in Berlin, Herr Metzner."[73] After the elections in 1935 Henlein asked the Berlin authorities for a special grant amounting to about 400,000 RM to cover the costs of the publication of the new party newspaper *Die Zeit*. The German Foreign Ministry was rather reticent, apparently because of a scarcity of available funds. It was due to the personal intervention of Rudolf Hess that the request of the Berlin Propaganda Ministry for a special grant "for subsidizing the new Prague daily, *Die Zeit*," was granted by the Minister of Finance on Feb. 3, 1936. The Foreign Ministry supported the request because "the Sudeten German Party would . . . suffer a severe blow" if the paper were forced to close. In such a case a Czechoslovak "judicial investigation of the financial affairs of the newspaper would . . . ensue, which naturally might easily lead to an exposure of the financial transactions of the Sudeten German Party. There would then arise the danger of the fact being disclosed that the Party has been receiving funds from sources for which it is not sufficiently able to account."[74]

In 1936 the SdP entered into contact with a special NSDAP section, the Parteischulung, which offered its indoctrination material to the head of the SdP education unit, Dr. Josef Suchy. Through so-called Schulungsbriefe, Dr. Suchy directed the indoctrination of the SdP in Nazi ideology. Similar communications were established in the field of sport and physical education and with the Reichsnährstand.[75] The SdP kept in close touch with the German legation in Prague and supplied it with confidential material. Henlein was also in personal

---

73. *Trials of War Criminals before the Nuernberg Military Tribunals under Control Council Law No. 10*, XII, 783. The collection will hereafter be cited as *TWC*. The memorandum of Altenburg is dated Feb. 15, 1937. See also *DGFP*, Series C, IV, 679, 614–15, 742. The German legation in Prague was informed by a senior official of the German Foreign Ministry on Nov. 16, 1935: "The sum earmarked for financing the Movement, fixed at 15,000 RM monthly, is further to be made available for disbursement, less 3,000 RM monthly which will be paid to the Party representative here. The sums still outstanding for October and November, which total 24,000 RM, are being sent to the legation with the next courier" (*ibid.*, IV, 821).
74. *Ibid.*, IV, 1026. See also *ibid.*, IV, 615, 742, 821.
75. *IMT*, XXXII, 10; *Anklageschrift*, p. 46.

contact with Foreign Minister Constantin von Neurath and briefed the latter on his London visits.[76] He had already received orders from the Reich to assist in espionage against the Republic, which he instructed reliable Germans to carry out.[77]

Henlein, Frank, and Dr. Fritz Köllner were empowered to issue so-called *Sonder-Aufträge*, through which carefully selected Germans, outwardly not belonging to the party, were entrusted with secret commissions and communications with Reich Nazi organizations such as the SS, SA, and HJ (Hitler Youth).[78] Various subsidies from the Reich were smuggled in or channeled through German business firms and banks, and there was some evidence that Nazi headquarters in Munich sent the SdP 960,000 Kč on Sept. 8, 1937, and 1,088,000 on Oct. 16, 1937.[79]

After Hitler had consolidated his position in Germany, he undertook the reorganization and centralization of the apparatus dealing with the problems of German minorities abroad. For this purpose, he set up a special office—the Bureau von Kursell—in 1935 as the central agency for more intensive contacts with Germans abroad.[80] In January 1937, SS-Obergruppenführer Werner Lorenz was appointed by Himmler as head of a new agency, the Volksdeutsche Mittelstelle, (VoMi), replacing the old Kursell Bureau. It was subordinate to Rudolf Hess but worked publicly under the supervision of Ribbentrop.[81]

The VoMi was entrusted with the direction of the activities of all Germans throughout the world. In July 1938 it took over the old VDA,[82] and Himmler's influence within the agency increased when many SS members joined its staff.[83] The SdP was subordinated to the VoMi and cleared all contacts with the Reich through the new

76. *DGFP*, II, 31; *DGFP*, Series C, IV, 742.

77. *Zpověď*, p. 39; *Koutek, Nacistická pátá kolona*, pp. 174 ff.

78. *Zpověď*, p. 34.

79. The deputy chairman of the Foreign Affairs Committee of the French National Assembly, Pezet, declared that there existed evidence that these sums were transmitted to help the SdP in the forthcoming municipal elections. (See the *Prager Presse*, Feb. 2, 1938, as cited in Henderson, *Eyewitness*, p. 113.) According to K. H. Frank, a part of the political and propaganda expenses was covered by subsidies from the VoMi and Sudeten German industrialists such as Dr. Kreibich, Liebig, Riedl, and Schicht, who reportedly gave 8 million Kč at the end of 1937 (*Zpověď*, p. 40).

80. The bureau was headed by Professor von Kursell, a high official in the Reich and Prussian Ministry of Education (*DGFP*, Series C, IV, 1115).

81. See above, pp. 52–53. The VoMi worked as a part of Section A of the Department of Cultural Policy in the Foreign Office (*DGFP*, II, 1039). Prof. A. Haushofer was taken over by the VoMi.

82. Koehl, *RKFDV*, pp. 37–39; *DGFP*, II, 1069.

83. Koehl, p. 37; De Jong, p. 282.

authority, which also handled the subsidies for German minorities.[84] It was the VoMi which directed the illegal activities of the SdP against Czechoslovakia that finally resulted in an open revolt.[85]

The all-out backing of the SdP by the Reich was strongly suspected in Prague. The Czechs thought, however, that the support of Prague by the Western Powers would localize and isolate the ferment roused by the peril of active Reich intervention. It felt confident to deal with the explosive situation in its own German areas, although it suspected Hitler of using the German question in Czechoslovakia as a propaganda gambit for the advance of the German thrust to the East.

Deteriorating relations between Germany and Czechoslovakia, intensified by a series of incidents,[86] made it difficult for Prague to implement the February program as quickly as it had intended. Czech public opinion and many civil servants resisted the conciliatory efforts of the cabinet because of a deep mistrust of German intentions. Hence the program, launched with propagandistic overtones, dragged.[87] The current German attitude confirmed Czech suspicions.

84. *DGFP*, II, 65. De Jong (p. 282) stated that from 1918 onward the Reich authorities secretly assisted German institutions abroad. Hitler centralized supervision over the assistance for Germans by forming the VoMi. According to De Jong, the real leading spirit of the VoMi was not Lorenz but Dr. Hermann Behrends, Lorenz's deputy. Koehl (p. 39), however, considered Lorenz to be "a skillful diplomat, tenacious, a kind of a social engineer." The VoMi received its policy lines directly from Hitler. It was supplied by funds, partly from German big business, through the so-called Adolf Hitler Spende. In 1937–38 alone, the VoMi received over 1.5 million RM from this source. Other funds came from the two million members of the VDA (De Jong, pp. 282–83).

85. There was still another organization dealing with Germans abroad, the AO (the Auslandsorganisation of the NSDAP), headed by Ernst Wilhelm Bohle from May 8, 1933. However, it was concerned solely with Reich citizens and seamen. It had branches in 45 foreign countries (*National Socialism*, pp. 287–89). De Jong (pp. 279–80) noted that it had a special section working with the Gestapo. In 1937 the AO set up a liaison section of the Abwehr "to use the ramifications of the AO for military espionage data." Gauleiter Bohle in his position as head of the AO was designated chief of the foreign organization in the Foreign Office on Jan. 30, 1937. He was without any influence whatsoever (*TWC*, XII, 801). For the activities of the AO on Czechoslovak territory, see Koutek, *Nacistická pátá kolona*, pp. 28–29.

86. See above, note 68.

87. It came as a surprise to no one when, on Nov. 17, 1937, Jaksch voiced criticism of the slow pace "at which the February Agreement is being put into effect" (*Survey 1937*, I, 458). Premier Hodža stated in Parliament, in November 1937, that out of the persons engaged in the first quarter after the conclusion of the agreement, 8.52 percent of Germans were engaged as state employees, and 14.83 percent as laborers. In the next quarter, the respective figures were 12.6 and 14.09. German firms supplied more than 40 percent of the requirements of the state railways. At the end of 1937, German-speaking candidates were admitted to the state police and gendarmerie even though they did not know Czech (*ibid.*, pp. 456–58; *Naše doba*, XXXXV [December 1937], 164).

A Sudeten German Party delegation participated in the Nazi Congress at Nuremberg.[88] Henlein visited London again (Oct. 10–15, 1937), and in conferences with Sir Robert Vansittart gained the impression that the Western Powers would not intervene in favor of the Czechs.[89] He therefore used an incident at Teplice-Šanov on Oct. 17, 1937, as ammunition for a frontal attack.

It was alleged by the Reich press that a truncheon assault had been made by the Czech police on SdP leader K. H. Frank in Teplice.[90] Henlein, still impressed with his London success and convinced with other SdP leaders that "the Teplitz incidents might afford the occasion to bring the Sudeten German question to a head with the help of the Reich,"[91] sent a letter to President Beneš protesting against the behavior of the police. "As the responsible and duly accredited spokesman of the Sudeten Germans," he demanded immediate appropriate steps to be taken for "self-administration and the performance of State executive functions by Germans in the German areas."[92] The fact that the Reich German broadcast had announced the text of the letter before it reached Beneš understandably aroused Czech opinion over this open connivance between Czechoslovak citizens and a foreign power. The German press and radio launched a violent campaign which was met by an official Czechoslovak protest in Berlin.[93] Czechoslovak attitudes visibly hardened, local elections were postponed, and all political meetings banned.[94]

88. *DGFP*, II, 3.
89. Hořec, p. 405. See above, note 69. After his return Henlein declared at the regional congress of the SdP at Teplice-Šanov: "The sympathies of England . . . are on our side. . . . The pre-condition to a good relationship between Prague and Berlin is a settlement of the Sudeten German problem. Berlin will never do anything without us and would always keep in mind our vital interests and rights" (*ibid.*). Eisenlohr reported on Oct. 22, 1937, that at least as late as Oct. 17 and 18 the Sudeten German leaders "were of the opinion that the Teplitz incidents might afford the occasion to bring the Sudeten German question to a head with the help of the Reich." Henlein stated that "no serious intervention in favor of the Czechs was to be feared from Great Britain and probably also from France" (*DGFP*, II, 22–23).
90. *Survey 1937*, I, 454. According to a confidential report of the SdP, "Deputy . . . Frank's nerves had in fact given way." The first blow had been struck by a policeman who was unaware that he dealt with the deputy, but "after that Herr Frank was not able to control himself and had then struck out at the policemen, from one of whom he had snatched a rubber truncheon" (*DGFP*, II, 27).
91. *Ibid.*, p. 22.
92. *Ibid.*, p. 21.
93. The *Völkischer Beobachter* wrote that "lies and hate, murder and terror stood beside the cradle of the Czechoslovak state and have never left it during its brief existence" (*Survey 1937*, I, 454).
94. *Ibid.; DGFP*, II, 21.

The SdP retreated, surprised by the vigorous and unanimous reaction of the Czechs, and its council of leaders issued a confidential directive to its members that "the Party must now readjust itself to present domestic political conditions." Ernst Eisenlohr, the intelligent and moderate German minister at Prague, noted:

> Obviously Konrad Henlein has come to realize that the time for the decisive struggle for power has not yet arrived, and that a too vigorously emphasized policy modeled on the Reich might involve the Party, and particularly their leaders, in dangers with which at present they feel unable to cope.[95]

The hope for a détente, which resulted in the first personal meeting between Henlein and Hodža on Sept. 16, 1937, suffered a severe setback as a result of the Teplice incident. Prague, undoubtedly influenced by the urging of the Western Powers, wanted to sound out the real German intentions, and in a frank discussion find out if there was any chance of bringing about a solution. While Henlein urged a fundamental reorganization of the state, Hodža offered the implementation of a gradual reform within the framework of the constitution.[96] At the meeting Henlein, still practicing duplicity, protested his loyalty to the Republic, although not long before he had declared at the annual meeting of the DAI in Stuttgart that the "happiness and future of the Sudeten Germans, as well as of all Germans in the world, are closely linked with those of the Third Reich, . . . and we have the inalienable right to unite ourselves on the basis of blood with our German brethren and to form one great national family."[97]

This two-faced policy—perfidy from the Czechoslovak point of view—was a stringent necessity because the SdP was conscious of the fact that no state could fail to crack down on a movement aimed at the destruction of its independence. There was no possibility of compromise if the party declared its real aims at the outset. Consequently, in order to prevent serious hindrance to their activities, Henlein and his aides consciously imposed self-restraint on themselves and the party. As they stated to Hitler, they had to "camouflage" their real purposes and to follow a cautious policy of conditioned loyalty.

95. Eisenlohr in his political report of Oct. 22, 1937 (*ibid.*, p. 23).
96. See Henlein's minutes of his first meeting with Hodža (*ibid.*, pp. 8–9). The minutes were duly transmitted to the German legation.
97. *National Socialism*, p. 129; *Německý imperialismus*, pp. 400–402. The DAI meeting was held during Aug. 11–15, 1937. In December 1937, Henlein stated at the Kronprinzenpalais in Berlin that the same German heart and spirit united the Sudeten Germans and the Reich (K. S. von Galéra, *Sudetendeutschlands Heimkehr ins Deutsche Reich*, p. 245).

Once they achieved unity of and control over the Germans in Czechoslovakia, they would be able to obstruct Prague's policies. By taking up both justified and unjustified German grievances,[98] the SdP was in a position to generate a dangerous psychological situation among the Germans.

During the years 1935–37 the SdP turned to the offensive simultaneously with the strengthening of Nazism in the Reich. The party continued to allege that it was neither conspiratorial nor totalitarian. Officially it pretended to stand aside from Nazi Germany, although acknowledging that the Nazi regime had carried out a number of constructive reforms. Its publicly voiced intentions served as a smokescreen. Operating as a power within the Republic which it sought to weaken and disintegrate, the SdP insisted it was not plotting at all. With the same breath, it specified such conditions for settling the outstanding issues as would entail the end of Czechoslovak independence. By 1937 most of its leaders[99] regarded the

98. The grievances of the SdP were listed in Henlein's report to Hitler (*DGFP*, II, 51–54). The most important ones were as follows: (1) The advance of the Czech language frontier into the German areas. (Thus, the decree of Minister of Defense František Machník of Jan. 28, 1936, stipulating that no workmen or employees belonging to political parties hostile to the state might be engaged in the armament industry. The SdP complained against the decree at the League of Nations on April 24. The complaint was rejected when the cabinet decided not to enforce the order.) (2) The Czech endeavor to weaken the Germans by its economic policy (the loss of more than 40,000 jobs by the blocking of the engaging of the Germans in state service, etc.). (3) The cultural policy of the government (inciting "the pupils against the German mother-race, its Reich and its Führer"). (4) The taking over by the state police of the administration in almost all German cities. (5) The National Defense Law of 1936 creating the frontier zone which covered most of the German areas and was "under permanent sway of exceptional legislation."

99. It has been stated repeatedly that there existed within the SdP a moderate autonomist wing which was ready to accept territorial autonomy within the frame of the Republic. This is also the thesis of H. K. G. Rönnefarth in his *Sudetenkrise*. Certainly the SdP was an amalgam of various nationalist shadings, some of them of a non-Nazi character. Most of the leaders, however, espoused the pan-German, authoritarian, antidemocratic, and anti-Czechoslovak objectives of Hitler. On the whole, it seems that the internal differences were more of a tactical order, i.e., whether German hegemony in Central Europe would be better advanced by the destruction of the Republic or by its strangulation as an independent state. According to Jaksch (*Europas Weg*, p. 490), the moderates were Dr. Kundt, Dr. Brand, Dr. Neuwirth, and Dr. Peters. Yet Dr. Kundt, for example, whose approach seemed to be more cautious than that of the radical group of Frank, became the leader of the Sudeten German group remaining in Czechoslovakia after Munich and closely followed the extreme National Socialist line. Whatever may have been his intentions, by his deeds he unfailingly supported the aims of the Henleinist policy until 1945. And Dr. Brand, in his report to Henlein on July 20, 1938, espoused the pan-German aims of Berlin. His alternative for Czechoslovakia was either to become a satellite of the Reich or to be destroyed (*Německý imperialismus*, pp. 306–309).

annexation of Czechoslovak German territories by the Reich as the most acceptable solution.[100] They would have settled for less if that had been Hitler's aim. However, they put themselves willingly in the service of pan-German ideas. The conspiracy against the Czechoslovak state, in which the SdP publicly claimed to play no role, continued meanwhile. Indeed the network of Nazi contacts and the amount of subsidies increased. The VoMi was instructed to establish a direct chain of command between Berlin and the residence of Henlein in Aš.

By the fall of 1937, Henlein and his close aides believed that the hitherto adaptable and flexible policy of the SdP had to assume a new degree of firmness. The incidents at Teplice and Henlein's favorable reception in London, coupled with the deep swell of Sudeten German nationalism, made them think that a new stage had been reached by the SdP which enabled them to come to a far-reaching political resolution. As "an understanding between Germans and Czechs in Czechoslovakia is practically impossible" and "a settlement of the German question is only conceivable on a German basis," and as such a settlement would have required the Reich German aid, Henlein sought a discussion with the only man who could make such a vital decision of principle, which would, in the final analysis, involve the whole structure of postwar Europe—Adolf Hitler. On Nov. 19, 1937, he delivered to Hitler and von Neurath his secret "Report for the Führer and Reich Chancellor Dealing with Questions of Immediate Interest to German Policy in the Czechoslovak Republic." Henlein claimed that the SdP could make an outstanding contribution "to the new order of Europe in the spirit of National Socialism and of the policy of the Reich." He asked the Führer for a personal discussion "involving the whole question of principle."[101]

The secret meeting took place after the annexation of Austria on March 28, 1938. On Nov. 5, 1937, Hitler notified his military chiefs that he had decided to settle the German question by force. "Czechia" and Austria would be annexed by the Reich, and the German food situation would be improved by the compulsory emigration of two million Czechs and one million Austrians. Hitler declared that almost

---

100. *DGFP*, II, 57.
101. *Ibid.*, p. 56. For Henlein's report, see *ibid.*, pp. 49 ff. Dr. Neuwirth affirmed that he and some other party leaders had never had any cognizance of the existence of such a report. They had also, he claims, been unaware of any secret meeting taking place between Hitler and Henlein in March 1938 (*Die Sudetenfrage in europäischer Sicht*, p. 172). This was undoubtedly due to the necessity for both protagonists to keep the highly sensitive matter strictly secret.

certainly Great Britain and probably also France had already tacitly written off the Czechs.[102] Military plans for the attack against Czechoslovakia were already drafted in June 1937.[103]

In November 1937, a decisive and fateful turning point was reached in Germany and Czechoslovakia that profoundly influenced European policy at a critical political juncture. Europe stood again on the verge of a serious political crisis in which the Sudeten German question was designed by Berlin and the SdP to play the central and dominant role. The resurgence of pan-Germanism in the past years had produced a sharp swing to the Nazis among the German minorities in Europe. An expression of this upsurge in Czechoslovakia was the virtual revolt against Activist policies and an eagerness to work in a still not yet publicly declared alliance with the Reich German Nazis. With tremendous pressure building up for Nazi intervention, the masses followed the SdP with enthusiasm on a course that led them further away from both the Republic and democracy.

It was also obvious that some legitimate grievances furnished ammunition to the SdP, and that the Czechoslovak party system was unprepared to cope quickly and efficiently with the explosive situation which confronted the state. The coalition system of government—in which any one of the major parties was strong enough to bar any important measure but not powerful enough to have its own way—made for an unwieldy and slow government. It forced the heads of the coalition parties to compromise. This gave great power to a handful of party leaders who maneuvered behind the political scene and parceled up the state machinery into spheres where the influence of the respective party was predominant. Such a tendency made it difficult to arrive quickly at an efficient program. It relegated the most

102. *IMT*, XXV, 402 ff. Hitler's declaration before the military leaders (von Blomberg, von Fritsch, Admiral Räder, Marshal Göring, and Minister von Neurath) was recorded in writing by Col. F. Hossbach on Nov. 10, 1937. It is therefore called the Hossbach Memorandum. (See also Friedrich Hossbach, *Zwischen Wehrmacht und Hitler 1934–38*, pp. 231 ff.) Hossbach tried to prove that the offensive war was not planned by the Wehrmacht.

103. Wolfgang Foerster, *Generaloberst Ludwig Beck. Sein Kampf gegen den Krieg*, p. 113; *IMT*, XXXIV, 732 ff. The German military chiefs favored war against Czechoslovakia in the event that France and Great Britain would not intervene. In his memorandum of July 16, 1938, General Beck, as chief of the General Staff of the army, stated that he did not see any chance of smashing Czechoslovakia without immediately provoking counteraction by France and England (*ibid.*, p. 118). Therefore, Beck insisted on the postponement of military action against the Republic until the fall of 1938, and resigned on Aug. 18, 1938. The differences between Hitler and Beck in this matter consisted in the fact that Beck, ready to smash Czechoslovakia alone, did not want the Reich to get involved in a European war.

important problems, those on which the conclusion of an agreement was difficult, to a slow process of partisan bargaining.[104]

Czechoslovak policy should have been more dynamic in its approach to nationality affairs. It failed grievously to undertake a major political and psychological offensive among the Germans. Usually it was thrown on the defensive, and its actions were largely reactions to the probing moves of the SdP. Instead of joining in a major public effort in all political, economic, and psychological spheres, the Czechoslovak leaders preferred to deal with the urgent problems behind closed doors.[105] Yet despite these weaknesses, the Republic was an oasis of national tolerance and refuge for thousands of German democratic exiles. Its leaders were doggedly devoted to the Western type of parliamentarian democracy, individual freedom, and preservation of human rights, and searched sincerely for peace in liberty in an era of totalitarianism and racial and national hatred.

From 1933 to 1937, Nazi power and influence abroad grew at an alarming rate. In the fall of 1937, Hitler considered the situation ripe for a showdown in Central Europe, and Henlein prepared to offer the services of his countrymen in implementing Hitler's aims:

> The Sudeten Germans are conscious of their particular political duty toward the anti-German mission and the policy of Czechoslovakia as ordained by the West and the Bolshevist East, and are resolved to be a factor in the National Socialist policy of the Reich.[106]

From this moment on, the Sudeten German Party, the spellbinder proclaiming the triumph of National Socialism in Czechoslovakia, emerged as a conscious instrument of an antidemocratic and anti-

104. Criticism of the party system was widespread and was shared by both President Beneš, who prepared—during the Second World War—a plan for a three-party system, and the resistance movement within Czechoslovakia after 1939. (See the program *Za svobodu do nové Československé republiky*, pp. 42–44.) Many Czech periodicals, such as *Demokratický střed (Democratic Center)* and *Naše doba*, voiced criticism of the party oligarchy before Munich. For example, see Prof. Josef Macek in *Naše doba*, XXXXV (March 1938), 321–25. (See also Eisenlohr's keen comments in *DGFP*, II, 116.)

105. The Communists critized the cabinet for its lack of decision and clear-cut policy (Gottwald, *Spisy*, VIII, 141). The Communist policy from 1935 on was based on a defense of the integrity and independence of the Republic against the Fascist peril. The party urged that stern measures against the SdP should be accompanied by large economic assistance to the distressed German areas and by national concessions to democratic Germans. See its memorandum to the government, Nov. 6, 1936 (*ibid.*, p. 275). The Communists, however, represented only one segment of the widespread criticism of the irresolute policy of the Hodža cabinet.

106. *DGFP*, II, 56.

parliamentary regime predicated on the magic of Hitler's personality. The voluntary yielding of the power of policy decision by the SdP, which enthusiastically abdicated even that modicum of free judgment it had hitherto exercised, had ominous portents for the whole of Europe. No less ominous were the conspiratorial methods it used to wreck a democratic state—a pivotal Western ally—while pretending to act on behalf of the right of self-determination. The great majority of Sudeten Germans handed over the decision on their fate to that aloof and inscrutable figure who bestrode the German scene—Adolf Hitler.

CHAPTER 5

Munich

It was long evident that the lowering Nazi storm would someday sweep beyond the German frontiers. And it was equally evident that when it blew across the Bohemian mountains, its political epicenter would be Konrad Henlein and his lieutenants.

Hitler began the active phase of his plans of conquest of Europe in 1937. Austria and Czechoslovakia, contiguous to the Reich, were selected as the first targets, since they formed the barrier to the German drive to the East. On paper, the Czechoslovak position looked formidable, supported as she was by France, Russia, and indirectly Great Britain. In reality, however, London was intent upon the settlement of the German question, and suggested strongly to Prague that it make extensive concessions.[1] Great Britain was interested in an accommodation in the Republic chiefly because a German attack upon it would result in French assistance to her ally and almost certain British involvement on the French side. London deemed it necessary, in fact, to counsel caution and to exert some pressure in Prague, because the problem of the Sudeten Germans could jeopardize European peace through the possible intervention of the Reich.[2] France was too weak to carry out a consistent policy of her own. The Soviet Union, distrusted by the West, faced the strong opposition of

1. In a long series of German-British talks, the Sudeten German question was constantly on the agenda. The British assured Berlin that pressure and influence were being used on Prague to promote a peaceful settlement (DGFP, I, 90, 132, 248, 259).
2. Theodor Kordt, the German chargé d'affaires in London, April 30, 1938 (ibid., p. 1103).

influential governmental circles in France and Great Britain which were trying to accommodate the Fascist dictators.

Henlein's public pronouncements had so far been imprecise and even Delphic. Various parties could read simultaneously in his spoken views much that might comfort both the radicals and the moderates. But at the same time they remained disturbed by his deliberate vagueness. This appears to have been exactly what Henlein and his staff intended. It was too early to announce a detailed plan for a radical solution. Henlein had to wait until Berlin served notice to the world that it was determined to protect German minorities at all costs. His New Year's message, published on Jan. 1, 1938, stressed the international implications of the German-Czech issue: "The Czech people must recognize that no settlement will ever be reached with our great neighbor, Germany, until the Sudeten Germans are satisfied."[3] This open threat of German intervention was coupled with a cautious article in *Venkov*,[4] the central organ of the Czechoslovak Agrarian Party, published on the same day.

Hitler's speech of Feb. 20, 1938, started the offensive: "Over ten million Germans live in two of the States adjoining our frontiers. . . . The fact that they are now citizens of other States should not deprive them of their rights as members of a national community." The Third Reich had to protect "those fellow Germans who live beyond our frontiers and are unable to ensure for themselves the right to a general freedom, personal, political, and ideological."[5] The menacing tone of the speech, referring to Austria and Czechoslovakia without expressly mentioning them, was met with firm opposition by the Czechoslovak press.

In subsequent conversations between Eisenlohr and Hodža it was apparent that, despite the threatening tones of Berlin, the Prague cabinet did not waver in its policy of moderation. Hodža outlined his program, consisting of a broad amnesty, the transfer of German officials to German areas, development of self-administration to the extent that in the future German officials would be employed in predominantly German territory, cessation of the building of minority schools in the German areas, holding of early elections, and the

3. *Die Zeit*, Jan. 1, 1938, as cited in R. G. D. Laffan (revised by V. K. Toynbee and P. E. Baker), *Survey of International Affairs 1938* (London, 1951), II, 51. The book is one of the best summaries of the Munich period.
4. The same issue of *Venkov* contained a message by the chairman of the Agrarian Party, Rudolf Beran, who pointed out that the SdP could no longer be ignored in the political life of the country. The message gave rise to a wave of excited dissent on the Czech side (*Naše doba* [January 1938], pp. 231–32).
5. *Documents on International Affairs 1938* (London, 1942), II, 12–13.

possible participation of the SdP in the cabinet.[6] The government was aware of the need for a better relationship between Czechs and Germans. It comprehended that this could be realized only after complicated and protracted negotiations with the SdP, which in turn had to be preceded by the reestablishment of contact between the party and the government.[7] Hodža's conciliatory talks with Eisenlohr were accompanied by a firm public stand. He reiterated before Parliament the will of Prague not to brook any interference in its domestic affairs. However, the following day (March 5), in an interview with the representative of the *Sunday Times*,[8] President Beneš took a conciliatory step backward by recognizing the moral right of Europe to protect the peace. Professor Laffan has rightly commented that it was very difficult "to reconcile Czechoslovak sovereignty" with the idea of the moral right of Europe to protect the peace. It seemed "to recall similar forms of words used in the past to cover Europe's dealings with the Eastern Question and to liken Czechoslovakia to the Ottoman Empire of the nineteenth century."[9]

Hitler's occupation of Austria did not upset Prague's endeavors toward a friendly settlement of the German question, although the change wrought in Czechoslovakia by the Anschluss was far-reaching. There were grave signs of potential troubles ahead for the Republic. The Reich completely encircled the Historic Provinces and controlled their principal trade lines to the south and southeast, and threatened to isolate Czechoslovakia almost completely from the West. The annexation evoked enthusiasm among the Czechoslovak Germans and, as the British consul at Liberec reported, it "has set in motion an avalanche of national feeling amongst the Sudeten Germans." He found a growing sentiment "that what is true for Austria must also be true for the Sudeten Germans."[10]

That Hitler had achieved extraordinary momentum by his annexation of Austria was indisputable. The question now was whether he could maintain the momentum in resolving the formidable problems that faced him in Czechoslovakia. Meanwhile, Eisenlohr criticized

6. Eisenlohr conferred with Hodža on February 23 and 26 (*DGFP*, II, 137–41, 143–46). For his summary of Hodža's reported aims, see *ibid.*, p. 179. One could, however, hardly believe that Hodža promised to employ only German officials in the German areas, as Eisenlohr reported, because Prague strongly defended its right to appoint officials of any nationality to any part of the state.

7. Hodža to Eisenlohr on Feb. 26, 1938 (*ibid.*, p. 144).

8. *Documents 1938*, II, 117.

9. *Survey 1938*, II, 61.

10. *DBFP 1938*, I, 68. The report is dated March 19, 1938.

the intransigent attitude of the radical wing of the SdP, with its insistence on what he called "demagogic demands of the Sudeten German Party, that is on Racial Protection Law and 'territorial autonomy' which are in practice unrealizable and are unacceptable to any Czechoslovak Government."[11] Considering the possibility that the SdP could draw the Reich into armed conflict by its irresponsible demands, Eisenlohr, who was clearly not initiated into Hitler's plans, insisted upon and received from Henlein and Frank assurances that the

> course of German foreign policy as communicated by the Legation is to be the sole determining factor for policy and tactical procedure of the Sudeten German Party. My instructions are to be strictly observed.[12]

Eisenlohr, with his moderate line of a gradual furthering of German interests, failed to understand the nature of the objectives of the SdP, intent on the concept of a Greater Germany. Henlein, not Eisenlohr, was the repository of Hitler's will and the trustee of Berlin.

The next day Henlein asked Reich Foreign Minister Ribbentrop for the opportunity of an early talk. He expressed gratitude "to all those who contributed to the success" of the Anschluss and assured Ribbentrop that the Sudeten Germans "shall render thanks to the Führer by redoubling our efforts in the service of the policy of Greater Germany."[13] The Henleinists remained grimly determined to achieve their Greater German dreams while Eisenlohr watched their program with deep misgivings. This difference in attitude epitomized the discrepancy between the exultant Sudeten German leaders, living in an unreal world of German power and believing that they were defending the patrimony of the Greater Fatherland, and the more pragmatic and prudent Reich German officialdom, not yet fully accustomed to the new National Socialist order.

As the SdP realized that only Hitler's assistance could ensure its success, it intensified its approaches to high Nazi officials and initiated conferences whenever possible with the hierarchy of the Reich. It passed outlines of its program to the Nazi leaders, supplied Berlin with a well-organized body of supporters, and opened the doors to Nazi penetration of the state. Motivated largely by the imposing dimensions of its pan-German program, it pledged aid to

11. *DGFP*, II, 155, 179.
12. The report of Eisenlohr of March 16, 1938 (*ibid.*, pp. 169–70).
13. The secret letter of Henlein (March 17) was submitted by F. Bürger, Henlein's representative in Berlin, on March 18, 1938 (*ibid.*, pp. 173–74).

Hitler in those areas of foreign policy which seemed to offer him a maximum of political and strategic advantages. There was actually a compelling need for discussion of basic objectives and a plan of action adapted to actual requirements. In default of such joint planning, there was danger that the eagerness of the Sudeten Germans might spark explosive demonstrations against the Czechs which could arouse democratic opinion in Europe and enable the Czechs to crush the German radicals and rout the SdP. The vigorous and insistent initiative of the SdP leaders coupled with the readiness of Berlin to promote their aspirations resulted in a joint venture cemented by direct and official conferences in Berlin on March 28–29, 1938.

The pivotal issue was Hitler's decision. He summoned Henlein and Frank to Berlin and at a three-hour audience on March 28 issued his instructions. Hitler announced that he had decided to solve the Sudeten German question "in the not-too-distant future" and expressed his full confidence in Henlein as "the rightful leader of the Sudeten German element." Henlein was made responsible for a policy which he was to follow in close cooperation with the German authorities, who could not intervene directly. The core of the instructions was summarized by Henlein: *"We must always demand so much that we can never be satisfied."* Henlein's successes in London were highly appreciated by Hitler, who asked him to go to London again "to continue to use his influence with a view to ensuring nonintervention by Britain."[14]

Next day the issue was discussed by Reich Foreign Minister Joachim von Ribbentrop.[15] Henlein was advised to maintain the closest possible contact with Ribbentrop, the head of the VoMi, SS-Obergruppenführer Lorenz, and Eisenlohr. The Reich government would refrain from appearing as the representative of the Sudeten demands, which would be presented only by the SdP. Henlein was assured of the full assistance of the Reich. The die was cast as the plotters embarked on what promised to be the big challenge of the

---

14. Henlein's report on his audience with Hitler on March 28 (*ibid.*, pp. 197–98). Present at the audience—besides Hitler, Henlein, and Frank—were Hess, Ribbentrop, and Lorenz. The purport of the instructions given by Hitler to the SdP was "that demands should be made by the Sudeten German Party which are unacceptable to the Czech Government."

15. *Ibid.*, pp. 204–205. The highest officials of the German Foreign Office, Eisenlohr, the representatives of the VoMi, and Henlein, Frank, Dr. Künzel, and Dr. Kreissl for the SdP, took part in the discussion. The SdP also maintained close contact with the supreme headquarters of the Wehrmacht and supplied it with information. One of the channels was F. Bürger in Berlin (*ibid.*, pp. 224, 232).

democratic powers, with Czechoslovakia selected for the first dramatic test.

No consideration of the Berlin meeting would be complete without reference to the absolute secrecy which enveloped the consultations. Europe remained in the dark not only about the results of the deliberations but also about their actual existence.

The Sudeten Germans, dizzy with the success of Hitler's recent experiments in politics, facilitated the Nazi breakthrough in the German areas of the Republic. When the SdP appealed to all Germans to join the party in view of the events in Austria, and the party press office announced that new members would be admitted only up to May 31,[16] the influx of new members was so great that at some places stocks of membership blanks were soon depleted.[17] Most Sudeten politicians engaged in acrobatics in an effort to jump on the Henleinist bandwagon. The head of the German Agrarian Party, Gustav Hacker, hailed the Anschluss and on March 22 fused with the SdP. The genuine believer in German-Czech cooperation, Minister Dr. Spina, resigned from the cabinet and abandoned political life. The next day, six Agrarian deputies took an oath of obedience to Henlein. Hacker became a member of Henlein's Führeramt.[18] The German Christian Socialists also suspended their activities on March 24 and their deputies and senators entered the SdP parliamentary club.[19] Almost all the bourgeois Activist movement voluntarily liquidated itself. None of the parties was able to withstand the nationalist temptation; their surrender to Henlein was rapid and complete. The third Activist party, the German Social Democrats, withdrew its Jewish minister, Dr. Ludwig Czech, from the cabinet, and Wenzel Jaksch replaced him as head of the party.[20]

The Social Democrats, Communists, and a few Liberals alone

16. *DBFP*, I, 64. The British minister in Prague to Viscount Halifax, the foreign secretary, on March 17, 1938. (See also *Naše doba*, April 1938, p. 425.)

17. Daubner, p. 80.

18. *Naše doba* (April 1938), p. 424; Daubner, pp. 80–82. The small German Traders' Party also dissolved itself.

19. Krofta, *Z dob*, p. 264. An enthusiastic promoter of German unity was Senator Canon Dr. Karl Hilgenreiner, who argued that the Sudeten German Catholics should not be less Catholic than Viennese Cardinal Innitzer, who ordered the ringing of all church bells on the occasion of Hitler's entrance in Vienna (*Naše doba*, April, 1938, pp. 385 ff.).

20. *Ibid.*, p. 425. The hard core of the German Social Democratic Party held firm against the SdP. There were 79,935 members of the party in 1931, and 82,425 in 1937 (César-Černý, *Politika*, II, 498). For the confidential report by Professor Pfitzner to Henlein (April 2, 1938) on his meeting with Jaksch, see *Mnichov v dokumentech*, II, 127–31.

remained to fight for democratic freedoms. They put up a brave anti-Nazi front, but were seriously hurt by the overwhelming support given to the SdP by the German masses. The German Social Democrats struggled valiantly to fashion a program that could command at least the support of the working classes. But it appeared that the nationalist excitement had already passed the point where moderate forces could have hoped to have any serious appeal. Activism ceased to pose an alternative. Against 55 Henlein deputies there stood only 11 German Social Democrats and five German Communists.[21] The SdP emerged as the real representative of the Germans in Czechoslovakia.

The general unrest in the German areas continued. Some 36 meetings of the SdP, with about a half million participants, were held on Sunday, March 27, 1938. According to Eisenlohr,[22] the demonstrations were characterized "by very violent outbreaks of enthusiasm on the part of Sudeten German people, who expect complete reshaping of their destiny." The German masses marched shouting, "One people, one Reich, one *Führer.*" Following orders, "Czechoslovak police and gendarmeries showed great restraint" and the German population "feels the behavior of the police to be helplessness and abdication of civil authority." The Germans even contemplated "direct Reich intervention." Another observer, P. Pares, the British consul at Liberec, reported on April 6 that "during the past weeks the majority of Sudeten Germans has ceased to be even nominally loyal to the State as the party leaders still profess to be."

Stimulated by the Austrian example, the Germans came to believe that nothing short of separation from Czechoslovakia would be acceptable.[23] Their state of mind became so violent that Reich authorities voiced apprehension. The entire German population was sharply critical of the negotiations between the Henlein Party and the government. Tension was "so great that a single shot for Sudeten Germans would suffice to start a blood bath among Czechs."[24] Henleinist party circles exerted brutal pressure to coerce every German to take an active part in the SdP. Whisper propaganda, newspaper attacks promoting hatred of the Czechs, commercial

21. *Naše doba* (April 1938), pp. 385 ff.
22. Report of Eisenlohr for March 31, 1938 (*DGFP*, II, 208).
23. *DBFP*, I, 123. Consul Pares noticed that "people in the streets give the Nazi salute openly, and greet one another with 'Heil Hitler.'"
24. The report of Eisenlohr of April 9, 1938 (*DGFP*, II, 226). The same day, two or three officials of the VoMi were ordered by Ribbentrop to go to "the disturbed areas to counsel reason" at the German borderland. The VoMi intervened also with the SA, urging it to refrain from incitement (*ibid.*, pp. 228–29).

boycotts inciting purchase only from German shops, violent interference with the activities of non-Henlein German parties, teachers'
propaganda in the German schools carefully cultivating national and
racial fanaticism and prejudice were some of the various forms of
pressure.[25] Abusive use of economic power was brought to bear upon
German employees, and threats of dismissal drove workers and
employees into the SdP. The varied patterns of intimidation were
signs of deep-seated turmoil, as one party abused the privileges and
rights of a democratic system in an effort to impress the German
population.

The reigning impression in the country was, however, one of
outward calm. So far, while there had been evidence of radicalism,
there had been no bloodshed, and even arrests were rare. Though the
Czechs gave the appearance of indifference to the crisis in their
day-to-day living habits, they were, of course, very much concerned
with what was going on in the German areas. They were confident,
however, that the strong international position of the country would
prevent any far-reaching concessions being granted to German
Nazism. Prague understood the necessity for a conciliatory attitude
toward the Germans. It balked, however, at any measure offering
territorial autonomy that would divide the state and leave a substantial area to the control of a movement whose subversive activities
were too well known to leave any ground for doubts as to its aim.
Autonomy would, moreover, leave about 380,000 Czechs within the
German regions—not counting the German democrats and Jews—and
some 730,000 Germans outside the German zone.

Hodža was ready to begin concessions with local elections which
would enable the SdP to place its members in municipal administration. Both he and Beneš even accepted the idea of eventually
admitting the SdP into the cabinet, provided it gave pledges that it
would pursue a sensible policy.[26] The problem was complicated, as
the national question blended with the issue of democracy versus
Nazism. The Czechs were ready to give the Germans satisfaction in
many important matters of principle but genuinely believed that they
could not be expected to refrain from defending the democratic
regime. Many among them advocated stronger measures to protect
the integrity of the state and its democratic liberties. They felt that
the state should not have tolerated any subversion and should have

25. Henderson, pp. 82–97. The author cited many concrete examples of pressure
   and intimidation.
26. Points made by Prime Minister Hodža to Basil Newton on March 21, 1938
   (DBFP, I, 76–77). Also see DGFP, II, 189.

cracked down on the SdP. The problem was, however, that the Henlein Party was careful to avoid doing publicly anything which might be construed as a conspiracy against the Republic. Although Prague was aware of some connection between the SdP and Berlin, the Czech-German question had become so grave a political and international issue that the government felt that it could not be solved by legal or penal measures only, but had to be fought out against an atmosphere of increasing pressure from the Western Powers on behalf of the Germans. The problem had long ceased to be an internal affair. Through the intervention of Hitler it had now become an issue of war or peace in Europe.[27]

The talks of the SdP with Prague served as excellent propaganda for Berlin in blackmailing London and Paris with demands for the right of self-determination for minorities. Prague—pressed by its Western friends[28]—had to produce concession after concession, although the real issue was not the Sudeten German question but the Nazi will to crush Czechoslovakia.[29] The correct assessment by

27. The scope of the present study prevents a wider analysis of the international background which formed an integral part of the internal history of the Czechoslovak Republic in 1938. For the international aspects of the Czech-German question, see the study by Laffan (*Survey 1938*, II). It is competent and scholarly, although it exaggerates the importance of the SdP, whose attitude and policy only reflected the ultimate decisive role of Berlin. The study by Boris Celovsky, *Das Münchener Abkommen*, presents an exhaustive and well-documented up-to-date survey, rightly stressing the primarily international character of the Munich crisis. The good treatment by John W. Wheeler-Bennett, *Munich. Prologue to Tragedy*, is obsolete in some points because it was written at a time when neither German nor British documents were available. It can still be read with profit, however. The most recent book by Rönnefarth, *Sudetenkrise*, is a thorough but biased compilation.

28. The British documents (*DBFP*) present the most instructive and the most eloquent story of appeasement. Relentless and merciless pressure was applied unilaterally on the Czechs. Although London was fully aware of the fact that the SdP was in Hitler's pocket (see, for example, Newton to Halifax, May 24, 1938; *DBFP*, I, 360), pretext after pretext was found for putting heavy pressure on Prague. British interest centered on the question of how to avert war at almost any price. The British diplomat William Strang (*ibid.*, p. 403) expressed the core of the policy of appeasement: "We did not want to get into the position of endorsing Dr. Beneš' plan (however good it might be) and then having to run away from it because the Germans rejected it and became violent again." If the Germans realized, as they did, this mood of the British Foreign Office, it was easy for them to maneuver at Munich. London did not care about who was right or wrong, but was interested solely in not being involved in war. It was completely indifferent, while using high moral terms, to the fate of democracy in Czechoslovakia. The evidence shows that London was treating Beneš more cavalierly than if he had been the chief of a tribe in Africa. See also the commentaries by W. N. Medlicott in the *Revue d'histoire de la deuxième guerre mondiale*, II (July 1952), 29–40 and IV (January 1954), 3–16.

29. Basil Newton noted (May 26–27, 1938) in a conversation with the head of

Prague of the real intentions of Berlin and the SdP made it unwilling to go along with any far-reaching proposal.[30] Grudgingly the cabinet retreated before the pressure and outright interference of London, which was bent primarily on the preservation of peace and basically disinterested in the integrity of the Republic.[31] Prague negotiated with Henlein under no illusions, aware only of its vital dependence on the Western Alliance.

The Czechs were sincerely willing to settle the whole German problem as an internal affair, but they realized the impossibility of a territorial autonomy which would allow the existence of an area administered on Nazi principles within the framework of a democratic state. They were well aware that, contingent upon the desire of Berlin, the whole area would sooner or later secede to Nazi Germany, and the Republic would be left at the mercy of Hitler without its fortifications. Prague felt that it defended not only its own independence but also the vital interests of the Western democracies. It was prepared to put up a solid defense against any German attack[32] and was confident about the outcome of a possible war if Czechoslovakia were assisted by France, Britain, and Russia.

Faced with the threat of Hitler, Prague set out to unify all provisions concerning nationality matters within one nationality statute. Hodža announced in a broadcast on March 28—the very day of the secret meeting of Henlein with Hitler—that the cabinet contemplated promulgating a minorities statute embodying in one act all existing minority legislation. It would form a legal basis for the

the Central European department of the Foreign Office, William Strang, that "even if there were not a single German in Czechoslovakia, the root problem of German-Czech relations would still remain, viz., a Slav state thrust into the heart of Germany. . . . The German Government . . . are using the Sudeten German question as an instrument of policy to strengthen their political and military position" (*DBFP*, I, 404). See also Celovsky, p. 166.

30. There were two main tendencies in the Prague cabinet: that of the Agrarian Party, which was intent upon bringing a solution by wide concessions (see the meeting of Eisenlohr with Beran on March 26, 1938; *DGFP*, II, 194–95), and the more intransigent tendency of the Czech center and leftist parties (*ibid.*, pp. 188, 195). The Catholic People's Party was implacable in its opposition to Henlein.

31. The British had considered, as early as 1938, that "the best standing ground for Dr. Beneš and for ourselves might be the early offer of a plebiscite," yet no guarantee for the remaining state would even be offered so far as Britain was concerned. (See the illuminating suggestions by William Strang in *DBFP*, I, 403.)

32. The Czechoslovak General Staff prepared for war "in the definite belief that it will come and probably in the not too far distant future." (See the report by the British military attaché, H. C. T. Stronge, from Prague, March 29, 1938; *ibid.*, p. 104.)

final settlement of grievances, based on the existing constitution, sovereignty of the state, and policy of nondenationalization. It would present the most advanced and perfect system of minority protection presently existing in Europe.[33] The speech encountered violent German criticism and was pronounced as absolutely unsatisfactory by the SdP at its meeting on April 5.[34] The SdP stated that it considered self-administration, compensation for damages suffered since 1918, and participation in the government of the state as indispensable prerequisites of any settlement.[35]

London too did not regard Hodža's proposal as an effective solution, and intimated to Prague its willingness to study a new Czechoslovak proposal.[36] It felt that the time had come when "a supreme effort must be made."[37] President Beneš had expected to solve the issue gradually, in the course of a decade. Under the impact of the absorption of Austria and the perilous situation, Beneš discussed the German problem with the Czech coalition parties and secured their consent to a new program which he communicated to London.[38] The cabinet also decided to move up the municipal elections which had been planned for May 22, 29, and June 12.

It would be wrong to infer too much from the Czech proposals and the German demands and counterproposals. The Czechs took pains to reassure the West that they favored a settlement, but a lot of persuasion would be needed to make them originate a whole new series of concessions and plans since each of their propositions seemed sufficient to clear the very last obstacles. Prague saw the whole Czech-German internal issue as a secondary element, wholly contingent upon the aims of Berlin. A corollary to this conviction was its belief that the Nazi interest in the Sudeten Germans was due primarily to Berlin's aggressive intentions, and that the Sudetens served merely as a tool of Hitler to help him crush Czechoslovakia and achieve German hegemony over Europe.[39] London and Paris, however, sought the answer to the question of the preservation of peace in Prague and were in no way inclined to look for it at the decisive spot, which was Berlin itself.

33. *Documents 1938*, II, 125; *DBFP*, I, 77; *DGFP*, II, 189.
34. *Ibid.*, p. 224.
35. *Ibid.*, p. 225.
36. *DBFP*, I, 118.
37. Newton to Beneš, April 22 (*ibid.*, p. 180).
38. *Ibid.*, pp. 188–95. On April 16, 1938, a political amnesty was signed by Beneš releasing 1,235 Germans from jail (*DGFP*, II, 235).
39. For example, see the speech of the head of the Czechoslovak Social Democratic Party, Antonín Hampl, for March 8, 1938 (Soukup, *Revoluce práce*, I, 69–73).

This insistence on Prague as the main target of diplomatic activities set the basic pattern of Western diplomacy for the whole pre-Munich period. As a result it altered the European balance of power and hid the reality under a screen of self-deception. The protracted negotiations between the SdP and Prague, which were held during the whole summer of 1938, created a curious atmosphere of ambiguity which surrounded the war preparations of Hitler and concealed the decision of the SdP to cripple Czechoslovakia.

The SdP congress, which took place at Carlsbad on April 23–24, 1938, was awaited with impatience by public opinion in Czechoslovakia and the chancelleries of Europe. The main event was the speech of Henlein[40] on April 24. The Sudeten Führer walked into the city Kurhaussaal through lines of Schutzkorps, and was greeted by the Hitler salute and roars of "Heil."[41] After reviewing German-Czech relations, he announced eight demands as the basis for the national settlement: full equality with the Czech people; recognition of the German ethnic group as a legal personality; recognition of the German settlement area; complete self-government; legal protection for those Germans who lived outside the German area; removal of injustices inflicted upon the Germans since 1918; recognition of the principle, "German officials in German territory"; and recognition of complete liberty to profess the National Socialist ideology.[42] Henlein stressed that

> German National Socialism is a political philosophy which has not only led the German Reich to renewed strength, but has also penetrated and organized the whole life of the German nation. . . . In it the German finds his conception of life and of morality. . . . The Sudeten German community, as a part of the German people . . . could not and would not stand aloof from a philosophy which all Germans in the world today delight to profess. . . . Like Germans throughout the world, we profess the National Socialist fundamental conceptions of life, which correspond to our whole way of feeling and thinking, and in accordance with which we desire to shape the life of our national group.[43]

40. *We Want to Live As Free Men Among Free Men. Speech Delivered before the Annual Congress of the Sudeten German Party on April 24, 1938 at Karlsbad* (Carlsbad-Leipzig, 1938). Dr. Köllner indicated that the SdP had 769,717 members, or 25.8 percent of the German inhabitants of the Historic Provinces, at the end of March 1938 (*Der Lebenswille*, pp. 56–57). He also announced that although the Aryan paragraph was introduced in 1938, it had been effective prior to this date (*ibid.*, p. 60).

41. Deubner, pp. 90–92.

42. *DGFP*, II, 242–43.

43. *Documents 1938*, II, 137.

Eisenlohr rightly commended the speech as being clear and fundamental.[44] In view of the excited state of mind of his followers, Henlein
asked Prague for concessions which he knew were so far-reaching
that they could not be granted, but he did not drive things to the
limit, leaving the door open for further talks. The Czech press was
outspoken in its disapproval of Henlein's program, with the liberal
and moderate *Lidové noviny* declaring on April 27:

> Berlin talked frankly through the voice of Henlein. The demands
> were written in Berlin and were official in the full sense of the word.
> Henlein conferred with the head of the Nazi Party in Berlin and
> received clear instructions. . . .
>
> These demands represent neither the maximum nor the minimum
> program of the German minority, but simply the foreign policy
> program of the Third Reich.[45]

The official reaction was more cautious. Hodža reiterated to Basil
Newton his policy of "negotiations wherever and whenever possible,"
but he did not expect that there would be any hope for serious
discussions before the coming local elections.[46]

The celebrations of May 1 were held at a series of mass meetings
throughout the country. Wherever Sudeten Germans gathered, their
attitude appeared to be favorable to the Carlsbad program. Henlein's
open espousal of Nazi principles seemed to reflect the growing
pressure of the rank and file.[47] He proclaimed at Liberec:

> Our confession [to National Socialism] was our most intimate
> matter. I could not tolerate any longer concealing our opinion. We
> are Germans and therefore we declare our espousal of German, that
> is National Socialist, ideas.[48]

SdP Deputy Georg Wollner spoke on the same day at Cheb and
explained that Henlein could not have professed Nazi principles
earlier, for tactical reasons. But today he and his followers did not

---

44. *DGFP*, II, 241.
45. In Christian Sigl, *Quellen und Dokumente. Ein Tatsachenbericht über die
Lage im sudetendeutschen Gebiet und über die Entwicklung der tschechoslowakischen Innenpolitik*, p. 11. For other voices of the Czechoslovak press, see
Survey 1938, II, 97–98.
46. On April 26 (*DBFP*, I, 195–96).
47. The report of Consul Pares from Liberec (*DBFP*, II, 249–50). Pares stated
that the rank and file of the party seemed to know little about Nazi principles
and confounded them vaguely with "allegiance to Hitler and the Third Reich."
He noted the paradox that members of the KB, like Henlein, Sebekowsky, and
Sandner, professed Nazism while the followers of Spann in Austria were
persecuted by the Nazis.
48. Krofta, *Z dob*, pp. 271–72.

need to pursue a two-faced policy any longer because they enjoyed the protection of Hitler and 75 million Germans.[49]

Demonstrations of other political groups were held in almost all Czech cities. The British correspondent Gedye, who eloquently described the Nazi manifestation at Liberec, witnessed the meeting of the German Social Democrats, the same evening when Jaksch called for work and bread "to defend democracy . . . [to] help us to bombard the Henlein position with bread."[50] Czechs massed in their cities to voice their opposition to any appeasement of Nazism. Tension increased as the battle lines seemed to be drawn more sharply than ever before.

The perilous situation in Central Europe led to a meeting of the British and French premiers and foreign secretaries in London on April 28–29. The British evaluation of the political and military aspects of the issues was pessimistic. Hence it was essential that every effort be made to reach a satisfactory settlement. In view of the Carlsbad eight points, British Foreign Secretary Viscount Halifax considered the recent Czechoslovak proposal for a nationality statute as an inadequate basis for negotiation. The French cabinet was more optimistic, but finally agreed that both governments should undertake a démarche in Berlin to learn more about German views while urging Prague to grant further concessions.[51] On May 11, Sir Nevile Henderson, British ambassador to Berlin, informed Foreign Minister von Ribbentrop that London was undertaking "an energetic démarche in Prague" and had urged the Czechs "to go to the limit of concession." He asked Berlin to use its influence with Henlein "in the direction of moderation." Von Ribbentrop replied that it was up to Henlein, who acted independently, to settle the issue.[52]

Basil Newton explained the depressing British view of the whole situation to Dr. Krofta on May 7 and urged Prague to advance toward recognition of the Republic as a state of nationalities.[53] In his

---

49. Krofta, p. 272. Deputy Dr. T. Jilly declared in Mikulov on May 1: "During the last three years I suffered for not having been able to profess National Socialism" (Silvestr Nováček, *Mikulovsko a Pohořelicko od nástupu nacismu k osudnému Mnichovu*, p. 150. This is an interesting, although biased, regional study).
50. Gedye, p. 399; Sydney Morrell, *I Saw the Crucifixion*, p. 23.
51. *DBFP*, I, 198 ff.
52. *DGFP*, II, 269–73. It was easy for the SdP to drive a hard bargain when it knew the British policy line.
53. *DBFP*, I, 265–71. Newton also conferred with Hodža, who assured him that the cabinet would do everything in its power "to ensure appeasement so far as Czechoslovakian policy was concerned" (*ibid.*, pp. 282–83).

audience with President Beneš on May 17, Newton was assured that the government was "convinced of the necessity of coming to an agreement without delay." However, Beneš regarded some points of the Carlsbad speech as inadmissible, i.e., "the incorporation of Sudeten Germans as a legal body and legal establishment of German areas within the state." He added that the London view of the situation in Czechoslovakia "was so black that the conclusion might be drawn that the only thing was to accept German domination with as good a grace as possible."

Beneš talked with candor in exposing his foreign policy. "Czechoslovakia must either accept German domination or continue in intimate connection with Western Europe." Conceding that British interest in Czechoslovakia was very limited, Beneš "was satisfied that Great Britain was sufficiently realistic to know that if Germany dominated Central Europe, Great Britain herself would in due course be seriously and fundamentally menaced."[54] Beneš was unaware that London based its policy upon a quite different conception of European policy:[55] Long before Munich the British government had decided to abandon the Republic to prevent Hitler from starting an armed attack.

The SdP and Berlin rightly assumed London to be the most sensitive spot, and Henlein continued to make good use of his British connections. He kept in touch with Sir Robert Vansittart, and indicated his willingness to come to London. Chamberlain and Halifax welcomed his visit, and Vansittart arranged for Henlein to see some members of the House of Commons, Winston Churchill included.[56] On his way to London (May 12) Henlein visited von Ribbentrop and State Secretary Ernst von Weizsäcker in Berlin. They agreed that Henlein would deny in London that he was acting on instructions from Berlin. He would stress instead "the progressive disintegration of the Czech political structure" in order to discourage any intervention on behalf of Czechoslovakia. He would present the

54. *Ibid.*, pp. 307–309, 313–14.
55. Chamberlain thought a settlement with Mussolini and Hitler possible (Lord Strang, *Home and Abroad*, p. 124). Chamberlain noted privately on March 20, 1938: "Nothing that France or we could do could possibly save Czechoslovakia from being overrun by the Germans" (Keith Feiling, *The Life of Neville Chamberlain*, p. 347). At the time of the Newton démarche at Prague, the New York *Herald Tribune* (May 15) received a dispatch from its correspondent Driscoll, based upon his talk with Chamberlain, reporting that Chamberlain was ready to consider the separation of the Sudetenland from Czechoslovakia. The report stressed that "Czechoslovakia cannot survive in its present form, the British are convinced" (*Survey 1938*, II, 113–15).
56. *DBFP*, I, 630. Vansittart was in regular contact with Dr. Brand, liaison officer of SdP (*DGFP*, II, 256).

eight demands of Carlsbad as the basis for negotiations and explain that Czech procrastination in this matter would lead only to an appeal for the right of self-determination.[57]

In London Henlein declared to Winston Churchill and Sir Archibald Sinclair that he had never received any recommendations or orders from Berlin, and that he saw only three possibilities of settlement: (1) autonomy within the Republic; (2) a plebiscite that would probably lead to annexation; (3) war. His objective was to arrive at autonomy.[58] In his conversations Henlein still gave the impression of an honest man genuinely interested in a speedy settlement.[59]

On his return from London on May 14, Henlein visited Hitler at Berchtesgaden. He returned to Aš on May 15, but went back again to Germany on May 22 to have a fundamental conference with Hitler.[60] The British seemed unaware of these connections, and Viscount Halifax even worried that Henlein, on account of his "reasonableness," could get into troubles with Berlin and his supporters.[61]

The naïveté of the British leader contrasted sharply with the conviction of Prague. The Czechoslovak press, politicians, and diplomats were asking whether the SdP really desired the settlement or only made "pretense of negotiating" and kept "raising new demands so as to make an agreement impossible, and then call for help from the Reich," as Eisenlohr reported on May 13. He realized that the overwhelming majority of the Czechs deeply mistrusted the SdP: "It seems generally assumed that the Sudeten German Party only acts on instructions from the Reich Government and that every point in Henlein's Karlsbad speech has been dictated by Berlin."[62] It was not until much later that the British found that Henlein had engaged in "an elaborate scheme of pretense to deceive the outside world as to the true objectives of his party."[63]

57. *Ibid.*, pp. 273–74.
58. *DBFP*, I, 297. For a full record of the conversations, see *ibid.*, Appendix II, pp. 630 ff. See also Winston Churchill, *The Second World War. The Gathering Storm* (Boston, 1948), pp. 285–86.
59. Halifax to Newton, March 16 (*DBFP*, I, 297–98). Wheeler-Bennett (p. 53) noted that the blond, bespectacled Henlein made an excellent impression during his visit to England.
60. *DGFP*, II, 310; *Survey 1938*, 118.
61. *DBFP*, I, 299.
62. *DGFP*, II, 276–79.
63. Strang, p. 128. William Strang wound up his diplomatic career as permanent under-secretary of state in February 1949. In perusing the British Documents one realizes that the Foreign Office had at its disposal many data showing the real situation in Czechoslovakia. Its interpretation, however, indicated a spirit of appeasement.

Prague reacted favorably to the démarche of May 7 and advised its allies (May 14) that its policy was aimed at a "more perfect development of its system of nationalities in the broad framework provided by the constitution."[64] A renewal of talks with the SdP was announced on May 13,[65] and the draft of the nationalities statute submitted to London included the promise of a reform of the language law, provisions against denationalization, proportional employment by the state, allocation of a proportional share of the various budget items, and wider educational autonomy.[66] On May 20, however, the political committee of the SdP moved to break off the negotiations.[67]

With the Nazi absorption of Austria, the exalted mood of the German population rose. Young Germans in particular indulged in provocations of Czech citizens.[68] Eisenlohr reported that the Germans were intoxicated by the Anschluss, and "they will neither await nor accept any other form of political situation. . . . The overwhelming majority, in fact, almost the whole population, hopes for Anschluss . . . and expects it in the immediate future." The Czechoslovak police were ordered, however, "to overlook minor offenses" and to avoid any coercive measures.[69] On May 14 the formation of a Freiwilliger Schutzdienst (FS; Voluntary Defense Service) was announced by the SdP. The FS was a replica of the Nazi storm troops. Willy Brandner, its chief of staff, proclaimed:

> The FS is not a body of troops for parades, but a body of soldiers on duty at all times. It is their duty to defend the Führer. . . . The FS men recognize . . . only one line of action: that of the German Socialist and soldier of the people. We march together with the men of the FS until the victory of our national group for its rights and Lebensraum.[70]

64. DBFP, I, 292.
65. DGFP, II, 310.
66. DBFP, I, 192–94.
67. Ibid., p. 331.
68. Ibid., p. 276. Newton reported to Halifax (May 10) that the attitude of the Germans in the district of Mariánské Lázně was "distinctly provocative," as he had learned from a member of his staff. The young Germans "are marching about in uniforms and ostentatiously giving each other . . . the Hitler salute."
69. DGFP, II, 295.
70. Bílek, p. 138. The FS took a leading part in the armed attacks against the Czechoslovak administration on Sept. 12–15, 1938. It was disbanded on September 15 (ibid., pp. 137–39). It was a grave error on the part of the Prague cabinet to permit its formation. For more information on the FS, see Koutek, Nacistická pátá kolona, pp. 199–203.

Czech public opinion looked askance at what seemed to be the retreat of Prague before Nazism. The press of all parties called upon the cabinet to take stern measures, and the Czech people united in their hostility against the German Nazis. Several hundred well-known Czech intellectuals published a manifesto, *We Remain Faithful,* in which they emphasized that there was no place for defeatists in a country which had to be ruled only by democrats. They urged all the citizens of the state to safeguard "the traditions of freedom and democracy."[71]

This, then, was the situation when Czechoslovakia was suddenly faced with her first crucial test. From May 19, Prague had been receiving reports of German concentrations of troops near Czechoslovak frontiers in Saxony and Bavaria.[72] (The first report had come from the British in Berlin.) The Czechoslovak General Staff believed that the German movements formed part of a plan of provocation and intimidation.[73] Moreover, von Ribbentrop called the Czechoslovak minister in Berlin, Vojtěch Mastný, to the Foreign Office at 7:30 P.M. on May 20 and announced that Hitler could no longer tolerate any oppression of the Germans.[74] The Prague cabinet met on the evening of May 20, and upon the insistence of the chief of the General Staff decided that the minister of Defense should at once call up one class of reserves in addition to certain specialists, a total of 176,000 men.[75]

The reports of German troop concentrations proved to be false.[76] However, the partial mobilization, carried out smoothly and quickly, and enthusiastically backed by the Czech population, strengthened enormously the authority of the state in the German areas. Newton reported to Halifax that the radical German elements were unpleasantly surprised and Germans everywhere were impressed by Prague's determination and swiftness of action.[77] Near the German border all

---

71. *DBFP*, I, 309. The initiators of the manifesto played an outstanding role in the Czech resistance movement during World War II.
72. *DGFP*, II, 340.
73. *Německý imperialismus*, p. 303. *DBFP*, I, 317–27.
74. *Ibid.*, p. 332; *DGFP*, II, 298–99.
75. *DBFP*, I, 367, 389; *DGFP*, II, 340–41. For an interesting survey of Dr. Brand's activities in Paris and London during the May crisis, see his letter of June 21, 1958, in the archives of the Collegium Carolinum, deposit No. 203.
76. For the May 21 crisis, see Gerhard L. Weinberg, "The May Crisis, 1938," *The Journal of Modern History*, XXIX (September 1957), 213–25. Weinberg concluded that "reports of really routine German troop movements were mistaken as presaging an . . . attack on Czechoslovakia."
77. *DBFP*, I, 354. During the night of mobilization, two Germans on motorcycles did not obey warning calls of the police sentry at Cheb and were shot dead when

bridges and crossroads were guarded and a large number of road-blocks were set up. Frontier light fortifications were manned at full strength. The army controlled all the frontier districts where Czechs and Germans had become bitterly antagonistic.[78]

The May crisis focused world attention on the so-called Sudeten German question, and showed that the Republic was determined to defend its integrity. In reasserting its authority over all German areas and disciplining the German extremists by a show of force, Czechoslovakia gave warning to the SdP and curbed the German interventionists who defied her authority. More than that, however, it showed that by these lightning measures Czechoslovakia believed that the main danger consisted in a sudden attack of German troops. The Czechoslovak General Staff knew that German war preparations would be disguised under the cover of training exercises, and interpreted any such move as a potential threat to the vital interests of the Republic.[79]

The partial mobilization of Czechoslovakia presented a direct challenge to Hitler. His plan Green continued to be a directive for military action against Czechoslovakia,[80] but with the annexation of Austria it was necessary to revise the earlier version. The chief of Supreme Headquarters of the Wehrmacht, General Keitel, after conferring with Hitler on April 21, prepared a new version of the directive for operation Green[81] which he submitted to Hitler for approval on May 20.[82] The main idea was to launch a surprise attack against Czechoslovakia in cooperation with the Sudeten German population, following an incident which would be created by Germany.[83] Undoubtedly Henlein's visit to Hitler on May 22 was connected with the preparation of a final draft and with instructions for the Sudeten leader. It was assumed, however, that the military attack would not be launched in the immediate future.

the sentry fired to halt them. The incident was exaggerated, and Hitler sent two wreaths to be laid by the German military attaché on the tombs of the victims (ibid., pp. 359, 360–61).

78. See the report of the tour of the frontier zone by the British military attaché in Prague (ibid., pp. 432–33). Consul Pares noted "the intense national hatred" (ibid., p. 437).

79. According to the British military attaché in Prague, the Czechoslovak measures were inevitable (ibid., p. 411).

80. The original version of plan Green against Czechoslovakia was issued on June 24, 1937 (DGFP, II, 358).

81. Ibid., pp. 239.

82. Ibid., pp. 299–303.

83. The version of April 22, 1938, mentioned expressly as one possibility of an incident, "the murder of the German Minister in the course of an anti-German demonstration" (ibid., p. 239).

On May 28, Hitler held a conference with his military leaders[84] and the new strategic directive for case Green was issued on May 30, beginning with Hitler's statement: "It is my unalterable decision to smash Czechoslovakia by military action in the near future." Its execution had to be assured by Oct. 1, 1938.[85] It is not clear to what extent the Czech challenge provoked Hitler to a shift in date. However, Professor Weinberg's opinion that the May crisis seemed to reinforce Hitler's previous determination to crush Czechoslovakia appears to be the most judicious in the light of available evidence.

In view of Berlin's decision, the showdown could not be far away, for Hitler had virtually reached the point of no return. The outlook for the Republic appeared dim. On the one hand, heavy pressure from the West for a settlement which would establish a Nazi state within democratic Czechoslovakia was forcing the cabinet to give way to the pan-German elements whose final objectives were the advancement of Greater Germany; while on the other hand, Nazi support of the SdP made a reasonable solution futile. The granting of any concession to the SdP meant for all practical purposes the attainment of new advantages by Berlin and the weakening of the Czechoslovak state. At the same time, however, it strengthened the position of those circles in the West who advocated assistance to democratic Czechoslovakia.

With Henlein and Hitler working in close relationship, it was virtually impossible for Prague to achieve any kind of settlement. Faced with these dilemmas, Prague followed the delaying tactic of retreat, offering to the Germans, under heavy Western pressure, more and more far-reaching concessions in the hope that the West would finally realize that the real issue had little to do with the Czechoslovak Germans. It was a unique spectacle. *The democratic Powers were utilizing all available means to press their democratic ally to capitulate before the totalitarian Nazi dictatorship.*

The mistakes were not completely unilateral, however. The Czechoslovak system of government was also at fault. Its coalition party system, while truthfully representing the kaleidoscope of various opinions, was clumsy and slow at a time of crisis when only a quick decision and a clear plan might have carried the day. After May 21, Hubert Ripka correctly judged the moment ripe to issue wider proposals and to carry them out quickly, with or without an agreement with the SdP.[86] By taking the initiative and simultaneously

84. *IMT*, XXVIII, 373.
85. *DGFP*, II, 357–62.
86. Hubert Ripka, *Munich: Before and After*, p. 23. The book is still useful. Dr.

making clear that it would fight for the integrity of the country under any circumstances, the government could have achieved an indisputable momentum and made the task of both the SdP and the Western appeasers much more difficult. Even if it had not managed to maintain the momentum, the willingness to act and the resolution to *fight, even alone,* for the integrity of the Republic and its democratic liberties would not have left open any possibility for the type of surrender which occurred on September 21.

Municipal elections were held at the end of May and the beginning of June under the sobering effects of the Czechoslovak mobilization. Voting was orderly and brought a dramatic, clear-cut victory for the SdP. Even though the elections did not necessarily prove that all of the votes cast for Henlein were wedded to the Nazi ideology, the German voters supported all the anti-Czech, anti-Semite, and anti-democratic tenets of the SdP, which gained 1,279,045 or 91.4 percent of the German vote.[87] When one took into consideration the fact that the Communists received some German votes, the SdP still appeared to win over 85 percent of the German votes.[88] Since all aspects of Nazism were known, there had seemed to be some reason for hope that there would be a falling away of German support for Henlein and Hitler. The event proved otherwise. It presented a unique fact to Europe: *At a free and democratic election, more than 85 percent of the Germans from Czechoslovakia identified themselves with Nazi aims.*

It was reassuring to the democratic way of life to note that the moderate Czechoslovak coalition parties, firmly attached to a compromise settlement of the German question, gained a large proportion of the Czech and Slovak popular vote. The small Fascist Party remained without any influence whatsoever, and the Communists strongly combated Henlein. The returns had provided a test of the maturity of the Czechs and Germans, in that both nations reached unhampered the judgments that would affect their fates. A surging feeling of national pride had found two quite different responses. The Germans assumed that the fault lay with the Czechs. They showed no

---

Ripka was an eminent Czech journalist, historian, and, later, minister. He died in London in 1958. A leader of the Beneš Party, he was one of the ablest Czechoslovak politicians and an expert on foreign policy.

87. *Osteuropa* (July 1938), pp. 717–21, as cited in MacAlister Brown's "Expulsion of German Minorities from Eastern Europe: The Decision at Potsdam and Its Background," unpublished doctoral dissertation, Harvard University, 1953, p. 68. The thesis is substantial and well written.

88. According to Karlgren (p. 97), Henlein obtained 88 percent of the German votes on May 22 and 29, and 81 percent in June. German-speaking voters of the Communist Party were not included.

understanding of the small Czech nation living under the shadow of the German colossus. They embraced National Socialism with exaltation. On the other side, the Czechs showed confidence in the future of their democratic state. They were willing to create more equitable conditions for their German partner because they understood that a reasonable settlement was a matter of survival. Amid intense national passions, menaced in their very existence, they voted for moderate forces and the democratic system of government. Surely this was an astonishing response to the overawing character of Nazi power.[89]

The main interest of the Western Powers was to prevent the rise of any conditions which would involve them in war. London, seconded by Paris, urgently pressed Prague to open talks on the basis of the Carlsbad eight points. Henlein put forward more moderate propositions during his May visit to London. These were regarded as reasonable, in that he had refrained from demanding a change in Czechoslovak foreign policy and had not insisted upon compensations and the implementation of Nazi ideology.

On May 31 Halifax warned Prague again that its unwillingness to accept these proposals would "exercise an immediate and adverse effect upon the interest taken in the problem . . . and upon the sympathy felt for the Czechoslovak government."[90] He did not confess, of course, that some influential British circles desired to channel German expansion to Southeast Europe at the expense of Czechoslovakia.[91] At the same time, both Western Powers pressed the Republic to disband the reservists which it had called up in May. Prague remained firm, stating that it could not weaken the army and jeopardize its already grave situation while the German Army was maintained at full strength.[92] The internal situation in the German area also required the continued reassertion of the state's power,

89. Not a few prominent Germans recognized the Republic as the harbor of democracy. See Dr. Franz Spina in the *Deutsche Landpost* (Sept. 15, 1937) and Erwin Zajíček in the *Deutsche Presse* (Sept. 15, 1937).

90. *DBFP*, I, 418. On May 25, Halifax stated that Czechoslovakia should offer autonomy on the Swiss model and adopt a position of neutrality in external affairs (*ibid.*, pp. 378–79).

91. Sir Horace Wilson, Chamberlain's chief adviser, told German chargé d'affaires Theodor Kordt (Aug. 23, 1938) that "a constructive solution of the Czech question by peaceful means would leave the way clear for Germany to exercise large-scale policy in the Southeast" (*DGFP*, II, 608). Sir Robert Vansittart exchanged frequent messages with Henlein (*DBFP*, I, 416, 418).

92. *Ibid.*, pp. 462–63. For the British and French pressure to disband the reservists, see *ibid.*, pp. 441, 467. Czechoslovakia proposed to extend the period of military service from two to three years in order to increase her army "to [the] bare minimum required to ensure Czechoslovakia against surprise" (*ibid.*, p. 463).

because the SdP had abused the indulgence of the government prior to the May crisis and had boasted that Prague had lost its authority and could not guarantee internal order.[93]

The talks between the party and the cabinet were resumed on May 24, when Hodža met Henlein.[94] Deputy Ernst Kundt discussed the propositions of Henlein in detail on May 30.[95] Berlin did not allow itself to be drawn into the talks as an interested party and continued to maneuver skillfully through the SdP. The new, more serious, stage in Czech-German negotiations prompted Henlein to review his policy and to make necessary preparations for joint action with the VoMi. He conferred with Lorenz in Berlin on June 3, asking for instructions in case the Czechs should accede to his demands. Aware that Prague was serious in its willingness to settle the problem,[96] Henlein reaffirmed that if Prague yielded, he would ask for a change in Czechoslovak foreign policy, and "the Czechs would never accede to that." [97]

The VoMi appointed an Austrian, Dr. Kier, as legal adviser of the SdP for its talks with Prague,[98] and Deputy Kundt was designated by Henlein as head of a special negotiating delegation which received its instructions from the VoMi. Their tenor was to give the impression that the SdP was conducting the negotiations seriously.[99] Actually, it was so anxious to please its Nazi masters and approached Ribbentrop so frequently for further instructions, that even he was obliged to complain on August 18 that "Henlein had already received clear instructions and therefore it was not fitting that one gentleman or another kept appearing from Prague at short intervals to obtain decisions on individual questions. Henlein and his people must learn to stand on their own feet. The answer . . . was contained in the general instruction given to Henlein, namely, always to negotiate and not to let the link be broken, on the other hand always to demand more than could be granted by the other side."[100]

93. *Ibid.*, p. 441.
94. *DGFP*, II, 353.
95. *DBFP*, I, 418.
96. *DGFP*, II, 403.
97. *Ibid.*, p. 384.
98. *Ibid.*, p. 556. Dr. Kier was a former Austrian Nazi lawyer employed at the Berlin Institute of Public and International Law (*ibid.*, p. 487).
99. *Ibid.*, pp. 562–63.
100. *Ibid.*, p. 587. The expenditures of the office of the party's representative in Berlin rose sharply due to the financing of journeys by Sudeten German deputies and agents to London, Paris, and Prague and to other propaganda activities. Consequently the Foreign Office increased its monthly subsidies from 3,000 RM to 5,500 RM (*ibid.*, pp. 594–95).

There is no need to discuss at length the development of the talks between Prague and the SdP.[101] They followed the pattern set by Berlin. The Germans always proposed more than Prague could accept, while the British used relentless pressure, threatening the Czechs with their désintéressement, in case Czechoslovakia did not yield. Thus, Prague found itself always giving way and always going further toward meeting the German demands. The SdP blindly followed the instructions of Berlin, while pretending that it sincerely aimed at a real settlement; and Berlin quickened its preparations for the invasion of Czechoslovakia. London continued its fateful policy line, never exerting any pressure whatsoever upon the SdP but forcing Prague to accept Henlein's measures.

Prague perceived the cynical play of Henlein and Hitler, and from the outset suspected that the Sudeten question was simply a Nazi device to pierce the Western alliance and to destroy its Eastern barrier.[102] Alas, with the exception of the Soviet Union, it stood alone in its opinion.[103] The Czechs hoped that during the negotiations the

101. Celovsky correctly points out that the negotiations between the SdP and the government were of importance only insofar as they made clear "die Bedenkenlosigkeit Henleins und seiner Freunde und Grad der Bereitschaft Prags" (Das Münchener Abkommen, p. 252).

102. Lord Strang belatedly called the program of autonomy of the SdP and the ensuing negotiations "a cynical farce and a highly successful one" on the German side. "Henlein threw off his mask in the first half of September 1938" (op. cit., p. 129).

103. The policy of the Soviet Union in the pre-Munich crisis was faithful to its engagements. The Soviet Union considered the Sudeten question to be the domestic concern of Czechoslovakia (DGFP, II, 604). In the middle of April, the Czechoslovak minister in Moscow, Zdeněk Fierlinger, urged that conversations be initiated for increased military assistance. Prague refused to enter into any direct Soviet-Czechoslovak military consultation out of fear that Paris would become suspicious. Krofta replied to Fierlinger on April 21, 1938: "In the relations among Paris-Prague-Moscow, there has always been the principle that Prague did not take any initiative and by itself would not discuss any military matters." On April 24, Fierlinger cabled Krofta that the situation was being discussed in the Kremlin by Stalin, Molotov, Voroshilov, Litvinov, and Kaganovich. It was decided that "the USSR, when asked, would be willing to take all steps pertaining to the security of Czechoslovakia in agreement with France and Czechoslovakia." At the beginning of September 1938, the Kremlin reportedly discussed the possibility of action without the participation of France (Zdeněk Tomeš as quoted in Soják, ed., pp. 336–37, 360). Klement Gottwald stated that Stalin told him expressly (in May) "that the USSR was prepared to give military assistance even if France could not do so, although this was a condition upon which Soviet assistance was made dependent: the support would have been given even in the case Poland and Rumania had refused the Soviet Army permission to pass through their territories. Stalin emphasized, indeed, that one condition would have to be fulfilled: namely that Czechoslovakia would defend herself and would ask for Soviet assistance. . . . Stalin entrusted me to inform President Beneš about this. This is what I did. Later on, the official Soviet

Germans would come out into the open with demands which would appear so preposterous that the West would be obliged to take a stand on Prague's side.[104] Prague did not know or appeared not to realize that already, during May and June, Chamberlain and Halifax had come to a decision to write off the Republic within its present borders.[105] The Munich solution was not a sudden decision, but rather the final link of a policy of accommodation and appeasement of Berlin and isolation of Soviet Russia (which was regarded as the chief potential peril).

Discussions between the SdP and Prague were carried out on the basis of the new Czechoslovak draft of the language and nationality bills, which had been handed to the SdP on July 28, and of the German memorandum presented to the cabinet on June 8.[106] The memorandum was based on the eight Carlsbad points which split the state into separate national units, rendering it virtually powerless. The Czechoslovak bills, on the other hand, sought to maintain it as a single unit with wide regional decentralization.[107] Prague was ready "to go to the extreme limit," so far as it was possible, to reconcile the democratic system with the Nazi doctrine.[108] The cabinet wished to

---

representative informed the Czechoslovak Cabinet about it" (*Pravda*, Moscow, Dec. 28, 1949, as cited in M. Gus, *Američtí imperialisté—inspirátoři mnichovské politiky*, p. 68). President Beneš stated the readiness of the USSR to come to his assistance alone, without France (*Mnichovské dny*, pp. 87–88). For the problem of Soviet assistance, see also F. Vnuk, "Munich and the Soviet Union," *Journal of Central European Affairs*, XXI (October 1961), 285–304; Otakar Odložilík, "Edvard Beneš on Munich Days," *Journal of Central European Affairs*, XVI (January 1957), 384–93; Max Beloff, *The Foreign Policy of Soviet Russia 1929–1941*, II, 151–66. Beloff's evidence is, however, contradictory. For the Communist side, see J. S. Hájek, *Mnichov*, pp. 105–106, 109, 126, 129; Čestmír Amort, "Die Sowjetunion und die Verteidigung der Tschechoslowakei gegen die faschistische Aggression im Jahre 1938," *Zeitschrift für Geschichtswissenschaft*, IX (1961), 1055–71.

104. *Survey 1938*, II, 181. Dr. K. Kříž wrote in *Právo lidu* (May 15, 1938) that the democratic world supported Czechoslovakia because of its own interests.

105. Also see Celovsky, p. 269; *Survey 1938*, II, 113–15; and *DBFP*, I, 403–12.

106. For the text of the SdP memorandum containing the "fourteen points," see *Documents 1938*, II, 151–62. For the Czechoslovak bills, see *Survey 1938*, II, 206–208.

107. For the Czechoslovak objections to the memo of June 7, see *DBFP*, I, 511. Newton himself stated that the Germans wished "to split [the state] up into separate units under cover of which they would be able to manage their own affairs on National Socialist lines."

108. For the Prague speech of Beneš on June 30, see *Documents 1938*, II, 164. K. H. Frank declared to British observers on July 9: "The official German view of the National Socialist world outlook today should be taught in the schools. . . . The personality of Herr Hitler should be permitted to be brought home to Sudeten Germans by pictures and other means and the Nazi flag be allowed to be flown" (*DBFP*, I, 555–56, 566, 572).

reach a compromise with the SdP, while mindful that it had to deal with a public opinion almost unanimously hostile to the granting of any wide concession.[109] The draft bills proposed to strengthen the provincial Diets and divide them into national curiae, and to enlarge the existing rights of nationalities; in effect, they presented generous concessions but still maintained the idea of a unified state. The bills were rejected by the SdP.

The existing gap between the sides brought a London decision that Prague must accept a British mediator.[110] Beneš protested that such a proposal seriously affected the sovereignty of the state "in a matter in which the Government . . . were going already to the utmost limits possible."[111] However, harassed by London, on whose attitude French policy depended, the Czechoslovak cabinet was forced to accept what was little less than an ultimatum.[112]

Shortly before the arrival of the British mediator, some 40,000 Sudeten Germans, together with the entire leadership of the SdP, participated in a national gymnastic festival at Breslau. On this occasion Henlein and Frank were received by Hitler (July 31), who discussed the situation in Czechoslovakia.[113] In Breslau Henlein made a violent pan-German address on July 29.

It is our firm conviction that Germany is singled out by history to institute that new justice among nations. . . . For this great spiritual unity we Germans have to thank one single man—Adolf Hitler. . . . Speaking for the largest German national group in Europe I can say . . . that we are all inseparable constituents of the great German people.[114]

Against this background it was difficult to expect that the presence of Lord Walter Runciman, the mediator,[115] would result in constructive developments or in an increase of goodwill between the two parties. Czech public opinion was unaware of the background and implications of the Runciman mission. Even prominent politicians

109. Oskar Ullrich (*Der grosse Irrweg der Tschechen*, p. 52) presented many extracts from the Czech press characteristic of the Czech attitude.
110. *DBFP*, I, 566, 572, 582. The British suggestion of a British mediator was conveyed to Beneš on July 20. Newton reported that Beneš was upset (*ibid.*, p. 600).
111. *Ibid.*
112. On July 23, 1938 (*DBFP*, I, 620). For the Runciman mission, see Robert Kvaček, *Osudná mise.*
113. *K. H. Frank*, p. 178; Celovsky, p. 288.
114. *Documents 1938*, II, 173.
115. Lord Runciman arrived in Prague on Aug. 3, 1938, with four members of his mission. F. Ashton-Gwatkin was his chief aide (*Survey 1938*, II, 211–12).

trusted the system of alliances which Prague had negotiated.[116] The Czech people were prepared to fight for their independence,[117] believing in the justice of their cause;[118] the government was, however, on the defensive. It proposed an enlargement of its own terms, which the SdP rejected on August 17.[119] The following day Henlein met Lord Runciman for the first time.

Runciman and the members of his mission were sympathetic to the German cause and friendly toward Nazi Germany.[120] They were also convinced of the honesty and integrity of Henlein,[121] to whom they

116. Ullrich (p. 107) rightly stated: "Der kleine Tscheche immer noch fest an die unwandelbare Bundestreue der Frankreich, England und Sowjetunion glaubte, als für die übrige Welt bereits die Situation klar war." Even Foreign Minister Krofta noted in his dispatch to the Moscow legation on August 13 that his first impression of the mission was good. "We are not afraid that [France and England] would deliver us to the tender mercies of Germany" (Zdeněk Fierlinger, *Ve službách ČSR: Paměti z druhého zahraničního odboje*, I, 122). The book contains very useful source material on Czechoslovak diplomacy in 1938–45. The second volume surveys the post-Munich period. Although valuable, it has to be read with caution, as it is biased.

117. Runciman stated to Halifax (August 10) that Prague displayed no signs of fear or nervousness: "the fabric here is of sterner stuff than was set up in Austria" (*DBFP*, II, 74). The British military attaché at Prague noted on August 22 that "the Czechoslovak General Staff had prepared the Army and the country for war in an almost masterly fashion. . . . Every civilian man and woman was ready to fight somehow" (*ibid.*, p. 147). He praised the morale of the army and nation. "They would fight for their very existence and for the maintenance of independence" (*ibid.*, p. 259). See also the manifesto by the Czechoslovak Officers Association (August 12), declaring, "We can die but we can give way no more. Not one step, not one foot" (*ibid.*, p. 81).

118. There was a close relationship between the democratic Germans and Czechs amid the nationalist frenzy. Hugh Seton-Watson described a joint meeting of the Czech and German Social Democrats in Pilsen. "The streets were lined on both sides with cheering crowds, . . . not party members but simple Czech citizens who shouted 'Long live our German friends.' And the Germans answered 'Long live the Czechoslovak Republic'. . . . Terrorized by Henlein's gangs for months past, these Germans enjoyed for a day the strange experience of being greeted as friends—by Czechs" (*Eastern Europe Between the Wars 1918–1941*, pp. 287–88).

119. After the Nationalities Statute—Plan No. 1—this enlargement was called Plan No. 2. It remained unpublished at the time.

120. *DGFP*, II, 592–93, 616. The correspondence of the British mission contains the most revealing evidence. For example, Ashton-Gwatkin wrote to W. Strang, on August 23: "We went to the Reichenberg Trade Fair. . . . The population lined the street and we were received with Nazi salutations and Heils and Sieg Heils. As I told Henlein next day, I had never felt so like Henlein before. . . . I like him [Henlein]. He is, I am sure, an absolutely honest fellow" (*DBFP*, II, 664).

121. In 1952, Mr. Ashton-Gwatkin commented in a letter to Sir Lewis Namier: "I believed that Henlein was genuine in his protestations that he was a man of peace. . . . He was a good-looking chap . . . not much education, but a copious flow of flatulent oratory, no political gifts or experience, but chosen as a figurehead by the Sudeten Party and those great landowners who hated the Czechs and feared 'bolshevism.' . . . The whole idea of the Runciman Mission was based on the assumption that freedom of negotiations between Czechs and

expressed their favorable views of Germany. The SdP and Hitler found them important indices of the British attitude.[122] Reports on the British views were sent to Hitler and, according to K. H. Frank, they "presented one of the most valuable political services rendered to the German Reich. They provided Hitler with invaluable information, indispensable for the carrying out of his international policy; he arrived at the conferences with the British with a strong card in his hand."[123]

As the reforms proposed by the Czechs were unlikely to satisfy the SdP, Lord Runciman sought to induce Prague to assent to the eight Carlsbad points, feeling that nothing short of this demand would be accepted by Henlein. Prague—in reality Beneš,[124] who had taken the leading part on the Czech side—produced on August 26 the so-called Third Plan envisaging the division of the state into 20 or more cantons. Since several cantons would contain predominantly German areas, the Germans were offered wide political autonomy. Furthermore, Prague promised to float a loan to assist distressed German areas.[125] The plan presented a great advance over previous governmental proposals, but there were no signs that the SdP would accept it, though even to the radical Frank it seemed to be "comparatively far-reaching."[126] In effect, the plan was rejected.[127]

The Sudeten tactics in dealing with Lord Runciman consisted in impressing on him the fact that the solution of the Czech-German problem was impossible within the present framework of Czechoslovakia; the Czechs were solely to be blamed as "the real disturbers of peace in Europe."[128] In the meantime, Berlin prepared for war.

Sudetens was possible." It appears that Ashton-Gwatkin had learned quite a lot in the meantime (Sir Lewis Namier, *In the Nazi Era*, p. 143).
122. Only a close circle within the SdP achieved direct contact with the Reich authorities. Frank paid visits to Hitler at the end of August (*DBFP*, II, 177). Henlein kept a direct line of communication to Hitler (*DGFP*, II, 616). Members on the negotiating delegation had an indirect contact with Henlein through Frank, who seemed to be the only one who knew Henlein's whereabouts (*ibid.*, pp. 556, 562). It might also be that Henlein cleverly left Kundt in the dark about the timetable of his course of action to make sure that Kundt would negotiate bona fide (Celovsky, *Abkommen*, p. 289). There is evidence, however, that the negotiating delegation was instructed by the VoMi to give an impression of being sincere (*DGFP*, II, 562). Frank also maintained contacts with Admiral Canaris, the chief of the Abwehr (*ibid.*, p. 577).
123. Wheeler-Bennett, *Munich*, p. 87.
124. *DGFP*, II, 633–47.
125. Vincent Urban, pp. 77–78, contains the text, which was unpublished at the time. See also *Survey 1938*, pp. 221 ff.
126. *DGFP*, II, 661.
127. On September 2 (Celovsky, *Abkommen*, p. 293).
128. *Ibid.*, p. 578. This was stated by Frank as the slogan of the delegation at the first preliminary discussion with the Runciman mission.

Unhampered by German sabotage of the talks, Halifax was encouraged to use Henlein as his messenger to Hitler to obtain approval for the continuation of negotiations.[129] Pretending to favor a peaceful settlement on the basis of autonomy, Henlein in reality was instructed by Hitler (whom he met on September 2) to continue the talks until further orders. Hitler assured the Sudeten leader that he would solve the problem himself, because he was now certain that Great Britain would agree to a settlement on his own terms.[130] On September 1, Lord Runciman informed Beneš that "he doubted whether anything less than the substance of [the] Karlsbad points would suffice to reach a settlement."[131]

The next day, the president received SdP leaders Kundt and Sebekowsky and held a fateful discussion with them lasting from 10:30 A.M. to 2:30 P.M.,[132] during which he offered to implement the principles of the so-called Fourth Plan. During the talks, Kundt pointed out that the Czechs did not seem to realize what had happened in Germany; that they were missing the real meaning of the epoch-making German National Socialist revolution. They evidently did not want to see that the Sudeten Germans could not but identify themselves with developments in the Reich. President Beneš gave a frank answer.

I, myself, and the great majority of our nation, are democrats and we will never accept Nazism and totalitarian doctrines. We see and comprehend only too well what is in the offing for Germany which is going through a terrible disease. Nazism is poison and doom. It

129. DBFP, II, 154, 177, 199–200, 231. The idea of using Henlein as a messenger of Lord Runciman to Hitler was rightly cited by Celovsky as a clear example of naïve and incompetent British diplomacy (Abkommen, p. 292).
130. K. H. Frank, p. 42. For the official communiqué from Berlin, see Documents 1938, II, 177.
131. DBFP, II, 207.
132. Prager Presse, Sept. 3, 1938. Mnichov v dokumentech (II, 413) puts the date at September 5. Wheeler-Bennett (Munich, p. 90) included a description of the discussion from the interview of G. E. R. Gedye with Beneš (published in the Daily Herald, London, Oct. 8, 1945). The date used—September 4—seems to be a mistake. According to Gedye, Beneš pushed "a blank sheet of paper toward Kundt and Sebekowsky. 'Please write your Party's full demands for the German minority. I promise you in advance to grant them immediately.' Kundt stared incredulously at Beneš. Sebekowsky sat in angry silence. 'Go on, I mean it. Write.' The Sudeten leaders, fearing a trap, were reluctant to commit themselves. 'Very well, if you won't write it down, I will,' said the President. 'You tell me what to say,' and he sat waiting." Beneš wrote down the principles of the Fourth Plan at their dictation. Jaksch (Europas Weg, pp. 308–309) calls the discussion a fabricated legend without giving cogent reasons. The same opinion is defended by Rönnefarth (Sudetenkrise, I, 479–80). The elaboration of the plan obviously took some time and Beneš did not pretend that the entire plan was prepared on September 2.

cannot end in Germany but by a great revolution inside or a terrific and catastrophic war. It will be a war of life and death . . . and its first victims will be our Germans. . . . They will then see what fate they have prepared for themselves through their own actions.[133]

The Fourth Plan, drafted under the personal supervision of President Beneš, was submitted to the SdP on September 7.[134] It applied the Carlsbad demands almost in their entirety.[135] Beneš made clear to Lord Runciman, in a special note accompanying his plan, that the application of the eight points "appeared to be utterly absurd, for it would establish for one section of the population a Totalitarian State within the democratic Czechoslovak Republic."[136] Prague—suspecting the real intentions of the SdP—expected that even this plan would be rejected and the real purpose of German actions would be revealed finally to the Western governments.[137]

The SdP was placed in an awkward position. In its view, the plan's proposals covered the most important principles of the eight points.[138] Deputy Kundt stated frankly that if the agreements based on the new plan were implemented, "the Germans will acquire such a position within the Bohemian-Moravian area, in conjunction with the encircling of this area by the Greater German Reich and full cooperation between Sudeten German and Reich German forces made possible" by such an agreement, that Czechoslovakia would come "not only to economic and intellectual, but also diplomatic and military subjection." Czechoslovakia would, indeed, become impotent.[139]

133. The address of Beneš on June 10, 1945 ([Czechoslovak] Ministry of Information, Lidická tryzna (Prague, 1945), pp. 20–21).
134. DGFP, II, 711. The government agreed to the plan on September 5. As England openly pressed for the acceptance of the plan, one wonders why Beneš did not make his agreement contingent on a British guarantee of Czechoslovak independence. British refusal would have made it harder for London to continue pushing Beneš.
135. The plan was prepared under formidable pressures from London and Paris. Newton declared to Beneš on September 4 that even if the outcome of the war were favorable "it was more than doubtful that Czechoslovakia would be reestablished in its present form or in such a readjusted form as may now be essential to avert war" (DBFP, II, 226–27). This kind of threat and blackmail was used freely by London from the spring of 1938 on.
136. The Czechoslovak government sent the text of the Fourth Plan to the Royal Institute of International Affairs in 1942. In an accompanying letter it commented upon the plan. This comment included the quotation from Beneš' note to Runciman (Documents 1938, II, 178).
137. Ibid.
138. DGFP, II, 711, 715, 719. Survey 1938 (II, 240–45) makes a comparison between the plan and the Carlsbad points. The Fourth Plan promised the establishment of large German cantons, proportional representation and compensation, and practically provided for German territorial autonomy.
139. DGFP, II, 716.

By accepting a valid agreement, the Bohemia-Moravia-Silesia area would either come unobtrusively under the exclusive influence of the Reich, or on the sudden violation of this agreement by the Czechs, there would remain the possibility of a solution by other means.[140]

Dr. Kier preferred acceptance to rejection, "since by skillful carrying out of this policy by the Sudeten German Party . . . the power of the State can be completely undermined from within."[141] Thus, the Sudeten Germans themselves gave evidence of their real aims, which were to destroy the Republic, and of the very nature of the Carlsbad points, which were completely misunderstood—with a great deal of willful intention—by the Western Powers. *The Sudeten German problem was not a cause of the conflict but its pretext.* The true reason, according to the Germans themselves, was the refusal of the Czechoslovak state to become a German vassal.

Hitler, Henlein, and Frank still desired more than the Czechs were willing to offer. They also had misgivings about Prague, which was suspected of seeking means to evade implementation of the plan.[142] As a result, the SdP created an incident at Moravská Ostrava on September 7, by staging a demonstration in which it protested that its deputy, Fritz May, was struck by a policeman.[143] Henlein used the incident as a pretext to break off negotiations with Prague,[144] obviously in order to await the results of Hitler's speech at the party congress at Nuremberg on September 12. The cabinet agreed even to the SdP's stiff terms and suspended the police officials at Moravská Ostrava, dismissed one policeman, and allowed the police president to resign. Kundt and Hodža agreed to resume negotiations on the day following Hitler's address.[145]

On Saturday evening, September 10, President Beneš made an address to the country, stating that the Republic was changing the speed, but not the spirit, of the course by which it strove to solve the problem of nationalities. If this problem were settled, then the state

140. *Ibid.*, p. 717.
141. *Ibid.*, p. 718. See also *DBFP*, II, 273.
142. This was feared by Kundt (*DGFP*, II, 715).
143. *DBFP*, II, 265. The British carefully investigated the incident and found that it was "deliberately staged by the Sudeten representatives." For the incident, see *Survey 1938*, II, 253; Rönnefarth, I, 485–86.
144. On September 7, the leading article in the *Times* suggested that Czechoslovakia might consider the cession of her territory. For the story of the article, see *The History of the Times. The 150th Anniversary and Beyond 1912–1948*, IV, 752–59.
145. *Survey 1938*, II, 257.

"will be one of the most beautiful, best administered, richest, and most equitable countries in the world."[146] On the eve of Hitler's address, tension increased and the German mobs sang Nazi songs and demanded a return to the Reich. The police exercised the "greatest restraint," according to the report of the German legation at Prague,[147] which obviously failed to state that (at the end of August) the leadership of the SdP had already issued instructions to stage these demonstrations and incidents.[148]

At the beginning of September, members of the SdP were briefed on the revolt planned for September 13–16. They were instructed that postoffices were to be seized first, then, in succession, the railway stations were to be occupied, next the gendarmerie stations and the state police stations, and, finally, the customshouses.[149] Hitler's speech served as the signal for the carefully prepared revolt.[150] In the evening, the German masses listened to Hitler, who called for a cessation of the oppression of the Germans in Czechoslovakia and for

146. See the extracts of the speech in Vincent Urban (pp. 83–86). The same day Marshal Göring called the Czechs "absurd pygmies" (*ibid.*, p. 86). On September 15 Beneš sent Minister Nečas to Paris with a secret suggestion that Prague might be willing to consider a cession of a small territory in return for the transfer of 1.5 to 2 million Germans to the Reich (Jan Pachta, Pavel Reiman, "O nových dokumentech k otázce Mnichova," *Příspěvky k dějinám KSČ,* I [No. 1, 1957], 104–33).

147. *DGFP*, II, 741–42. Bílek (pp. 220–21) published a report by a nonactive Czech politician on the situation in the German area. He found there "a kind of fanaticism, whipped up to a hysterical degree." He witnessed German women falling on their knees and raising clasped hands toward Henlein, calling out "The day will come." He pointed out that almost all German schoolmasters and teachers and about two thirds of the priesthood belonged to the most active Henleinist agitators.

148. Whenever a reliable member of the SdP feared his arrest, he could easily escape to the Reich. The local party headquarters provided him with a special stamp on his party card, which served in place of a passport (Bílek, p. 119).

149. *Ibid.*, p. 140.

150. The German Army recruited its German agents in Czechoslovakia. For details on the preparations and activities of the Abwehr in Czechoslovakia, see De Jong, pp. 286–87; Bílek, pp. 10–11, 104–108. The German refugees from Czechoslovakia and some German citizens of the Republic living in the Reich were organized in Germany as the Sudeten Legion and the Sudeten Freikorps (*ibid.*, pp. 92–100).

On August 18, 1938, the headquarters of the FS (stormtroopers of the SdP) issued the following directions: ". . . (b) everything necessary for the rebellion should be secured from the appropriate district leader. . . . The agreed objects should be fetched only by persons who have sworn a special oath and should always be stored at places close to the Reich German frontier. The German frontier guard should be informed . . . ; (g) the starting point for rebellion will be announced three times . . . ; (i) Members of the FS should immediately occupy the prescribed points in the greatest possible order" (*ibid.*, p. 116).

the application of the right of self-determination. The vitriolic tone of his address aroused the assembled storm troopers and the masses of Sudeten Germans, who poured into hundreds of villages and cities and attacked customshouses, gendarmerie posts, and railway stations. They smashed the windows of the Jewish and Czech shops, assaulted the German democrats, and shot policemen. Swastika banners were hoisted. The drama unfolded toward a still unpredictable dénouement. The German masses were rebelling, both physically and spiritually. Crowds marched in the streets singing and shouting. The next day, the Czech police and army struck back and quickly restored order, almost without shooting.[151] The government imposed martial law on several German districts on September 13, and extended it on September 14 and 15.[152]

On September 13 the SdP handed Prague a six-hour ultimatum demanding the withdrawal of the state police, repeal of martial law, confinement of the military to barracks, transfer of control of the security forces to municipal authorities, and an announcement of these measures over the radio.[153] Hodža promised to comply with all the demands, provided the SdP leaders came to Prague to discuss the maintenance of public order.[154] In reply Henlein, upon his return from Nuremberg where he had conferred with Hitler,[155] relieved the SdP negotiators in Prague of their functions, marking a bitter end of the Czech-German dialogue. Henlein then left for Germany to direct the action against Czechoslovakia, and on September 15 proclaimed through the German news bureau:

> We wish to live as free Germans! We want peace and work again in our homeland! We want to return to the Reich![156]

151. Gedye (p. 431) witnessed the disturbances and the restoration of order. "The main streets of Karlsbad were a wreckage of broken glass and shattered plate-glass windows and the German mob was in control of the town. Then a car with Czech gendarmerie . . . drove onto the square at Karlsbad and the men began slowly to get out. Before half a dozen were on the pavement and had quietly lit up their cigarettes, there was not a Henlein hero, not a Swastika within sight." There were 11 deaths during the demonstrations of September 12–13 (DBFP, II, 316). For the uprising, see also Henderson, pp. 179–85.
152. Documents 1938, II, 198. During the period of martial law, no one was executed. Martial law was applied to only 16 German districts (Survey 1938, II, 315). The SdP headquarters at Cheb was captured on September 14. Two armored cars had to intervene and six people were killed by German machine-gun fire (Bílek, p. 54). The most violent riots occurred in the districts of Cheb and Krumlov.
153. DGFP, II, 751–52.
154. DBFP, II, 313.
155. On September 13 (Survey 1938, II, 261). Henlein flew to the Reich on September 6 and returned with Hitler's instructions the next day, when the Ostrava incident occurred (Wheeler-Bennett, p. 92).
156. DGFP, II, 802.

Two days later, he issued a call to arms against "the Hussite-Bolshevik criminals of Prague."[157] Overt insurrection failed, however, and the balance of forces tilted toward Prague. The executive committee of the SdP fled across the border, and other leading party officials either were arrested or went into hiding.[158] The leaderless German population became a prey to depression.[159] The Czechoslovak authorities were now masters of the situation. Anxious members of the SdP quickly professed their loyalty toward the state.

On September 16 the SdP was dissolved, and the following day the government introduced a state of emergency. The Reich authorities in Czechoslovakia were deeply concerned over the situation in the predominantly German areas. With defections within the SdP ranks, there was growing danger that the Czechs would succeed in splitting the German nationalist camp. A new national council of Sudeten Germans, composed of members of the German political parties, issued a manifesto welcoming the Fourth Plan.[160] A hard core of German democratic forces was formed by the German Social Democrats, who fought courageously on the side of the Czechs against the Nazis in special defense units. Their heroic defense of democracy conveyed a picture of brave men who, in a time of crisis, rose above their own nationality to defend human freedom.

In the meantime Henlein and his aides, bent upon union with the Reich, prepared the foundation of paramilitary units. On September 15 Henlein proposed to Hitler, as a preliminary to a conference with Chamberlain, that he ask for "immediate cession of regions having more than 50 percent of Germans in their population and their occupation by Germans within 24 hours."[161] On September 17 Henlein

---

157. *Documents 1938,* II, 208.
158. *DGFP,* II, 822.
159. *Ibid.,* pp. 824, 826, 828.
160. Joan and Jonathan Griffin, *Lost Liberty,* pp. 42–46. The guiding spirit was Jaksch.
161. *DGFP,* II, 801. The SdP held that the census of 1910 should serve as a basis for any plebiscite. Only those who were born in this area before 1918 should be entitled to vote. The Sudeten police should be entrusted with the maintenance of public order (*ibid.,* pp. 824–44). On September 17, Henlein sent deputies Dr. Rudolf Schicketanz and Wolfgang Richter to Berlin to elaborate plans for the cession of the Sudeten territory. One believed that the plebiscite should follow the cession of certain designated zones. The SdP even entrusted Erwin Winkler with the preparation of a map outlining Sudeten demands, which was dispatched to Hitler at Berchtesgaden by a special airplane about September 19. The map served Hitler as a basis for his conversations with Chamberlain at Godesberg and for his demand of the so-called Godesberg line (National Archives of the United States, Records of the German Foreign Ministry, *Captured German Documents* [Container 2443, frames E, 239, 927]; the memorandum of Altenburg, Oct. 17, 1938). In a special memorandum submitted

formed the Sudeten German Freikorps (FK) from his cadres, subordinated directly to Hitler and undertaking terroristic raids from Reich territory.[162] Its strength increased, finally amounting to some 34,000 men. The attacks, raids, shootings, and killings continued at the German-Czechoslovak border until October 1.[163] On September 22 the FK occupied the salient of Aš, from which the Czechoslovak military personnel had been withdrawn. Following Hitler's instructions, the SS troops then marched into the city of Aš.[164]

With the flight of Henlein and his lieutenants, further decision was left to Hitler, who until now had directed the course of events from behind the scenes. His inflammatory speech, coupled with violent press and radio campaigns and the open revolt of the SdP, gave the needed impetus to the manipulation of European diplomatic machinery; the first fruit of German policy had ripened. At once, the British Prime Minister, Sir Neville Chamberlain, decided to discuss the deterioration in European relations with Hitler personally. Chamberlain's subsequent trip to Berchtesgaden (September 15) and the succeed-

to Hitler before September 19, the SdP suggested that the remaining Czech rump state be tied to the Reich by an economic and customs union and "be subject to German military supremacy" (*DGFP*, II, 845). This was only one of the many SdP propositions and plans.

162. *IMT*, XXV, 482, 486–87, 490–91, 496. The Freikorps (FK) was under the direct orders of Hitler, subordinated to the army, and assisted by the SA. Chief of Staff of the SA Schepmann swore in the leaders of the FK in Dresden on September 24. On September 30 it was subordinated to the SS. (See also *IMT*, XXVIII, 381–82.) The real head of the FK was Chief of Staff Senator Anton Pfrogner. Each group of the FK had a special Meldekopf which received reports from underground Green cadres on Czechoslovak territory.
Director Otto Hermann was instructed to remain in Prague to collect intelligence reports, which were transmitted through the German legation (*Zpověď*, p. 45).

163. *IMT*, XXXVI, 356–364. Doc. 366-EC. The document contains a very informative report by Lt. Colonel Köchling, the liaison officer of the OKW at the FK. The delegates of the SA and SS, Max Jüttner and Gottlob Berger, had sharp differences over the question of control over the FK. The activities of the FK were stopped on October 1. The 33,954 members of the FK were distributed 13,545 rifles. The headquarters of the FK was situated at Castle Donndorf near Bayreuth. Admiral Canaris was calling on Henlein almost every second day. (See also the affidavit by SS-Oberführer G. Berger in *IMT*, XXXI, 498–500.) Lt. Colonel Köchling listed 52 men as lost, while 110 of the enemy were reported killed in more than 250 different actions on Czechoslovak territory (*IMT*, XXXVI, 363). Prominent SdP leaders headed the FK groups: Fritz Köllner, Franz May, Willy Brandner, and Fritz Bürger. See also the article by Martin Broszat, "Das Sudetendeutsche Freikorps," *Vierteljahrshefte für Zeitgeschichte*, IX (January 1961), 30–49. Bílek (pp. 146–92) collected official Czechoslovak documents on the disturbances from September 16 to September 30, 1938.

164. On September 27 Aš was in German hands. *DGFP*, II, 880, 968–69; *IMT*, XXVIII, 386.

ing conference at Godesberg, emphasized his determination to prevent war at almost any price. Until Munich, the only question had been how Hitler would obtain by peaceful means and political agreement what could otherwise be had only as a result of military action.

On September 19, the day after the Franco-British consultations, both London and Paris proposed to Prague the direct transfer to Germany of areas with more than 50 percent of German inhabitants,[165] and Britain indicated its willingness to join in international guarantee of the new boundaries. The Czechoslovak government rejected the proposals "made without consultation with the representatives of Czechoslovakia." It proposed instead arbitration based on the Locarno Peace Pact. The Anglo-French proposals, said Prague, would destroy the balance of power in Europe.[166] To overcome Czechoslovak resistance, the French and British ministers arrived at Hradčany Castle, the president's home, at 2:00 A.M. on September 21, and delivered a note to Beneš amounting to an order, insisting that he should accept the proposals without reservations. He was told that the joint démarche "had the character of an ultimatum in the sense that it represented final advice . . . and the last possible moment for acceptance" of the advice of both governments "if this country was to be saved." The audience terminated at 3:45 A.M.[167]

165. For the text of the proposals, see *DGFP*, II, 831–32. The reactions of Beneš are described in *DBFP*, II, 416. Lord Runciman, who left Prague on September 16, recommended in his report to Chamberlain that the agitations of parties and persons antagonistic to Germany should be forbidden, and that the state should be declared neutral and should cede the frontier districts. However, he placed responsibility for the final break upon the shoulders of the SdP. He declared that "Czechoslovak rule in the Sudeten areas for the last twenty years though not actively oppressive . . . has been marked by tactlessness, lack of understanding, petty intolerance, and discrimination, to a point where the resentment of the German population was inevitably moving in the direction of revolt" (*ibid.*, pp. 675–79).

166. The text is in Vincent Urban, pp. 96–98.

167. *DBFP*, II, 441–42, 449–50; Beneš, *Mnichovské dny*, pp. 21–22; Václav Král, *Pravda o okupaci*, pp. 74–76, hereafter cited as *Pravda*. This thoroughly informative study is marred by the absence of any references and footnotes. However, it brings a wealth of data.

There were indications that Prime Minister Hodža, convinced of the impossibility of fighting alone, asked Britain and France to deliver a sort of ultimatum to persuade the cabinet to yield. There has been controversy on this point, and Hodža denied having voiced any such demand (Beneš, *Mnichovské dny*, pp. 49–52). See also *DBFP*, II, 425; Wheeler-Bennett, p. 121; *Les événements*, pp. 268, 273, 821, 2639–40, 2713; Rudolf Beckmann, *K diplomatickému pozadí Mnichova*, pp. 159, 193; Paul Reynaud, *In the Thick of the Fight*, pp. 188 ff.; Zdeněk Tomeš as cited in Soják, ed., p. 368; Hájek, *Mnichov*, pp. 100, 107–108; Michal Múdrý, *Milan Hodža v Amerike. Medzi Americkými Slovákmi. Články, reči, štúdie. Hodža a stredná Europa*, pp. 82–84; Henri Noguères, *Munich ou la drôle de paix* (29 septembre 1938), pp. 150–55.

Late on the same day the Soviet Union notified Beneš that it was ready to come to the assistance of Czechoslovakia as soon as the League of Nations was formally served with the Czechoslovak complaint against the aggressor. It assured Beneš that it would not wait for the final decision but would go immediately to the support of the Republic.[168] Beneš was afraid, however, that Czechoslovakia would become a second Spain and that the alliance with the Soviet Union would alienate the West, whose apprehensions of the USSR played a considerable role in its attempt to appease Hitler. Moreover, he considered that even with Russia's assistance Czechoslovakia would be defeated.[169] The weak and vacillating members of the Czechoslovak government "proved to be too much the civilized and intellectual product of the last war, too thoroughly 'men of Geneva,' to be able deliberately . . . to pick up a brutal bully's gage thrown at their feet" by the French and British ministers.[170] The irresolute cabinet and helpless political leaders bowed before the pressure and accepted the Anglo-French proposals despite their past pledges that they would defend every inch of Czechoslovak territory.

168. Beneš, *Mnichovské dny*, p. 86–88. See also *Mnichov v dokumentech*, II, 229. For the controversial question as to whether the USSR was willing to assist Czechoslovakia even without the aid of France, see John A. Vnuk, "Munich," pp. 292 ff.; John A. Lukacz, *The Great Powers and Eastern Europe* (New York, 1953), pp. 166–89; Čelovský, pp. 374–82; Ministry of Foreign Affairs of the USSR, *Documents and Materials Relating to the Eve of the Second World War*, p. 203–204; *Mnichov v dokumentech*, II, 217, 229; Hájek, *Mnichov, passim;* Tomeš, as cited in Soják, ed., pp. 360–67, 369; Fierlinger, I, 152, 167; Max Beloff, pp. 151, 158, 162; Beckmann, pp. 169–70, 177; Vladimir Potiemkine, ed., *Histoire de la diplomatie* (Paris, 1946–47), III, 664–66; General Gamelin, *Servir*, II, 341, 346, 348, 360; Hodža as quoted in Múdrý, pp. 84–85. There are still many problems open to discussion, i.e., why the Soviets remain silent on this subject despite favorable evidence, and why the Communist historians are rather reticent with regard to the Soviet readiness to give assistance even without France. See Král, *Pravda*, pp. 97–98. A review of the evidence seems to indicate that the USSR was ready to give material aid to Czechoslovakia even without French assistance. Because of the lack of direct communication between the Republic and the Soviet Union, the possibilities of efficient assistance, with the exception of aircraft aid, were estimated as slight. The only available railway line across Rumania was in very bad shape, and both Poland and Rumania refused to allow Soviet forces to cross their countries (Beneš, *Mnichovské dny*, p. 93; Fierlinger, I, 87, 88, 131, 161, 167). After September 24 Soviet Air Force officers and specialists came to Czechoslovakia to make preparations for the landing of Soviet airplanes.

169. *Mnichovské dny*, pp. 88–91. Beneš recognized the fact that the Soviet Union was the only country which had supported Czechoslovakia in the Munich days. The real intentions of the Soviets, however, remain unknown.

170. Hamilton Fish Armstrong, "Armistice at Munich," *Foreign Affairs*, XVII (January 1939), 238. This excellent survey still remains one of the best reviews of the Munich crisis. Churchill stated that he had always thought that Beneš was wrong to yield (*The Second World War*, I, 302). See also Reynaud, pp. 189–90.

The news of the capitulation was met by an outburst of national indignation, with the largest demonstrations taking place in Prague. All factories stopped work and mass rallies continued, with the people calling for a strong military government and defense of the integrity of the state.[171] The cabinet of Hodža was forced to resign, and Gen. Jan Syrový became premier of the new government which, however, regarded itself bound by its predecessor's acceptance of the surrender of its territory.[172] Unlike most of their leaders, the Czech people displayed a determination to fight for the preservation of their independence, resolved that a bitter battle was before them.

During the month of September, the Reich concentrated troops for a mass attack on Czechoslovakia.[173] Prague was strongly advised by London and Paris not to do anything which could be construed as a repetition of the measures of May 21.[174] Only in the face of the huge German war preparations and on the urgent insistence of Prague, did Paris and London finally admit that they could not continue "to take [the] responsibility of advising" Prague not to mobilize.[175] On September 23, at 10:20 P.M., the Czechoslovak radio broadcast the

171. Ripka, Munich, pp. 108–10; Gedye, pp. 452–53. A group of young politicians—Dr. Ladislav Rašín, Dr. H. Ripka, Ferdinand Richter, Josef Patejdl, etc.—took a resolute stand against capitulation and urged the army to take power and defend the integrity of the Republic against Hitler. The Communists held the same view. See Křen, Do emigrace, pp. 54–58, 66–70, 78–84. At Prague more than 100,000 people assembled before the House of Parliament. Dr. Rašín, whose father had been slain by a Communist, declared in a characteristic speech: "At this fatal hour, I recognize no parties and I am ready to work with everybody, even with the Communists, for the defense of our endangered country. Those who are not ready to fight and die for it are not worthy of freedom" (Ripka, Munich, p. 109). Dr. Rašín was the leader of a right-wing party. For a description of the manifestations, see the articles in the Příspěvky k dějinám KSČ, 1958, No. 5, 121–30; December 1961, 653–72.
172. The new government was largely a shadow cabinet of experts. The real power still remained with the heads of the parties and the leading members of the former Hodža cabinet (Ripka, Munich, p. 110). Dr. Petr Zenkl, the mayor of Prague who became a minister in the new government, gave the inside story of the Syrový government in the Prague daily Svobodné slovo, for May 21–24, 1946. General Syrový was a weak figurehead. For a very interesting description of the pre-Munich days in Prague, see Pierre Buk [F. C. Weisskopf], La tragédie tchécoslovaque. De septembre 1938 à mars 1939; Křen, Do emigrace, pp. 52 ff.
173. The task of the Wehrmacht was "to prevent retreat of [the] Czechoslovak Army from [the] Moravia-Bohemia area" and "to bring about [a] rapid decision." A pincer attack would be effected on northern and southern Moravia (DGFP, II, 727–30). Five German armies with 37 divisions were massed on the frontiers (DBFP, II, 544–45, 551–52, 592). The Reich Security Main Office made preparations for the invasion and occupation of the Republic and provided for the enlistment of the Sudetens to assist the Gestapo and Sicherheitsdienst (SD) in the occupied territory. A total of 12 special Einsatzkommandos were prepared along the frontier (IMT, XXXIX, 536–44).
174. DBFP, II, 319, 368, 369.
175. Ibid., pp. 460–61; Gamelin, II, 349.

decree of general mobilization. Popular response to the call was enthusiastic,[176] and the mobilization progressed smoothly. By September 28 more than one million men were under arms. Over 9,000 fortified posts, ranging from machine-gun posts to heavy fortresses, guarded the Historic Provinces alone.[177] Four armies stood prepared.

The Czechoslovak strategy called for a retreat from Bohemia. The Moravian barrier was to be held against the expected pincer attack from Austria and Silesia.[178] The First Army, with 11 infantry divisions defended Bohemia; the Second Army, with six divisions and several frontier regiments, and the Fourth Army, with nine divisions, defended northern and southern Moravia, respectively, where the main strategic reserve of four divisions and one rapid division was situated. The Third Army was deployed against Hungary, with six divisions and one rapid division.[179] Czechoslovakia became a war camp.[180] All the main roads were mined and blocked. A total blackout covered the country. The remaining SdP officials were arrested and confined in

176. Bílek, p. 69. The streets of the cities were immediately filled with reservists hurrying to their destinations. For the enthusiastic response of the Czech and Slovak population, see M. Lvová, "Lid chtěl bojovat" *Příspěvky k dějinám KSČ*, August 1963, III, 542–56. A large part of the German reservists failed to take up military service. For example, some 60 to 70 percent of the German reservists of the First Czechoslovak Army Corps failed to report (*ibid.*, pp. 545–46).

177. Hájek, *Mnichov*, pp. 72, 104. Some of the inside equipment was not completed (*Denkschrift*, pp. 28–36). The fortifications greatly impressed the German generals (Bullock, *Hitler*, p. 430). But see also *DGFP*, IV, 70–71.

178. The chief of the French General Staff, General Gamelin, concluded that the Czechoslovak Army could have resisted efficiently and could have even succeeded in constituting the pillar of the Eastern Front (Gamelin, II, 352, 354–57).

179. *Historie a vojenství*, XI, 1964, No. 1, 102–103; Interview with Gen. Antonín Hasal, Washington, D.C., May 1, 1958. (See also *DBFP*, II, 609–10, 575, 591–92.) The description of the deployment of the Czechoslovak Army in Jaksch (*Europas Weg* pp. 322–23) is incorrect. (See also the deposition of General Faucher in *Les événements*, V, 1200–10.) The Czechoslovak officer corps was only 5 percent German, and German soldiers were scattered throughout the Czechoslovak units.

180. When Hitler occupied the provinces of Bohemia, Moravia-Silesia, and western Slovakia on March 15, 1939, the German Army seized 1,582 airplanes, 501 antiaircraft guns, 2,175 guns, 469 tanks and armored cars, 43,876 machine guns, 1,090,000 rifles, 114,000 pistols, and a vast amount of other war material (Hitler's speech, April 28, 1939, in *Dokumente der deutschen Politik*, VII, part I, 150). For a different figure, see Miloš Hájek, *Od Mnichova k 15. březnu*, p. 153. The list did not include vast supplies of material which remained within Slovakia and Ruthenia, and which were either sold or seized by Germany in 1939. Gen. Heinz Guderian commented upon the Czech armored equipment: "It was to prove useful to us during the Polish and French campaigns. During the Russian campaign it was finally replaced by heavier German equipment" (*Panzer Leader*, p. 64).

internment camps.[181] The diplomatic corps prepared to move to the new seat of government at Turčanský Svätý Martin in Slovakia.

Beneš regarded the green light given to him by the West for mobilization to be the long-awaited proof that the West had at last grasped the meaning of the German objectives. He realized, as did the entire nation, that this war would be a life or death struggle. Nevertheless, the morale of the entire Czech population was superb. Beneš was asked to spend the night of September 27–28 in his new secret quarters near Prague, because the government expected Hitler to bombard the city that very night. However, soon after his arrival he was recalled to Prague. Disturbing news had come from the Western capitals.[182] London was striving to stave off the war through the proposal of a new timetable for the German occupation of the German areas, differing in some points from the original proposals of September 21.

The Czechoslovak Army decided to fight. About September 28 there was a conference of high military leaders at the Supreme Army Command Headquarters at Račice, near Vyškov. At this meeting the generals agreed to install a military government which would resist any capitulation and defend the integrity of the Czechoslovak territory, provided Poland would not intervene.[183] On September 29, after hearing reports of the Munich conference, representatives of the four armies arrived in Prague to see President Beneš, their supreme commander, and demanded that he reject capitulation. "They entreated, threatened, begged, some wept."[184] They stated unanimously:

> We must go to war regardless of consequences. The Western Powers will be forced to follow us. The entire nation is united, the Army is firm in its decision to fight. And even if we were left alone, we must not yield; the Army has the duty to defend the national territory even at the price of a war.[185]

181. *DGFP*, II, 971.
182. Beneš, *Mnichovské dny*, pp. 67–69. The British timetable followed the speech of Hitler of September 26, declaring that after the cession of the Sudetenland "there are no more territorial problems for Germany in Europe" and emphasizing that Herr Beneš had to hand over this territory to Germany on October 1.
183. Interview with General Hasal and the author's recollection of a discussion with the commanding general of the Second Army, Gen. Vojtěch Luža, in 1944. See also Křen, *Do emigrace*, pp. 62–63, 68–70. For the mood of the army leaders, see *Mnichov v dokumentech*, II, 206–208, 251–54.
184. Beneš in London, on Jan. 8, 1941 (*Central European Observer*, XVII, Jan. 17, 1941).
185. Beneš, *Mnichovské dny*, p. 115. Beneš listed Generals Krejčí, Vojcechovský,

Beneš, visibly shaken, hesitated for a while. Finally he declined their proposal, saying that the war would come quickly anyway, and it was necessary to save the existence of the nation. "The generals left dissatisfied, embittered, and in a desperate mood." Beneš "pondered seriously once more the question: Have I made the right decision in this terrible crisis?"[186] The question continued to pursue him for the rest of his life.

At Munich, on September 29, the Four Powers decided on the surrender of Czechoslovak territory; the Republic was neither invited nor even consulted.[187] Following a meeting of Czech party leaders and the cabinet on September 30, Foreign Minister Kamil Krofta received the ministers of France, Great Britain, and Italy and declared without letting them speak:

> The President and the Government submit to the conditions of the Munich Agreement which has come into being without Czechoslovakia and against her.

An attempt by de Lacroix, the French minister, to express condolence was cut short by Krofta.

> We have been forced into this situation; now everything is at an end; today it is our turn, tomorrow it will be the turn of others.[188]

Luža, Votruba, and Prchala. According to General Hasal, neither General Votruba nor General Prchala was present. The presence of General Krejčí is subject to doubt. (See *Mnichov v dokumentech*, II, 254, 419.) The chief commanders of the Fourth Army sent General Ingr as their representative to Prague. General Ingr arrived too late, as the Munich agreement had already been accepted. (See also Svaz, *Generál Ingr*, p. 3.)

186. Beneš, *Mnichovské dny*, p. 117.

187. Germany, Great Britain, France, and Italy agreed that the cession of the Sudeten territory would start on October 1 and be completed by October 10. The conditions of the evacuation would be laid down by an international commission composed of the representatives of the Four Powers and Czechoslovakia. The occupation should be carried out gradually in the four zones marked on the map. The fifth zone should be determined by the commission and be occupied by October 10. The commission should also ascertain the territories in which a plebiscite would be held and should determine the definitive border line (*DGFP*, II, 1014–16). The agreement was harsher than the Anglo-French proposals of September 21. The Czechoslovak representatives were told the results at 2:15 A.M. on September 30. It was "a sentence without right of appeal and without possibility of modification." For the report of Hubert Masařík, one of the representatives, see Ripka, *Munich*, pp. 224–27.

188. *DGFP*, IV, 4–5; Ripka, *Munich*, pp. 230–31. In the afternoon, a committee of the coalition parties, consisting of about 50 members, met in Parliament, and complied with the Munich agreement, which had never passed Parliament as the constitution required. Those politicians who urged that the Munich agreement

The prime minister broadcast the news to the nation at 5 P.M.

We have had to choose between making a desperate and hopeless defense, which would have meant the sacrifice of an entire generation of our adult men, as well as of our women and children, and accepting, without a struggle and under pressure, terms which are without parallel in history for their ruthlessness. . . .

We were deserted. We stood alone. . . . It is our sacred duty to preserve the lives of our people, in order that it may not emerge weakened from this age of terror, and in order that we may not be obliged to abandon our belief that our nation will rise again, as it has done so often in the past.[189]

European public opinion enthusiastically welcomed the agreement; responsible American circles were pleased.[190] Under German pressure

---

be rebuffed met, but their attempts failed (Buk, p. 146; Král, ed., *Politické strany*, pp. 159–64). Also the army chiefs declined to take the responsibility for a military coup as, in their opinion, the hostility of Poland made any resistance hopeless. Yet as late as October 3 there was an attempt to install a new anti-Munich government headed by General Krejčí and the members of the younger political generation who opposed the capitulation in Munich (Křen, *Do emigrace*, pp. 78–83).

189. *Survey 1938*, II, 447.

190. The American attitude during the Munich crisis was somewhat mixed. The reports of the American correspondents from Czechoslovakia supported the Czechoslovak point of view (CBS, *Crisis—A Report from the Columbia Broadcasting System*). The American minister in Prague, Wilbur Carr, reported accurately. For example, on September 28, he stated to Secretary of State Cordell Hull: "The Sudeten problem would never have become a menace to peace or even the cause of an international conflict . . . except for the inflammatory activities of the German press and propaganda. . . . The conflicts in the Sudetenland have been conceived and directed by the Sudeten Germans and the participants have been equipped, organized, and supported by the Reich Germans" (*Foreign Relations of the United States. Diplomatic Papers. 1938*, I, 610). The ambassadors in Paris and London, William C. Bullitt and Joseph P. Kennedy, were strong appeasers (*ibid.*, pp. 494–95, 510–11, 514, 565, 595, 621). John McVickar Haight, Jr., noted that the impact of American foreign policy upon France was to "weaken the spirit of resistance in France" ("France, the United States and the Munich Crisis," *The Journal of Modern History*, XXXII, December 1960, 358). President Franklin Delano Roosevelt's appeals to Hitler and Beneš on September 26 for the continuation of the negotiations and for "a peaceful, fair and constructive settlement of questions now at issue" (*ibid.*, p. 658) practically put the causes of Nazi Germany and Czechoslovakia on the same level. For Beneš the appeals presented "the last heavy blow" because "an agreement in the concrete situation could only lead toward the destruction of the Republic" (*Mnichovské dny*, pp. 105–106, 108). Learning about the cable of Chamberlain informing Hitler that he was willing to come to Munich, President Roosevelt sent a message to the British prime minister saying, "Good man" (*Foreign Relations*, p. 688). The Department of State commented upon the Munich agreement on September 30: "As to immediate peace results, it is

President Beneš resigned on October 5 and left the country shortly thereafter. A world of freedom and tolerance had passed away.[191]

Very few happenings are so decisive that they split the history of a nation into two definite parts. Such events, if they occur, leave their mark forever on the soul of a nation; they nurture a new state of mind, for nothing can be the same after such explosions. Munich was such a cleavage for the Czech nation, and it still remains buried beneath the surface of the national consciousness. It presented the supreme moment of modern Czechoslovak history which found the entire nation ready to defend its independence. The Czechoslovak government capitulated only because it was abandoned by the allies who had been presented to the Czech people for twenty years as guardians of international morality. The surrender of Czechoslovakia did not save her from humiliation and degradation, and the possible gain in human lives was more than balanced by the loss of national dignity. Subsequent developments showed clearly that the Czech people had been right—against the prevailing opinion of their political leaders— in wanting to fight despite hopeless odds, even at the price of the greatest bloodshed. To use the words of an outstanding Czech patriot, the moral ideas of a truly independent and free state had to be preserved even at the price of Czechoslovakia's becoming another Thermopylae and Beneš another Leonidas. Conditions dictated after a lost war would not have been very different from those of an agreement that sacrificed hundreds of thousands of Czechoslovaks to oppression within Nazi Germany and delivered a democratic country to the mercy of its enemies.[192]

unnecessary to say that they afford a universal sense of relief" (*ibid.*, p. 703). Roosevelt seemed to be pleased with the Munich agreement. (See also Charles Callan Tansill, *Back Door to War. Roosevelt Foreign Policy 1933–1941,* Chicago, 1952, p. 428, and William L. Langer and S. Everett Gleason, *The Challenge to Isolation, 1937–1940,* New York, 1952, pp. 32–35.) *The New York Times* (September 30), the *Christian Science Monitor* (September 29), and other papers hailed the Munich agreement (Tansill, pp. 42–43). It is interesting to note that on September 22 the United States stated its readiness to assume the protection of the Czechoslovak citizens and interests in the Reich, Poland, and Hungary in case of war (*U. S. Foreign Relations,* p. 634).

191. The editorial in the last issue of the Jewish German Prague daily, *Prager Mittag* (October 19), was symptomatic. "They now demand the closing down of a paper whose loyalty to democracy, whose work for a true friendship between Czechs and Germans of this Republic, spoke from every page that it ever published. And now we are told that precisely for this reason we are unpopular, even a hindrance on the new way which must be followed. That is the point at which we must resign" (Griffin, p. 181).

192. Letter of Nov. 7, 1938, by Dr. Ladislav Rašín to Beneš (Beneš, *Memoirs,* pp. 95-96). The Communists also preferred war to capitulation. See Gottwald's

Munich also marked the collapse of the French system of alliances and the end of the traditional French influence in East Central Europe. Liberation of 40 German divisions only increased the German threat to the West. The belief that British interests were not directly involved in the dismemberment of Czechoslovakia and that peace could be purchased at the expense of a small nation proved to be a grave and fatal mistake. The "Beneš system" of staking the existence of the state almost unilaterally on an alliance with France collapsed with Munich.[193] There was, however, no real alternative for the policy of Beneš. The subsequent fate of Colonel Beck, Milan Stojadinović, and Leopold III showed that it was unlikely that any reasonable settlement could have been reached with the Nazi Reich. The betrayal by the West, which had assisted in the destruction of a democratic state, its staunchest ally, wasted an immense capital of esteem for the Western democracies. In the future, no responsible Czechoslovak statesman could fail to draw appropriate conclusions from the lesson learned so bitterly at Munich.

Czechoslovakia's share of the guilt lay in the fact that the Republic had not understood how to forge an efficient instrument out of its only possible alternative: sufficient insistence on—even bilateral— military agreements with France and Soviet Russia. Beneš was a tough negotiator, but he was too often on the defensive in dealing with the West. He neglected to make absolutely clear to his allies that he would not abandon one inch of Czechoslovak soil under any condition. This alternative course—feared by London as it increased the danger of Britain's involvement in war, and by Paris because France was bound to come to the assistance of her ally—that Czechoslovakia would fight even if she were left alone, had *never* been used as an argument to induce London to press the SdP for a détente. Moreover, while having moral, political, and strategic advantage on its side, Czechoslovakia failed to undertake any serious propaganda effort to impress Western public opinion. She gave way to humiliating British blackmail, grudgingly yielding ground, and step by step coming

address on October 11 (*Spisy*, VIII, 268–73). For very interesting comments by a Communist author on the Munich capitulation and its impact on the Czech nation, see Křen, *Do emigrace*, pp. 85–97, 105–13.

193. There was no military agreement between France and the Republic, and there was not any joint plan of operations or mobilization. There existed only a stipulation providing for the possible stationing of one group of French aircraft on Czechoslovak airfields. Only after May 21 did General Krejčí ask General Gamelin for a discussion of measures to be taken with regard to coordination of mobilization plans. He received an evasive answer (Beneš, *Memoirs*, p. 42). For Czechoslovak policy before Munich, see the critical commentary by Karel Lisický, *Československá cesta do Mnichova*.

closer to the fatal end. Prague should never have accepted the first Anglo-French ultimatum. Its assent sealed its ultimate fate. Even after the mobilization, it tolerated the invasion of Czechoslovak territory by the armed Reich forces and neglected to take appropriate steps to wipe out German SS troops occupying the Czechoslovak salient of Aš. Here was a unique opportunity given to Beneš to prevent Munich and to force the allies to come to his assistance. On the whole, the Czechoslovak guilt lay in neglect of opportunity and lack of strong will on the part of her leaders.

A comparison cannot be drawn between the consistent policy of this democratic outpost, valiantly struggling to stave off the Nazi menace, and the course of action taken by France and Britain. President Beneš, despite all his weaknesses, remained a towering figure beside the Chamberlains, Horthys, Bonnets, Becks, and Stojadinovićs, with their political cynicism and ignorance. On the domestic front, Prague—mainly through the influence of the right wing of the Agrarian Party—allowed full freedom to the enemies of democracy and the state. Its indulgent attitude toward the subversive activities of the SdP, whose leaders were relatively free to spread chaos and anarchy and to undermine the integrity and unity of the state, dangerously weakened its power among the German people, whose traditional respect of firm order and discipline was all too well known. By allowing the SdP and its storm troops to become the fifth column[194] of the Nazi Reich, the democratic regime abdicated its power and let the SdP form a state within the state. The Republic showed remarkable restraint, but this was of no avail against Nazi duplicity. Compromises and concessions were futile against German intrigues and planted incidents.

In the predominantly German areas, the German democratic minority was caught in the meshes of civil war and was exposed to Nazi reprisals for its loyalty to democracy. During the disturbances of September, the German democrats fought valiantly on the Czechoslovak side.[195]

The SdP had attained its first goal after a long and brilliantly conducted political campaign. Its success was assured through the confidence and allegiance it gained from the majority of its country-

194. De Jong (p. 294) uses the Austrian NSDAP and the Czechoslovak SdP as examples of the fifth column. It is interesting to note that the term "fifth column" was coined in the Spanish Civil War. When General Franco launched his troops in four columns against Madrid, General Mola declared that the fifth column already in Madrid would open the attack on the government (*ibid.*, p. 3).
195. *U. S. Foreign Relations*, pp. 690, 721. For the refugee camps, see *CBS, Crisis*, p. 37.

men. Thus the SdP set the pace for other German groups in Europe, and its demands became the pattern for subsequent claims of German minorities in other countries.[196] The paradox consisted in that the very advantage of being able to appeal to the mother country induced the German minorities to sacrifice their own interests and to become closely dependent on the Reich. In the case of the Sudeten Germans, misuse of the democratic rights which they enjoyed under the Czechoslovak Republic destroyed the very conditions in which Czech-German cooperation could have flourished. The abuse of the right of self-determination by the Sudeten Germans, who used it as an instrument to promote their nationalist aims, proved that the idea of self-determination was a limited and qualified concept which varied according to specific circumstances in each nation and the actual historical situation.[197] It ought to have been used only to establish conditions which would prevent national oppression and enable each nation to constitute its own state.[198] Such a conception of national self-determination would have left enough room for the establishment of the Czechoslovak Republic in its historic frontiers, and prevented the application of the principle to any national group whose real aim was to serve as the spearhead of a foreign power.

The conflict between Czechs and Germans had become mortal. Munich was merely a pause. The plan for the treatment of the Czech nation prepared by the SdP for the case of a German military victory over Czechoslovakia in 1938 displayed a degree of viciousness that was rare even at the time of Hitler.

In the so-called Grundplanung OA (Basic Plan), some SdP leaders proposed to solve the German-Czech historic dispute once and

196. See the agreement between Germany and Rumania of Oct. 23, 1940, recognizing the legal personality of the German ethnic group, its national registration, the special position of its leader, and the right to hoist the swastika. The local NSDAP constituted the executive organ of the ethnic group (*National Socialism*, p. 141).

197. Alfred Cobban presented a lucid discussion of the principle of self-determination in its historical context in his *National Self-Determination*. When the well-known German philosopher F. W. Foerster visited London he was told by a member of Parliament: "You can hardly expect us, who in every part of the globe have stood for national self-determination, even for Ireland . . . to oppose self-determination for the Sudeten Germans." Foerster replied, "But if the Irish lived on the east coast of Great Britain and if on the continent a vast Irish empire had armed to the teeth and if the leader had proclaimed himself head of all Irishmen throughout the world, would you then have granted independence?" . . ."An awkward silence followed" (F. W. Foerster, *Europe and the German Question*, pp. 378–79).

198. I follow Cobban's thesis.

forever: After the occupation of the Historic Provinces, the leader of the Sudeten Germans would become their governor. The annexation of the provinces was to be proclaimed from Prague. After a period of military administration, which would last for five years, the leader of the Sudeten Germans would take over the administration of the whole area. The German population would be settled in a zone stretching from the Dyje Valley over Brno, Vyškov, and Olomouc to the Oder, and thus would isolate the Czechs from the Slovaks. There would be only German schools; the Czech language would disappear. The plan recommended that the Sudeten Germans refrain, for tactical reasons, from discussing the elimination of Czech at this time. Czech agriculture and industry would be increasingly dominated by Germans, and German immigration would be fostered while every assistance would be offered to Czech emigration.[199] Other plans of the SdP made preparations for cooperation with the Reich German authorities in the case of an outbreak of war or of a peaceful occupation of the "Sudeten German areas." They put forth propositions for an annexation and Germanization of the Czech areas of Olomouc and Moravská Ostrava in case the Czechs were granted "a political independence in the interior of Bohemia and Moravia."[200]

At the present juncture, Munich was considered by ruling circles in Europe as the basis of a new settlement in Central Europe. Yet the tone and content of the SdP plans as well as of many of Hitler's activities were not such as to encourage even very cautious hopes that progress had been made in Munich toward the laying of the groundwork for a more permanent order. What further disasters were yet needed to shake the Western democracies out of their incredible complacency? For the moment, the mutilated Czechoslovak state was left alone in the middle of an apathetic Europe.

199. The plan was found in the archives of the bureau of Henlein in Aš in 1945, and was used at the indictment of K. H. Frank. It was prepared in the period May–July, 1938, and was written at the bureau (Václav Král, *Otázky hospodářského a sociálního vývoje v českých zemích v letech 1938–1945* [3 vols.], I, 34; hereafter cited as *Otázky*. This is a Communist-biased but extremely informative survey). It is not known whether the views expressed in the plan reflected the opinion of the radical wing only or of the SdP itself. For the text of the plan, see Institut für Internationale Politik und Oekonomie, *Die Vergangenheit warnt*, pp. 27–38; hereafter cited as *Vergangenheit*.
200. František Štěpán, ed., "Nové dokumenty o protičeskoslovenských plánech dnešních revanšistů z let 1938–1939" (*Příspěvky k dějinám KSČ* [December 1961], pp. 729–33).

CHAPTER 6

The Dismemberment of Czechoslovakia

The German troops under Col. Gen. Wilhelm von Leeb crossed the Czechoslovak frontier at the Bohemian Forest at 2 P.M. on Oct. 1, 1938.[1] Other units followed according to the Munich timetable. Twenty-five German divisions occupied the former Czechoslovak territory by October 10,[2] and the annexed areas were reorganized and integrated into the Reich.[3] Hitler entered the annexed zone on October 3 and toured the country amid enthusiastic masses of Germans.[4] When the German Army concluded the occupation of the Sudeten territory, Henlein pledged to Hitler Sudeten support for the Nazi plans.

> Our assurance that we will not perish but will be called upon, as the German guard in the East, to enter the victorious path of the future with the whole of the German nation, is all due to your work.[5]

1. *Dokumente der deutschen Politik*, VI, part 1, 367; hereafter cited as *Dokumente*. See also the official publication of the NSDAP, *Mit dem VII. Korps ins Sudetenland* (Munich, 1939).
2. [Czechoslovak] Ministry of Information, *Československo a norimberský proces*, p. 294.
3. *Dokumente*, VI, 371–73. The incorporation was supervised by the Zentralstelle in the Reich Ministry of the Interior under the direction of State Secretary Dr. Stuckart. Henlein was appointed Reichsstatthalter on April 14, 1939, and Liberec became the capital of the Sudetengau. In November 1938, Hans Krebs, Wilhelm Sebekowsky, and Friedrich Zippelius were appointed government presidents at, respectively, Ústí nad Labem, Carlsbad (later at Cheb), and Opava. They were subordinated to Henlein (*Dokumente*, VI, 373).
4. *Dokumente*, VI, 376. For the enthusiastic welcome of the annexation, see *Endlich befreit. Sudetendeutsche Jugend erzählt von der Befreiung ihrer Heimat* (Liberec, 1939).
5. At Liberec on Oct. 10, 1938.

However, Munich again proved that the territories of the Sudeten Germans did not form a single unit and were not capable of independent existence. In view of this indisputable fact, Berlin broke up the annexed areas into several parts and decided that the southern Moravian territories would fall to Austria, and southern Bohemia to Bavaria. The remainder formed a Reichsgau, called the Sudetengau. On the basis of the Munich agreement the Reich occupied an area of 28,996 sq km[6] containing 2,822,899 Germans and 738,502 Czechs and Slovaks.[7] Parts of the territories were divided among Silesia, Bavaria, Niederdonau, and Oberdonau;[8] the largest part formed the Sudetengau.[9]

The same territorial division was followed in the organizational setup of the NSDAP. The SdP was incorporated into the NSDAP on Dec. 11, 1938,[10] and SdP officials took over corresponding functions in the NSDAP. The SA (brown shirts) were constituted under the leadership of former Deputy Franz May and enlisted some 190,000 members. Sudeten German youths, who were organized in the Deutscher Turnverband, became members of the Hitler Youth in April 1939. This reorganization of the SdP and of the other party groups according to the NSDAP model was assisted by scores of Reich Germans.[11] The NSDAP of the Sudetengau was given jurisdic-

6. *Sudetenland*, p. 15.
7. *Central European Observer*, XVI (Dec. 16, 1938). A total of 3,576,719 Czechoslovak citizens were ceded to the Reich. The figures were approximate, as they were based on the 1930 census. The Germans estimated the number of Czechs—also according to the same census—at 676,478 persons on Nov. 17, 1938. There were, in addition, 32,274 Czech nationals living in the Reich (*DGFP*, IV, 152). The difference in figures may have been caused by the emigration of many Czechs after September 21. One has to keep in mind when working with statistical data that a certain degree of restraint is necessary in handling the figures. Statistics are not strictly accurate and differ frequently. However, the figures are indicative of the nature of the real situation.
8. The German provinces were given 317 sq km, 1,675 sq km, 2,678 sq km, and 1,718 sq km, respectively, with 52,967, 90,332, 224,806, and 97,157 inhabitants (*Sudetenland*, pp. 16, 21; Statistisches Reichsamt, *Statistisches Jahrbuch für das Deutsche Reich*, pp. 15–16).
9. The Sudetengau included 2,943,187 inhabitants on the basis of the census of May 17, 1939 (*Statistisches Jahrbuch*, p. 16). According to this census (Bohmann, *Sudetendeutschtum*, pp. 124, 133) 3,405,168 inhabitants were incorporated into the Reich. These figures included Czechs, so that the number of Germans would actually be much lower.
10. Rudolf Hess issued the order on November 5. Henlein was appointed Gauleiter and K. H. Frank his deputy on October 30 (*Dokumente*, VI, 378–79; Karl Viererbl, ed., *Sudetenland im Reich*, p. 39). Richard Lammel (*ibid.*) pointed out that the incorporation was greatly facilitated by the fact that "Die SdP war schon in der Tschechenzeit nach den Grundsätzen der Bewegung im Altreich aufgebaut, soweit das unter Tschechen möglich war." Henlein was appointed SS-Gruppenführer and Frank, SS-Brigadeführer.
11. Viererbl, ed., p. 40.

tion over the remaining parts of Bohemia and Moravia after the establishment of the Protectorate in 1939,[12] and the SA-group "Sudeten" and other trained Sudeten Germans formed special units which took part in the campaign against Poland.[13] On Dec. 4, 1938, at the election for the Reichstag, 2,467,944 persons voted yes and 27,485 voted no, and 41 Sudeten deputies entered the Reichstag.[14] The Gleichschaltung had been carried out speedily and with full success.

The SdP began a program to encourage the exodus of all Czechs. Its officials were ordered to attach derogatory posters proclaiming "Tschechisches Geschäft" and "Jüdisches Geschäft" to Czech and Jewish shops,[15] causing many Czechs, democratic Germans, and Jews to abandon their properties and leave for the Republic;[16] and during the night of November 9–10, anti-Jewish demonstrations were led by the SdP on direct orders from Berlin. The properties of those who had fled to the Republic were allotted to reliable German nationalists. The Land Reform of 1919 was declared invalid, and ten months after Munich some 150,000 ha were redistributed among members of the

12. Franz May as cited in Viererbl, ed., pp. 55–56.
13. The Abwehr retained those Sudetens who were trained to be used against Czechoslovakia and formed them into special battle and sabotage troops. The Breslau office of the Abwehr trained some 3,000–5,000 Sudetens who clandestinely crossed the German-Polish frontier before the German offensive and occupied important industrial plants and mines in cooperation with the Polish Germans (De Jong, p. 154; Georg Wagner, Sudeten-SA in Polen).
14. Dokumente, VI, 393. For SdP propaganda activities among the Czechs in the Sudetengau, see the Library of Congress, Manuscript Division, "The Rehse Collection" (Container 468).
15. Ibid. For example, the district office of Liberec sent circulars on Oct. 24, 1938, stating: "Die Partei hat ein Interesse daran, dass alle volksfremden Elemente aus dem Sudetengau entfernt werden. Ich erinnere noch einmal an die mündlichen Aufträge, die allen politischen Leitern wegen der Plakate 'Jüdisches Geschäft,' 'Tschechisches Geschäft' gegeben wurden." (See also Svobodné slovo, Aug. 15, 1946.)
16. Up to Nov. 4, 1938, there were 91,625 refugees in the Czechoslovak Republic from the territories ceded to Germany and Poland, among them 72,912 Czechs, 10,817 Germans, 6,765 Jews (Central European Observer, Nov. 25, 1938). Up to May 1939, the provinces of Bohemia and Moravia accepted some 23,000 Jewish refugees from the Sudetenland (Jacques Vernant, The Refugee in the Post-War World, p. 60). The Historic Provinces received for the period 1933–39 some 216,000 refugees from the Reich, Saarland, Sudetenland, Austria, Danzig, Memel, and Spain (Malcolm J. Proudfoot, European Refugees 1939–52. A Study in Forced Population Movement, p. 27). See also Eugen de Witte, "Die Sudetendeutsche Emigration 1938" in Preidel, ed., pp. 373–79. Theodor Procházka ("La Tchécoslovaquie de Munich à mars 1939," unpublished doctoral dissertation, Université de Paris, 1954, p. 135) estimates the figure of Czech refugees from the Sudetenland to the Historic Provinces after the cession of the Sudeten territories at 116,000 Czechs and 12,000 Germans. Ripka (Munich, p. 252) also put the number of German refugees at 12,000 toward the end of January 1939. According to Jaksch (Europas Weg, pp. 338–39), about 7,000 to 8,000 German democrats were put into Nazi concentration camps. Another 5,000 emigrated.

SdP through the special Fund of Reparation of the Land Reform.[17] The industrial properties of Czech banks and concerns were sold below their real prices, and the branches of the Czech banks were taken over by German banks. Czech inscriptions were torn away, Czech societies, clubs, and associations abolished, and their property confiscated.

Prior to March 15, 1939, the date of the occupation of the remaining part of Czechoslovakia, several Czechs were slain and others seriously wounded during a series of anti-Czech demonstrations.[18] The SdP, oblivious of the privileges it had enjoyed in the democratic state, exhibited a hostile attitude toward everything Czech. Its activities revealed to the world the value of its allegations on the right of self-determination.[19]

Moreover, during negotiations on the final delimitation of the new Czechoslovak-German borderline, the SdP urged Reich German authorities to push through their own demands for Czech territory without attention to ethnographic considerations. Their attitude caused even the Wilhelmstrasse to become incensed against both the arrogant behavior of the Sudeten representatives and their demands for incorporation of purely Czech communities.[20] Henlein meanwhile established a special bureau in Berlin, directed by Dr. Quido Klieber,

17. Pierre George, Le problème allemand en Tchécoslovaquie, p. 70. Henlein affirmed on July 9, 1939, at Žatec, that 150,000 ha were restored to the former proprietors, i.e., the German high aristocracy (Josef Hanč, "Czechs and Slovaks since Munich," Foreign Affairs, XVIII, October 1939, 110).
18. The demonstrations took place at Most, Duchcov, Bílina, Teplice-Šanov, Znojmo, Pohořelice, etc. See "L'oppression des Tchèques dans les districts sudètes," Les nouvelles tchécoslovaques (July 1939), as cited in Radomír Luža, Odsun, p. 13. For the first wave of persecution of the Czechs, in October and November 1938, see Mnichov v dokumentech, II, 313, 317–18, 320, 326–31; Král, Pravda, pp. 100–101. Hans Krebs reported regularly on the behavior of the Czech population in his region during the occupation. He boasted that Czech schools remained only in the districts of Liberec, Jablonec, and Vrchlabí. There were 42 Czech elementary schools with 2,654 pupils; only 18 Czechs attended higher schools and 69 Czechs other schools ("The Trial of the SdP Deputies," Svobodné slovo, Dec. 10, 1946). There were 152,103 Czech pupils in schools in the annexed territories prior to Sept. 30, 1938 (Král, Otázky, I, 35). For persecution in the lignite areas of Most and Duchcov in the period 1938–39, see the series of articles by Fr. J. Den, "Pohraničí za okupace" (Czech Borderland during the Occupation) in Svobodné slovo, Aug. 13, 1946 ff.
19. DGFP, IV, 133–34, 140–42.
20. National Archives of the United States. Records of the German Foreign Ministry, Container 2444, frames E 240,662–63; 240,665–66; 240,721–22; 240, 743–45. The Sudeten Germans arbitrarily occupied parts of the Czech territory near Svitavy on Jan. 19, 1939, and also near Moravská Třebová (ibid., E 240, 823–27). See also DGFP, IV, 179. For an adequate description, see Theodor Procházka, "The Delimitation of Czechoslovak-German Frontiers after Munich," Journal of Central European Affairs, XXI (July 1961), 200–18.

a member of the Reichstag, who collected all demands for the rectification of the frontier and undertook appropriate intervention with the Berlin authorities.[21] The local Sudeten German Party officials even contemplated provoking disturbances in Brno in order to induce the Reich to occupy this largest Moravian city.[22]

The SdP objectives had been met in part by the Munich agreement, but it had fallen short of what was desired by the party leadership. Indicative of the party's real state of mind was the new memorandum prepared by the staff of Konrad Henlein, advocating the incorporation of the Bohemian-Moravian area into the German Reich.[23] It also suggested four alternatives for the solution of the Czech question, but rejected the first two in favor of either the incorporation of the Czech state into the Reich or the formation of a satellite state. By thus advocating the subjection of the Czech state, the SdP crossed the line between politics and adventure. Now, symbolizing the specter of an aggressive, threatening Germany in the midst of the Czechs, it increased the atmosphere of national war and exposed the extent of Sudeten German nationalist discontent.

At the beginning of October 1938, Prague was preoccupied with the question of its frontier. Its politicians were aware that Munich had opened up the whole problem of the Czechoslovak frontiers, including those in common with Poland and Hungary, which also had to be appeased. Yet the German question overshadowed everything. The findings of the International Commission in Berlin (October 5) as to the Fifth Zone which was to be occupied by Germany from October 7 to 10 were extremely unfavorable to Czechoslovakia,[24]

21. K. H. Frank informed von Ribbentrop on Oct. 17, 1938, that the Sudeten material to back the demands for local rectifications of the frontier was collected at Liberec and dispatched to Dr. Klieber in Berlin, who became a member of the special Committee on Frontier Delimitation in the Reich Ministry of the Interior (National Archives of the U.S., Container 2443, E 240,133–34). The German Foreign Office stated on October 22 that Dr. Klieber "hat sich bisher mit besonders weitgehenden Forderungen bei den internen Besprechungen hervorgetan" (ibid., E 240,136). Henlein also intervened to Hitler, for example on Nov. 19, 1938.
22. Dr. Wolfgang Branczik, the city councilor at Brno, presented such a memorandum to Marshal Göring on October 8 (ibid., E 239, 799). The SdP officials in Brno contemplated provoking the Czechs in order to force the intervention of the Reich (ibid., E 240,141–44). See also Štěpán, ed., "Nové dokumenty," pp. 733–35.
23. National Archives of the U.S., Container 2443, E 239,784–90, Staff of Konrad Henlein (Abteilung V-A).
24. The figure of the census of 1910 was taken as the basis of the national delimitation. Even Viscount Halifax declared such demands "grossly unfair" (DBFP, III, 93), but this line of occupation was presented to Prague as an

which accepted them under duress. With the Fifth Zone Czechoslovakia handed over to Germany the Czech districts of Hlučín, Hodonín, Bílovec, and Opava,[25] to mention only the province of Moravia-Silesia. Strategic considerations again played a decisive role. Almost all the main railway lines of Bohemia and Moravia had to traverse territory occupied by the Germans. Yet even this zone had been enlarged by the Wehrmacht[26] in more than 300 places, and the final German proposal of November 3 set forth new demands based on military considerations which would involve taking over purely Czech territories.[27] Another new demand for what was to be called the Sixth Zone caused consternation at Prague for, according to the resolution of the International Commission, the final delimitation of the frontiers should have been negotiated by both governments. It was accepted by the cabinet only after "hours of difficult and impassioned debate."[28]

On Nov. 20, 1938, Germany and Czechoslovakia signed the minutes relating to the final delimitation of the borders.[29] This agreement settled all frontier questions between the two states without a plebiscite. However, the new indefensible frontier lines confirmed that the strategic consequences of Munich were considered by

---

ultimatum agreed upon in advance by the Four Powers under strong German pressure (*Documents 1938*, II, 336; *DGFP*, IV, 27–28, 33–34, 41–42).

25. On Oct. 31, 1938, Dr. Bohuslav Ečer, deputy mayor of Brno, presented a memorandum to several members of the House of Commons in London. According to the memo, the district of Hlučín was 95.16 percent Czech, that of Hodonín, 88 percent, Bílovec, 73.80 percent, and Opava, 55.85 percent, if the 1930 census were taken as the basis. Even on the basis of the 1910 census, Hodonín was 87.09 percent Czech, Bílovec 67.28 percent, and Hlučín 80.51 percent. Besides these Czech districts, many Czech cities were occupied, such as Hodslavice (99.9 percent Czech), Štramberk (98.62 percent), Polička (96.84 percent), Příbor (95.14 percent), Klímkovice (92 percent), Moravský Krumlov (89.46 percent), Hlučín (89.18 percent), Kopřivnice (86.3 percent), Břeclav (83.4 percent), Zábřeh (68.7 percent), and Znojmo (64.29 percent) (*Československo a norimberský proces*, pp. 87–91; Luža, *Odsun*, p. 13). For the report of the Czechoslovak delimitation subcommittee of Nov. 11, 1938, see *Mnichov v dokumentech*, II, 323–26, 425–26.

26. *DBFP*, III, 117, 207. In the negotiations on the Fifth Zone "the German staff officer got up and barked a lot of orders" (*ibid.*, p. 117). The supreme command of the Wehrmacht thought that "even now, in the event of war," Czechoslovakia would "pin down some 25 German divisions at the beginning." It estimated that the Czechoslovak armed forces at war strength comprised 750,000 men and 1,360 airplanes (*DGFP*, IV, 53–58, 109–10).

27. *Ibid.*, pp. 129–32.

28. *Ibid.*, p. 145. The Sixth Zone contained, in four small areas, 5,615, 11,379, 4,000, and 2,913 Czechs, while respective figures for the Germans were as follows: 539, 254, 0, and 63 (*ibid.*, pp. 129–31).

29. *Ibid.*, pp. 164–65.

Germany as the most important part of the agreement.[30] The territorial losses to Germany sustained by the Czechoslovak Republic were tremendous. In addition, large amounts of its territory were ceded to Hungary and Poland. The loss of territory also included 33 percent, or 4,922,440, of the country's population. A total of 1,161,616 Czechs and Slovaks were left in the Third Reich, Poland, and Hungary.[31] The Republic now measured 38,190 square miles and had 9,807,096 inhabitants, including 377,830 Germans.[32] The fact that even the new Republic contained a German minority while losing more than one million of its own nationals showed clearly that in Central Europe it was impossible to arrive at a nationally homogeneous state unit.

The real measure of the Nazi policy was the gap between its contention in the pre-Munich period and what actually happened when the foundations of Czechoslovak democracy were undermined. The Czech gloomy prophecies were fulfilled. It was not the German minority but the Czechoslovak Republic itself that had been the key objective of Hitler and Henlein. It was not the right of self-determination but eastward expansion that directed Nazi policies. The almost pathetic attempt of the SdP, encouraged from Berlin, to justify a policy of subversion and violence on the basis of national self-determination proved to be only a smoke screen. The true reason behind the Sudeten German question was not exasperation with the Czechoslovak authorities but the savage racial and emotional character imparted by German nationalism to its Czech relations. That the Sudeten German leaders, inspired by pan-German aspirations, bore responsibility for the Czechoslovak crisis appears to be an indisputable fact established by all available evidence.

The economic picture of the new Republic looked black. It had lost about one third of its industrial potential. The most staggering loss

30. The diplomatic correspondent of the *Manchester Guardian* noted: "The bearing of the German representatives on the military subcommittee of the International Commission has only one parallel—namely the bearing of the German military chiefs at Brest Litovsk in 1918" (Elizabeth Wiskemann, "Czechs and Germans after Munich," *Foreign Affairs*, XVII, January 1939, 294).

31. Czechoslovakia ceded 738,502 Czechs and Slovaks to the Reich, 134,311 to Poland, and 288,803 to Hungary according to the census of 1930 (*Central European Observer*, Dec. 16, 1938). The Vienna award (Nov. 2, 1938) by Germany and Italy determined the new Czechoslovak-Hungarian frontier. Some 1,027,000 inhabitants fell to Hungary. About 241,698 inhabitants were lost to Poland, which occupied the largest Czechoslovak industrial basin in the Těšín territory.

32. The census of 1930 was taken as the basis. In view of natural increase, the official estimate of the population was put at 10,300,000 inhabitants in 1938. The Germans were divided as follows: 99,256 stayed in Bohemia, 135,542 in Moravia, 134,317 in Slovakia, and 8,715 in Ruthenia (*ibid.*).

was that of nearly all the lignite mines (93 percent) and of more than one half of the coal mines (55 percent). Czechoslovakia also lost about 46 percent of her supply of electric energy. In comparison with the pre-Munich situation, the new state had to spend more than 1 milliard Kč for the import of coal and some 180–360 million for imported electric energy. The major part of the export industries (paper, glass, jewelry, pottery, and textiles) was left in the Sude-tengau. Industrial export capacity amounted to only 48.3 percent of the pre-Munich total. The ensuing sharply unfavorable trade balance clearly indicated the extent of the impoverishment.

The Republic remained agriculturally self-supporting, but its tim-ber reserves—in the Historic Provinces alone—declined by 42.4 percent. The mutual dependence of the separated territories and the remaining part of the Republic was evidenced by the necessity of large imports of lignite and coal to the new state. Comparing the figures from Jan. 1, 1939, to April 30, 1939, it can be seen that 33.22 percent of the total Czechoslovak imports were contributed by the Sudeten territories; and the exports of the Republic—from March 15, 1939, when it became the Protectorate—to the Sudeten areas amounted to 25.32 percent.[33]

In 1940, Henlein remarked that "the strengthening of our co-operation with the Protectorate, with which we have been bound by hundred-year-old ties, remains our special problem. We must hope that the further development after the establishment of the customs union [of the Protectorate with the Reich in 1940] will draw closer these two economically mutual dependent territorial units."[34] Yet even in comparison with the Czech market, the prospects for the antiquated small-scale Sudeten export firms' competing effectively with the modern Reich German textile, glass, or pottery industries remained gloomy. Only the war with the development of new needs saved the unbalanced Sudeten economy from an acute crisis.

Centuries-long economic cooperation within one geographical unit could not be destroyed by a simple stroke of the pen. The annexed territory and the rump state of Czechoslovakia could be divided by an artificial line on the map, but the many economic ties and mutual dependencies could not be broken even by Nazism. For the moment, economic unity was stronger than man-made decisions.

33. The data are taken from an instructive study by the Československý studijní ústav (Czechoslovak Research Institute), *Hospodářské následky Mnichova*, p. 72. See also *DGFP*, II, 856, 865–66, 912–15.
34. The official Prague daily, *Der neue Tag*, for Feb. 1, 1940, as quoted in the *Central European Observer*, XVII (April 1, 1940). See also Deutsche Bank, *Das Sudetenland im deutschen Wirtschaftsraum*.

After Munich, the Republic was reconstituted on a federal basis as Czecho-Slovakia. The former provinces of Slovakia and Sub-Carparthian Ruthenia received wide autonomy, with their own cabinets and diets. The central government in Prague was entrusted with the administration of the Historic Provinces although only foreign affairs, national defense, and finances were controlled from Prague.[35] The very existence of the new state depended on the friendly disposition of Berlin. Prague's new foreign minister, Dr. František Chvalkovský, therefore planned to pursue a policy of cooperation with the Reich. The Agrarian Party, which became the directing political force, was anxious to establish good relations with Berlin, and the cabinet headed by Gen. Jan Syrový, strove to remove points of friction with the Reich in order to prevent German complaints and retain a modicum of independence.

Munich created a new political situation within the country. In a prevailing atmosphere of severe criticism, gloom, desolation, discouragement, and ideological confusion, many of the former leading politicians went out of public life. The center of power moved from the democratic-liberal group around Beneš toward the right. The

35. At the beginning of October, the Slovak political groups under the direction of the semi-Fascist Hlinka Party met at Žilina and asked for the creation of a Slovak cabinet consisting of a president and four other ministers. Dr. Jozef Tiso became the first Slovak premier on Oct. 6, 1938 (*Documents 1938*, II, 342). On November 22, the new constitutional law establishing autonomy for Slovakia and Ruthenia passed in Parliament. After Munich, Slovakia came under the influence of the totalitarian autonomist Hlinka People's Party which cooperated with the SdP from the winter of 1937–38 on. A separatist Nazi-minded wing developed within the party and was gaining ground under the impact of Nazi successes at Munich. Its leaders entered into direct contact with the Reich (*DGFP*, IV, 86–93). This faction, led by Dr. Vojtěch Tuka, Dr. Ferdinand Ďurčanský, and Alexander Mach, received subsidies from Berlin (*DGFP*, IV, 171). The best study on the modern history of Slovakia, with special focus on the post-1938 period, is by Jozef Lettrich, *History of Modern Slovakia*. See also Král, *Pravda*, pp. 111–16, 127–32, and the interesting memoirs by a member of the cabinets of General Syrový and R. Beran, Dr. Ladislav Feierabend, *Ve vládách Druhé republiky*, pp. 54–57, 93, 105–22, 137 ff.

The German minority in Slovakia (the Carpathian Germans) embraced the Carpathian Party, which was a part of the SdP. Its leader, Franz Karmasin, became state secretary in the Slovak cabinet. After Munich the Carpathian Party was reorganized and renamed the German Party. It formed an outpost of the NSDAP. Karmasin received a monthly subsidy of 30,000 RM until April 1, 1940, when it was reduced to 15,000 RM. It is not clear at what date the subsidy started. The VoMi deposited 300,000 RM for Karmasin in Bratislava in the fall of 1939. The governor of Austria, Dr. Seyss-Inquart—a Sudeten—also granted Karmasin a subsidy. The activities of Karmasin were characteristic of the fifth column. As an agent of Berlin, he carried out its orders. Today, Karmasin is active in the Sudeten movement in West Germany (*Československo a norimberský proces*, pp. 344–45; *DGFP*, VIII, 476–77; *National Socialism*, p. 480).

system of liberal democracy was being replaced by an oligarchical regime whose axis was formed by a conservative coalition between a large part of upper bourgeoisie and a few scattered groups of urban and rural middle classes. The party system was simplified by the fusion of all bourgeois parties into a new Party of National Unity under the leadership of the Agrarian Rudolf Beran; the Left founded the Labor Party. The two-party system replaced the former multiplicity of parties, the Party of National Unity forming the government, the Labor Party its constructive opposition. When the resignation of President Beneš left the presidency vacant, Dr. Emil Hácha was elected president on November 30.[36] On Dec. 1, 1938, the cabinet of General Syrový was replaced by a new government headed by Rudolf Beran.[37]

Prague was aware of the fact that any overt hostility against the Reich would lead to the end of its independence.[38] Its aim therefore was to adapt the country to the changed conditions without renouncing Czechoslovak sovereign rights.[39] Abandoned by all, her frontier still unguaranteed despite the promises of the Munich agreement, Czechoslovakia strove to regulate her relations with Berlin and fulfill the far-reaching demands of Germany in order to maintain at least formal sovereignty. Held in dependence at sword's point by Germany, Czechoslovakia intended to endure the present situation with patience until a change in the international climate would make it possible to improve her position.

On November 19 Prague signed the German-Czechoslovak Protocol on the Construction of the Oder-Danube Canal and the treaty for a Breslau-Vienna highway giving Germany extraterritorial privileges in Czechoslovak territory.[40] The highway was to be included in the Germans customs and passport area. In January 1939 the Reich arranged for free transit of its property in sealed cars through the

36. Hácha was born in 1872. He was president of the Supreme Administrative Court in Prague and never participated in politics. Hácha was an able lawyer bent on scholarly pursuits and fond of music and art. For a portrait, see DGFP, IV, 175–76.

37. Beran was born in 1887. He was a clever political tactician of a rather provincial caliber, without much imagination and with no pretense to the cultural polish and intellectual sophistication of the Beneš and Masaryk circle. He was definitely not a personality to lead the state in its moment of supreme crisis.

38. For the post-Munich attitude of the Czech people and their politicians, see the interesting reports by German chargé d'affaires Hencke (DGFP, IV, 104–108, 173–77, 182–83).

39. Compare the address of Beran before the National Assembly on Dec. 3, 1938 (Documents 1938, II, 364).

40. DGFP, IV, 153–54.

Republic between Breslau and Vienna.[41] On November 20 a treaty was signed between the two governments covering the right of option and the acquisition of German nationality. A German-Czechoslovak declaration on the protection of the respective national minorities was also signed.[42] (The form of a declaration was preferred by the Nazis to the more formal treaty because the Reich had no intention of granting to the Czechs the position the latter had permitted the German element to enjoy in the Republic.)[43]

According to Hitler, who explained his views to Chvalkovský, after Munich there were only two alternatives left to Prague. The first was to arrive at a friendly agreement with Berlin, since Prague was a vital part of the German sphere of influence. The second was to follow a policy of unfriendly activities toward the Reich (which could not tolerate the presence of a hostile country at its southern flank). The guarantee of Czechoslovakia's security should not be her now superfluous army but the friendship of Berlin. Hitler regarded the Republic as an agricultural country which would supply Germany with its products in exchange for German industrial goods.[44] Should Prague follow an anti-German policy, it would be liquidated quickly. Hitler, however, did not seem to have made a final decision so far as Prague's fate was concerned, although as a preparatory measure he issued a general directive for a surprise attack on Czechoslovakia.[45] Further, the German Foreign Office prepared a draft on an Entente Cordiale between Berlin and Prague. It presented the view of the more conservative section of the Wilhelmstrasse.[46]

Czechoslovakia should become a satellite of the Reich. In all questions of foreign policy Prague was to serve the policy of Berlin.[47] Dr. Ernst Woermann, under-secretary and head of the political division of the Wilhelmstrasse, prepared a commentary on the draft explaining the German desiderata. Prague should carry out an extensive adjustment of its policy to the internal German structure in

41. Ripka, *Munich*, p. 273.
42. For the text, see *DBFP*, III, 649–53.
43. *DGFP*, IV,141.
44. Hitler to Chvalkovský on Oct. 14, 1938 (*DGFP*, IV, 69–72).
45. On Oct. 21, 1938 (*ibid.*, pp. 99–100).
46. *TWC*, XII, 931.
47. *Ibid.*, pp. 833–35. The undated draft was prepared by Dr. Gaus during November. This draft was supplemented by a draft of an economic agreement prepared on December 9, and a draft of a secret military clause from December 9. These drafts already included all the demands which were to be implemented by the establishment of the Protectorate on March 15, 1939 (Heinrich Bodensieck, "Der Plan eines 'Freundschaftsvertrages' zwischen dem Reich und der Tchecho-Slowakei im Jahre 1938," *Zeitschrift für Ostforschung*, X, September 1961, 464 ff.).

economic and political matters, particularly with regard to the Jewish question.[48] Yet even this wide-ranging proposal of vassalage was not considered satisfactory and it vanished in the files of Ribbentrop. With his mind set on war, Hitler obviously could not leave Czechoslovakia wedged in the heart of the Reich. In view of his war plans it would be very difficult indeed to embark on a military campaign with hostile Czechoslovakia pointed at his flank.[49] He realized that many Czechs indulged in plans and dreams of extending their present frontiers and that they were opposed to the Nazi Reich by the inescapable facts of their geographical position and different ideology. The Czechs could not become pro-German when their everyday life reminded them of the impossible solution at Munich. They would use the first opportunity to rise against Hitler because they had everything to gain from his defeat and nothing to lose from his victory.

Any agreement on paper could not change the facts of history, political life, geography, ideology, and power realities. Czechoslovakia did not intend to attack Hitler in 1938 or 1939, but her place was determined by circumstances beyond her control. Her interests were opposed to those of Berlin, but her destiny was interwoven with that of Nazi Germany in the sense that every German defeat was a Czechoslovak victory. The mere existence of the Czechoslovak Army with its modern equipment presented a serious potential danger to the Nazi Reich, involved as it would be in a European war. Despite all the paper promises, such an army could not but strike at the Nazi Reich when a favorable opportunity arose. Hitler could not be expected to put up with such a danger when embarking on an offensive war. He therefore felt that the occupation of the Czech barrier would guarantee the heart of the Reich. Its control by Germany would be tantamount to German hegemony in East Central and Southeastern Europe.

Any German government bent on aggressive plans in Europe could not tolerate the existence of an independent Czechoslovakia in the center of the German space. It had to enter into an alliance with her or neutralize her. The pan-German aspirations to take possession of the Czech promontory and the brutal force of Nazism determined the way for attaining the neutralization of the Republic in a manner habitual to Hitler: by assassination. Thus, it was between the end of November and the middle of December that Hitler made the final

48. *TWC*, XII, 835–39. The comment was prepared on Nov. 25, 1938.
49. See the arguments used by Hitler during the audience with Chvalkovský on Jan. 21, 1939 (*DGFP*, IV, 190–95).

decision to crush Prague. In the middle of December he ordered the OKW to prepare the liquidation of Czechoslovakia.[50] The remaining German minority in the Republic and the Nazi-minded Slovak and Ukrainian elements again were selected to assist Germany.[51]

The remainder of the German minority in Czechoslovakia was disappointed to learn that it could not share the lot of its countrymen. With exaggerated and invented reports it strove to induce the Reich authorities to annex new areas. It openly criticized the SdP for not having represented Sudeten interests more efficiently. The attitude of the Czechs was hostile and tensions between both groups continued, but there was no persecution or any organized drive against the Germans. Many Czechs boycotted German shops and goods.[52] Some Germans were dismissed from private Czech enterprises because the Czech refugees and many thousands of Czech employees coming from the Sudeten area, Slovakia, and elsewhere had to be given new jobs. The precarious economic situation of the state, which was carrying out the demobilization of a million soldiers, made it almost impossible to give special attention to German complaints in view of the greater tasks of reconstruction which lay ahead.[53] The Sudeten Germans were instructed by Berlin[54] to abstain from exercising their rights of option for Germany because they had to perform "the responsible and at the same time advantageous mission . . . as coguarantors" of Czechoslovak dependence on the Reich.[55]

The German minority was represented by a new group assembling the remaining five deputies and three senators of the SdP in a parliamentarian club of the German National Socialist deputies and senators in the Czecho-Slovak Republic. Deputy Ernst Kundt became its chairman and new leader of the Sudeten German group.[56] The

50. The directive of December 17 by General Keitel (*DGFP*, IV, 185–86).
51. The VoMi was charged with underground activities in Ruthenia (*ibid.*, p. 138). The German Security Service (SD) reported on November 29 about its useful connections in the Republic. As a result, the SD financed journeys of the Slovak separatists (Ďurčanský, etc.). The German Foreign Office refunded some of the expenses (*ibid.*, pp. 171–72).
52. *Ibid.*, pp. 179–81. I use the report of Hencke of Dec. 10, 1938 (*ibid.*).
53. The memorandum by Deputy Kundt of Dec. 16, 1938 (*ibid.*, pp. 183–85). The new frontier cut off the economic lifelines of the remaining Germans with the Sudeten territories. The Reich dispatched 10 million Kč for a special welfare fund on December 7. Up to Feb. 6, 1939, the sum of 8,183,334 Kč was turned over to Kundt (*ibid.*, pp. 177–78, 187–88).
54. *Ibid.*, p. 189.
55. Hencke in his report of December 10 (*ibid.*, p. 181).
56. *Naše doba*, XXXXVI (November 1938), 100.

Sudetens continued their pre-Munich course of action. On December 14 Kundt asked in the National Assembly for the establishment of a new relationship with the Third Reich. He felt that the Czechs should realize that the Sudeten Germans were members of the German National Socialist community under the leadership of Adolf Hitler.[57]

After Munich the German campaign unfolded under more adverse conditions for the Czechs, despite the fact that the latter had adopted a conciliatory attitude from the outset. The Henleinist methods of pressure were faithfully reenacted with all the familiar techniques of intimidation, concealed threats, and hackneyed arguments. The German University at Prague solemnly celebrated the beginning of the winter session with Nazi manifestations on Jan. 11, 1939. The German element in Czechoslovakia (wrote Kundt the same day) did not consider itself a minority but an upholder of German rights entrusted with a special mission.[58] He specified German demands on January 17 in his article "What We Want": the right of free political activities as National Socialists; employment of all Germans; exclusion of Jews in any interaction of German-Czech relations; establishment of close political and economic relations between the Reich and the Czechs; and the development of a good relationship between the Sudeten Germans and the Prague cabinet.[59] Kundt's arrogant tone aroused the Czech press,[60] which made comparisons between the critical situation of the Czech minority in the Reich and the privileged status of the Germans in the Republic.[61]

A new consciousness of rising pressure and of the approaching political storm dominated Prague. This feeling, stemming from the tense international situation, had been building up since the Republic had weathered the series of German, Hungarian, and Polish territorial annexations in the fall of 1938, thus showing a surprising degree of resilience and opposition to the forces that were pulling the new state apart. The principal problem for Czech political leaders was how long they could prolong their resistance to German demands and how

57. *Ibid.* (January 1939), p. 172.

58. *Ibid.* (February 1939), pp. 228–29. Kundt's article was published in the *Prager Zeitungs-Dienst* on January 11.

59. Ripka, *Munich*, pp. 279–80.

60. *Národní politika* (January 18) commented that "the German attitude has to change in the new Czecho-Slovakia," and *Lidové listy* (January 18) stated that "Kundt does not facilitate his task by using the old tone" (Procházka, "La Tchécoslovaquie," p. 173).

61. The Czechoslovak Germans were provided with one university, two institutes of technology, 14 secondary schools, 13 training colleges for teachers, 31 schools for apprentices, 38 higher elementary schools, and 124 elementary schools (Ripka, *Munich*, p. 281).

quickly and sharply pressures would be built up to make them bow.[62] The government watched anxiously the whispering propaganda of the Germans as they spread a rumor of the early incorporation of the Republic within the Reich. Kundt's statement made on December 14, to the effect that the Germans had held on for twenty years and had to be patient for a few more months, was felt to be an ominous preview of things to come.[63] In a country contiguous to Germany and with not one single ally anywhere, the problem was not only of remaining independent but also of forestalling possible German actions. Probably the last thing in the world Prague wanted was to give Berlin the impression that it was failing to follow its new policy of cooperation. It was wary over the increasingly aggressive tone of the Sudeten Germans.

The prevailing uncertainty about the designs of Berlin induced Prague to send Foreign Minister Chvalkovský to Berlin to confer with Hitler and Ribbentrop in order to obtain a guarantee of the present Czechoslovak frontier. Both Nazi leaders complained to the Czechoslovak minister of sinister symptoms of a general trend in the Republic that might lead to fatal consequences. A section of the Czech press looked upon the present situation as temporary, Chvalkovský was told, and many Jews and old Beneš officials and sympathizers were still serving in influential positions. A speedy reduction of the army was regarded as essential. Hitler and Ribbentrop stated emphatically that the new Czech policy of rapprochement was not shared by many Czechs, exhorted Chvalkovský to eliminate the spirit of Beneš and the influence of the Jews, and warned him of the grave consequences which would result from any display of anti-German tendencies.[64] Berlin left all basic problems open and did not clarify its intentions. When Chvalkovsky asked for a guarantee of frontiers, Ribbentrop was evasive.

From the Czech point of view, Chvalkovský's visit to Berlin was disappointing. Prague had expected to buy the guarantee of its frontiers even at the price of great sacrifice. Insecurity concerning the future was deepened by the fact that all fundamental questions

62. There were, indeed, differences within the Czech political camp. Some right-wing bourgeois groups sought to install a more authoritarian regime, and hit at Masaryk and Beneš. The Fascist movement was without any influence. Under the shadow of Berlin, the left lowered its voice and the right became vocal in its demands and attacks against the humanist principles of the pre-1938 Republic. For a useful survey, see Feierabend, *Ve vládách*, pp. 61, 66, 77, 92, 94.

63. *DGFP*, IV, 188–89.

64. Chvalkovský's conversation with Hitler and Ribbentrop took place on Jan. 21, 1939 (*DGFP*, IV, 190–202).

remained unanswered.[65] Chvalkovský urged the Czechs to accede to German wishes. He reported the distrust voiced by Berlin, and restated his conviction that any failure to meet German demands would lead to greater political and economic pressures. The cabinet grudgingly resolved to recognize the Franco government *de jure,* to curb the press attitude toward the Reich, to recognize the organization and the activities of the NSDAP on Czechoslovak territory, and to set up a special committee to settle the grievances of the German minority.[66] Yet Prague still declined to abandon its treaty system. Above all, it strove to secure recognition of its neutral status and a guarantee of its frontier. In spite of the evasive answers from Berlin, Prague approached all four Munich Powers on February 22, asking them to guarantee the frontier of the Republic, which would in turn proclaim its neutrality.[67]

The pressure from Berlin was accompanied by Kundt's increasingly violent tone. He declared at Prague on February 17 that the Germans in the Republic wanted to exist and work as the Kulturträger of their nation.

> The Germans should be free people, who shall live, work and expand according to National Socialist laws . . . and according to National Socialist justice in private and public life.[68]

Premier Beran concluded an agreement with Kundt—who was obviously a mouthpiece of Berlin[69]—in which the legal status of the Sudeten German group would be discussed by Kundt and two

65. The report by Hencke of January 21 (*ibid.,* pp. 203–204).

66. *Ibid.,* pp. 204–206. General Krejčí, chief of the General Staff, resigned on February 19, and the expenditure for the army for 1939 was reduced by one third (*ibid.,* pp. 205, 213–14). The army was supposed to have a strength of 120,000 men (*ibid.,* p. 228). The National Bank surrendered to the Reichsbank the gold coverage for Czechoslovak bank notes withdrawn from circulation in the Sudeten territory (*ibid.,* pp. 215, 242–43). It was also decided to issue regulations for the Jewish question and to dismiss various high officials of the Beneš era (*ibid.,* p. 205). For Czech resistance to German pressures, see Heinrich Bodensieck, "Das Dritte Reich und die Lage der Juden in der Tschecho-Slowakei nach München," *Vierteljahrshefte für Zeitgeschichte,* IX (July 1961), 249–61.

67. *DGFP,* IV, 215–16.

68. Ripka, *Munich,* p. 282.

69. Kundt worked under the supervision of the VoMi to which he sent reports, some of which were addressed to Hitler. Copies were also dispatched to the German legation at Prague (*DGFP,* IV, 217). Kundt also took care of intelligence reports, prepared lists of unreliable Czechs, and so forth. The German espionage agency at Dresden, the Sudetendeutsche Kontrollstelle, directed activities against Czechoslovakia (Procházka, "La Tchécoslovaquie," p. 233).

members of the cabinet.[70] At the end of February, Kundt's *Press Bulletin* noted that Berlin considered the Republic's "attitude against Bolshevism and the Jews" as the criterion of Prague's disposition toward National Socialist Germany.[71] There was a general feeling in Prague that some kind of agreement with Berlin was necessary to prevent the situation from getting a lot worse. The internal stabilization and consolidation of the country urgently required a definitive settlement of its relations with Berlin. This was considered undesirable in Berlin, however, in view of Hitler's determination to smash the Republic. To obtain some clue to the German policy line, Chvalkovský dispatched Dr. Herbert Masařík, his chief of cabinet, to Berlin, with broad concessions. Masařík, however, was allowed to confer only with a relatively minor offical of the Wilhelmstrasse on March 1.[72] Berlin clearly intended to avoid any closer commitment and to leave Prague in the dark while preparing the ground for the final blow.

The Nazi plan called for the encouragement of a Slovak separatist revolt against the Prague government. It intended to create German demonstrations so that the Reich might appear compelled to intervene against Czech "lawlessness and anarchy" and assist the Germans against their "persecutors." Finally, Hungary would be given Ruthenia and thus Berlin would firmly ensure Hungarian support.[73] Hitler and Göring received the Slovak extremist leaders, Tuka, Ďurčanský, and Mikuláš Pružinský (who undertook the trip without the consent of the Prague government), and promised them German assistance if Slovakia would proclaim herself an independent state.[74]

The subversive activities of the Slovak and Ukrainian Fascists and the secret negotiations of the Slovak ministers with the Reich could not be allowed to develop further. Prague demanded that the Slovak

70. Ripka, *Munich*, p. 281.
71. *Ibid.*, p. 289. Kundt declared in Berlin in February that the Germans in Czechoslovakia played an important role in the Reich policy in Southeastern Europe (*Německý imperialismus*, pp. 498–99).
72. *DGFP*, IV, 221–24. See also the description by Dr. M. Schubert as cited in Feierabend, *Ve vládách*, pp. 179–96.
73. Hungary continued to agitate against Czechoslovakia even after the Vienna award. In the period from November 3 until the end of 1938, Hungarian terrorists carried out 19 armed attacks against Czechoslovak territory (*DGFP*, IV, 222; *Naše doba*, February 1939, p. 229).
74. Hitler received Tuka and Karmasin on February 12 (*DGFP*, IV, 209–13). Göring conferred with Ministers Ďurčanský and Pružinský at the beginning of March (*ibid.*, pp. 230–31). Wilhelm Keppler, state secretary at the German Foreign Office, supervised the developments in Slovakia from Vienna with the assistance of Josef Bürckel, the Austrian Gauleiter, and Arthur Seyss-Inquart, the governor of Austria (Lettrich, pp. 105–108, 124–29).

ministers refrain from all propaganda activities against the Republic and associate themselves openly with the present constitutional order. When the Slovak extremists continued their agitation, President Hácha dismissed Slovak Premier Tiso and his ministers from their posts on the night of March 9, and the Czechoslovak Army was instructed to maintain public order in Slovakia. The Slovak nationalist Karol Sidor, who favored union with the Czechs, was appointed the new Slovak prime minister.[75] Ďurčanský, who fled to Vienna, and Tiso were summoned to Berlin where they were told bluntly by Hitler that if Slovakia "hesitated or refused to be separated from Prague, he would leave the fate of Slovakia to events" and allow her occupation by Hungarian troops.[76] Ribbentrop set Tiso a time limit: He would await a report from Tiso by 1 P.M. on March 14, informing him that the Slovak Diet had proclaimed the independence of Slovakia.[77] The Fascist wing of the Slovak Hlinka party, bent on the destruction of the Republic, was used by Berlin to cover another aggression of Hitler through the slogan of the right of self-determination. Berlin considered an independent Slovakia weak and thought that such a state would "best further the German need for penetration and settlement in the east." Oriented toward the Reich, it would serve the Nazi aggressive plans against Poland and Southeastern Europe. It would also be helpful in completely isolating the Czechs.

While the Slovak part of the Nazi plot worked smoothly, the Czechoslovak General Staff was receiving reports that Germany was preparing military action against the Republic. By March 10, the General Staff secretly obtained the German plans for a military deployment against Czechoslovakia and the information that March 15 was the date of occupation. Foreign Minister Chvalkovský, however, derided the intelligence. He believed that Germany would not violate the Munich agreement because of her self-interest in the temporary status quo and that she would merely exert strong pressure to force Czechoslovakia to reduce her army and cut her ties with the

75. DGFP, IV, 229–31, 233, 237, 238, 247–48; Ripka, Munich, pp. 361–68; Feierabend, Ve vládách, pp. 137 ff.

76. The conversation was held on March 13, 1939 (DGFP, IV, 243–45).

77. Lettrich, p. 129. For the German plans, see the memorandum submitted by under state secretary Dr. Ernst Woermann to Hitler on Oct. 7, 1938. Dr. Woermann stated that "a slogan of [the] 'right of self-determination'" should be used "for the outside world" (DGFP, IV, 46–48). To conceal the German intentions, Hencke affirmed in Prague that the support of the Slovak Fascists was a matter of a faction of the NSDAP which in no way represented the official German policy (Feierabend, Ve vládách, pp. 138–39, 141; DGFP, IV, 231).

West.[78] Prague did not realize that by moving the bulk of its troops to Slovakia it fell into the German trap and denuded the Historic Provinces of the necessary military cover. It was also obviously unaware of the fact that Hitler had ordered the OKW to make military preparations to implement an ultimatum to Czechoslovakia on March 10, the very day the Czechoslovak Army occupied all military points in Slovakia.[79]

In view of the progress of the antidemocratic campaign in Slovakia, it was now the turn of the Sudeten Germans to foment new manifestations in other parts of the Republic. The VoMi and its Sudeten agents organized German demonstrations on March 12 in all the Czech cities with a German element.[80] There were some skirmishes in Prague and Brno, but it was difficult to rouse violence among the Czechs.[81] The core of the demonstrators was formed by German students who took over the tasks of the old FS. They secretly organized special units in Prague and Brno and staged anti-Czech and anti-Jewish demonstrations.[82] Berlin set off simultaneously a violent press and radio campaign. The propaganda machine worked with full speed, furiously protesting against alleged persecution of the Sudeten Germans and attacking what it called the revival of the Beneš spirit. On March 13, Hitler secretly offered a free hand to Hungary in Ruthenia.[83] The right of self-determination—as soon as it ceased to serve Nazi objectives—became a dead letter.

The declaration of the new Slovak state by the Slovak Diet at Bratislava added an even more ominous note to the critical situation.

78. *Právo lidu*, Feb. 19, 1947; *Svobodné slovo*, Feb. 19, 1947. The new chief of the General Staff, Gen. Bohuslav Fiala, and the head of its intelligence section, Col. František Moravec, warned Chvalkovský on March 10 and 13. Czechoslovak intelligence received the first warning from the French Second Section before March 10. Two days later, new intelligence stated that the Slovak separatist action was but a part of the German plan against Prague. (See also Procházka, "La Tchécoslovaquie," p. 239.)
79. The terms of the ultimatum prepared by the OKW on March 11, 1939, were handed over to Hácha and Chvalkovský on March 15 (*DGFP*, IV, 234–35).
80. The demonstrations took place at Prague, Brno, Olomouc, Jihlava, and Ostrava (Václav Buben, ed., *Šest let okupace Prahy*, p. 15; *DGFP*, IV, 239, 246; *Německý imperialismus*, pp. 504–505).
81. The Reich sent the so-called Vorkommandos clandestinely to prepare the occupation (*K. H. Frank*, p. 186).
82. K. H. Frank, "The SS in March 1939," *Böhmen und Mähren*, III, May 1941, 179.
83. Admiral Horthy's remark is indicative of the low degree of international morality in Hitler's Europe. "On Thursday the 16th of this month a frontier incident will take place, to be followed on Saturday by the big thrust" (*DGFP*, IV, 241).

Faced by Hitler with two alternatives, independence or Hungarian domination, the Diet decided for independence on March 14, and the Fascist faction of the Hlinka People's Party assumed practical control of Slovakia. The larger autonomist group favoring union with the Czechs submitted to the less unfavorable alternative.[84] Slovakia thus became the first satellite of Nazi Germany.[85]

Since March 10, Prague had watched the German backstage maneuvering with increased anxiety. It was also deeply concerned by the chaotic situation at home. During the last days all its efforts to isolate and solve the Czecho-Slovak problem had failed through the interference of Berlin. Prague awoke too late to the fact that the Reich had used the Slovak Fascists to cause dissension between Czechs and Slovaks, thus diverting the attention of Prague from German preparations. Government circles were hard at work trying to understand the puzzle which these developments presented. The prevailing line of reasoning still held that the current quarrel was simply another form of pressure destined to weaken—not to abolish—the sovereignty of the Republic. On March 13, at a meeting of the cabinet, Chvalkovský confessed that he had no adequate explanation for the current crisis and suggested that President Hácha go to Berlin.[86] After delays due to Ribbentrop's instructions to the German legation in Prague to break off all contacts with the Prague authorities, Chvalkovský managed to send a written communication on March 14 asking for a personal meeting between Hácha and Hitler.[87]

The special train with Hácha and Chvalkovský, both still considering the future in terms of a small Czech state, left Prague at 4 P.M.,

---

84. Dr. Jozef Tiso, a Catholic priest, headed the first cabinet. He was elected president of the Slovak Republic on Oct. 26, 1939. After the war Tiso declared before the National Court (March 17, 1947): "Without the pressure exercised by Hitler, the Slovak Diet would never have voted in favor of the independence of Slovakia" (Lettrich, p. 133). The Hlinka Party became a Fascist party. For its side of Slovak history, see Joseph A. Mikuš, La Slovaquie dans le drame de l'Europe. Histoire politique de 1918 à 1950; House Report, 83rd Congress, 2nd Session, No. 2684. The latter report was prepared with the assistance of Georgetown University and a group of "experts" and is a biased survey presenting the Fascist Hlinka Party as the true voice of Slovakia.

85. German troops occupied the western part of Slovakia, where they seized huge stocks of war material (DGFP, IV, 259; Lettrich, p. 136). The German-Slovak treaty on the protective relationship between the Reich and Slovakia was signed in March.

86. The deposition of Rudolf Beran at his trial (Svobodné slovo, Feb. 4, 1947).

87. For the story of the German evasive reactions to Hácha's visit to Berlin, see DGFP, IV, 247, 248-49, 255.

March 14, and arrived in Berlin at 10:40 P.M.[88] Meanwhile (at 5:30 P.M.) the troops of the German Eighth Army Corps had crossed the Czechoslovak border near Moravská Ostrava and at 6:40 P.M. the SS-Leibstandarte had occupied the industrial center of Moravská Ostrava.[89] There was no Czech resistance, since no Czechoslovak Army units were stationed in the city. When the first Czech troops were encountered, however, they offered fierce resistance.[90]

Hácha learned about the German invasion in Berlin. He had been received by Hitler in the presence of Göring, Ribbentrop, Keitel, and other high officials at 1:15 A.M. on March 15, 1939. At the interview, Hitler informed Hácha that in view of the Czech "provocations" and of the state of confusion following the break of Slovakia, "he had given the order for invasion by German troops and for the incorporation of Czechoslovakia into the German Reich." The invasion would start at six o'clock in the morning.[91] Bewildered and amazed by the sudden calamity, Hácha called Premier Beran in Prague to announce this "terrible blow," and explain Hitler's ultimatum and threat of bloodshed.[92]

The Czechoslovak cabinet met in Prague after 2 A.M. Armed resistance was regarded as impossible, since the Republic was defenseless without fortifications. In Berlin, Hácha's resistance forced Göring to use threats of destroying Prague by an air attack unless Hácha surrendered. At last, after strong opposition, Hácha signed the German military conditions requiring the capitulation of the Czechoslovak Army and instructed Prague to take measures to prevent any bloodshed. After the military ultimatum had been signed, Ribbentrop presented his Czech visitors with another draft containing a declaration by both governments. Hácha called Prague again. Beran and his cabinet asked Hácha to refrain from signing the declaration placing the fate of the Czech nation in the hands of Hitler, as it would be a clear breach of the constitution. While resisting, Hácha fainted. Finally he finished by signing the fatal document at 4 A.M.[93]

88. *Ibid.*, p. 260.
89. *Ibid.*, pp. 261–62. The Germans occupied this area because they feared that Poland would seize it for herself. This was confessed by Göring to Sir Nevile Henderson (*IMT*, XXXI, 246).
90. Beneš, *Memoirs* (p. 58), on the fight of the 8th Silesian Regiment at Místek.
91. *DGFP*, IV, 263–69; *IMT*, XXXII, 15. For Hácha's report on the meeting, see *Mnichov v dokumentech*, II, 392–95.
92. *Svobodné slovo*, Feb. 4, 1947.
93. *Ibid.* The indictment at the trial of the Protectorate government included a description of the fateful night in Berlin (*ibid.*, April 30, June 12, 1946). Dr. Paul Schmidt was present as Hitler's interpreter. For his description, see Schmidt, *Hitler's Interpreter*, pp. 122–25.

The conviction was unanimously expressed . . . that the aim of all efforts must be the safeguarding of calm, order and peace in this part of Central Europe. The Czechoslovak President declared that, in order to serve this object and to achieve ultimate pacification, he confidently placed the fate of the Czech people and country in the hands of the Führer of the German Reich. The Führer accepted this declaration and expressed his intention of taking the Czech people under the protection of the German Reich and of guaranteeing them an autonomous development of their ethnic life as suited to their character.[94]

Prague was caught unprepared by the unexpected catastrophe. It had thought that the topic of the conference would be the secession of Slovakia. Yet even after the signing of the declaration it still imagined that Hitler would leave some kind of sovereignty to the Czech state and that the main reason for the German occupation was to disarm the army.[95]

During the night of March 14–15, a snowstorm raged through Bohemia and Moravia, preventing many Czechoslovak airplanes from taking off.[96] Only the intelligence section of the General Staff did succeed in escaping with its secret files by air to London. The occupation had come so suddenly that there was not time even to destroy the military stock. In Prague, the General Staff and many state offices burned confidential material throughout the night.[97] Hitler, with Henlein, came unannounced to Prague on the evening of March 15.[98] In the early morning of the same day, specially trained groups of Sudeten Germans assumed police authority or instructed the Czech police officers to follow their orders pending the arrival of the

94. *DGFP*, IV, 270.
95. Dr. Jaroslav Krejčí at the trial of the Protectorate government (*Svobodné slovo*, May 1, 1946). See also Procházka, "La Tchécoslovaquie," p. 289.
96. It is instructive to note Hitler's statement: "In 1939 I gave them [the Czechs] an ultimatum . . . otherwise German aircraft would be over Prague. I would have irremediably lost face if I'd had to put this threat into execution for at 6 o'clock fog was so thick over our airfields that none of our aircraft could have made its sortie" (*Hitler's Secret Conversations*, p. 168).
97. See the second volume of the memoirs of Dr. Ladislav Feierabend (*Ve vládě Protektorátu*, pp. 12–13). Dr. Feierabend, a member of the Protectorate government, fled to England in 1940 and became a minister in the Czechoslovak cabinet in exile until he resigned on Feb. 28, 1945.
98. The commanding officers of Army Groups 3 and 5, Generals Blaskowitz and List, took over the administration in Bohemia and Moravia respectively. K. Henlein and J. Bürckel were entrusted with civil affairs (*Dokumente*, VII, 501).

Wehrmacht.[99] The Gestapo opened headquarters in major cities and began the first wave of arrests.[100] The cheering Sudeten Germans, wildly hailing the German Army, contrasted sharply with groups of weeping Czechs.

During the night of March 15–16, Hitler, Ribbentrop, Frick, and Lammers conferred on the future of the country at Castle Hradčany in Prague, former seat of Bohemian kings and Czechoslovak presidents. They compiled the decree proclaiming the establishment of the Protectorate of Bohemia and Moravia which was announced by Ribbentrop on the Prague radio on March 16. Neither President Hácha nor the Czech cabinet was consulted.

> For a thousand years the provinces of Bohemia and Moravia formed part of the *Lebensraum* of the German people. They were arbitrarily torn from their ancient historic setting by force and folly and, by their ultimate fusion into the artificial structure of Czechoslovakia, became a center of constant unrest. . . . The German Reich, however, cannot tolerate continuous disturbance in these areas which are of such vital importance for its own peace and security. . . . It is therefore in keeping with the law of self-preservation that the German Reich is now resolved to intervene decisively to rebuild the foundations of a reasonable order in central Europe.[101]

According to Hitler's decree, the new Protectorate formed a part of the Greater German Reich, and its German inhabitants became citizens of the Reich and subject to its jurisdiction. The Protectorate was autonomous and self-governing. The Führer would appoint a Reich protector as his direct representative. The Reich took over control of foreign affairs and military protection and exercised direct control over transportation, posts, and telegraphs. It was entitled to issue legal measures valid for the Protectorate and to take all steps necessary for the assurance of security and order.[102]

99. K. H. Frank in *Böhmen und Mähren*, III, 1941, 179. Some of the German students were already members of the SS. Their activities were highly appreciated by Himmler and Heydrich, and the members of the special groups were admitted immediately into the SS (*ibid.*). See also *IMT*, XXXIX, 276.

100. *IMT*, XXIX, 271.

101. *DGFP*, IV, 283–84. The Protectorate treaty of France with Tunisia from 1881 served as the model for Hitler's decree.

102. *Ibid.*, pp. 284–86. See also the ordinance of June 27, 1939, stating that the Reich protector was entitled to change this decree as well as to take whatever measures he regarded as necessary whenever there was a danger of procrastination. The decree of March 16, 1939, introduced the regime of capitulations by declaring the Germans exempt from Protectorate jurisdiction.

Hácha was able to read the decree only after its promulgation. Hitler asked Hácha to come to see him, and assured him that his position as president remained unaltered.[103] Soon thereafter Hitler left Prague for Olomouc, Brno, and Vienna, where he received K. H. Frank and Konstantin von Neurath, whom he appointed, respectively, state secretary in the Protectorate and Reich protector of Bohemia and Moravia.[104] On March 16, Prof. Dr. Josef Pfitzner was appointed deputy mayor of Prague and his signature was required on all city documents.[105] Other Czech cities followed the example of Prague. The Germanization of Czechoslovakia was off to an early start.

Nazi occupation brought to a climax the anti-German sentiment prompted by the aggressive tactics of the Sudeten Germans and their overeagerness to embrace Nazism. In all strata of Czech society there developed a perceptible resolve to checkmate the Germans. President Hácha and the government banned the small pro-Nazi group Vlajka (Flag), and even the leader of the Czech Fascists, Rudolf Gajda, agreed to disband his movement. With the full backing of the Czech political leaders, Hácha constituted a new movement—the National Rally—which replaced old political parties and presented a united counterblock against the Germans. In a sort of national plebiscite, 99.79 percent of Czech men voluntarily applied for membership by May 3, 1939.[106] Important factors in the trend toward close national union were the fact of the German occupation, the arrogant behavior of the Sudetens, the basic prodemocratic orientation of the people, the general desire to resist a traditional enemy, and the common understanding that the Czech people had entered the final stage of the struggle for their national survival. National unity through firm resistance to the Nazi occupation became a matter of vital importance for a nation engulfed in a German sea. It was almost unanimously felt

103. Procházka, "La Tchécoslovaquie," p. 293.
104. *Die Zeit*, March 19, 1939. Frank was nominated despite the pledge given by Hitler to Hácha that no Sudeten German would be appointed. (See the manuscript of Ladislav Feierabend ("Paměti," Washington, 1956, p. 177) and *IMT*, XXXII, 18. On May 5, Frank was designated der Höhere SS- und Polizeiführer in Böhmen und Mähren (*Naše doba*, July 1939, p. 556). In this function Frank was subordinated directly to Berlin and commanded the German police forces in the Protectorate.
105. The German language became the second official language of the city of Prague on March 20 (*Naše doba*, May 1939, p. 415).
106. Hácha dissolved Parliament and designated the executive committee of the National Rally on March 21 (*Naše doba*, May and July 1939, pp. 418, 558). To a certain extent, the rally became a cover for the Czech underground movement. By 1941 it had ceased to function (Král, *Pravda*, pp. 189–95, 209).

that it might constitute the difference between life and death.

In the five and a half months following Munich, the rump state of Czechoslovakia had succeeded in achieving a certain degree of economic consolidation. A chance for relative freedom was still given to millions of Czechs and Slovaks. Yet after Munich it was apparent that the country lay at the mercy of its mighty neighbor. The obligations of the signatories of the Munich agreement were not honored, and the question of guarantees was still on the agenda when Hitler occupied Prague. The Republic had to fear renewed invasion because Munich had not solved the real problem constituted by the continued existence of the Czechoslovak state in what many Germans considered to be their living space. Soon it became evident that the Nazis had no intention of permitting a real settlement. Even the pro-German policy of Chvalkovský did not satisfy Berlin, intent on its advance toward hegemony over Europe. Even while discussing the easing of German-Czech tensions, the Reich and the Sudeten Germans in the Republic were preparing their murderous assault.

On March 15, the terms of the Munich pact were flagrantly flouted by Hitler and his Sudeten auxiliaries. Nazi Germany was ready to embark on her imperialist policy, and the Czech promontory had to be occupied, since, through her unique position, Czechoslovakia epitomized the European balance of power. The American military attaché in Berlin rightly grasped the wider significance of the occupation:

> The military and strategic advantages which Germany has gained by the occupation of Bohemia, Moravia and Slovakia are enormous. Strategically Germany has placed herself between Poland and Hungary. . . . [Germany] commands the gateway to Krakow . . . and the Russian Ukraine. Her new position now places her armies on three sides of Poland . . . with respect to Hungary, Germany also threatens Budapest from the north and west and her armies are in a position to march directly into the fertile plains of Hungary, or through Hungary to Roumania.[107]

The surrender of Prague was a logical consequence of Munich. It showed again that the leaders who refused to fight to the bitter end under more favorable circumstances prior to Munich had engaged on a course of amoral drifting that could end only in a new series of surrenders. In March 1939, without fortifications, it would have meant national suicide to go to war even if the Czechoslovak policy had been conducted by much more capable leaders than the haughty

107. *Nazi Conspiracy and Aggression,* IV, 396.

and naïve Chvalkovský or the crafty and unpopular Beran. The military chiefs and those courageous politicians who wanted to defend the Republic in 1938—as the Abyssinians had defended their country in 1935—proved to have been right in the Munich days when they pressed the irresolute Beneš and the vacillating cabinet and party leaders to resistance up to the last stand. The Republic was defeated in the September previous, not in March.

Certainly the task of the post-Munich conservative and in many ways reactionary regime had been hard and ungrateful, devoid as it was of popular support. It had tackled many problems but failed to solve the main issue: the establishment of firm control over the opposition forces that challenged the legitimate government. No doubt Berlin was the main agent in rousing these disruptive forces, since without German interference Prague could have mastered its crisis by constitutional means. However, responsible circles misjudged the situation completely and up to the last minute believed that Germany would not stage a coup d'état. Through maladroit bungling they sent the old and inexperienced Hácha with the incompetent Chvalkovský to Berlin, where Hitler and Göring were obviously free to exert every kind of pressure upon them. Without doubt, Hácha and Chvalkovský should have refused emphatically to sign what amounted to the surrender of Czechoslovak independence, and the cabinet should have fled the country.[108] The fate of Czechoslovakia was a clear example of a depressing but palpable fact: a small country cannot afford the tragic luxury of committing those errors which larger countries commit with impunity. But these blunders were merely the last link in a chain of events which had enveloped the unfortunate country in forces largely beyond its control.

The Nazi action, carried out despite Hitler's assurances at the time of Munich that he had no further territorial claims in Europe, struck a formidable blow against the spirit of Munich. The appeasers rightly considered it a "lamentable disaster"[109] when one of the chief signatories of the Munich agreement had made it a scrap of paper in less than six months. The peace purchased at the sacrifice of Czechoslovakia had lasted no more than a few months.

The Great Powers, guaranteeing Czechoslovak independence at least morally, did not move in March, although they were made aware of what Hitler had in store for them. However, the American, Soviet, British, and French governments realized that the new

108. For Hácha's opinion, see Feierabend, *Ve vládě*, pp. 54–56.
109. French Foreign Minister Georges Bonnet (*DGFP*, IV, 283).

situation was illegal, and condemned the extinction of free Czechoslovakia in unusually strong terms.[110] Politically, the true meaning of the subjugation of Czechoslovakia was that the German Nazis were resigned to a deterioration of their relations with the West. In the light of the Czechoslovak strategic and economic position, the move revealed that Berlin was prepared to strike a hard blow against Europe. Disinterested as it had been in "far-away" Czechoslovakia, as Chamberlain had referred to her, London would soon feel compelled to offer its assistance to Warsaw and Bucharest. In effect, the occupation of Prague was the final warning signal for the Western democracies and awakened them to the Hitlerite peril.[111]

The dreadful news of the German invasion reached former President Beneš in Chicago. On March 16 he cabled protests to President Roosevelt, Prime Ministers Chamberlain and Daladier, Commissar Maxim Litvinov, and Joseph Avenol, secretary general of the League of Nations.[112] Three days later Beneš called the attention of world public opinion to Germany's brutal violation of her pledges in Central Europe.

Do not believe that it was a question of self-determination for a minority. From the beginning it has been a battle for the existence of the State. . . . With the subjugation of Czechoslovakia, freedom is being guillotined.

Germany had established her government in Prague, and

has cynically claimed to have done all this in the name of peace in Europe.

Beneš warned that the world was in danger of losing the concepts of morality, freedom, and decency. "A society which goes on tolerating this state of affairs will be annihilated and will disappear."[113]

The Czechoslovak legations in Washington, Moscow, London, Warsaw, and Paris refused to recognize the new status of the Republic and withheld their offices from Nazi authorities. Connections were established with the resistance movement in Czechoslovakia. The intelligence officers who had fled Prague on March 14 placed themselves at the disposal of Beneš and continued to operate one of the best intelligence networks in Europe. Additional thousands

110. Beneš, *Memoirs*, pp. 68–70.
111. *DBFP*, IV, *passim;* Reynaud, pp. 204 ff.
112. Beneš, *Memoirs*, p. 65.
113. *Ibid.*, pp. 66–67.

of officers and soldiers fled their homeland to fight for the liberation of
their country from outside its borders. Beneš assumed the leadership
of the Czechoslovak political movement abroad, declaring that
Czechoslovakia continued to exist legally and was bound neither by
the Diktat of Munich nor by the illegal establishment of the Protectorate and puppet Slovakia.[114]

114. *Ibid.*, pp. 63 ff., 298–300. Beneš had a long conversation with President
Roosevelt on May 28. Roosevelt stated that he considered Beneš still to be
president of Czechoslovakia. A valuable description of the beginnings of
Czechoslovak action abroad was given by Křen (*Do emigrace*).

Part III

DECISIVE YEARS

CHAPTER 7

The Protectorate of Bohemia and Moravia
and the Forces of Germanization

The establishment of the Protectorate[1] reflected the harsh element which the Germans injected into their dealings with the Czechs. Scrapping any idea of compromise, the Nazis tightened their control of the Bohemian area. The implications seemed clear enough: A period of intensified Czech-German conflict was in prospect with a new hardening of the Nazi policy throughout Europe.

Nazi policy was guided by the conviction that the Czechs had to be dominated. Any friendly attitude would be taken by them as a sign of weakness.[2] The Nazi leaders were too steeped in brutality, too remote from moral sentiments, to be able to calculate the effect of their actions and policies. Even the conservative Neurath thought it necessary to show a firm hand, "for the Czechs were thick-skulled and treacherous."[3] With the coming of war in 1939, it was in the Nazi interest that calm prevail, so that all possible profit could be garnered from the vast industrial potential of the Protectorate. Hitler decided to avoid anything which might provoke the Czechs, but stated clearly to Reich Protector Neurath that "any Czech defiance must be crushed

1. According to the estimate of Oct. 1, 1940, there were 7,485,000 inhabitants in the Protectorate (*Statistisches Jahrbuch für das Deutsche Reich*, p. 17). It was estimated that there were 226,720 Germans in the Protectorate on March 1, 1940, and 284,360 on April 1, 1944 (*Statistický Zpravodaj* [Statistical Bulletin], VIII, 1945, 83–84). The Protectorate had an area of 48,925 sq km (*Sudetenland*, p. 26). For different estimates, see Bohmann, *Sudetendeutschtum*, p. 194.
2. K. H. Frank to Wilhelm Stuckart, state secretary in the Reich Ministry of the Interior, according to Stuckart's memo of May 2, 1939 (*TWC*, XII, 894 ff.).
3. *DGFP*, VIII, 723–24.

with the harshest means from the outset."[4] The Protectorate was thought to be only a provisional regime in time of war. Actually, this period developed into the most divisive period in Czech-German relations.

Considerable concern was expressed in responsible German circles over the future of the Czech territory and its inhabitants after establishment of the Protectorate. The staff of Rudolf Hess, the Foreign Ministry, the Reich Ministry of the Interior, the offices of various Gauleiters, and the branches of the Protectorate administration and of Berlin ministries each planned a different program.[5] These plans tended toward the abolishment of the Protectorate and the division of the Czech territory in order to hasten its Germanization. As early as July 12, 1939, General Friderici, representative of the Wehrmacht at the Reich Protectorate in Prague, had sent his plan to the OKW recommending peaceful Germanization of the country through assimilation and emigration.[6] High level differences of opinion reached the point where Hitler alone could make the final decision. The fall of France apparently speeded that decision. On Aug. 31, 1940, Neurath asked for an audience with Hitler and sent him Frank's and his own memoranda defending the maintenance of the unity of the Protectorate as a precondition for a successful Germanization of the Czech territory. Frank proposed complete Germanization as a policy goal of the Reich in the Protectorate.

4. *DGFP*, VIII, 538. Report by Dr. Ziemke, Prague representative of the German Foreign Office, for Dec. 15, 1939.
5. See the memo by Frank (*IMT*, XXXIII, 264). For example, the Gauleitung Niederdonau suggested the separation of Moravia from Bohemia and its union with the province of Niederdonau (*ibid.*). See also the so-called Jury Plan—Dr. Hugo Jury was the Gauleiter of the Niederdonau—elaborated in the spring of 1941 (*Československo a norimberský proces*, pp. 206–207). For the text of the various plans, see *Vergangenheit, passim*. In June 1939, the Foreign Ministry believed the aim of the Reich policy to be the destruction of the Czech will to have its own state (Král, *Pravda*, pp. 152–53). In 1939, the NSDAP Gauleitung in Liberec prepared a plan for a division of the Czech territories into six cantons, with the objective of bringing about their Germanization (Štěpán, ed., "*Nové dokumenty*," pp. 735–39). Himmler made a proposition on May 30, 1939, to move Germans from South Tyrol into Moravia. "Ich könnte mir vorstellen, dass im böhmisch-mährischen Raum—am besten in Nordmähren—einmal durch Massnahmen des Deutschen Reiches bzw. des Herrn Reichsprotektors ein solches Gebiet geschaffen werden könnte, das den Vorteil hätte, dass Mähren, das wieder voll und ganz deutsch werden muss, einen wertvollen Zuwachs von 200,000 gutrassigen, sehr bewusst deutschen und kämpferischen Volkselementen bekäme" (Conrad F. Latour, *Südtirol und die Achse Berlin-Rom 1938–1945*, Stuttgart, 1962, p. 34).
6. *IMT*, XXVI, 377. Friderici stated frankly that as the German nation was master in the Czech territory it should take steps to solve the Czech problem forever.

Such a process of Germanization would provide for:

(1) The national mutation of racially suitable Czechs;

(2) the expatriation of Czechs who cannot be racially absorbed and of the stratum of the intelligentsia hostile to the Reich, or Sonderbehandlung these and all destructive elements;

(3) the resettlement of the space freed in this manner with fresh German blood.[7]

Czech schools would be abolished gradually and Czech would cease to be the official language. All these methods could succeed provided they were planned and carried out by a responsible central agency.[8]

Konstantin von Neurath agreed completely with Frank's plan. In his own memorandum he set forth the objectives of Nazi policy.

> From a state political point of view this goal can mean nothing else than complete incorporation into the Greater German Reich; from a national political point of view it means the occupation of this area by German men and women.[9]

He sketched three solutions: expulsion of the Czechs from Moravia, their expulsion from the whole area, or their Germanization; and recommended the third solution, which was approved by Hitler.

> Assimilierung des Tschechentums, d.h. Aufsaugen etwa der Hälfte des tschechischen Volksteile im Deutschtum. . . . Diese wird u.a. auch durch vermehrten Arbeitseinsatz von Tschechen im Reichs- gebiet . . . also durch Zerstreuung des geschlossenen tschechi- schen Volksteiles erfolgen.
>
> Die andere Hälfte des tschechischen Volksteiles muss auf die verschiedensten Arten entmachtet, ausgeschaltet und ausser Landes gebracht werden. Dies gilt besonders für die rassish mongolischen Teile und den Grossteil der intellektuellen Schicht. . . .
>
> Elemente, die der beabsichtigten Germanisierung entgegenarbei- ten, müssen scharf angefasst und ausgeschaltet werden.
>
> Die aufgezeigte Entwicklung setzt naturgemäss ein vermehrtes

7. IMT, XXXIII, 266. The memo was dated Aug. 28, 1940 (ibid., pp. 260–71).

8. Ibid., pp. 268–69.

9. Ibid., p. 253. Neurath advocated the application of merciless methods against the Czech minority in the Sudetengau. "The Czechs who live outside the Protectorate in the adjoining Gaue are, in comparison to the mass in the Protectorate, insignificant splinters. Their Germanization or elimination can, therefore, proceed at a completely different pace, and the methods used for such a minority can also be different. These differences will not cause any trouble" (ibid., p. 258). For the Germanization of the Czech minority in the Sudetengau, see Josef Orlík, ed., Opavsko a severní Morava za okupace, pp. 36–37, 112–14, 169, 188, 201–205.

Hereinströmen Deutscher aus dem Reichsgebiet in das Protektorat voraus.[10]

Hitler ordered "that while the semblance of the Protectorate autonomy was to be maintained, Germanization had to be carried out centrally by the office of the Reich protector."[11]

Thus in the early fall of 1940,[12] the fate of the Czech nation was determined: *the Nazi victory would bring about its physical destruction* through assimilation, deportation, colonization, and extermination. This plan remained the basis of the Nazi policy during the war.

The Rasse-Siedlungshauptamt SS (the Race and Resettlement Main Office of the SS) was entrusted with carrying out the necessary preparations for Germanization.[13] As early as Oct. 9, 1940, Himmler ordered a special questionnaire on the racial composition of the Czech people.[14] Being in the middle of the war, the Nazis did not want to stir the Czechs to any desperate action by an early enunciation of their plans. Therefore, they concealed their investigations under cover of a general health examination.[15] The examination of the Czech children in the schools was to be followed by X-ray tests of the Czech population under the pretense of a campaign against tuberculosis.[16] The obligatory exchange of personal identity cards ordered by Acting Reich Protector Reinhard Heydrich in the spring of 1942 aimed at obtaining personal and racial data important

10. Report by General Friderici (Oct. 15, 1940) on the result of the visit of Neurath and Frank to Hitler (*IMT*, XXVI, 375–76). The same was reported by Dr. Ziemke on Oct. 5, 1940 (*IMT*, XXXV, 439–40).

11. *IMT*, XXVI, 377.

12. According to Král (*Otázky*, I, 40), Hitler received Neurath and Frank on Sept. 29, 1940, and Frank alone on Oct. 11–12, 1940.

13. *Československo a norimberský proces*, pp. 211–15. See also the address by SS-Obersturmführer Dr. Hussman from the Prague branch of the Main Office at Wasserburg on June 29, 1942 (*IMT*, XXXIX, 362–64).

14. The National Archives of the United States. Federal Records Center. *The Himmler Files*. RG 1010 EAP 161-b-12/42. The Main Office prepared a provisional estimate on Oct. 23, 1940, according to which 45 percent of the Czechs were destined for Germanization (Král, *Pravda*, p. 159).

15. *The Himmler Files*. Himmler stipulated expressly, "Der Bogen soll die bekannten harmlosen und die für uns wichtigen Fragen enthalten." In January 1941, Himmler wrote to Frank: "Wir sprachen vor längerer Zeit . . . dass in Schuluntersuchungen eine Bestandsaufnahme des gesamten tschechischen Volkes vorgenommen werden müsste. Ich habe nunmehr einen solchen Fragebogen für tschechische Schulärzte entwerfen lassen. . . . Wenn wir diese Schuluntersuchungen durchführen, haben wir damit zum ersten Mal praktisch eine rassische Bestandsaufnahme des tschechischen Volkes."

16. Report by Heydrich to Bormann, May 18, 1942, as reported in Král, *Otázky*, I, 41. Heydrich emphasized that "to cover this activity one has to emphasize . . . the necessity of the struggle against tuberculosis."

to the process of Germanization.[17] The measures were intended to work out a racial criterion for selecting Czechs for assimilation and deportation or extermination.[18]

The coming of the new Acting Reich Protector and General of the police, SS-Obergruppenführer Reinhard Heydrich, marked a more active phase in the implementation of the Hitler decision. Heydrich reiterated the Nazi plan for the solution of the Czech question in his secret address to German officials of the Protectorate on Oct. 2, 1941. The long-range policy was to Germanize the area. Hostile and racially doubtful Czech elements were to be expelled; hostile but racially reliable Czechs were to be Germanized. If they maintained their opposition, they would be liquidated. However, the war required that all the measures for Germanization be concealed in order that the Czechs might not be led to resort to open revolt.[19] One year later, the stubborn resistance of the Czechs induced Frank to indicate publicly what was in store for them.

If the Czechs do not submit, then a day will come when it will be definitely too late for a change of heart. They will then no longer be in a position to disturb order and peace in the heart of the fighting Reich. . . . It is ridiculous to believe that then it would be a matter of some political haggling, autonomy or so-called Germanization.[20]

After the death of Heydrich, the influence of Frank and the Sudeten Nazis did not fail to increase. The urgent need of the total war effort overshadowed all other problems but one: In 1943, the new German State Ministry headed by Frank concentrated the implementation of all the measures and plans of Germanization in the hands of Frank who, as the SS-Obergruppenführer and chief of the SS and

17. *Ibid.*
18. See the text of the documents in *Vergangenheit*, pp. 134 ff., and the lecture of Dr. Hussman (*IMT*, XXXIX, 362).
19. For the text of the address, see *Vergangenheit*, pp. 122 ff. See also Král, *Pravda*, p. 253.
20. *Čechoslovák*, Oct. 28, 1942, a London weekly. The extract was taken from Frank's speech in Prague on Oct. 18, 1942. The Sicherheitsdienst (SD) branch in Prague regularly published secret reports describing Czech public opinion. The report for the period of March 15, 1939 to March 15, 1940, stated that the Czech nation "is completely opposed to the Protectorate, National Socialism and the German nation" (Král, *Otázky*, I, 32). More than one year after Frank's address, the daily report of the SD in Prague, Nov. 4, 1943, affirmed that "bei den Tschechen der weitaus grösste Teil der tschechischen Population heute ausgesprochen deutschfeindlich eingestellt ist" (*The Himmler Files*. T 81 250-a/196; *Stimmungsberichte* by the Main Security Office, *Amt III* [SD Inland]).

police in the Protectorate and the Sudetengau, enjoyed the full confidence of Hitler and the SS. Thus, one central agency directed the Germanization of the Historic Provinces. As late as April 1944, Frank, in his secret address to officials of the Sudetengau headed by Henlein, reiterated the annihilation of the Czech nation and its Germanization as a firm aim of German policy.[21]

Only the outcome of war deprived the Nazis of the opportunity to carry through their policy. They succeeded, however, in seriously impairing the development of the Czech people by a series of steps which touched all aspects of national life. As Vincent Urban put it: "The autonomy of Bohemia and Moravia . . . was really only a screen behind which the extensive machinery of the German occupation authorities, centered in the office of the Reich protector and acting through the SS detachments and the Gestapo, carried out one of the greatest attempts at denationalization of modern times."[22]

Obviously the Czech system of education was one of the main Nazi targets. Using the mass anti-German demonstrations of October 28 as a pretext, the Nazis closed all the Czech universities on Nov. 17, 1939. When a Czech delegation asked Frank in 1942 to reopen the universities, it was told:

> If the war is won by England, you will open your schools yourselves; if Germany wins, an elementary school with five classes will be enough for you.[23]

Since the goal was to deprive the Czechs of their intelligentsia, the main attack was directed against the secondary schools. The number of secondary schools—159 in the school year 1938–39 with 95,164 students—was reduced to 118 schools with 42,838 students in 1943–44.

21. For the text of this address, see *Vergangenheit,* pp. 163 ff. For the mood of the Sudeten Germans in the Sudetengau favoring this final solution, see *Opavsko,* pp. 112–14.

22. *Op. cit.,* p. 34. For a description of various methods of Germanization, see Václav Král, "The Policy of Germanization Enforced in Bohemia and Moravia by the Fascist Invaders during the Second World War," *Historica II* (1960), 273–303. As late as Sept. 8, 1944, the Race and Resettlement Main Office of the SS arranged for the registration of Czech children in the German schools (*The Himmler Files.* RG 1010 EAP 161-b-12/42). The Germans did not hesitate to strive to Germanize children "whose fathers or parents had to be executed as members of the resistance movement" (*TWC,* IV, 1028–29. Himmler to SS-Colonel Sollmann, June 21, 1943). A special section of Himmler's staff, the Lebensborn—the Well of Life Society—took care of the children designated for Germanization.

23. *IMT,* XXVI, 467. See also Heydrich's secret address on Feb. 4, 1942 (*Vergangenheit,* pp. 145–48).

The teachers' training institutes declined from 53 to 22 during 1943–44. Attendance at the higher elementary schools dropped from 258,031 pupils in 1938–39 to 190,506 in 1944–45; at the elementary schools, from 654,515 pupils (in 5,710 schools) to 587,794 (in 5,467 schools) in the same period. On Sept. 9, 1940, Neurath forbade the hiring of any new Czech teachers, and his approval was required for the construction of Czech schools.[24]

The Nazi cultural policy displayed the same hostility in a more concealed way. It pretended to help the Czechs provided they accepted the German claims to predominance and became reconciled to their inferior position. Since the idea of national independence was affirmed to be a grave error, it was suggested that the Czech people adapt themselves to the German frame of mind and acquiesce in German protection.[25] The Czech press, literature, and other branches of cultural life were curbed by strict censorship and a threat of concentration camp for violators. After 1942 a very limited number of papers and periodicals were allowed to be published, most of them edited by Czech collaborators. The situation was similar in the publishing field, in the theater, and in music. On Sept. 1, 1944, all Czech theaters were closed down. The German language was assigned absolute precedence over Czech, with German alone to be used in correspondence with German authorities. All official correspondence between the Czech authorities had to include a German translation, and German alone or German and Czech were to be used whenever a German corporation or authority was concerned.[26]

The Nazi concept of Germanization favored German ownership of Czech land. The Czech Land Office was taken over by the Nazis,[27]

24. Král, *Otázky*, I, 43–44. In April 1941, Frank intimated that only 35 percent of the pupils from elementary schools might register at the higher elementary schools (*ibid.*).
25. See the address of Reich Minister Dr. Lammers in Prague on Nov. 20, 1940, or the articles by Neurath on Dec. 1, 1940 and March 15, 1941 (*Naše doba*, December 1940, February, April 1941).
26. Král, *Otázky*, I, 42; Shiela Grant Duff, *A German Protectorate. The Czechs under Nazi Rule* (p. 196), which gives an incomplete but still interesting survey of the early phase of the German occupation; Arnold Toynbee and Veronica M. Toynbee, eds., *Survey of International Affairs 1939–46. Hitler's Europe* (London, 1954), p. 589, with a section on partitioned Czechoslovakia written by Elizabeth Wiskemann.
27. The six leading Czech officials were arrested prior to the takeover (*Naše doba*, July 1939, p. 556). In 1942, Frank formed a land office for Bohemia and Moravia with the task of administering the state estates and forests. He stated on June 4, 1942, that this office "steht unter deutscher Leitung und hat deutsche Bodenpolitik zu verfolgen" (Leopold Chmela, *Hospodářská okupace Českoslo-*

and the forests and estates section of the Ministry of Agriculture was removed from Czech control. The German Settlement Society in Prague acquired 53,100 hectares (some 131,000 acres) of land in the areas of south Bohemia and Moravia alone by September 1940.[28] Under the responsibility of the reorganized Land Office, a long-range program was started to resettle the land with Germans. Compulsory German management was imposed upon a number of large Czech farms (totaling 337,000 hectares) in 1943. By Feb. 26, 1943, 4,931 German peasant-resettlers were installed in the Protectorate.[29] Czech peasants were driven from their lands by the establishment or enlargement of the German military training camps. (The area of the new SS-training camp near Benešov amounted to 55,000 hectares.) Sixty-two parishes fell victim to the new policy and some 37,000 Czechs were turned out in 1942 and later.[30] In the Moravian district of Vyškov more than 20,000 Czechs were evacuated from 33 parishes.[31] With the confiscations at the district of Rokycany and at Milovice it was estimated that the Germans had appropriated some 80,000 hectares for military purposes, evacuated 245 parishes, and turned out some 80,000 Czechs.[32] The expropriation of Czech land

venska, p. 108; hereafter cited as *Okupace*). Chmela's book presents a competent survey of German economic policy in the Protectorate. In some aspects it has been superseded by the recent study by Král (*Otázky*) which is, however, strongly Communist-biased. For the German settlement program, see Koehl, pp. 42–43; Král, *Pravda*, pp. 156–57.

28. Czechoslovak Ministry of Foreign Affairs, *Czechoslovakia Fights Back* (p. 47), presents a useful survey. See also Duff, p. 203. In the fall of 1941 about 100 families of German resettlers from Bessarabia were settled in the district of Mělník where some 3,000 ha were confiscated (*TWC*, XIII, 608). For other German documents see *Vergangenheit*, pp. 86, 118 ff.

29. Address of Frank on Feb. 26, 1943 (*Böhmen und Mähren*, IV [March–April 1943], 38). For the tasks of the land office, see *Vergangenheit*, pp. 118–19, 136–37. For the compulsory management of Czech farms, see Král, "The Policy of Germanization," p. 302. Some 35,000 ha of the confiscated land belonged to about 25 Czech aristocratic families who had refused to register as Germans (Král, *Pravda*, pp. 168, 255).

30. *Tisky k těsnopiseckým zprávám o schůzích Prozatimního Národního shromáždění republiky Československé*, No. 82, Dec. 18, 1945. See also a useful study by Čestmír Amort, *Partyzáni na Podbrdsku*, pp. 49–50.

31. *Tisky*, No. 202, Feb. 21, 1946. The evacuation started on March 31, 1941, and ended by April 1, 1943. (See also *ibid.*, No. 163, Feb. 11, 1946.) For other evacuations, see Amort, p. 31.

32. *Tisky*, No. 224, Feb. 27, 1946. The evaluation of the property involved amounted to two and a half milliard K. Karel Šedivý (*Why We Want to Transfer the Germans*, p. 38) and Vincent Urban (p. 37) used the same figures, although they differ from those used by this writer: a total of 119,845 ha of land confiscated and 45,524 Czechs driven out. They did not indicate their source, but it appears to be an official Czechoslovak estimate reached toward the end of the war.

was closely connected with the gradual and systematic Germanization of Czech properties.

If we read the decrees by which German agents were established in former Jewish commercial and industrial firms in the years 1940, 1941 and 1942; if we read the names and origins of the persons who appeared in the lists of the newly nominated and "elected" members of the administrative and supervisory councils of industrial firms, co-operatives and banks we find everywhere that Sudeten Germans from Liberec and Jablonec, from Ústí and Rumburk, from Cheb and Aš appear side by side with Germans coming from various parts of the Reich. Sudeten Germans entered the Czech districts to direct the local administration, they were given the businesses, factories, etc., of Czechs who had been carried off to concentration camps or to execution.[33]

Through the process of Aryanization,[34] Jewish capital amounting to more than 6 milliard K was confiscated and German commissars were assigned to Jewish firms.[35]

Hand in hand with this move went the Germanization of Czech industry and finance.[36] During the Neurath era of 1939–41, Reich German capital assumed control of Czech financial and industrial concerns chiefly through forced purchases of securities. One result of

33. Vincent Urban, p. 42. The recent competent study by Theodor Schieder, ed., *Die Vertreibung der deutschen Bevölkerung aus der Tschechoslowakei,* forming volume IV/1 of the *Dokumentation der Vertreibung der Deutschen aus Ost-Mitteleuropa,* p. 17, states: "Zu einem grossen Teil waren die Dienstverpflichteten in der Rüstungsindustrie des Protektorats Sudetendeutsche. Das gleiche gilt für die im Protektorat eingesetzten Verwaltungsbeamten." The volume will hereafter be cited as *Dokumentation.*
34. The term Jewish was defined by the decree of Neurath on June 21, 1939. A firm was regarded as Jewish if a director or a partner was Jewish or one quarter of the capital was supplied by a Jew (Duff, p. 136). It is of interest that the Protectorate government unanimously refused three times to follow the order of Frank that it issue the anti-Jewish Nuremberg laws. It forced the Reich Protector to issue the laws in June 1939 (Feierabend, *Ve vládě,* pp. 44–45).
35. Král, *Otázky,* I, 69–76.
36. The main instruments of economic Germanization were the German banks. The Germans also sequestrated property of "persons, companies and associations who have fostered activities deleterious to the Reich" (decree of Oct. 4, 1939. *Reichsgesetzblatt (RGBl)* 1939, I, 1938). Most of the Czech industrial concerns—such as the Škoda Works, Vítkovice Iron Works, Brno Small Arms, etc.—became a part of Göring's concern. Reich German and Austrian capital funds (Sudeten capital not included) in the area of the Protectorate increased from 415,627,000 Kč in 1938 to 2,375,073,000 K in 1945, or to 571 percent (1938 = 100). German participation in industry was as follows (according to the report of May 9, 1941): wool, 60 percent; cement, 90 percent; paper, nearly 100 percent; chemicals, 30–40 percent, etc. (Král, *Otázky,* I, 54–55).

the appointment of Heydrich to Prague and the corresponding as-
cendancy of Frank had been to favor the expansion of rival Sudeten
German capital. The violent rivalry among Reich banks and concerns
for the exploitation of the enormous Czech booty was sharpened in
1941–42 by new moves of Sudeten capital, which felt itself gravely
hurt by the inroads of Reich capital into an area considered its
exclusive sphere of influence.

With the prolongation of the war questions of ownership were
made subordinate to the increasing needs of total economic mobilization. The direct transfer of ownership was replaced by the assignment
of German directors and executives to key positions in Czech industrial undertakings and financial institutions.[37] The deteriorating situation on the Eastern front dictated rapid concentration and centralization of Czech industry.[38] A total of 3,200 industrial enterprises were
shut down and 8,500 workshops and trades and 3,500 businesses were
closed.[39] Since almost 99 percent of the closing orders concerned small
Czech firms, the Czech small bourgeoisie was decimated and German
control of concerns and monopolies became almost absolute.[40]

German capital investments were guided by both national interests
and the necessities of war. The one-sided expansion was dictated
solely by German plans without regard for the economic structure of
the Czech lands.[41] The militarization of the Czech economy increased

37. I follow Král (Otázky, II, 14–16, 222 ff.). Dr. Bernard Adolf, Frank's friend,
became chairman of the Association of Manufacturers. Erich Sturm became
director of the National Bank. On Sept. 30, 1941, 739,000 employees worked in
12,900 enterprises. There were 32,000 Germans (4.38 percent) among them, but
only 3.3 percent of the workers were Germans. Some 35 percent of the
employees of the central administration of large concerns were Germans (ibid.,
I, 54–55). Large Czech banks were forced to liquidate in favor of the German
banks. Many savings banks and other financial institutions were closed or seized
by the German banks (Chmela, Okupace, pp. 72–90). The SS took possession—among other things—of a part of the furniture and wood industries.
Its protectorate enterprises formed one of the most important branches of its
economic activities (Enno Georg, Die Wirtschaftlichen Unternehmungen der
SS, Stuttgart, 1963, pp. 72 ff.).
38. The concentration program was started in 1942. It brought another wave of
Germanization through the introduction of German card indexes, printed matter,
and forms (Leopold Chmela, The Economic Aspect of the German Occupation
of Czechoslovakia, pp. 110–11. This book is an English version of the Czech
edition but is in some sections more up to date). See also Král, Otázky, III,
206 ff. The orders for the closing or restricting of industrial enterprises were first
promulgated in 1939, when 211 such orders were issued (ibid., I, 207).
39. Ibid., p. 210.
40. Ibid., pp. 216–17.
41. Chmela, Economic Aspect, pp. 117–18. For example, the new aircraft industry
employed some 100,000 men although only about 5,000 men were needed in
Czechoslovakia (Chmela, Okupace, p. 98). In the years 1942–44 approximately
330 new industrial enterprises were opened (Král, Otázky, III, 265).

its dependence on Germany. Berlin fully realized the vital importance of the Czech industrial capacity, and it was this awareness that formed one of the factors in its decision to occupy Czechoslovakia in 1939.[42]

When the Nazis took control of the Czech areas they extended their grasp over the Czech nation through the introduction of a planned economy. These steps required the conversion of the Protectorate to a war basis, geared to Germany by a plan covering all aspects of production, distribution, and consumption. The totalitarian Nazi economic policy was relentlessly carried out through a reorganization of the economic structure of the Protectorate. The economy was strictly regulated through the imposition of compulsory economic bodies which controlled and directed all aspects of economic life.[43] Planned control reached full efficiency by the concentration of control over industry, consumption, trade, and labor on Jan. 15, 1942, in the new Ministry of Economics headed by Dr. Walter Bertsch, who became the first German minister in the Protectorate government.

Czech currency was used to bolster the German economy. A decree of March 21, 1939, determined the rate of exchange between the Reichsmark and the Protectorate crown: one mark equaled ten crowns.[44] Because the real rate was 1 RM to 6–7 K, the Germans purchased Czech goods for two thirds of the cost. The gold reserve of the Czech National Bank was taken over by the Reichsbank and paid in marks.[45] Establishment of a customs union with the Reich on Oct. 1, 1940, carried out against the tenacious opposition of the Protectorate government, guaranteed that Germany would get everything in exchange for her paper currency. The customs union increased the influx of Czech goods into Germany in return for worthless marks or credits with the Reichsbank account. The German tax system was

42. Field Marshal Göring declared at a conference of the representatives of the various Reich ministries (July 25, 1939), "Dass die Einbeziehung von Böhmen und Mähren in den deutschen Wirtschaftsraum u.a. auch deswegen erfolgt sei, um durch Ausnützung der dort befindlichen Industrie das deutsche Kriegspotential zu steigern" (*IMT*, XXXVIII, 368).
43. Chmela, *Okupace*, pp. 18–20; 96–97.
44. *TWC*, XIII, 652.
45. On March 18, 1939, the National Bank was forced to ask the International Bank at Basel, where most of the Czech gold was deposited, to transfer its gold to the account of the Reichsbank. The amount of gold involved in this complex transaction, which led to violent discussions in England because of the involvement of the Bank of England, was 23,087 kg. Besides this gold, during the period between May 15, 1939 and April 20, 1940, the National Bank was forced to sell 12,768.96 kg of gold to the Reichsbank (Chmela, *Okupace*, pp. 44–45). See also Křen, *Do emigrace*, pp. 434–37.

introduced. The Protectorate crown lost its independent position with regard to foreign countries, and the price level in the Protectorate went up by 70 percent because of the increase of prices and taxes dictated by the Nazis.[46] From 1940 on, the Protectorate was forced to contribute a special yearly fee to assist the Nazi war effort. By 1945, the total sum amounted to 53.5 milliard K.[47]

The requirements of war intensified German control of the labor market. The working day was extended; the entire Czech labor force was conscripted; and workers were tied to their jobs. From Dec. 18, 1941, all Czechs could be called up for war work anywhere in Germany.[48] In 1942, there was a total mobilization of manpower. Finally Minister Bertsch mobilized all the men from 16 to 65 years and all the women from 17 to 45 years for work in Germany.[49] It is estimated that less than 500,000 Czechs were sent—willingly or by force—to Germany to be used as laborers.[50] In the early months of 1945 some 10,000 Czechs were sent to work on fortifications in Austria, 2,000 to the Sudetengau, and 50,000 to the construction of field fortifications in the Protectorate itself.[51] The mobilization of Czech technical and manpower resources was accomplished by the merciless pressure of threats and police terror. The result was influenced by the fact that war emergency needs transcended all considerations of cost and utility.

Production expanded in war industries while consumer industries lagged because of low priorities. The price paid for the results was, however, high. Equipment, machine tools, and plants were used up, and the Czech industry was fully converted to wartime production

46. *K. H. Frank*, p. 54; Chmela, *Okupace*, pp. 157–58.

47. The contribution amounted (in milliards of K) to: 1940, 3; 1941, 5; 1942, 8; 1943, 10; 1944, 12.5; 1945, 15. Out of the total amount of 53.5 milliard K, more than 42 milliard were paid (*ibid.*, pp. 60, 68). It is interesting to note that while the Protectorate covered 60 percent of its budget by taxes, this coverage amounted to only 40 percent in the Reich (*ibid.*, p. 61). The Protectorate also delivered large amounts of grain, fodder, sugar, and cattle to the Reich and took care of the German troops stationed in its territory.

48. *IMT*, XXVI, 485.

49. *Ibid.*, on Feb. 2, 1943.

50. The figures pertaining to the number of Czechs compelled to forced labor in Germany vary according to the authors. The figure used in the official Czechoslovak report of Sept. 29, 1945—750,000—appears to be exaggerated (*ibid.*, p. 486). Chmela (*The Economic Aspect*, p. 134) used the figure of 600,000 persons published by the Ministry of Social Welfare. Král (*Otázky*, I, 190) put the figure at 374,211 persons in 1939–1943. It was estimated that there were 140,000 Czechoslovak workers in the Reich in January 1945 (*IMT*, XXX, 588).

51. Chmela, *The Economic Aspect*, p. 135.

and integrated with the German economy. Inadequate maintenance and replacement confronted the expanded industry and presented a grave drawback.

The Nazis made heavy demands upon the capacity of Czech agriculture and forestry. As rationing was instituted in 1939, agricultural production demands, under pressure of German requirements, were extended and speeded to potential capacity. Exhausted forests and soil and worn-out machinery presented an immediate cost. Nazi concern, as in all economic fields, was not in long-range possibilities which would take the Czech farmer into consideration but rather in immediate results as required by the Nazi war machine.

Forced labor, the prohibition of strikes, and close control by the National Labor Center served only to strengthen the Czechs' bitter distaste for the regime under which terror, coercion, and jail were regular practices. The Nazi policy of stick for the intelligentsia and carrot for the farmer and workman failed to lessen Czech labor's hatred for a system which had brought national catastrophe. The organizational efficiency of the Nazi economic machine was seriously impaired by Czech awareness that the only economic criterion was the welfare of Germany. Germanization, economic subjugation, and police terror with executions and arrests drove the Czechs to passive resistance. Hence, the Nazi economic policy was made increasingly dependent on sheer police methods. The Nazis never understood and never really strove to achieve any dialogue with the Czechs. Even their economic policy presented only a means to subjugate the Czech area in their own interest. They regarded any permanent modus vivendi with the Czechs as impossible, if not undesirable. This lack of understanding of the Czech state of mind ultimately affected the very organization and efficiency of the Nazi administrative regime.

The autonomy of the Protectorate was in reality only a device by the Nazis to regulate and supervise the administration of the country. The Czech bureaucratic apparatus was maintained but put under Nazi control by the appointment of Germans to key positions.[52] Thus, ultimate decisions rested with the Germans. The Reich protector was the highest authority in the country, entitled to issue decrees or to restrict rights whenever German interests demanded it.[53] His

52. There were 1,884 German high officials in the Protectorate in 1942 (Král, *Otázky*, I, 23). The list of the Gestapo members who dealt with the Czechs contained 5,861 names (report of Minister Prokop Drtina to the Constituent Assembly on May 27, 1947, as quoted by *Těsnopisecké zprávy o schůzích*).

53. Duff, p. 98. See the ordinance on legislation in the Protectorate of Bohemia and Moravia, June 7, 1939 (*RGBl*, Berlin, I, 1039). The Reich Protector's

office was divided into departments roughly corresponding to the Protectorate ministries. German officials were placed in each ministry and other central offices.[54] Their consent was mandatory for any act to become official. The state president and Protectorate government were subordinated to the protector, who used the government as a convenient channel to pass his orders. Because of the obvious pragmatic and propaganda value of this façade, which the Nazis were anxious to keep, the government and president had some bargaining power at the beginning and could cushion the harsh impact of some stringent measures.[55]

The country was divided into regional districts (Oberlandratbezirk), each headed by a district commissioner (Oberlandrat),[56] who dealt with the affairs of the local Germans and supervised Protectorate offices.[57] Germans were appointed as deputies to the provincial presidents of Bohemia and Moravia. The largest Czech cities—Brno, Jihlava, Olomouc, Moravská Ostrava, Pilsen, and České Budějovice— were administered by Sudeten German commissars.[58] In some Czech cities Germans were nominated to the Czech municipal councils.[59] Most of the district administration offices had German officials in

deputies were a state secretary—K. H. Frank—and an under state secretary—Kurt von Burgsdorff. The basic decree on German administration in the Protectorate was issued on Sept. 1, 1939 (RGBl, 1939, I, 1691). See also Documents on International Affairs 1939–46. Hitler's Europe, pp. 306–308.

54. Gradually the Germans took over the Supreme Price Control Office, the Statistical Office, the direction of the State Estates and Forests, the head offices of the Railways and Posts, the police headquarters, the labor office, etc. (Šedivý, p. 34).

55. State President Hácha sent three memoranda (April 25 and Oct. 13, 1939, Sept. 12, 1940) to the Protector or to Hitler. He complained against German interventions in the internal affairs of the Protectorate (Král, Pravda, pp. 182–85; Feierabend, Ve vládě, pp. 98–101). The premier of the first Protectorate government was Gen. Alois Eliáš, appointed by President Hácha on April 27, 1939. For an interesting account of the anti-Nazi activities of Dr. Hácha and his government, see Feierabend, Ve vládě, passim. For a critical evaluation, see Král, Pravda, pp. 181 ff.

56. Documents 1939–46, II, 307. Several Czech districts formed a German regional district, of which there were 15. In 1942 this amount was reduced to 7 (Král, Pravda, p. 143).

57. Documents 1939–46, II, 307.

58. Duff, 119. For example, Oskar Judex was the commissar in Brno, Leo Engelmann in Jihlava, Fritz Czermak in Olomouc, Josef David in Budějovice, etc. Dr. Schwabe became regional president in Moravia. In 1940 there were more than 140 Czech cities and communities administered by German commissars. This amount rose to 200 at the beginning of 1943. Toward the end of 1940, some 2,000 German officials were employed in communal administration (Král, Pravda, pp. 162, 167).

59. For example, on July 20, 1940, three Germans were appointed to the city councils in Chrudim and Vysoké Mýto (Naše doba, September 1940, p. 612).

leading positions. Germans also headed such important social corporations as the Institute of Pensions, the Accident Insurance Institute,
and other social security bodies. Through a liaison office with the
Reich protector's office they supervised the trade unions. All large
cooperative organizations as well as the Union of Handicrafts, the
Agricultural Union, and the Central Association of Manufacturing
Industries were dominated by the Nazis.[60] The Nazis were thus able,
with a relatively small administrative apparatus occupying key
positions, to direct and supervise the Protectorate bureaucratic
machinery.

The Protectorate Germans acquired German citizenship on March
16, 1939. They were subject to the Reich criminal and civil laws and
were removed from the jurisdiction of the Czech courts.[61] The Czechs
were subject to German law when the other party was a German or if
the act was committed on German premises. All political crimes and
acts of resistance were tried in German courts.[62]

The backbone of Nazi occupation was the security police and the
SS. Nazi rule developed into a genuine police administration supervising every aspect of Czech public life. The thin layer of German
bureaucracy would never have been able to operate without recourse
to a security apparatus to maintain an atmosphere of fear, intimidation, and nervous tension in the entire Czech nation. Police forces in
Bohemia and Moravia were subordinated to the Reich Security Main
Office in Berlin (Reichssicherheitshauptamt; RSHA) commanded by
Reinhard Heydrich. State Secretary K. H. Frank was made head of
police and controlled the SS in the Protectorate. The Reich protector
himself gave basic political directions. Executive orders of the
security organs were given directly from Berlin. The secret state
police (Gestapo) and the criminal police were the agencies of the
central administration of the Reich.[63] All officials were ordered to

60. I follow Vincent Urban, p. 35. See also Frank's explanation in *Vergangenheit*,
    p. 168.
61. Raphael Lemkin, *Axis Rule in Occupied Europe. Laws of Occupation—
    Analysis of Government—Proposals for Redress*, pp. 346, 347–50. Lemkin's
    useful reference book presents an analysis and the text of laws and regulations of
    the German and Italian occupational authorities.
62. Lemkin, pp. 348–49; Duff, pp. 123, 126. There were special Reich German
    courts in the Protectorate, the so-called Amtsgerichte, Landgerichte, and
    Oberlandgericht in Prague (Duff, p. 127). Political crimes were tried at the
    Sondergericht in Prague and at the Volksgericht in Berlin and Dresden (Buben,
    ed., *Šest let okupace Prahy*, p. 150).
63. In 1945 Frank explained the functioning of the Gestapo in the Protectorate:
    "Die Gestapo war ein Teil der Sicherheitspolizei mit zwei voneinander
    unabhängigen Chefs, einer in Prag—zeitweise Dr. Geschke—und der andere in
    Brünn. Beide erhielten ihre Instruktionen und Befehle direkt vom Reichssicher-

comply with directives issued by the Gestapo.[64] The independently operating Sicherheitsdienst (SD; Security Service), another branch of the Reich Security Main Office, engaged in political intelligence.[65] The uniformed Ordnungspolizei, of whom there were eight or nine battalions in the Protectorate, were entrusted with the maintenance of order.[66] SS units were also stationed in the country, and two regiments were raised from among the ranks of Protectorate Germans.[67]

The successor of Neurath, Acting Reich Protector SS-Obergruppenführer Reinhard Heydrich, inaugurated a series of reforms streamlining the administrative apparatus. He appointed a new Protectorate government on Jan. 20, 1942. Dr. Jaroslav Krejčí became head of a new cabinet which included a German member, Dr. W. Bertsch, and a Czech Quisling, Emanuel Moravec, as chief of propaganda. At the same time the office of the premier was dissolved and the cabinet ceased to be a collective organ. The German chiefs of departments at the Reich protector's office became permanent deputies of the ministers and directors of the respective ministries.[68] As Heydrich put it, the Prague cabinet became a purely German instrument.

> The Czech Minister is in our sense no Minister at all. As we all know very well, they [the ministers] just carry out our orders. I cannot tolerate that my instructions be discussed by the Czech Cabinet.[69]

---

heitshauptamt in Berlin. Ausser diesen Gestapochefs gab es einen Befehlshaber der Sicherheitspolizei im Protektorat—zeitweise Dr. Rasche—der aber nicht das absolute Recht hatte, diesen Gestapochefs Instruktionen zu geben" (*IMT*, XL, 529). See also Král, *Pravda*, p. 144.

64. For more data on the Gestapo, see *Documents 1939–46*, II, 308; Gerald Reitlinger, *The SS. Alibi of a Nation*, p. 213, a useful but somewhat inaccurate book; *Zpověď*, pp. 74–75; Delarue, *Histoire de la Gestapo*, pp. 327 ff.

65. *Zpověď*, p. 75.

66. Duff, 79; *TWC*, XII, 895.

67. The SS-Standarten 107 and 108 in Jihlava and Prague (Duff, p. 83). The Protectorate government maintained a special government militia, totaling 6,887 men, at Prague, Brno, and Hradec Králové (*ibid.*, p. 73; Král, *Otázky*, I, 13). For its transfer to northern Italy because of its political unreliability, see K. H. Frank, p. 212.

68. *Ibid.*, p. 66; "The Trial of the Protectorate Government," *Svobodné slovo*, June 6, 7, 1946; Král, *Otázky*, I, 21–22. The leading German officials in the Protectorate ministries were Danko, Staehly, Scholtz, Schmeisser, and Reischauer. Premier Krejčí was replaced by Richard Bienert, who was informed by Frank of his appointment on Jan. 19, 1944 (*Svobodné slovo*, May 16, 1946). The trial brought out evidence that the public addresses of the ministers were written by Nazi ghost writers and handed to the ministers, who were ordered to read them in public.

69. Feb. 4, 1942. Král, *Otázky*, I, 20.

The policy line was clearly stated by Heydrich in his report to Martin Bormann:

> The policy line of all measures is to pretend that there is an autonomy but simultaneously to liquidate this very autonomy from the inside. We have to demand of the Czechs to take those measures which will arouse indignation while we adopt measures which are popular.[70]

The simplification of the Protectorate administrative machine was established by Hitler's decree of May 7, 1942, ordering the Reich protector to undertake measures "to make possible the adaptation of the administration . . . to any situation which may arise."[71] The number of Oberlandrats was reduced to seven, and most of their jurisdiction was delegated to local authorities who acted on behalf of the Reich in specific matters.[72] The final stage of the reform was reached on Aug. 20, 1943, when former Reich Minister Dr. Wilhelm Frick became the new Reich protector[73] and K. H. Frank was appointed minister of state in charge of the Ministry for Bohemia-Moravia, which superseded the protector's office. The Reich protector became nominal head. All power rested with the state minister, who held the position of a Reich minister.[74] State Secretary and SS Police Chief SS-Obergruppenführer K. H. Frank became at the same time supreme head of the Nazi machine of brutal repression. Thus it was a Sudeten German who personally applied terrorism. In the eyes of an ordinary Czech he embodied the archetype of an arrogant and ruthless Sudeten German.[75] Ultimately what at the outset had been marked as the protective role of the greater German Reich revealed itself as simply naked brute force.

From 1939 on, K. H. Frank's spirit pervaded the everyday dealings of the occupational power with the Czech people. His conception of discipline was to repress with strictest measures, extensive arrests,

70. Nov. 6, 1941 (*ibid.*).
71. Lemkin, p. 347.
72. Král, *Otázky*, I, 22.
73. SS-Oberstgruppenführer Kurt Daluege, head of the Ordnungspolizei, succeeded Heydrich on May 27, 1942, as deputy of the Reich protector. He was weak and exercised no influence ("The Trial of Kurt Daluege," *Svobodné slovo*, Oct. 10, 12, 17, 1946).
74. *K. H. Frank*, p. 208; *Vergangenheit*, p. 168; *IMT*, XXVII, 199.
75. See the characteristics of Frank in Vincent Urban, pp. 40–41. Frank wrote from his prison after the war: "The curse of the Sudeten Germans, who will be expelled from Czechoslovakia, is called down on me" (*K. H. Frank*, pp. 108–109). According to Neurath, it was wrong to bring a Sudeten German to such a leading position as that occupied by Frank, since he could not be impartial because of his former attitude toward the Czechs (*IMT*, XL, 528).

and executions what he called the "Czech mob" because "the Czech would take any friendly treatment and any favors as due to German weakness."[76] Such a spirit, indeed, made Czech-German coexistence utterly impossible. The Nazi regime in Czechoslovakia seemed to have only one *raison d'être:* to conclude the historical conflict by the destruction of the Czech nation. The awareness of prolonged secular collision affected the everyday course of the two peoples. In the shops and streets, in the offices and workshops, the two nations avoided each other, the Czechs stepping aside, the Germans keeping aloof from any unnecessary contact with their despised fellow citizens.[77] The national dispute seemed to transcend everything. The *Drang nach Osten* policy aimed at the total domination of the Czech area.

> Bohemia and Moravia and the peoples settled in this area lie and have always lain in Germany's political and national *Lebensraum.* The area of these countries forbids them to have political independence, at least as a state, or a political form with an anti-German conception. The inability of the Czechs to organize themselves permanently is caused by the features of the area which they inhabit. Any German Reich must have the possibility of making political decisions regarding this area and its inhabitants; as far as the security of the German *Lebensraum* to the east and possibly the southeast is concerned this is simply a fundamental law.[78]

If such was the conception of the Nazi Eastern policy, the rule of terror was indeed necessary.

76. Report by State Secretary Stuckart to Reich Minister and Chief of the Reich Chancellery H. Lammers, May 2, 1939 (*TWC*, XII, 895).
77. The Germans from the Reich were almost always considered by the Czechs as being less involved, more correct, and less vindictive than the Germans from Czechoslovakia.
78. K. H. Frank's address at the Eastern Institute in Cracow on June 24, 1941 (V. Urban, pp. 33–34).

CHAPTER 8

Terror and Resistance

Retribution and ruthless police methods were applied by the Nazis from the beginning of the occupation.[1] The first Czech reactions were expressed by a series of spontaneous mass manifestations on the occasion of various religious and national commemorations in the spring and summer of 1939, by many demonstrations of public anger and revolt, and by the appearance of a multitude of underground resistance groups.

The German repressive response did not immediately assume a mass character. With the outbreak of war, 8,000 Czech public figures were arrested as political hostages around Sept. 1, 1939.[2] Czech resistance assumed sharper forms. Following the instructions of the underground movement, Prague became the center of anti-German demonstrations on the anniversary of Independence Day (October 28). Czech masses marched through the inner city singing the national anthem and shouting slogans. Groups of Germans began to

1. A total of 4,639 persons were arrested in the period from March 15 to May 23, 1939 (Král, *Otázky*, I, 24). At the end of June 1939, Prague Acting Mayor Dr. Otakar Klapka (executed in 1941) asked Henlein in an address: "I beg you to cooperate with me toward the general political amnesty. Mutual understanding would not be possible if there stood the barrier of a political prison between us" ([Czechoslovak] Ministry of the Interior, *Persekuce českého studentstva za okupace*, p. 25; hereafter cited as *Persekuce*. The volume contains valuable documents and is indispensable for an understanding of the events of October and November 1939 in Prague).
2. *IMT*, XXXII, 339; Král, *Otázky*, I, 24. The lists of hostages were prepared in August 1939 (*K. H. Frank*, p. 61).

provoke the Czechs, hurling insults and tearing the national badges off the marching Czechs; some Germans even started firing. One Czech was killed, 15 were seriously wounded, and hundreds were injured.[3] Yet no serious damage resulted and the demonstrations never took the form of a riot. In the evening the streets of Prague were calm again.[4] By 5 P.M. of the same day, K. H. Frank delivered a special message from Hitler to Hácha. The Reich could not tolerate further demonstrations, and if the Czech police proved unable to master the situation, Hitler would be forced to abolish the autonomy of the Protectorate. Actually, Frank and Hitler intended to use the Czech indignation over the German shooting to provoke new demonstrations which would enable them to strike a blow against the Czechs.[5] They soon found their opportunity.

Jan Opletal, a Czech medical student who had been injured on October 28, died on November 11. His funeral on November 15 gave rise to new students' demonstrations in Prague. Neurath and Frank were called to Berlin, and Hitler ordered those responsible for the latest incidents to be shot. The SD prepared a list of leading student officials and Frank designated nine of them to be shot. On the evening of November 16, the leading functionaries of the National Student Association were arrested, and without any trial they were shot on the morning of November 17.[6] The same morning all the Czech universities were occupied by the SS and all students living in student homes arrested; more than 1,200 students were sent to concentration camps.[7] The Czech population was given an explanation in the official proclamation signed by Neurath on Nov. 17, 1939:

> On account of acts of violence against Germans by a group of Czech intellectuals, the Czech universities have been closed for three years; nine participants have been shot and a large number have been arrested.[8]

3. Report by Dr. Stahlecker, head of the German security police (*Persekuce*, pp. 35–42).
4. In all, some 400 persons were arrested. For a description of the demonstrations of October 28, see *Persekuce*, pp. 35 ff.
5. Letter of Frank to Himmler, Nov. 4, 1939 (*K. H. Frank*, p. 229).
6. *Ibid.*, pp. 201, 203. There was no investigation of the incidents of November 15, nor any examination of the arrested students, who had been selected arbitrarily.
7. *IMT*, XXXIII, 249–51.
8. *IMT*, XXXIX, 534. The universities were reopened in 1945. The closing affected 18,998 students, 1,223 professors, and 10 universities and institutes (*Persekuce*, p. 105; *IMT*, XXXIII, 245). November 17 was proclaimed International Student Day after the war in commemoration of the spirit of the Czech students.

The brutal and unjustified severity of the Nazi measures intensified anti-German sentiment among the Czechs.[9] Berlin, it was clear, had no intention of ameliorating in any way the blow to Czech-German relations caused by the occupation of Prague.

The crackdown signaled a new campaign of pressure and intimidation. Hitler laid down his directives to Neurath. The Protectorate would not be abolished and there would not be any large-scale settling of the country with Germans at present, "because the Germanization of the new German East has precedence and there are hardly enough settlers available even for that program."[10] Through the winter of 1939–40 a wave of arrests swept through the Protectorate. Neurath held that "it was necessary to rule with a firm hand."[11] The Nazi policy took an increasingly ominous shape through 1940. Almost daily arrests heightened the pressure.[12] The declaration of war against Yugoslavia and the entrance of the Soviet Union into the war aroused the expectations of an early victory among the Czechs, who responded by a series of sabotages and strikes. Despite the first Soviet setbacks the resistance movement initiated several mass campaigns in September 1941. The boycott of the Czech Protectorate press, supported by the efficient and popular Czechoslovak London broadcast service, turned out to be effective.[13] Heydrich himself confessed that the wave of sabotage, the slackening of work, and the activities of the resistance groups had reached a point where "the unity of the Reich was definitely threatened." As the alarming reports about the deteriorating situation in the Protectorate reached Hitler, he invited the head of the security service, R. Heydrich, and K. H. Frank to a conference on September 21–22.[14]

9. *Persekuce*, pp. 78–79. Premier Eliáš learned about the executions only in the afternoon (*ibid.*, p. 87). The cabinet offered its resignation, but Hácha refused to accept it (Feierabend, V*e vládě*, pp. 112–15).

10. *DGFP*, VIII, 538.

11. *Ibid.*, pp. 723–24. It appears that the conservative Protector von Neurath defended a more moderate policy against the brutal approach of Frank. See also Král, *Pravda*, pp. 200–201.

12. *K. H. Frank*, p. 63. For example, on Feb. 22, 1940, the Gestapo of Brno arrested 224 Communists; nine of them were executed on March 3, 1940. Up to the end of May 1941, the Germans jailed 5,796 Communists (Král, *Otázky*, I, 25).

13. [Czechoslovak] Ministry of Foreign Affairs, *On the Reign of Terror in Bohemia and Moravia under the Regime of Reinhard Heydrich*, p. 13. For the wave of sabotage and strikes in the summer of 1941, see Král, *Pravda*, pp. 228–29.

14. *Ibid.*, pp. 229–32. See Heydrich's address on Oct. 2, 1941 (*Vergangenheit*, pp. 128 ff.). "Neurath let himself be completely diddled by the Czech nobility. Another six months of that regime and production would have fallen by 25 percent. Of all the Slavs, the Czech is the most dangerous, because he's a worker.

The Nazis were ready for a decisive showdown. On Sept. 27, 1941, Berlin announced that Reich Protector Konstantin von Neurath had asked the Führer for sick leave. "The Führer has acceded to von Neurath's request and has entrusted the exercise of the office of Reich Protector to Obergruppenführer Heydrich for the period of von Neurath's leave." The nomination of the head of the German security police did not augur well. On his arrival in Prague Heydrich issued two decrees. In the first decree, "in order to put an end to incidents of an extraordinary character," he proclaimed that the Reich protector was entitled to declare a civil state of emergency, apply martial law, and install summary courts.[15] He could order the death penalty, hand over a prisoner to the secret state police, or order his liberation. There was no appeal from his verdicts. The second decree declared that from September 28 a civil state of emergency was in effect through most of the Protectorate. It further stipulated:

> All actions violating public order, security, economic life or peaceful work, as well as the intentional possession of firearms or explosives or ammunition, are subject to martial law. . . . Whoever learns of such action or intentions without immediately reporting them . . . is also guilty and thus subject to martial law.[16]

The comment of the German official daily *Der neue Tag* for September 29 displayed the wide gulf between the Czechs and Germans:

> The Czech people still have not got enough common sense to realize the consequences of their existence in the middle of a

He has a sense of discipline, he's orderly. . . . Now they will work, for they know we're pitiless and brutal" (Hitler, on Jan. 23, 1942 in *Hitler's Secret Conversations*, p. 192). Hitler mixed his hatred with a strange kind of admiration. "The Czech State . . . was a model of honesty. Corruption practically didn't exist amongst them. Czech officials are generally inspired by a sense of honour. That's why a man like Hácha is more dangerous than a rogue of a journalist" (*ibid.*). The same state of mind applied to Frank, who called the Czechs "the masters of underground activities" (Frank's secret speech of April 1944, *Vergangenheit*, p. 169).

15. The summary courts were not courts at all. They consisted of members of the Gestapo, Kripo, or SS. The Gestapo prepared lists of Czech victims which were transmitted for approval to Prague. Being placed on the list equaled the death sentence. The Prague Gestapo set the total number of Czech victims which the local Gestapo offices had to deliver. Heydrich or Frank signed the lists as current mail without caring for more details or reasons. Besides the summary courts, "working" only during states of emergency, the most common practice used by the Gestapo was the so-called Sonderbehandlung, i.e., putting a person to death without any trial (*K. H. Frank*, pp. 134, 137, 205).

16. For the text of the decree, see *Národní politika* (*National Politics*), Sept. 30, 1941.

Europe led by Germany. Therefore they will have to learn to understand what realism and loyalty mean.[17]

Prime Minister Alois Eliáš was arrested and accused of high treason, and the first six executions were carried out on September 28.[18] Every day the papers printed the names of Czech officers, journalists, teachers, workers, farmers, clerks, and artisans executed in Prague and Brno. At Brno the executions took place at a former student home. Tickets were sold for 3 RM to Germans who wished to attend. German women, in particular, enjoyed the "spectacle."[19] In many cases the only reason for a death sentence was listening to a foreign broadcast. During the night of October 7–8, more than 800 leading functionaries of the Czech Sokol (gymnastic organization) were arrested. Within eight months only some 60 to 70 remained alive. On October 8, the Sokol was dissolved and its property confiscated.[20] From September 18, the Jews had to wear the star of David in a conspicuous place, and all contact with them was prohibited.[21] From September 28 to the end of December 1941, 414 Czechs were reported as executed.[22] Thousands more were deported to concentration camps or put to death without any sentence (the so-called Sonderbehandlung). Daily announcements of the executions sent a wave of repulsion through the country. Many Czechs vowed that when their day should come they would have no mercy for any German. The dose of Heydrich terror curbed the Czech nation but did not crush it. The Czech resistance movement was crippled, but not completely destroyed.

Early on the morning of Oct. 4, 1941, the first Czechoslovak parachutists were dropped into the country. Soon they were followed by others. They were officers and soldiers of the Czechoslovak Army in Great Britain who had volunteered for intelligence and sabotage activities on Czechoslovak territory in cooperation with the local resistance groups. On October 5 the Czechoslovak authorities in London took the decision to prepare an attempt upon Heydrich's

17. *On the Reign of Terror*, p. 56. The SD situation reports indicated approval of the Nazi measures on the part of the Sudeten population (Král, *Pravda*, p. 248).
18. *Národní politika*, Sept. 30, 1941. Two Czechoslovak generals were executed first.
19. Habřina, ed., *Žalm Moravy*, pp. 16–17.
20. K. H. *Frank*, p. 64. From June to December 1941, 5,162 persons were arrested in Bohemia and 5,164 in Moravia (Král, *Pravda*, p. 145).
21. *On the Reign of Terror*, p. 50.
22. *Ibid.*, p. 22. The executions were carried out by the troops of the Waffen-SS (*IMT*, XXIX, 185–86).

life.[23] On May 27, 1942, at 10:35 A.M., two parachutists wounded Heydrich in his car as he proceeded to Prague.[24] Heydrich died several days later. German response was instantaneous. Frank immediately imposed a civil state of emergency and left to report to Hitler.

The new deputy of the Reich protector, SS-Oberstgruppenführer and General of the Police Kurt Daluege, ordered all Czechs to report at special offices to have their identity cards stamped. Those who failed to register and those who sheltered them were to be executed. All Czech sport, theater, and other public gatherings were prohibited. More than 5,000 communities were subjected to a house-to-house search and 4,715,501 persons went through the process of identification; 1,148 were arrested and 657 shot dead on the spot.[25] A reign of terror was instituted,[26] as summary courts worked at full speed. On June 10, 1942, the German radio announced that the Czech mining village of Lidice had been razed. A total of 192 men and 7 women had been shot, 195 women deported (of whom 52 died), and some 100 children sent to a concentration camp.[27] There had been no direct connection between any inhabitant of Lidice and the shooting of Heydrich; the village had been selected merely to set an example.

On the occasion of the memorial service for Heydrich in Berlin, State President Hácha and the members of the Protectorate cabinet were informed by Hitler that if any other such event occurred he

23. For the activity of Czechoslovak parachutists in 1941–42, see the report by the RSHA, Aug. 5, 1942, *Attentat auf den Chef der Sicherheitspolizei und der S. D. Stellvertretenden Reichsprotektor SS-Obergruppenführer Heydrich*. This unique document is at the YIVO Institute for Jewish Research, New York. OCC E Ha/-5. See also J. B. Hutak, *With Blood and with Iron. The Lidice Story*, pp. 62 ff.; Král, *Pravda*, pp. 259 ff.
24. The pertinent facts were ignored by S. Harrison Thomson in his otherwise excellent volume, *Czechoslovakia in European History*, (p. 414). Reitlinger (*The SS*, pp. 215, 217) gives May 29, the wrong date.
25. *Attentat, Anlage B and C*. The Germans were exempted from martial law and restrictions. See also Czechoslovak Ministry of the Interior, *Lidice. Čin krvavého teroru a porušení zákonů i základních lidských práv*, p. 22. This is a basic collection of documents reconstructing the liquidation of Lidice. See also Král, *Otázky*, I, 26.
26. This psychosis was a part of the German plan to pacify the Protectorate. Fear and tension were rising every day as rumors were spread intentionally that every tenth Czech would be shot (*Attentat, Anlage F*).
27. The actual burning and killing are described in *Lidice*, pp. 18, 52, 62–63. The Germans shot even those inhabitants who were outside of Lidice with their friends, in hospital, etc. The Lidice children were gassed in Chelmno in July 1942 (*Rudé právo*, Jan. 26, Feb. 2, 1963). For Lidice, see also *Attentat, Anlage D*, and *TWC*, IV, 79–84). On June 24, 1942, the entire village of Ležáky was burned down. All the inhabitants, men and women, numbering 33 persons, were shot because they had offered shelter to the parachutists (*K. H. Frank*, p. 208).

would deport the whole Czech population.[28] Hitler ordered the execution of 30,000 politically unreliable Czechs if the culprits were not discovered. Even Frank lodged protests at this decision and in personal discussion prevailed upon Hitler to rescind his order.[29]

During the state of emergency, 1,357 Czechs were executed and 3,188 arrested.[30] An atmosphere of revenge, fear, shock, and brutality pervaded the daily life of every citizen. A well-known journalist, Julius Fučík, described the period as he saw it from the Prague prison.

The route from Pankrác to the Petschek Palace [seat of the Gestapo] and back now becomes the daily Calvary for thousands of prisoners. The SS men, acting as overseers in the cars, are taking revenge for Heydrich. Already before the prison car has made its first mile, blood of dozens of prisoners is flowing from their bruised faces and mouths beaten with pistol butts. . . .

There is nothing horrifying in that any more. Every night one hears the roll call downstairs in the corridor. Fifty, a hundred, two hundred people whom they will load bound hand and foot into lorries like cattle for the slaughterhouse and carry away . . . for mass executions. The guilt? Above all they are not guilty. They were arrested, they are in no way connected with any of the major cases, neither are they needed for further investigations; they are, therefore, suited for death. . . .

A post-office employee arrested by mistake is standing downstairs

28. *Secret Conversations*, p. 452. It is not clear, however, whether Hitler meant his threat seriously. Frank made a note on his visit to Hitler May 27, 1942: "As a measure of atonement, 10,000 suspect Czechs, or people who have been guilty of anything in the past, are to be arrested or, if they are already detained, shot in concentration camps" (Král, *Otázky*, I, 26). See also the instruction of Himmler in the collection of documents of unequal value, *Zločiny nacistů za okupace a osvobozenecký boj našeho lidu*, p. 42. Prior to his visit to Hitler, Frank jotted down his own suggestions. In case of a failure to solve the death of Heydrich before the end of June, Frank proposed to abolish Czech autonomy and to shoot a large number of Czechs (*K. H. Frank*, p. 96). Michel de Bouard ("Mauthausen," *Revue d'histoire de la deuxième guerre mondiale*, IV, July–September 1954, p. 57) reported that the Czech prisoners in the camp of Mauthausen were subjected to a terrible vengeance after the death of Heydrich. Out of 3,000 in 1942, there remained 300 in 1944. They were "très unis et dignes."
29. Hitler's order was transmitted by Himmler between June 12 and 18. Frank flew to Hitler to persuade him to rescind his order because it would make the situation in the Protectorate intolerable (*Zpověď*, p. 145).
30. The state of emergency was lifted on July 3, 1942. The number of those hanged or shot does not include the inhabitants of Lidice and Ležáky. (See the report of Daluege to Lommers in *TWC*, XII, pp. 899–901, and the report of Frank to Hitler, *Vergangenheit*, p. 155.)

near the wall and awaiting his release. He hears his name called out
and says "Present." He is made to join the batch of people
condemned to death, taken away and shot, and only the next day is
it discovered that it was merely a coincidence of names, that a
namesake of his was to be executed. To ascertain accurately the
personal data of people who are to lose their lives—who could be
bothered? And what is the use, anyway, when their purpose is to
kill off the whole nation. . . .

Death by bullet stalks the country like a plague and makes no
distinction among its victims.[31]

The Germans from the Protectorate hailed the wave of terror and
expressed satisfaction with the energetic measures taken by their
leaders:

The center of interest yesterday among the population of Bohemia
and Moravia was the announcement of the retaliatory action
against the village of Lidice (OBL Kladno). This measure has
evoked great satisfaction and in many instances open joy among the
entire German population. There is, above all, a feeling of satisfaction, especially because energetic measures have now "at last" been
taken. The opinion prevails that action of this kind should have
been taken sooner.[32]

On June 16, one of the parachutists surrendered voluntarily and
named the hiding place of the other seven (two of whom had killed
Heydrich) as the Orthodox Church of Saint Charles Borromeo in
Prague. On June 18,[33] after several hours of violent battle with the
German police and the Waffen-SS, all seven Czechs died. The bishop
of the Orthodox Church, three clergymen, and those members of the
Resistance and their families who had assisted the parachutists were
executed, and the Orthodox Church was dissolved. The German
police report stated that "the prisoners belong to the best racial
representatives of the Czech people. They affirm that they are proud
to die in this way for the Czech nation."[34] Daluege hailed the German
policy in his report to Berlin:

---

31. Julius Fuchik, *Notes from the Gallows*, pp. 72–74. Fuchik was a Communist
   journalist who was arrested on April 24, 1942, and executed on Sept. 8, 1943.
   The notes were written in prison and smuggled out.
32. Situation report of the Prague SD of June 12 (*Vergangenheit*, pp. 153–54).
   See also the Prague SD report of June 9 (*ibid.*).
33. Two of them were shot and five committed suicide (*Attentat*, pp. 31 ff.). The
   information given by Delarue (*Histoire*, p. 333) is inaccurate.
34. *Attentat*, pp. 41 ff.

The contribution of the policy hitherto adopted—severe treatment, individual police measures, the frame of mind we have artificially produced, and the intentionally applied nervous tension of the Czechs, stimulating an increase of fear until rumours of an intended decimation of the entire nation were spread—proved correct.[35]

In September 1942, the relatives of exile and Resistance leaders were placed in internment camps.[36] On Feb. 17, 1943, the closest friends and relatives of Beneš were sent to concentration camps. On March 10, 1943, the shortwave bands were ordered to be removed from radio sets.[37] The head of the SD and the security police in Prague (Jan. 20, 1943) made preparations for the expected wave of sabotage and instructed his men to compile new lists of Czechs for concentration camps and execution.[38] In April 1944 Frank boasted that some 100 Czechs were sentenced to death every month, not counting many executed without being sentenced.[39] These almost desperate measures showed clearly the extent of Nazi failure. With the most brutal methods the Nazis could not crush the national spirit of the Czech people. They never succeeded in devising any means of meeting legitimate Czech complaints. It is impossible to escape the conclusion that the blame for this wretched situation has to be laid to monumental mismanagement of the whole Czech policy by the Nazis. When things went from bad to worse, Hitler and Frank blamed the Czechs for the woes of the country, implying that once the underground was smashed, all would be well. The appearance of Heydrich in Prague and the continued violence following his death almost annihilated the cadres of the Resistance movement, but the use of police methods alone, insistently set forth by Frank, who was the real *spiritus rector* of the Nazi policy,[40] could not solve the Czech problem.

The tragedy consisted in the fact that the Czech, living in his own

35. *TWC*, XII, 899–901.
36. *K. H. Frank*, p. 69.
37. *Ibid.* Král gave some figures of arrested persons: May 1942, 2,007; June, 2,043; July, 2,442; August, 1,864 (2,489 of the four months' total were Czech workers arrested in the Reich). In March 1943, 2,955 persons were arrested (1,047 were Czech workers in the Reich) (*Pravda*, pp. 145–46).
38. *Vergangenheit*, pp. 157–58. Himmler directed Daluege (Feb. 3, 1943) to deport 500 Czechs to concentration camps as a preventive measure (*ibid.*).
39. *Ibid.*, p. 170.
40. When Frank complained about the nomination of Daluege and affirmed that he considered himself the guarantor of the political line of the Führer and SS in the Protectorate, Hitler explained to Frank that Frank was the permanent element in the Protectorate, and no political action could be taken without his approval. See the notes of Frank on his audience with Hitler, May 28, 1942 (*K. H. Frank*, p. 140).

country, had no opportunity to avail himself of what should have been his birthright. Derisive slogans were shouted by the German masters, but flamboyant national hatred was no adequate substitute for genuine concern for the welfare of the people. In 1942 it seemed obvious that when the Czechs won back their independence, basic national, political, economic, and social changes would be imperative. National coexistence between Czechs and Germans would no longer be possible. The Czech fight against the Nazis was bound to be a fight to the finish.

The natural reaction of the Czech people to the occupation of their country was the broadest possible organization of a Resistance movement. Out of the welter of Resistance groups which sprang up throughout the country, four leading organizations emerged:[41] Obrana národa (Defense of Nation) was a military organization covering the entire Czech territory with a vast detailed network; Politické ústředí (PÚ; Political Center) was the central agency of the leading political personalities; Petiční výbor Věrni zůstaneme (PVVZ; Committee of the Petition "We Remain Faithful") embraced socialists and trade unionists, focused its attention on the ideological front, and elaborated the program Za svobodu (For Freedom), which was accepted as the program of the Czechoslovak Resistance movement.[42] The fourth unit, the Communist Party, worked separately, and until the Soviet-German war in 1941 combated both the Nazis and the West and was strongly critical of the Czechoslovak Resistance movement and President Beneš.[43]

41. The beginnings of the Resistance movement dated back to the Munich crisis, when communications were established between Beneš and his followers and collaborators in the country who formed the core of the Czechoslovak Resistance until most of them were either executed or arrested in 1940–42 or fled abroad. See the article by one of them, Dr. Jan Jína, "P. Ú," *Svobodné slovo,* June 8, 1947; Křen, *Do emigrace, passim.*

42. For the Czechoslovak Resistance movement, see Karel Veselý-Štainer, *Cestou národního odboje. Bojový vývoj domácího odbojového hnutí v letech 1938–45.* The book is indispensable for the second phase of the Resistance, from 1942, but has to be read with caution; Vladimír Krajina, "La résistance tchécoslovaque," *Cahiers d'histoire de la guerre* (February 1950), 55–76. See also the latter's articles in *Svobodné slovo* (June 8, 1947). Krajina was a member of the ÚVOD. The Czechoslovak Social Democratic Party published a brief survey *Kapitoly z historie odboje* (Prague, 1946). Other studies are Vozka, *Hrdinové domácího odboje;* Jaroslav Jelínek, *PÚ. Politické ústředí domácího odboje;* Feierabend, *Ve vládě;* Křen, *Do emigrace;* Král, *Pravda;* Amort, *Partyzáni na Podbrdsku;* Antonín Benčík et al., *Partyzánské hnutí v Československu za druhé světové války.* The last volume is strongly Stalinist.

43. For the Communist underground movement, see Ústav dějin KSČ, *Za svobodu českého a slovenského národa. Sborník dokumentů k dějinám KSČ v letech 1938–1945 a k IX., X a XI. svazku spisů Klementa Gottwalda.* The volume of Amort is also useful, although it deals only with a particular region. For the anti-Beneš campaign, see Beneš, *Memoirs,* pp. 160–162.

In November 1939 the first arrests were effected in the inexperienced leadership of the Political Center, and some of its members fled
abroad. The arrests continued, but the various organizations succeeded in regrouping themselves after every German coup. By
January and February 1940, conditions throughout the country were
ripe for the union and streamlining of all non-Communist Resistance
groups, in one loosely connected central organization called the
ÚVOD (Central Committee of Home Resistance).[44] The Defense of
Nation dealt with the military side of the Resistance and busily
prepared for national insurrection.[45] The chief activity of the Political
Center was to gather the intelligence which was regularly dispatched
to Beneš in London. The PVVZ centered on the elaboration of the
program which was adopted by the ÚVOD in 1941.

In the fall of 1941 and 1942, a series of arrests played havoc with
the ranks of the ÚVOD and other smaller organizations. Mass arrests,
deportations, and executions during the first and second martial laws
of 1941 and 1942 destroyed almost the entire network of the underground. Only fragments remained of what had been well-organized
networks. The Communist underground was liquidated as well. But
the Nazis succeeded in crushing the Resistance movement only
momentarily. As a matter of fact, the fragmentation of the Resistance
made it more difficult for the Nazis to liquidate all the underground
groups. In 1943 and 1944, the Czechoslovak underground was reorganized, and from the middle of 1944 on it stepped up its action
in unison with the progress of the Allied armies. Throughout its
first phase—1939–42—the ÚVOD had registered the most incisive
of its political successes: the creation of an excellent intelligence
service which formed the most important field of its activity. On
Aug. 12, 1939, secret radio contact was started with the Czechoslovak exile movement in England and France. For example, one
network, *Sparta I*, operated 12 radio transmitters, sent more than
20,000 cables to London or elsewhere, and received some 6,000 cables
in 1940–41.[46]

44. Dr. Feierabend gave a vivid description of the first amateurish phase of the
   activities of the PÚ (*Ve vládě*, pp. 67 ff.). The organizations continued to exist
   separately. Their union was effected by the constitution of a committee
   consisting of two members from each of them (Krajina, "La résistance," p.
   62).
45. A special group carried out sabotage. The attempt against Hitler's life in
   the Munich brasserie was reportedly prepared by this group (*ibid.*, p. 63). See
   also Vozka, pp. 105 ff.
46. Krajina, "La résistance," p. 58. For the transmitter group Sparta I, see *ibid.*,
   p. 65. After the Germans had succeeded in smashing the radio groups of the
   ÚVOD, radio contact was maintained by Czechoslovak parachutists flown from
   Britain. See also Beneš, *Memoirs*, p. 158.

Owing to the excellent intelligence work of the Czechoslovak underground, Beneš was supplied with a mass of first-rate information on the situation in the country and in Germany. Until the arrest of a senior member of the Abwehr, Paul Thümmel,[47] direct reports from the German General Staff were often received by Beneš from the Political Center. Hitler's preparations for the invasion of Great Britain in 1940, his plans of campaign in the Balkans and of his attack on Soviet Russia, and details on the German intelligence networks in Great Britain, in the Soviet Union, Turkey, and the Balkans were relayed to London. According to Beneš they were "of immense usefulness in the guidance of our liberation movement abroad."[48] Direct contacts were established with the Soviet intelligence in Prague in 1940 and very valuable reports were given to Moscow— among others, the exact date of the imminent German attack against the USSR.[49]

The Resistance at home and the Czechoslovak liberation movement abroad were in close contact from the very beginning. Beneš was regularly informed about political opinion in the country and the ÚVOD received valuable information on the situation abroad. Some of the addresses of Beneš were first transmitted for comment to the ÚVOD.[50] The regular and frequent contact between the Czechoslovak underground movement and Beneš,[51] who had been almost unanimously recognized as the leader of the movement of the liberation, made for mutual agreement on all basic political principles. In his political activity in exile Beneš always gave careful consideration to the mood of the country. During the war his popularity increased to an all-time high, and he became the universally revered symbol of the Czechoslovak struggle for freedom and independence.

47. Paul Thümmel was a member of the Abwehr in Prague, where he headed the section on the Balkans and East Europe. He was reportedly arrested in February 1942. See the letter by Vladimír Krajina to the author, May 26, 1958; his French article, p. 65; Král, *Pravda*, p. 245; the narrative by Dušan Hamšík and Jiří Pražák, "Bomba pro Heydricha," in *Plamen* (*Flame*), IV, July 1962, 45 ff.
48. Beneš, *Memoirs*, p. 158; Král, *Pravda*, pp. 244–45.
49. *Ibid.*, pp. 211, 224, 244; Krajina, "La résistance," p. 66. Contact was established in the spring of 1940.
50. Vozka, p. 19; Beneš, *Memoirs*, p. 158.
51. Contact by way of secret radio transmitters was but one of the methods of communication. Many foreigners, Czechs, and, above all, Slovak Resistance members smuggled microfilms, letters, and reports across the frontier. Communications evolved in two phases. The first one—until 1942—was characterized by the predominance of the ÚVOD radio transmitters; the second one—1942–45— was built mainly from abroad, by Czechoslovak parachutists. For the various means of contact, see the address of Minister Dr. Drtina in *Svobodné slovo* (Dec. 10, 1945).

The Czechoslovak underground movement was not restricted to its wide-flung network of military, political, and economic intelligence. Through a series of channels, thousands of Czechs and Slovaks were helped to escape from the country. During 1939 and 1940, many prominent politicians left Czechoslovakia in order to help to organize the liberation movement abroad. Illegal presses,[52] actions of various Resistance groups,[53] strikes and acts of sabotage,[54] and the providing of shelter for those who were obliged to go underground,[55] as well as relief and assistance for the families of the imprisoned and deported,[56] belonged to other fields of activity of the underground movement. The underground organizations proceeded cautiously along the same path as in the other subjected countries of Europe. They had not yet found the proper opportunity for an open fight. By diversive actions and various campaigns the Resistance boosted the morale of the country and acquired political significance. Its activities centered on political, economic, and psychological fields where the greatest harm could be done, although it could not be counted simply in terms of Germans slain or trains wrecked. The lack of opportunity to achieve large immediate results was compensated for by the serious embarrassment of the Nazis through excellent intelligence, passive resistance, and pinprick tactics.[57]

52. Among the most widely read illegal papers were *V boj* (*Into Battle*); *Český kurýr* (*Czech Messenger*); *ČSR* (*Czechoslovak Republic*); *Rudé právo* (Amort, p. 33; Jelínek, p. 109).
53. The Czech press reported on April 26, 1939, that the use of hydrochloric acid had caused damage to the uniforms of 30 German soldiers. The Germans arrested 100 persons in reprisal (*Naše doba*, June 1939, p. 496). Neurath issued a proclamation in August 1939, warning that all sabotage activities, including the dissemination of rumors and disobedience, would be punished with the greatest severity (*IMT*, XXXIX, 535–36). On June 8, 1939, after one German policeman had been shot dead by unknown persons, 107 Czechs were arrested in the city of Kladno, among them 41 members of the municipal council. Thirteen of them never returned from concentration camps (*K. H. Frank*, p. 201; Alois Pěnička, *Kladensko v boji za svobodu*, p. 32). For a good description of the actions of the Resistance in 1941, see Král, *Otázky*, III, 210 ff.
54. There were many acts of sabotage such as the cutting of telegraph poles and wires, railway sabotage, damage to military vehicles, etc. For examples in the region of Brdy, see Amort, *Partyzáni*, pp. 21, 30–31. The Abwehr brought up some figures on Czech sabotage: from September to the end of 1941, 582 cases; in 1942, 470; in 1943, 585 (Král, *Pravda*, p. 258).
55. The providing of shelter for members of the Resistance had been punished by death since May 1942.
56. For instance, the mayor of Prague, Dr. Klapka, used city funds to assist such families. He was executed in October 1941 (Vozka, p. 37). Hácha gave 500,000 K in 1939 and Eliáš used 7 million K of his own funds for the same purpose (*Svobodné slovo*, May 24, 1946; Feierabend, *Ve vládě*, pp. 147–48).
57. Frank and Heydrich were highly impressed by both the methods and the achievements of the Resistance (*Vergangenheit*, pp. 128, 169).

The Resistance influenced all strata of the population and reached as high as the Protectorate government. The premier, Gen. Alois Eliáš, was one of its most prominent members. From the beginning he was in regular contact with President Beneš and the ÚVOD, and his activities were carried out in full agreement with Beneš, who had asked Eliáš three times not to resign.[58]

General Eliáš adopted a line of simulation and perseverance. He transmitted—with some other members of the cabinet—valuable information to Beneš and arranged for the transfer of funds to the Czechoslovak movement abroad.[59] He secretly provided relief to the families of imprisoned patriots and took an active part in the political match against the Nazis. His pattern of national conduct was to maintain surface compliance in the new situation while making all preparations for the final military insurrection. The national task was to beat the Germans when a favorable moment arose in the international situation, since Eliáš was anxious not to evoke reprisals prematurely. In the meantime, he used his high post to obstruct German demands and to assist the efforts of the Resistance in many other ways. He was finally tracked down by the Gestapo, arrested on Sept. 27, 1941, and executed on June 19, 1942.[60]

Throughout 1939 and 1940 the Czechoslovak liberation movement abroad and President Beneš welcomed contacts with Hácha and Eliáš and other members of the Protectorate cabinet who recognized Beneš as the supreme authority.[61] Beneš cautioned them that they would be

58. "The Beran trial," *Svobodné slovo*, Feb. 28, 1947. For contacts among Beneš and Eliáš and Hácha see Král, *Otázky*, III, 214 ff.; Král, *Pravda*, pp. 195 ff.; Feierabend, *Ve vládě, passim;* "The Trial of Frank," *Svobodné slovo*, April 28, 1946.

59. "The Trial of the Protectorate Government," *Svobodné slovo*, June 14, 1946. The Protectorate minister of Finance, Dr. Josef Kalfus, helped to finance the Resistance movement. Kalfus was the only minister who transmitted regular secret messages to London even after the arrest of Eliáš (*ibid.*, June 16, 26, 1946).

60. His conception was open to criticism (Král, *Pravda,* pp. 233 ff.). For the Eliáš trial on Oct. 1, 1941, see Helmut Heiber, "Zur Justiz im Dritten Reich. Der Fall Eliáš," *Vierteljahrshefte für Zeitgeschichte*, III (July 1955), 275–96. General Eliáš was under surveillance by the SD from the spring of 1940. Frank urged his arrest as early as Feb. 26, 1941, in a letter to Himmler. Some days prior to his arrest, Eliáš received a message from Beneš asking for the resignation of his government. The Germans got wind of it and Neurath reported it to Berlin, where Hitler ordered the arrest of Eliáš and a change of Reich protector (*K. H. Frank*, pp. 89, 95, 159, 205). The Protectorate cabinet met on Sept. 28, 1941, and considered its resignation and the abdication of Hácha as a protest against the imprisonment of its premier. By a close majority against four ministers it was decided to stay in office for fear that the Germans would replace the cabinet by Quislings (*Svobodné slovo*, May 28, 1946).

61. President Hácha was also in contact with London until September 1941

obliged to resign when the political situation required it. In September 1941, he asked for the resignation of the cabinet. After Heydrich's arrival in Prague, all mutual contacts broke down. Beneš felt strongly that both the cabinet and Hácha should have resigned in protest against the mass executions ordered by Heydrich. After that date, the continuing existence of the Prague cabinet and its servile subjection to almost all Nazi wishes clearly worked in favor of Berlin.

With the homeland in grave peril, thwarted in their national aspirations, and fighting with desperate courage, resistance forces at home nourished themselves on the hopes of reconstituting a new Czechoslovakia. The dream of a better life in a new Republic exercised a magnetic attraction on the masses. The Czechoslovakia of their vision bore little relationship to the tragic realities of the post-Munich period. The patriots envisioned a republic, again free and independent, allied both with East and West. They saw a strong democratic state, with two or three major political parties. They strove for a just and progressive social and economic order that would distribute national wealth more equitably. They invoked the tragic memories of the Sudeten German threat to internal security and demanded a new national state without the Germans.

The removal of the Germans from the territories of the Republic became the aim of the majority of Czechs. The Nazi terror, executions, and daily arrests, the slow agony of a powerless people, and the cruel repression immeasurably reinforced Czech antagonism to everything German. The way to reconciliation was closed. Coexistence between Germans and Czechs was now deemed unthinkable. Only one alternative remained. It was to liberate the nation from the German grip once and for all. The idea of transfer absorbed the minds of the Czech people. It would uproot the Nazi-tainted, sinister group which had planned and executed the destruction of the Republic on behalf of a merciless regime. The idea of the transfer of the Sudeten Germans gained widespread approval in the underground movement and among the Czech masses. There existed no area of substantial disagreement within the Resistance leadership to this particular demand. Already in the first half of 1939, the soldiers and officers who had escaped from Czechoslovakia to Poland asked the reconstitution of Czechoslovakia "without national minorities . . ." on a national

---

(Feierabend, "Memoirs," p. 656). Hácha, who regarded himself as a temporary deputy of Beneš, became seriously ill; by 1943 he moved only in a wheelchair and was unable to sign his name. He died shortly after the return of Beneš in 1945 (*Svobodné slovo*, May 25, 1946).

basis. The minorities who committed treason were to be expelled.[62] The illegal central committee of the Social Democratic Party, always inclined to be tolerant in nationality questions, set forth the same demand in a secret message sent abroad on Jan. 30, 1940:

> We inform you that with the vast majority of the Czech and Slovak people we would welcome the establishment of the old historical frontiers . . . and the transfer of the major part of . . . the Germans.[63]

The military prepared a plan for the occupation and colonization of the borderland. Each Czech district was to contribute a fixed quota of Czech families to be sent into the German areas.[64] The ÚVOD incorporated the demand for transfer of the Sudeten Germans in its program, *For Freedom,* compiled by leading members of the Social Democratic underground in 1940–41:[65]

> Nationality problems are to be arranged to the effect that no repetition of the internal causes of the fall of the First Republic can occur again. The scope and extent of such arrangements depend on the outcome of the war, particularly on the extent of the German defeat. On no account will there be place in the Republic for those Germans who have assisted the Henleinists or Nazis in any way or have enjoyed any advantages from them. . . . The Government of National Revolution will immediately take all necessary measures pertaining to state citizenship, property, indemnities and restitution of the legal state.[66]

The illegal newspaper of the ÚVOD, the *Czech Messenger,* stated on Sept. 30, 1941:

62. R. Kopecký, *Československý odboj v Polsku v roce 1939,* p. 35.
63. The private papers of the late former Czechoslovak Minister František Němec (Montreal). For the radical mood of the non-Communist underground on the Sudeten German question, see Křen, *Do emigrace,* p. 555.
64. A part of the plan was sent abroad in 1940. It was revived in the decisive phase, 1944–45 (Veselý-Štainer, p. 214).
65. The author of the original text was Prof. Dr. Josef Fischer. This text went through a process of amendments by the collective leadership of the PVVZ. The final text was approved by the representatives of the Obrana národa, PVVZ, and Political Center. Almost all of the authors were executed by the Germans. A summary of the program was sent to London. The program itself was published in 1945. It is extremely valuable, for it indicates the ideological basis of the Resistance (*Za svobodu do nové Československé republiky. Ideový program domácího odbojového hnutí vypracovaný v letech 1939–41*). The program demanded restoration of the historical frontiers, the reform of the state machinery, and the end of the old party system.
66. *Ibid.,* p. 76.

The Third Republic will be a national state. . . . Czechoslovakia cannot tolerate any more the old conception of the minority policy. . . .

Therefore it is absolutely necessary to solve the German problem by way of the transfer of the German minority from the territory of Czechoslovakia.[67]

The transfer of the Sudeten Germans from Czechoslovakia was a guiding principle for Resistance groups throughout the Nazi occupation.[68] The demand was not only the result of a lingering desire for national independence, but also the outcome of the collective experience. It arose from the necessities of Czechoslovakia at a time when no one knew whether the Czech people would have a chance to survive. Girded with its program, the Czech Resistance entered the year 1941 confidently. It expected that the war would eventually exhaust Germany, which would then be assaulted by the joint forces of the Allied armies and the Resistance at home. The liberated Republic would be ruled by a government of national revolution constituted mainly of the leaders of the democratic forces of the Czech and Slovak underground at home and enlarged by a few prominent members of the liberation movement in exile under the leadership of Beneš.[69] The democratic Resistance movement would provide a working basis for the new Republic.

Early in the fall of 1941, everything changed. The slaughter spread across the country, and in several weeks the Czech fighting elite was decimated by a series of swift actions directed by Heydrich. The massacres of 1941 and 1942 shifted the center of political activity to the Czechoslovak exiles abroad. The decision about the future political regime—as far as the Czechs were concerned—no longer lay within the country. Unfortunately it was the exile movement, not the

67. Jelínek, pp. 147–48.
68. Prof. Dr. Vladimír Krajina stated in a letter to the author (May 26, 1958): "I cannot remember that I have ever met anybody in the Resistance movement who would not agree completely with the transfer of the Germans." The author, who worked in the underground movement until May 1945, can only confirm the statement of Professor Krajina. The transfer of the Germans also belonged to the basic demands of the Rada 3 (Council of the Three), the largest Resistance group existing in the Historic Provinces in 1944–45 (Veselý-Štainer, pp. 131, 159). The demand became a commonplace for anybody working in the underground. See also the 1943 plan of one of the groups of the Political Center, demanding that the statutes through which the Czechoslovak Germans became Reich citizens be considered valid (Jelínek, p. 176). It also asked the sequestration of all German property on Czechoslovak territory (ibid., p. 178).
69. For the plan of the PVVZ, March 19, 1941, see Veselý-Štainer, pp. 68–69.

Resistance at home, which ultimately provided the nucleus of the postwar government. Thus more or less skillful politicians, who lived in the midst of the exile intrigues and did not face real danger, became the leaders of the country in 1945. The destruction of the flower of the Czech intelligentsia, Army, and workers' movement, who had been the prime movers in the struggle for liberty and national revival, cleared the way for the postwar regime. Thus, the key to the capitulation of the democratic forces in February 1948, and to the absence of strong independent-minded personalities within the Czechoslovak Communist Party, is to be found, to a large extent, in the Nazi policy of terror in 1938–45.[70] That policy, too, shaped the Czech national will to remove the Germans by transfer.

70. The German post-1945 version of the activities of the Czech Resistance was strikingly different. Many German authors gave free rein to their imagination and prejudices without even a perfunctory examination of the available documents. They alleged that the Resistance movement was practically nonexistent and that the Czechs were satisfied with Reich German protection. This state of mind is not very likely to promote the essential principles of historical research in the Federal Republic. Walter Görlitz (Der Zweite Weltkrieg 1938–45, II, 122) stated: "Blieb das Protektorat Böhmen-Mähren bis zur letzten Stunde des Krieges ruhig. Partisanen gab es hier nicht." Ludwig Schreiber (Die Vertriebenen. Die Tragödie einer Heimat, p. 145) affirmed: "Denn die Deutschen [in 1939–45] an den Tschechen keine wie immer geartete Vergeltung geübt, . . . sondern sie gut und menschlich behandelt, sofern sie sich gegen die gültigen Staatsgesetze nicht vergangen hatten." Erich Kern (Das andere Lidice. Die Tragödie der Sudetendeutschen, p. 6) wrote that Czech autonomy was almost complete. On the whole, "blieb Böhmen und Mähren eine Insel der Ruhe und des inneren Friedens. Kein einziger Strassenüberfall auf deutsche Kolonnen erfolgte . . . keine einzige Brücke zerstört" (ibid., p. 84). Prof. Rudolf Schreiber (in Preidel, ed., p. 98) gave a description of the situation in the Protectorate: "In Protektorat waren die kleine stille wirtschaftliche Sabotage . . . und Schiebereien an der Tagesordnung, hingegen fehlte dort jeder leidenschaftlich-heldische Zug der Widerstandsbewegung. . . . Konnte selbst Heydrich in wenigen Monaten beträchtliche Werbeerfolge unter den tschechischen Arbeitern und Bauern erringen." Dr. Wilhelm K. Turnwald affirmed that "during the war the Czech population neither offered any considerable resistance nor practiced any effective sabotage against war industry. The Czechs were exempted from military service. The food was no worse, perhaps even better than in Germany. As in Germany, the Gestapo in Bohemia and Moravia interned obvious opponents in German concentration camps. No active resistance to the German armies of occupation . . . was ever observed, not even in the last weeks of war. . . . The Sudeten Germans, as a national group, had no share in the happenings" (W. K. Turnwald, ed., Documents on the Expulsion of the Sudeten Germans, p. XIX). Prof. Eugen Lemberg (Osteuropa und die Sowjetunion. Geschichte und Probleme, p. 255) stated: "So gut es ihnen [Czechs] unter Hitlers Herrschaft äusserlich ging," and enumerated "the advantages."

CHAPTER 9

The Czechoslovak Political Movement Abroad and the Preparations for International Recognition of the Republic

The primary aim of the Czechoslovak liberation movement abroad during the first war years was to achieve international recognition of the Czechoslovak Republic within its pre-Munich frontiers. The problems inherent in securing this objective were of major concern to the exile movement. The constitution of the Czechoslovak Army and the creation of the state machinery presented many difficulties which the outbreak of war had put into increasingly sharp focus. Beneš, whose popularity at home was unmatched as a symbol of national unity, had to cope with both the cool attitude of the British government and the hostility of the French cabinet.[1] The power of the Munich appeasers still predominated in both capitals. The Czechoslovak exile movement itself faced much jockeying for position and a shifting of personalities and political groups, and it was only gradually that a more complete degree of unity developed. It was not until after the fall of France that Great Britain recognized the provisional

1. The book by R. H. Bruce Lockhart, *Comes the Reckoning*, and his article, "The Second Exile of Eduard Beneš," *Slavonic and East European Review*, XXVIII (November 1949), 39–50, present a fair description of the British attitude toward Beneš and the Czechs. (See also Beneš, *Memoirs*, pp. 81 ff.) Bruce Lockhart was liaison officer of the Foreign Office and later on the British representative with the provisional Czechoslovak government. A useful although somewhat biased survey of the political situation in regard to the Czechoslovak exiles up to the outbreak of World War II was given by Křen (*Do emigrace*).

Czechoslovak government (July 21, 1940).[2] Beneš resumed his functions as president of the Republic. On the day of the British recognition, Beneš nominated the new government under the premiership of Msgr. Jan Šrámek[3] and established an advisory body, the Czechoslovak State Council, to act as an auxiliary organ of control. A special agreement on military matters was signed with Great Britain on Oct. 25, 1940.[4]

The next task was the placing of Czechoslovakia on an equal footing with other Allied governments. Her provisional status evoked some discriminations. It was, however, only after long discussions and on specific orders from Churchill and Eden that London decided to extend full and definitive recognition to the Czechoslovak government abroad.[5] The move was precipitated by the act of the Soviet Union, which recognized the Republic with its pre-Munich frontiers and concluded a treaty of alliance with the Czechoslovak government. A race developed between the British and the Russians to recognize Czechoslovakia first. They put their signatures to the recognition acts on the same day, July 18, 1941.[6] The restoration of the Republic to its

2. "The view of the Foreign Office was not, at that time, that Beneš would be welcomed back." The Czechoslovak representatives were subjected to "irritating delays and minor humiliations" (Lockhart, *Reckoning*, p. 106).

3. Monsignor Šrámek was the leader of the moderate Catholic People's Party. A member of the last pre-Munich cabinets, he belonged to the firm adherents of the tough line against Henlein and the Western appeasers. He was deputy premier in the post-1945 cabinets. Caught when trying to escape from the Republic after the Communist take-over in 1948, he died in confinement.

4. Beneš, p. 115. The Czechoslovak Army was constituted in France and participated in the battles of June 1940. Czechoslovak pilots distinguished themselves in France and during the Battle of Britain. The Czechoslovak Tank Brigade participated in the battles of Tobruk and Dunkerque in 1944. Some 350 parachutists were dropped over Czechoslovakia. Two Czechoslovak Army corps were organized on the Eastern front. The First Army Corps lost 6,000 men during the battle at Dukla in 1944. Out of 1,500 active Czechoslovak airmen in Great Britain, some 500 were killed (Bohuš Štefan Mastný in *Sklizeň* [*Harvest*], V, October–November 1957).

5. The statement by R. H. Bruce Lockhart is worth quoting. "The plain truth was that, had there been no Churchill and no Eden, there would have been no Czechoslovak Government, no President Beneš, no Foreign Secretary Masaryk, and no gratitude from any Czechoslovak to Britain and still less to the United States who in the matter of recognition had lagged behind us all the way" (*Reckoning*, pp. 130–31). For the story of the recognition see *ibid.*, pp. 133 ff.; Beneš, *Memoirs*, pp. 123 ff.

6. Lockhart, *Reckoning*, pp. 119. After the invasion of Russia by Hitler (June 22, 1941), Moscow immediately contacted Beneš and declared itself ready to renew diplomatic relations. (For the draft of the treaty, see Beneš, *Memoirs*, p. 157.) It also gave permission for the formation of a Czechoslovak Army in the USSR. Full recognition of the Czechoslovak government was implied, as no mention was made of any provisional cabinet (Eduard Táborský, *The Czechoslovak Cause. An Account of the Problems of International Law in Relation to*

full international status placed it on an equal legal basis with other governments in exile. It presented a significant step forward in the final liquidation of the Munich agreement—a liquidation which was the foremost objective of Beneš.[7] The heart of the Czechoslovak thesis lay in the contention that the Republic continued to have a legal existence and did not accept the Munich dictate, which had been, as far as the Czechoslovak state was concerned, invalid from its inception.

Most of the Czechoslovak political leaders felt with Beneš that their fight could be understood best if taken as a struggle for basic democratic and human values and as a part of a prolonged series of social revolutions involving the whole world. They realized that in the years immediately following the war the world would be confronted with immense social, economic, and political changes.[8] Within this framework Czechoslovak policy had to aim toward close cooperation with both the Western powers and the Soviet Union. The achievement of a friendly relationship with the smaller powers in Central Europe, particularly with Poland,[9] was also regarded as important. Great stress was laid upon international cooperation based on the principles of collective security, peaceful settlement of international disputes, and equality of rights for all nations.[10]

Past events compelled Beneš and his followers to review the whole nationality problem of the state. In the fall of 1938, as he went into exile, Beneš had weighed the basic question: "When Munich is liquidated . . . how can we solve our nationality problem once and for all and, as far as possible, justly?" Viewed alone, the problem justified a critical reassessment of the Czechoslovak German policy and a search for its solution. Beneš, aware that the problem was of

---

Czechoslovakia, p. 100). The volume presents a lucid analysis of the juridical problems involved in the international position of the Republic. The United States recognized the provisional government on July 31, 1941. Its definitive recognition was given as late as Oct. 26, 1942 (*ibid.*, pp. 100–101).

7. Beneš, *Memoirs*, p. 197, noted: "From September, 1938, sleeping and waking, I was continuously thinking of this objective—living for it, suffering on its account and working for it in every one of my political actions. In fact, it was already my only aim in life."

8. Táborský, p. 9. Address of Beneš, Dec. 11, 1940 (*Central European Observer*, XVII, Dec. 16, 1940).

9. There were serious negotiations between the Polish and Czechoslovak governments in London regarding the establishment of a confederation. For the question, see Piotr S. Wandycz, *Czechoslovak-Polish Confederation and the Great Powers 1940–43* (Bloomington, Ind., 1956).

10. Hubert Ripka, "Principles of Czechoslovak Policy, Past and Future," *The Central European Observer*, XIX, Jan. 23, 1942.

truly vital importance, felt that Czechoslovakia "must either solve it at whatever cost or succumb." He took the relevant decision:

In order to preserve pre-Munich Czechoslovakia it would be necessary to adopt the principle of a very radical reduction in the number of its minorities.[11]

Beneš pursued this objective, persistently adapting his tactics to the historical situation and political developments. He saw in the removal of the Sudeten Germans a hard measure, but perhaps the only one which would lead toward the stabilization of the Central European area. He was ready to make the solution acceptable to and dependent upon the approval of the Great Powers, because only then could it be of permanent value. As the war progressed, Beneš pressed his aim at first cautiously and then energetically. The increasingly patent brutality of Nazism, the prolongation of the war, the continued solid support of Hitler by the Sudeten Germans, the terror in the country, and the rivalry among the Great Powers united in making a very impressive case.

The presence of a small but very active Sudeten German Social Democratic Party in exile in Great Britain, with its leader Wenzel Jaksch, led to new quarrels and difficulties.[12] In the first months of exile, Jaksch counted on a short war and social revolution in the Reich.[13] Jaksch himself affirmed:

For the Sudeten Germans we demand also the right to decide freely whether they want to live as an autonomous sector of the historical provinces of Bohemia and Moravia, that is to say, in a closer State-union with the Czechs, or whether they want to be attached as a province to a federal Reich.[14]

11. Beneš, *Memoirs*, pp. 211–12. A suggestion of Beneš to Minister Nečas on Sept. 15, 1938, had already indicated the possibility of a transfer (see above, p. 141). Hubert Ripka reported that he held a discussion on the transfer with Beneš in December 1938 (Elizabeth Wiskemann, *Germany's Eastern Neighbours. Problems Relating to the Oder-Neisse Line and the Czech Frontier Regions*, p. 63. This volume gives a rather sketchy account of the transfer.)

12. The Jaksch group numbered 975 members on June 1, 1942. (See a circular of the Treugemeinschaft sudetendeutscher Sozialdemokratie, end of June 1942. The papers of Němec.) There were other groups of democratic Sudetens and German Communists.

13. Beneš, *Memoirs*, pp. 213–14, 328. See also Jiří Hronek, *Od porážky k vítězství*, II, 173 ff. Hronek describes the rather liberal Czech exile attitude toward the Germans during 1939.

14. *Was kommt nach Hitler* (London, 1939), p. 16, as cited in Beneš, *Memoirs*, p. 328.

In his first discussion with Beneš (Aug. 3, 1939), Jaksch called for a federalization of the Republic on the basis of the so-called Fourth Plan from 1938. Although representing a mere fraction of the people at home, Jaksch pretended to speak in the name of more than three million Sudetens. The conference of the Sudeten German Social Democrats demanded the application of the right of self-determination to the Sudeten Germans and the recognition of their autonomy within a federal state with their own Diet and government.[15] Jaksch recommended that the party members enlist in the British Army because "the question of the Sudeten territory belonging to the Czechs is open and a fresh decision will not be taken without our participation."[16]

The Sudeten German Social Democrats agreed to participate in the liberation movement under the condition that Beneš give them a pledge concerning the future political status of the Germans within the Republic. They took full advantage of the hesitations displayed by London and Paris toward Beneš. Jaksch, retaining the immediate objectives of the Henlein movement, believed that Germany would be a party at the final settlement of Europe.[17] Working in the political background against Beneš, he sponsored a program which invited strong Czech criticism, seriously weakened the position of the Sudeten Germans themselves, and revealed an utter lack of understanding of the vicissitudes occurring in the Czech homeland.[18] Instead of practicing his past political convictions, Jaksch incited

15. On March 10, 1940. For the text of the resolution, see *Die Brücke*, April 4, 1959. See also J. W. Brügel, "Die Aussiedlung der Deutschen aus der Tschechoslowakei," *Vierteljahrshefte für Zeitgeschichte*, VIII (April 1960), 143 ff.; Jan Křen, "Revanšisté s protinacistickou minulostí," *Československý časopis historický*, IX (1961), 46 ff.

16. Jan. 7, 1940 (Beneš, *Memoirs*, p. 330). Jaksch criticized the Reich German Socialists for their recognition of the pre-Munich Czechoslovak frontiers (*Europas Weg*, p. 353).

17. It is interesting to note that the plans of the Reich German resistance counted on the inclusion of the Sudeten territory. Ulrich von Hassell's terms for the peace settlement, sent to Chamberlain on Feb. 22, 1940, asked "to have the union of Austria and the Sudeten with the Reich out of any discussion" (*Diaries 1938–1944*, p. 118; John W. Wheeler-Bennett, *The Nemesis of Power. The German Army in Politics 1918–1945*, London, 1954, pp. 488–89). Carl Goerdeler prepared three plans for a peace settlement. On May 30, 1941, he asked for the inclusion of Austria and the Sudetenland within the frontiers of 1914. On March 26, 1943, he still defended the maintenance of the hegemonic position of Germany in Europe. As late as the fall of 1943, Goerdeler still held the same view (Gerhard Ritter, *Carl Goerdeler und die deutsche Widerstandsbewegung*, pp. 569, 571, 587).

18. In the midst of Nazi persecution in the Protectorate, the group around Jaksch prepared plans for winning back "many moderate Nazis" (circular by Jaksch, London, Oct. 23, 1940; papers of Němec).

trouble for himself, split his party, and missed the opportunity to win German representation in the cabinet and state council.[19] By raising old issues and inflaming passions, he exercised extraordinarily bad judgment. His masked imitation of Henleinist dreams did a grave disservice to the German democratic movement.

In his conversations with Jaksch, President Beneš maintained the necessity of an absolute equality of Czechs, Slovaks, and Germans, and asked for the unconditional and unreserved cooperation of all citizens irrespective of parties or nationalities. He explained that "in the question of allegiance to the State and the fulfilment of civic duties . . . no conditions are any more admissible now than they were in 1938."[20] It was impossible, Beneš felt, for anyone to set conditions for the acceptance of the state, as neither he nor any exile government was authorized to make unilateral decisions on problems which only the people at home could decide. From the outset he favored the inclusion of the anti-Nazi Germans in the liberation movement, and offered Jaksch six seats in the state council. The Sudeten German Social Democratic Party intimated again that its acceptance was conditional on negotiations pertaining to future relations between the Czechs and Sudeten Germans.[21] As a practical matter, such a demand entailed the retention of Sudeten territory under Henleinist rule, as the great majority of the Sudeten Germans supported the SdP. The discussions continued during the winter of 1940–41. On Dec. 11, 1940, President Beneš announced to the state council:

> I stress that as occasion arises I will accept as a matter of course the participation of some politicians and groups not yet among us today. I have discussed this with some politicians from among our German fellow-citizens. I have offered them participation and I have obtained an affirmative answer. . . . I therefore suppose their representatives [German Social Democratic Party] will join the State Council in [the] near future.[22]

Yet no agreement could be reached with Jaksch's group, which lived under the impression that the British would make their backing of Beneš dependent upon his conclusion of an agreement with Jaksch, who thus might be able to exercise a sort of veto power.[23]

19. A group of Sudeten German Social Democrats led by Josef Zinner broke away and formed the Deutsche Sozialdemokratische Arbeiterpartei in der Tschechoslowakischen Republik, Oct. 18, 1940. It disagreed with the policy of Jaksch.
20. Beneš, *Memoirs,* pp. 312–13.
21. *Ibid.,* p. 311.
22. *Ibid.,* p. 308.
23. *Ibid.,* p. 216.

Beneš pondered the modalities of a solution of the Sudeten German problem during the winter months of 1940–41. Fearing the possibility of the conclusion of a separate peace treaty between Great Britain and Germany, he sought the best way to safeguard the security of the Republic while still giving full satisfaction to the Germans. Beneš appeared to regard both aims as his greatest concern.[24] On Feb. 1, 1941, he sent the fruit of his reflections, the secret "Memorandum Pertaining to Our Peace Aims," to the members of the cabinet for discussion. Beneš' conception of suitable peace aims can be summarized in four points: (1) to insist upon the historic frontiers of the Republic; (2) to form an area within the state which would be inhabited by the Czechs; (3) to remove the Germans from this area; and (4) to extend the German area from the Czech zone to the frontiers.[25] The plan of Beneš met strong criticism and even outright refusal to accept the principle of a closed German territorial unit. Minister Dr. Ladislav Feierabend stated that a system of international protection of the minorities was no more acceptable. He wanted to impose an obligation upon the Reich to accept as its citizens all those Germans who would be expelled from the Czechoslovak Republic.[26]

The Social Democratic minister of Social Welfare, František Němec, favored transfer as a method for solving the national problem but disagreed with the idea of a purely German area. He recommended the strengthening of the security of the state through Czech resettlement of German borderlands, although he admitted that there would still remain some German districts which would have to be split up and surrounded by Czech territory.[27]

The Slovakian Social Democrat Ján Bečko thought that any compact German area would be attracted by its proximity to the Reich. As the Germans inhabiting the Republic were Reich German citizens after 1938–39, they would become unwanted foreigners after the war. Hence, the Reich should take care of all of them. As her minimum demand Czechoslovakia should be permitted to expel all those Sudeten Germans who served Hitler directly, in addition to the internationally approved number of Sudeten Germans removed from the Republic through regular transfer.[28]

The minister of National Defense, Gen. Sergěj Ingr, put forward

24. Feierabend, "Memoirs," p. 620.
25. Papers of Němec. Jan Křen put the date of the memorandum at February 3. Beneš mentioned his plan in his report to the home Resistance on Nov. 18, 1940 ("Revanšisté," p. 51).
26. Feierabend, "Memoirs," p. 634. His answer was sent in March 1941.
27. Papers of Němec.
28. The reply was sent to Beneš in March–April 1941 (ibid.).

another scheme: (1) to cede the salients of Aš, Cheb, Šluknov, Frýdlant, Broumov, Frývaldov, and Osoblaha to the Reich in order to get rid of about three quarters of a million Germans; (2) to carry out the transfer of one million Germans as a compensation for the territorial cession; (3) to expel immediately one quarter of a million Germans; (4) to crush the economic power of the remaining one and a quarter million Germans through confiscations and other measures; and (5) to resettle the formerly German area with Czechs and Slovaks.[29]

The Social Democratic minister, Jaromír Nečas, rejected the idea of a compact German settlement area. He proposed to abandon the German salients and to ask for the transfer of one and a half million Germans and the acquisition of the territory of Kladsko and Ratibořsko (Silesia) as compensation. The Germans should be given two alternatives, either to remain Reich citizens, possessing all the rights belonging to aliens, or to become Czechoslovaks.[30]

Through the spring of 1941 there were further informal discussions between members of the cabinet and Beneš. Beneš himself was disposed to abandon some of the salients to the Reich. Minister Ripka resolutely advocated the transfer of the Germans,[31] because to his mind the war presented a unique historic opportunity which the Czechs ought to use to secure their national existence once and for all.[32] As the first Czechoslovak political leader, he voiced his opinion publicly on May 17, 1941.

> We hope that this war will produce an opportunity for settling, once and for all, the question of the Sudeten Germans. . . . It will be necessary, with all the appropriate means, including also possibly an organizational application of the principle of the transfer of populations, to prevent Germany from misusing her national minorities for her Pan-German aims.[33]

29. *Ibid.* On April 8,1941.
30. *Ibid.* On Feb. 25, 1941.
31. Feierabend, "Memoirs," p. 657.
32. *Ibid.*, p. 881. MacAlister Brown reported that according to Dr. Ripka a secret plan originated in the spring of 1941, worked out by Beneš, Masaryk, and Šrámek. It called for the expulsion without compensation of the active members of the SdP, the transfer with compensation of other Germans, and the retention of anti-Nazis. The existence of such a plan is not borne out by the available evidence ("Expulsion of German Minorities," p. 218).
33. Lecture at the Alliance Française, Manchester, England, on May 17, 1941 (Czechoslovak Ministry of Foreign Affairs, *Czechoslovakia in Post-War Europe. Problems of Reconstruction*, p. 61; *Central European Observer*, May 30, 1941). Dr. Beneš noted the transfer as an instrument to solve national problems in his lecture at Oxford on May 23, 1941, as reported by J. W. Brügel ("Die Aussiedlung," p. 145).

Beneš still remained cautious. Great Britain was fighting alone against Hitler. The Soviet Union stood aloof, and the United States displayed little interest in Central Europe. The winning of the necessary support of Britain was to be made easier by the ceding of the Czechoslovak salients. Even under these circumstances, Beneš felt, Czechoslovakia would emerge in a greatly enhanced position. There were, however, still many imponderables in the war situation, since complex and powerful forces had been set in motion everywhere. While waiting for them to take effect, Beneš carefully weighed the various aspects of the tactics to be used in resolving the German question.

Meanwhile, the Czechoslovak government adhered to the principles of the Atlantic Charter with some reservations stated on August 29, 1941. The observation was made that "the vital interests and sovereign rights" of the Republic should be safeguarded. Translated into plain language it meant that the right of self-determination of the Sudeten Germans would not be recognized because, as Beneš put it, "such a concept of self-determination is a priori a denial of the right of self-determination of ten million Czechoslovaks and precludes the very existence of an independent Czechoslovak State."[34] In September 1941, in a London review, Beneš went a step further.

I accept the principle of the transfer of populations. . . . If the problem is carefully considered . . . the transfer can be made amicably under decent human conditions, under international control and with international support.[35]

He adopted a more uncompromising attitude because his position became stronger through the recognition of his government by Great Britain and the Soviet Union. The same reasons led Jaksch toward the abandonment of his former conditions. In the summer of 1941 he agreed to enter the state council without reservations, while keeping his "former fundamental view of the relations" of the Germans to the Republic.[36] On Sept. 22, 1941—as yet before the rule of Heydrich— Beneš conferred with Jaksch, to whom he read dispatches received from the Resistance at home. These made no secret of the fact that Nazi brutality had only stiffened its demands. They indicated that any participation of the Sudeten Germans in the liberation movement was impossible. Although still in favor of German representation in

34. Beneš, *Memoirs*, pp. 315–16.
35. "The New Order in Europe," *The Nineteenth Century and After*, CXXX (September 1941), 150–55.
36. Beneš, *Memoirs*, p. 325.

the state council, Beneš asked Jaksch for a postponement of the nominations to a more favorable psychological moment.[37]

The arrival of Heydrich aroused Czech hatred against the Germans, and even the group around Jaksch began to realize the seriousness of the savage dispute taking place in the country. The massacres in the Protectorate shattered the Czech people once again and cast a lurid light on the horror, savagery, and perfidy of the Nazi regime. The endeavor of Beneš to win the cooperation of Jaksch was at its end. Both sides recognized the temporary impossibility of proceeding with the nomination of German Social Democrats to the state council.[38] Beneš' moderate stand, advocating a restricted application of the principle of transfer at the outset of 1941, thus underwent a distinct change. Nazi brutality increased the anti-German mood in all Allied countries. When a nation's existence is in peril, its government is bound to analyze all possibilities, no matter how farfetched they may seem. Heydrich confronted Beneš with a new wave of terror. Czech people were shot in cold blood. Beneš responded to the sharpening situation with his usual caution in his address to the state council on Nov. 25, 1941:

> I have also had negotiations with some political elements among our democratic Germans. . . . By mutual agreement their co-operation on the floor of the State Council has been postponed for the time being in view of events at home. . . . The State Council is an organism which has as its first and most important mission to unite all political elements of all former political lines of thought

37. *Ibid.*, pp. 216, 325; Jaksch, *Europas Weg*, pp. 364–65. According to the former secretary general of the Foreign Office in Prague, Arnošt Heidrich, on Sept. 17, 1941 Beneš informed the Resistance movement that he would consider it useful to include Jaksch and another Sudeten German among the members of a state council and inquired about the possible reaction of the Czech population. The dispatch from Prague stated that the mood of the Czech people excluded any such move (interview with Arnošt Heidrich, Washington, D.C., June 26, 1956). By the end of January 1941, more than 14,000 secret messages had been exchanged between Beneš and the underground movement (Lockhart, *Reckoning*, p. 112).

38. Beneš, *Memoirs*, p. 325. For the conference of the Jaksch group on Sept. 28, 1941, see a circular by Jaksch dated Aug. 8, 1942 (Papers of Němec). The group also agreed "to inaugurate abroad that measure of co-operation with the Czechoslovak State organization which is rendered possible by psychological conditions at home"(The Resolution of the Executive Committee of the Jaksch group, June 7, 1942, in Beneš, p. 303). Beneš, however, nominated the German Communist Karl Kreibich to the state council in October 1941, with the explanation that Kreibich was nominated as a Communist and not as a member of German nationality (*ibid.*, p. 309). Clearly this was an excuse. Kreibich wholeheartedly approved the idea of transfer.

and of all nationalities in the Republic owing allegiance to the State.

As for the ultimate fate of the German inhabitants of Czechoslovakia after the defeat of Nazism, Beneš emphasized that

> It will especially be necessary to punish all those who, directly or indirectly, have participated in acts of treason and bestialities perpetrated by the Henleinites, the Nazis and the Gestapo.[39]

The mass tragedy of the Czech people at home and the demands of the underground for the expulsion of all German culprits exercised a decisive influence on the policy of Beneš, who recognized that a substantial reduction in the number of Germans remaining in the Czechoslovak state had become a sheer necessity.[40] On Jan. 7, 1942, in a discussion with Jaksch and his group, Beneš endorsed the principle of the transfer of those Germans who had gone over to Nazism. Beneš explained that the minimum demands of the Czech people included the removal of Germans from the country. He himself, after careful consideration of various possibilities, came to the conclusion that

> . . . it will be necessary to rid our country of all the German bourgeoisie, the pan-German intelligentsia and those workers who have gone over to Fascism.[41]

Jaksch disagreed. The differences were argued out thoroughly in a series of talks and letters. The last talk took place on Dec. 1, 1942, in which Beneš made the Czechoslovak stand clear.

> Never forget what efforts I made for an agreement with you during the struggle over Munich! But what did Hitler prepare for us—and with him more than 80 percent of your German co-nationals in Bohemia and Moravia, the representatives of whom you claim to be today? . . . We can draw but one calm, but stern conclusion: A just *retribution for all direct and indirect, active and passive war criminals as a lesson for the future and — complete separation!* . . . Only in this way will we be able to meet again later . . . as

39. *Ibid.*, pp. 311–12.
40. Feierabend, "Memoirs," p. 880. Minister Feierabend himself advocated the transfer of the German peasantry, assimilation of the working classes, and cession of the German salients (*ibid.*, p. 760).
41. Beneš, *Memoirs*, pp. 217–18. In his article on "The Organization of Postwar Europe," Beneš stated that "it will be necessary after this war to carry out a transfer of populations on a very much larger scale than after the last war. This must be done in as humane a manner as possible, internationally organized and internationally financed" (*Foreign Affairs*, XX, January 1942, 238).

neighbours and live each in his new home without bitterness and in peace, separated, *side by side* with one another.

In that connection I shall never forget that you, the true German Social Democrats . . . have never sullied the German name during this great historical crisis.[42]

This proved to be the end of the Czech-German dialogue.

The idea of transfer was inseparably linked with the question of the punishment of the Nazis and Henleinists. Because more than 85 percent of the Germans in Czechoslovakia had lent themselves to the purpose of Nazi subversive activities against the Republic, any measure of retribution concerning those who had directly or indirectly helped to destroy the Republic would necessarily strike a great number of people. Unable to live "with a German revolver permanently" aimed at their breast, the Czechs decided not to allow a repetition of Munich. The exodus of those Germans who helped Hitler and Henlein and Frank presented the best solution. Only the anti-Nazis who remained faithful to the democratic state could remain.[43] Responsible Czechoslovak leaders whose role was particularly outstanding in the diplomatic preparations of the transfer— besides Beneš, Minister of State Dr. Hubert Ripka was the architect of the transfer—were aware that the removal of the Germans was not exclusively a Czechoslovak question. Two million Germans had to be transferred to the Reich, which would be occupied by the Allies; therefore, approval had to be sought from the Allied governments. The measure should form an indispensable part of the postwar settlement. No Great Power accepted the idea of international minority protection any more. The Czechoslovak authorities realized that during this stage of war only the general principle of transfer

42. Beneš, *Memoirs*, pp. 220–21. The Appendix to the *Memoirs* contains the text of the important correspondence exchanged between Jaksch and Beneš. The last letter from Beneš was dated Jan. 10, 1943. The British annulment of Munich caused Jaksch to lodge a protest at the Foreign Office on Aug. 9, 1942. He asked the British cabinet to prevent the occupation of the Sudeten borderland after the end of war and to entrust the Jaksch group with the administration of the Sudeten territory. If this proved to be impossible, then an international administration should be put in charge of the territory for the period between the end of war and the conference of peace (*Europas Weg*, pp. 373–74). A protest was also sent to the State Department in Washington, D.C. In September 1943, Jaksch and some other Sudeten exiles pleaded for the provisory autonomous administration of the Sudeten territory after the end of the war (Papers of Němec).

43. Speech of Beneš at Mělník, Oct. 14, 1945; Beneš, *Memoirs*, pp. 317–18.

could be approved by the Allies, while the measure itself and its modalities and procedure would have to be worked out at the end of the war.[44]

The problem of the Czechoslovak frontiers and the question of the fate of the Sudeten Germans necessarily arose again when Beneš started discussions with the British Foreign Office on the liquidation of the Munich treaty. London was still unwilling to condemn the Munich dictate outright. Negotiations were prolonged indefinitely. Again the Soviet Union came indirectly to Beneš' aid. On June 9, 1942, he conferred with Soviet Foreign Minister Molotov in London, and the latter declared that the USSR had never recognized nor would it recognize what had happened at Munich and after. He also promised to give support to the demand to reduce the number of Czechoslovak Germans.[45] This binding declaration prodded the British Foreign Office and hastened the conclusive phase of the protracted negotiations with Beneš which started in April 1942. The final conversations between Foreign Secretary Anthony Eden and President Beneš took place on June 4 and 25, and July 7, 1942.[46] Beneš pointed out that the liquidation of the Munich dictate was a part of a vaster problem which involved the fate of the German minorities in Central Europe. He argued that the transfer of the German population would prevent the recurrence of Munich, since it concerned only those who had assisted the aggressors. It would be carried out in a humane way.[47] The new Republic would form a homogeneous state whose independent existence would guarantee the maintenance of order in Central Europe.

At this time, the British minister with the Czechoslovak government, Philip B. Nichols, informed Beneš that "the British Government had given careful consideration" to the Czechoslovak "attitude in the matter of the transfer" from the Republic "of minority populations which had conspired against" it. "At the time of the final solution of . . . minority problems after the victorious end of the war the British government did not intend to oppose the principle of transfer of the minority population from Czechoslovakia in an endeavour to make Czechoslovakia as homogeneous a country as possible from the

44. *Ibid.*, p. 315; Smutný, *Němci v Československu*, p. 73.
45. Fierlinger, *Ve službách*, II, 75–76. The cable from Beneš informed Fierlinger that Molotov had recognized the expulsion of Germans as an internal problem of the Republic. (For the declaration of Molotov, see Beneš, *Memoirs*, p. 204).
46. *Ibid.*
47. *Ibid.*, p. 206. See also a commentary by Smutný (*Němci*, p. 73).

standpoint of nationality."[48] On July 7, 1942, Eden informed Beneš that "his colleagues agree with the principle of transfer."[49] Shortly thereafter, the decision of the British cabinet, that it had no objection to the principle of the transfer of the Sudeten Germans, was communicated to Beneš.[50]

The massacres in the Protectorate following the attempt on the life of Heydrich, and the slaughter of the inhabitants of Lidice, sent a wave of revulsion throughout the world.[51] The tragedy of thousands upon thousands was now rendered comprehensible in terms of the personal tragedy of the innocent citizens of Lidice. The implications of the latest Prague and Brno executions went beyond the fate of the individuals involved. Berlin decided again to spurn world opinion, and the terroristic methods of alien rule indicated clearly the perilous situation of the Czechs. On June 17 the Czechoslovak cabinet made personally responsible for all the Nazi crimes not only the German authorities but all Germans "who aided the culprits though only indirectly, or approved of their conduct." Special courts would be set up to judge and punish the criminals after the end of war.[52]

The shocking situation in the Protectorate put further pressure upon London. In an exchange of notes on Aug. 5, 1942, Great Britain declared that it did not feel itself bound by the pledges and consequences of the Munich agreement, and that at the final settlement of Czechoslovak frontiers it "would not be influenced by any changes effected in and since 1938."[53] The chapter of Munich was closed. Nullification of the Munich pact and British approval of the principle of the transfer of the Germans dramatically illustrated the new international climate. Czechoslovakia was emerging from the war, if as yet merely on an international-juridical basis, as a fully independent state. There were grave and complex issues in need of adjudication, among them the fate of the Germans. The problems

48. Beneš, p. 206. The quotation is taken from the Beneš report and is given in his words. Jaksch expressed his doubts on the validity of the report of Beneš (Der europäische Osten, I, July–August 1955, 416–19).
49. Letter by the British Foreign Office to Rudolf Storch (Der Sudetendeutsche, Oct. 29, 1955) in Smutný (Němci, p. 71).
50. Beneš, Memoirs, p. 207.
51. For instance, American Secretary of the Navy Frank Knox declared in Boston (June 13, 1942) "If future generations ask us what we were fighting for in this war we shall tell them the story of Lidice." On June 14, Secretary of State Cordell Hull issued a statement expressing shock over this "wanton butchery of hostages and brutal torture of innocent women and children." The Illinois town of Stern Park Garden was renamed Lidice on July 12. Wendell Willkie was the speaker (Central European Observer, June 26, July 24, 1942).
52. Ibid.
53. Ibid., Aug. 21, 1942.

they posed were too difficult for easy solution. The demand for a homogeneous state was approved by Great Britain. Other Great Powers were still to be brought to the realization that they should take Czechoslovak aspirations into account.[54]

After having effected some changes in the composition of the government on Nov. 13, 1942, Beneš asked the members of the new cabinet to prepare concrete proposals for the future Czechoslovak frontiers and of the relationship of Czechoslovakia with Germany.[55] Beneš fought off any attempt to put forth demands for territory. He was still ready to cede some Czechoslovak territory to Germany, particularly those areas between the mountains and the historic frontiers. In the talks between Beneš and some members of the Šrámek cabinet, the majority defended the integrity of the Republic and were ready to agree to some small territorial losses only in exchange for the approval of the transfer of a large number of Germans to the Reich. At an informal meeting on Dec. 8, 1942, some members of the cabinet formulated a plan according to which Czechoslovakia would cede the salients of Cheb, Šluknov, Frýdlant, and a part of the salient of Broumov and would agree to some rectifications of the northern Moravian frontier, provided that Germany would be willing to take over two million Sudeten Germans.[56] The plan was influenced by the prevalent mood in Great Britain where some officials opposed the principle of transfer. Other governments in exile, however, favored the idea of transfer.[57] Minister of Finance Ladislav Feierabend elaborated a proposal for indemnification of the Germans. The principal provisions of his plan were as follows: (1) All personal property would remain in possession of the transferees, who would determine the part they desired to take with them; they would be compensated for the remaining part; (2) the equipment and installations of various enterprises could be removed only in exceptional cases; (3) all agricultural equipment, cattle, and domestic animals would remain; (4) the indemnity paid by the state should be assessed

54. The French Committee of National Liberation revoked the Munich agreement on Sept. 29, 1942. It declared it null and void from the beginning and recognized the pre-Munich frontiers. General de Gaulle went all the way to annul Munich, further than the British Foreign Office was ever willing to go (Beneš, *Memoirs,* pp. 227 ff.). For the implications of the nullification of Munich, see Hubert Ripka, *Likvidace Mnichova.*

55. Beneš' authority in the exile movement was of decisive importance. He set forth its program and activities and directed its foreign policy. He also maintained almost a monopoly in the matter of connections with the Resistance at home.

56. Feierabend, "Memoirs," p. 927. Premier Šrámek did not participate in any of these discussions (interview with Dr. L. Feierabend, Sept. 24, 1963).

57. Feierabend, "Memoirs," p. 928.

in generous terms and should be paid out of the large Czechoslovak claims against the Reich.[58] Beneš agreed with the memorandum of Feierabend and stressed the importance of the favorable economic conditions of the transfer. He desired it to be carried out in an exemplary way.[59]

The willingness of some Czechoslovak exile politicians to offer even some of the smaller parts of the country to the defeated Reich for the removal of the Sudeten Germans showed clearly the vital emphasis put upon the solution of the German question. It showed also the regrettable propensity, particularly on the part of the vacillating Beneš, to regard the territorial integrity of the state as a pawn to be sacrificed in exchange for other political aims. This policy of easy abandonment, violating by unconstitutional propositions the very thesis of the integrity of the Republic upon which its legal existence had been based, grew from roots which could be traced well back in time. The Munich state of mind still prevailed. Indifference to the integrity of the state encouraged easy abuse at the hands of its adversaries.

As the balance of forces shifted in the vast and terrible war, Beneš revealed his aims in his interview with C. L. Sulzberger of *The New York Times* on Feb. 19, 1943: In the East Central European area independent states should be established first, their safety secured by transfer of fifth columns. The remainder should be entitled to enjoy all human and democratic rights.

> In the future it should not be possible in Europe . . . to create by the use of minority treaties or minority laws a special State in another State and prepare large fifth columns for a period of crisis or war.[60]

As the Czechoslovak international position improved after Allied repudiation of the Munich pact, Beneš seized the initiative and strove

58. *Ibid.*, p. 972.
59. *Ibid.*, p. 973. Beneš frequently dealt with the problem of transfer in public addresses. On April 28, 1942, before the Foreign Press Association in London, he affirmed: "I am prepared for the grim necessity of population transfers" (Oscar I. Janowsky, *Nationalities and National Minorities*, p. 137). In his address at the University of Manchester on Dec. 5, 1942, Beneš stated: "We cannot altogether rule out the possibility of certain population transfers as a condition for establishing the equilibrium of a permanent peace. Transfers are a painful operation. They involve many secondary injustices. The framers of the peace settlement could not give their consent unless the transfers were humanely organized and internationally financed" (*The Way to Victory*, p. 14). The statements of Czechoslovak political leaders pertaining to the idea of transfer are to be found in Louise W. Holborn, ed., *War and Peace Aims of the United Nations*, I, 434, 438–39, 443–44, 446; II, 997–98, 1021–22, 1023, 1024–39, 1036, 1037, 1042, 1043, 1045, 1048.
60. *Ibid.*, p. 998.

to obtain American and Soviet backing for his idea of transfer. This move was in keeping with Beneš' contention that peace and security had to be safeguarded by the actual solving of international problems, not merely by empty declarations. The Czechoslovak argument, conducted both in public and behind the diplomatic scene, was to be given a new practical turn in the United States and the Soviet Union. Since the policy of Beneš was predicated upon continued understanding between East and West, the independence of Czechoslovakia was to be secured by close cooperation with the Great Powers having interests in Europe: the Soviet Union, the United States, and Great Britain. His main preoccupation was to offset the Red Army's fast progress toward East Central Europe, which might result in a de facto determination of the future of the area by the Soviets' mere presence. Beneš was anxious to reaffirm Czechoslovak independence by concluding a Soviet-Czechoslovak treaty as soon as possible. He felt that he now had an excellent opportunity to come up with something positive that would answer the needs of the area most directly concerned—Czechoslovakia and Central Europe—and at the same time would offer some hope that the region would not become the focus of some anti-Soviet or anti-Western bloc.

Beneš' visit to the United States in May and June 1943, was intended to point up the newly won international status of the Republic and to find out more about the intentions and policies of the American government. Being aware of the importance of the Soviet-American rapprochement, Beneš was eager to reach a deeper understanding of the Soviet attitude so that his forthcoming visit to Washington might enable him to be more specific about Czechoslovak policy toward both the Soviet Union and Germany. He therefore put several questions to Soviet Ambassador Bogomolov on March 19, 1943, asking him to transmit them to Moscow. "Was Moscow ready to conclude with Czechoslovakia a treaty similar to the Anglo-Soviet pact and adapted to Czechoslovak conditions? Would Moscow consider it possible to stress in the treaty the mutual obligation of both partners not to interfere in the internal affairs of the other partner? Could the Soviet Union tell us in principle what its attitude towards Germany would be after the war and could it support our view of the necessity to transfer" at least a part of the Germans? The British government—Moscow was told—resolutely supported the last demand.[61]

On April 23, 1943, Bogomolov reported the Soviet answer. Moscow

---

61. Beneš, *Memoirs*, p. 242; Fierlinger, *Ve službách*, II, 119–20. See the evasive replies of Soviet Deputy Foreign Minister Korneichuk (*ibid.*, pp. 128–29).

asked Beneš to submit a draft of the desired treaty to the Soviet government. The reaction toward the problem of the transfer of Nazi Germans was not negative, but Moscow had not yet reached any definite decision. The same evasive answer was formulated on the Soviet policy toward Germany. However, on June 5, during the visit of President Beneš to the United States, Bogomolov called on Minister Ripka and informed him that the Soviet government "was now definitely in favor of the transfer of the German Nazi population from Czechoslovakia."[62]

The official visit of President Beneš to the United States was highly successful. The conversations showed full agreement on all principal points. Beneš twice discussed with President Roosevelt the problem of the Czechoslovak Germans. On May 13, Roosevelt agreed to a reduction in the number of Germans in Czechoslovakia by way of transfer;[63] on June 7, Roosevelt reiterated his agreement with the transfer of the German minorities from eastern Prussia, Transylvania, and Czechoslovakia,[64] and concurred in the Czechoslovak view of a Soviet-Czechoslovak treaty. Beneš gave him detailed information on his negotiations with the Soviets and his future plans in relation to the USSR. "Our treaty was regarded by the American government as typical of what the Soviet Union's other neighbors should do, in time, so as to secure their independence and non-interference in their internal affairs . . . on the side of the Soviet Union."[65]

The visit of President Beneš to the United States had been worthwhile. He had initiated a reappraisal and reorientation of Czechoslovak minority policies. The details might be worked out later on, and more formal meetings and conferences had to set their seal on agree-

62. Beneš, *Memoirs*, pp. 243, 286. Ripka and Beneš used the American approval of transfer on May 13 to prod Moscow to follow suit. Moscow did.
63. *Ibid.*, p. 193.
64. Beneš cabled to his government. "He [Roosevelt] agrees to the transfer of the minority populations from Eastern Prussia, Transylvania and Czechoslovakia. I asked him again expressly whether the United States would agree to the transfer of our Germans. He declared plainly that they would. I repeated that Great Britain and the Soviets had already given us their views to the same effect" (*ibid.*, p. 195). There exists no minutes of the conversations of Beneš with Roosevelt in the Roosevelt files. The director of the Franklin D. Roosevelt Library, Hyde Park, New York, Herman Kahn, wrote to this writer on Feb. 10, 1958: "We have been unable to find any documentation of the conversations with visitors, and only very rarely were any notes made of such conversations. Usually, our information on such matters has come from what President Roosevelt's visitors have said about their meetings with him." The biographer of Beneš, Compton Mackenzie, was told by Beneš in May 1944, that Roosevelt had stated to Beneš on the matter of transfer in 1943: "You will have no difficulties from our side. Go right on and prepare it" (*Dr. Beneš*, p. 293).
65. Beneš, *Memoirs*, pp. 186, 193, 243.

ments previously reached. But in the summer of 1943, Beneš had succeeded in having the principle of the transfer of the Germans accepted by the three Great Powers. Beneš proceeded cautiously, and in his diplomatic activities displayed both adaptability and moderation. These two qualities were the hallmark of his policy and both seemed to offer necessary reassurances to Czechoslovakia's allies. As was his practice, and to maintain a wide area for flexibility, he outlined his program for the solution of the German question through transfer in the most general terms, as a general principle to be applied in the most humane manner possible, against those German inhabitants of the Republic who were not actively opposed to Nazism.

Beneš was aware that Munich had proved that the West alone was unable and unwilling to defend the Czechoslovak state. Even after the Soviet-German pact he believed that the Soviet Union would ultimately range itself in the Western camp against Hitler. The alliance between Czechoslovakia and Soviet Russia was regarded by both the Resistance at home and Beneš as natural and mutually profitable. The correct and loyal attitude of the USSR at Munich had left an indelible impression on the minds of the Czech people, who had displayed their traditional sympathy toward their Slav big brother in the brave struggle of the Russian people and the Red Army against the Hitlerite invaders. The alliance with Russia was extremely popular among all strata of the population. The victorious march of the Red Army toward the West had been followed with enthusiasm by the reorganized Resistance at home, which fully supported the idea of an alliance which would safeguard the future security and integrity of the Republic.[66]

Beneš regarded the Soviet-Czechoslovak alliance as a natural response to the new problems created by German expansion, but he was wise enough to realize that the alliance should be supplemented by friendly relations and cooperation with Western democracies, so that the cooperation of West and East should form a guarantee of Czechoslovak independence.[67] Since 1942, Beneš had been anxious to conclude a written agreement with the Soviet Union in order to secure firm assurances of Soviet noninterference in Czechoslovak

66. For the first phase of the war relations between Beneš and Moscow, see the article by Eduard Táborský, the wartime secretary of Beneš, "Beneš and the Soviets," *Foreign Affairs*, XXVII (January 1949), 302–314.
67. Eduard Táborský, "Beneš and Stalin—Moscow, 1943 and 1945," *Journal of Central European Affairs*, XIII (July 1953), 156. This article is of much value as it is based on primary sources, mainly Beneš' papers.

internal affairs. Now he desired to forestall the entry of the Red Army into Central Europe by written guarantees.[68]

After his return from Washington, Beneš encountered British opposition to the timing of his visit to Moscow, where the treaty was to be signed. Following the Conference of Foreign Ministers in Moscow, however, the British dropped their reservations.[69] Soon thereafter, the Teheran conference dealt (apparently) with spheres of influence for the Eastern and Western fronts.[70]

President Beneš arrived in Moscow on Dec. 11, 1943. The next day he participated with Stalin and Kalinin at the solemn signing of the Soviet-Czechoslovak treaty of friendship, mutual aid, and cooperation. Both states pledged mutual assistance in the present war against Germany and her allies and against any future German policy of *Drang nach Osten*. They exchanged promises of mutual noninterference in internal affairs.[71] Beneš was lavishly entertained and Stalin lost no opportunity to emphasize his friendship for Beneš and Czechoslovakia.[72] On Dec. 16, 1943, Beneš conferred with Molotov and, on December 18, with Marshal Stalin.[73] Beneš prepared, among other items, a memorandum for the Soviet government dealing with the transfer of the Germans from the Republic. It contained in ten points the basic scheme of his plan of transfer. All the German inhabitants of the Republic would remain Reich citizens. The Czechoslovak government would be entitled to determine who would be allowed to keep or to apply for Czechoslovak citizenship. Removal of the Germans would be effected under a five-year plan, with the main phase of the transfer being carried out in two years. No district in the state was to contain a Slav population of less than 67 percent. Within the first few months the German elements most responsible— the functionaries of the former Henlein Party, SS, Gestapo, officials, etc.—were to be expelled. The property of the members of the Nazi Party would be confiscated. The less directly involved Germans were to be permitted to take part of their property to Germany. The remainder of their possessions would be credited to them as a part of

68. According to E. Táborský, President Beneš realized that Stalin's assurance was not a foolproof guarantee. Yet he regarded written obligations as preferable to complete uncertainty (*ibid.*, p. 155).
69. The conference was held from October 19 to November 1, 1943. London did not oppose the treaty as such, but it regarded its timing as unfortunate and detrimental to the Poles (Beneš, *Memoirs*, pp. 244, 254).
70. The Teheran conference took place from November 28 to December 1, 1943. For the spheres of influence, see *ibid.*, pp. 252–53.
71. *Ibid.*, pp. 255–57.
72. Táborský, "Beneš and Stalin," pp. 159, 162.
73. *Ibid.*, p. 166.

German indemnities, to be reimbursed to them by postwar Germany. Czechoslovakia would become a national state in which the members of former minorities would enjoy all democratic and individual rights. The schools were to be Czech, Slovak, and Ukrainian only, with the exception of the German elementary schools.[74]

"That is a trifle, that's easy," replied Molotov.[75] Stalin and Molotov fully agreed with the Czechoslovak demands. Stalin even took Beneš to a large map of Europe hanging in his office and, holding a red pencil in his hand, asked the latter to make further demands for German territory. Eduard Táborský described the scene.

> Beneš was not one of those who wanted to grab as much foreign territory as possible. He was even prepared to trade some Czech frontier areas for German districts if that could straighten out the boundary and facilitate the transfer of the Germans. . . . When, with his pencil ready, Stalin was waiting for Beneš to express his wish, the Czechoslovak President repeated that he would only desire to straighten somewhat the boundary line, and as an example thereof he pointed to the Glatz region. Hardly concealing his astonishment at Beneš' moderation Stalin marked off that region for Czechoslovakia.[76]

Beneš was elated over the results of his Moscow trip. He had secured Moscow's acceptance of his proposals for transfer and recognition of the historic frontiers. The Soviets agreed to leave the occupation of the Czechoslovak territory to Czechoslovak troops and to hand over

74. The text of the memorandum handed to Molotov (as supplied by E. Táborský to the author) is identical with the ten-point scheme given by J. Smutný (pp. 64–68). According to Wiskemann (*Eastern Neighbours*, p. 69) and *Dokumentation* (IV/1, 181–83), this scheme originated in 1944. The date appears to be a mistake, as the scheme was given to Molotov in December 1943, and had to be prepared prior to the trip to Moscow, probably in the fall of 1943. For the text of the memorandum, see Eduard Táborský, "Pravda zvítězila" (Truth Won), the manuscript of the third volume. See also his letter to the author, Jan. 13, 1953.

75. Táborský, "Beneš and Stalin," p. 167. The favorable mood of Moscow toward transfer passed through different phases. Thus on Aug. 28, 1941, Ambassador Maisky asked Beneš why Czechoslovakia required the Sudeten-German districts and "if their possession would not prove disadvantageous." He further asked whether Beneš would not change his opinion "in the event that Germany would be different after this war, for example revolutionary and socialistic" (*ibid.*, p. 165). This information weakens the description of the Communist attitude given by Bohuslav Laštovička in his unfair and tendentious book V *Londýně za války* (p. 80).

76. Táborský, "Beneš and Stalin," p. 167. In another memorandum, Beneš strove to win Soviet support for the inclusion of the principle of transfer of the Germans in the armistice agreement (Laštovička, p. 307).

the liberated territory to the Czechoslovak civil administration.[77]
From London he reported to the Resistance at home:

The Moscow negotiations . . . have given me complete satisfaction. The Russians will support us in all the principal questions. . . . This covers also . . . carrying out the transfer of the
guilty minority population from the Republic on the largest scale
possible.[78]

During his stay in Moscow Beneš conferred with Czechoslovak
Communists to ascertain their views. They agreed in principle with
Beneš that the government in the liberated country should devolve
mainly upon the Socialist parties. However, the Communists desired
to play the most influential part in the new government, and opposed
the return to Prague of the present Czechoslovak government in
London.[79] In the parleys the German question was broached, but the
Communist policy was circumspect. As late as 1942, the Comintern
School near Ufa still comprised a special Sudeten German group in
addition to the Czech and Slovak groups.[80] The Kremlin was publicly
reserved and advised Beneš to shun publicity on the whole idea of
transfer.[81] When Beneš outlined his plan of transfer before the
Czechoslovak Communist leaders, they preferred to retain the anti-
Nazi line.

Their viewpoint was set forth in a letter by their leader, Klement
Gottwald,[82] on Dec. 21, 1943: (1) The Republic will punish all

77. Beneš, Memoirs, pp. 263, 267.
78. Táborský, "Beneš and Stalin," p. 168.
79. Letter from Klement Gottwald to Václav Nosek, Dec. 21, 1943 (Naše cesta, Vienna, March 1955).
80. Wolfgang Leonhard, Die Revolution entlässt ihre Kinder (Cologne-Berlin, 1955), p. 193.
81. Zdeněk Fierlinger wrote from Moscow to the Social Democratic Left in London (Dec. 21, 1943) that the Kremlin did not want any publicity on the question of the transfer of the Sudeten Germans. He advised them to avoid any public discussion which might be misused, but he defended the transfer. There exist two different texts of the letter by Fierlinger. His own version was published in his book, Ve službách, II, 206. The introductory sentence reads: "On the whole, the Kremlin took up a positive standpoint towards the question of the transfer of German and Magyar populations." The text of the letter preserved by Minister Němec runs as follows: "On the whole, the Kremlin took up an entirely cold standpoint towards the question of the transfer. . . ." Obviously the meaning is quite different. However, this might have resulted from an error in the writing of either text, as the Czech words for positive and cold are similar: kladný and chladný. On the other hand, Fierlinger might have deliberately changed the original text in order to cast a more favorable light on the Soviet stand.
82. For the text, see the papers of Němec; Gottwald, Spisy, XI, 270–71. There are slight differences in the wording but the sense is identical. The letter was

traitors and active helpers of Hitler. These will be expelled and their property confiscated; (2) other Czechoslovak citizens of German origin will be free to choose either Germany or Czechoslovakia, and the government will retain the right of decision in each individual case; (3) the German anti-Nazis and anti-Fascists who have actively participated in the struggle against Hitler will be automatically entitled to claim their citizenship; (4) the whole plan will be carried out with the participation of the German anti-Fascists. Clearly, the Communists put a brake on the more complete solution envisaged by the democratic exiles in London and wanted to wait till the political situation cleared up sufficiently for them to decide. Their plan left the door open for either a moderate or a radical solution. Beneš did not oppose the Communist stand because he believed that what mattered was putting the general principles into effect and that the Communists would subscribe to his views there.

President Beneš returned from Moscow almost jubilant. The Soviet policy for Central Europe offered, Beneš thought, a constructive framework which would guarantee a strong and independent Czechoslovak democracy. The new treaty would safeguard the Republic against any new German thrust to the East.

> The foundation of our future foreign policy is . . . the geographic position of the Republic in its pre-Munich frontiers. Its cornerstone will be our Treaty with the Soviet Union, which will form the basis of our post-war security. It will be completed by a second essential pillar of post-war European policy, i.e., the British-Soviet Treaty by which we are automatically bound to a very close and friendly cooperation with Great Britain.[83]

Beneš felt that he had accomplished a great deal in 1943. The United States and the Soviet Union recognized nothing that had happened in 1938 and 1939. Both Great Powers regarded the problem of the Sudeten Germans as a Czechoslovak internal affair and expressed their approval of the principle of transfer. Obviously the mere formulation of a principle in general terms was not the same as putting it into practice. The practical problems involved were enormous. Yet to appreciate the dimensions of the Beneš triumph one

---

addressed to Václav Nosek, head of the London Communist group. Beneš brought this letter with him to London—together with the letter from Fierlinger. Both letters remained open to make clear that Beneš was well acquainted with their contents. For the Beneš version of the negotiations with the Communists, see *Memoirs*, pp. 268 ff.

83. The fourth message by Beneš to the state council, Feb. 3, 1944 (Holborn, ed., II, 1029).

needs only to consider that the acceptance of the method of transfer by the Three Powers represented a basic change in thinking. It was one more important result of the shock administered by Hitler.

The recognition of the general principle still left the most difficult task unresolved: the formation of a workable transfer plan acceptable to the Great Powers. This was where the real problem of the immediate future lay in 1944.

The European Advisory Committee of Great Britain, Soviet Russia, and the United States was constituted on the basis of the agreement reached at the Moscow Conference of Foreign Ministers, and one of its tasks consisted in preparing the final terms of the articles of capitulation for the Reich.[84] At the end of July 1944, the committee asked the Allied governments to submit their proposals for the capitulation of Germany.[85] The Czechoslovak memorandum, which was delivered on Aug. 24, 1944,[86] proposed a concrete plan of transfer: Some 1,600,000 Germans were to be removed to Germany and about 800,000 Germans, regarded as politically reliable, were to retain their citizenship. The memorandum evaluated the war casualties of the Sudetens at 250,000 persons, and estimated that about 500,000 Henleinists and Nazis would escape the country prior to the end of the war.[87] Those Germans who preferred to stay in the Republic had to apply for Czechoslovak citizenship, while the active anti-Nazis were automatically accepted as citizens. They were to enjoy all democratic and human rights but would be denied minority rights. The transfer would take place within two years. The transferees would be allowed to take with them all movable property and would receive compensation for their immovable property either directly from the Republic in Reichsmarks or out of the Czechoslovak claims against the Reich.[88] Furthermore, the Czechoslovak government requested the committee to insert the principle of transfer in the armistice conditions of the German capitulation. This would guarantee the acceptance of the transfer by Germany, which would engage itself to admit the Sudeten Germans.

During the months of December 1944 and January 1945, Ripka urged Soviet Russia to support the Czechoslovak request of putting the principle of transfer into the articles of armistice with Hungary.

84. Beneš, *Memoirs,* pp. 249–50.
85. MacAlister Brown, "Expulsion," p. 226.
86. Fierlinger, *Ve službách,* II, 421–22.
87. Karel Lisický as quoted in Jaroslav Stránský, *Odsun Němců z ČSR s hlediska národního i mezinárodního,* I, 26; Brown, "Expulsion," p. 228.
88. Lisický, as cited in Stránský, p. 26.

Ripka wanted thus to establish a precedent. At the beginning, Moscow remained lukewarm.[89] Ripka gave a short acccount of the transfer measures to the correspondents of the Swedish and Swiss press for the first time on September 14.[90] The Czechoslovak memorandum containing the plan of transfer—already presented to the Advisory Committee—was delivered to the three Great Powers on Nov. 23, 1944.[91] The tenor of the replies suggested that the Great Powers preferred to discuss the matter among themselves before arriving at any binding proposition.[92] The British government replied in January 1945 that it had studied the plan "with care and sympathy." Because the memorandum dealt with problems which could not be settled by Great Britain separately without her allies, it reserved its answer for the time when all problems were to be settled by negotiations among the principal Allied Powers.[93] The Czechoslovak government received a note from the government of the United States on Jan. 31, 1945:

> The American Government fully appreciates the injuries suffered by Czechoslovakia at the hands of Germany and of the German minority during the past decade or so and is prepared to examine the problem in an effort to seek a satisfactory solution for the future. This solution, of course, will have to take into account the needs of Czechoslovakia referred to in your note, and also the broader aspects of the problem in its relation to general measures

89. Fierlinger, *Ve službách*, II, 421–22, 431, 433, 434, 437.
90. Holborn, ed., p. 1036.
91. It was presented to the United States embassy in London on Nov. 23, 1944 (Brown, "Expulsion," p. 309). Brown used several unpublished State Department papers. According to the final recommendation of the State Department, transfer was to be accepted only when it was "conducive to improved relations and greater political stability" (*ibid.*, p. 207). The Czechoslovak plan was evaluated in a special paper in December. The authors of the paper asserted that the transfer should not concern loyal Germans and called it "a choice between evils" (*ibid.*, p. 309).
92. The postponement of binding recognition of the transfer of the Germans might have been the reason for the purported Beneš order to the General Staff in January 1945, to prepare as an alternative a plan for the retention of 800,000 Germans in the Republic and the removal of some 600,000 Germans, with their territory, to the Reich. About 1,700,000 persons should have been expelled (Lisický, as quoted in Stránský, I, 30).
93. Fierlinger, II, 545. On Jan. 16, 1945, Balfour, the British representative in Moscow, sent a letter to Molotov informing him of the British reply. The British Ministerial Armistice and Post-War Committee headed by C. Attlee discussed in early July 1944 the possibility of transfer of German populations from East Europe. "The Committee thought that, although on a long term such transfers might be an advantage to all the countries concerned, the short-term difficulties were so serious that they might cause a German economic collapse" (Sir Llewellyn Woodward, *British Foreign Policy in the Second World War*, p. 466).

for the future peace and security of Europe as a whole, as well as
the particular problem which will face the Governments accepting
the unconditional surrender of Germany, which thereby become
responsible, as occupying powers, for the control and administration of Germany.

There will also undoubtedly arise related questions with regard
to the transfer of Germans from other territories. Since this problem
may therefore involve an aggregate of some millions of people, it
would be a matter of major concern to the occupying powers in the
maintenance of order in Germany during the absorption of such
people from abroad simultaneously with the repatriation or resettlement of millions of displaced persons now within Germany.

The American Government therefore feels that transfers of the
kind contemplated in your Excellency's note should only be carried
out pursuant to appropriate international arrangement, as suggested in your Excellency's address of October 8, 1944, and under
international auspices. It also agrees with the Czechoslovak Government that any process of transfer should be a gradual one, in order
to provide facilities for the orderly settlement of transferred persons. Pending such international arrangements, the American Government feels that no unilateral action should be taken to transfer
large groups, and understands from the statements cited above
that the Czechoslovak Government does not envisage any unilateral
action to do so.[94]

During the second visit of Beneš in Moscow in March 1945,
Molotov reminded Beneš of the Soviet full support of the idea of
transfer given in 1943. He was ready to enter into negotiations with
London on this matter.[95]

In their latest effort to wrestle with the Sudeten problem, the three
Great Powers were confronted with an issue that reached beyond the

94. *Foreign Relations of the United States. The Conference of Berlin 1945*, I,
648; hereafter cited as *FRUS 1945*. See also the memorandum of the United
States Mission in Budapest (H. F. Arthur Schoenfeld), June 12, 1945 (Hungarian Ministry for Foreign Affairs, *Hungary and the Conference of Paris*,
II. *Hungary's International Relations Before the Conference of Paris*, pp. 4–5).
95. Soviet Russia appeared to back the Czechoslovak demand. (See the
affirmations of Molotov in his conference with President Beneš on March 21,
1945, in Fierlinger, II, 595). E. Táborský, reporting on the conversation, stated
that Beneš refused to consider any enlargement of the Czechoslovak territory.
"We do not want the Germans in, we want them out." The eager willingness of
Molotov in 1943 to give full support to the Beneš plan of transfer seemed to have
faded (Táborský, "Beneš and Stalin," p. 178). The attitude of the Czechoslovak
Communists, the subsequent policy of Moscow, and the narration of Fierlinger,
who participated in the conference, cast doubts on the statement of Táborský
concerning the lack of eagerness of the Soviets.

Czechoslovak area and involved the basic character of the settlement of the entire German issue.[96] A Big Power agreement appeared to be an essential precondition, because the occupational authorities of the Allies in the defeated Reich would be held responsible for the care of an additional more than two million people. There arose also some doubts concerning the Republic's ability to adjust itself to a serious reduction in manpower. Being agreeable to the general principle of the transfer of Germans, the Great Powers desired to work out specific conditions of the transfer which would be carried out under international auspices to guarantee its humane and nondiscriminatory character.[97]

Note

The concept of transfer of population did not originate during World War II. The first population transfer in modern history took place before World War I, when the first international treaty on the exchange of population was concluded in November 1913 between Bulgaria and Turkey, followed by the Greco-Turkish agreement on

96. In connection with the problem of the western and northern frontiers of Poland, the Western Powers expressly recognized the transfer of Germans from the newly reconquered territories. Winston Churchill declared to the House of Commons on Dec. 15, 1944: "The transference of several millions of people would have to be effected . . . as well as the expulsion of the Germans . . . from the area to be acquired by Poland in the West and the North. For expulsion is the method which . . . will be the most satisfactory and lasting . . . I am not alarmed by the prospect of the disentanglement of populations, nor even by these large transferences, which are more possible in modern conditions than they ever were before" (House of Commons Debates, 5th series, vol. 406, col. 1483, in Wiskemann, *Germany's Eastern Neighbours*, p. 82).

The United States government position was stated by Secretary of State E. R. Stettinius on Dec. 18, 1944. "If . . . the Government and people of Poland decide that it would be in the interest of the Polish state to transfer national groups, the United States Government in cooperation with other governments will assist Poland, in so far as practicable, in such transfers" (Z. Jordan, *Oder-Neisse Line. A Study of the Political, Economic and European Significance of Poland's Western Frontier*, London, 1952, p. 129).

97. The State Department prepared a brief to be used by the American delegation at the Yalta conference. It recommended "that although this Government should not oppose a general transfer of the German minorities from neighboring states, it should, wherever possible, favor a selective transfer. Such action, if carried out gradually, in an orderly manner, and under international supervision, would contribute to better relations between the states concerned" (*Foreign Relations of the United States. The Conferences at Malta and Yalta, 1945*, p. 179). For more information on the transfer of German minorities, see *ibid.*, pp. 189–90. The State Department recommended, in respect to Czechoslovakia and Germany, "that the pre-Munich frontiers . . . be in principle restored, subject to any minor rectifications which the Czechoslovak Government might wish to propose" (*ibid.*, p. 189).

the exchange of populations in 1914. Both treaties, however, simply regularized the status quo, because the inhabitants had already abandoned their homes before the conclusion of the agreements.[1] Against this background, the idea of mutual exchange of populations developed as an efficient method of settling minority problems in the Balkans. The Convention of Neuilly (Nov. 27, 1920) on the reciprocal exchange of inhabitants between Bulgaria and Greece followed the already established pattern.[2] A mandatory type of transfer gradually replaced the free and voluntary feature of the original measure. The largest transfer, involving nearly one million Greeks and 400,000 Turks, took place between 1923 and 1933. Its direct cause was the defeat of the Greek Army in Asia Minor and the ensuing determination of Turkey to establish a national state. The Convention of Lausanne (Jan. 30, 1923) made all necessary provisions for a compulsory population exchange between Greece and Turkey.[3]

These examples show that a removal of population took place whenever it was warranted by the interests of security, peace, and stability in the respective regions. The Munich agreement spoke of transfer as did the German-Czechoslovak Treaty of Nov. 20, 1938, dealing with the question of option.[4] It was the address by Hitler on Oct. 6, 1939, that inaugurated the transfer of German minorities.[5] Germans were removed from the areas where troubles could develop. The majority of the resettlers were established in the annexed Polish provinces.[6] About one and a half million Poles were expelled to make room for the German resettlers. The transfers did not touch other smaller states of Central and Southeastern Europe, where the local German minorities supported the policy of the Reich.

The idea of transfer found both supporters[7] and opponents.[8] One

1. This discussion is based on the excellent account by Joseph B. Schechtman, *European Population Transfers 1939–1945*. Schechtman defines the transfer as "the organized removal of an ethnic group from its country of residence and its subsequent resettlement in territories under the sovereignty of its ethnic homeland" (p. x).
2. *Ibid.*, p. 13.
3. *Ibid.*, p. 16.
4. *Ibid.*, pp. 40–41.
5. *Ibid.*, p. 39. The speech of Hitler was followed by the conclusion of a series of treaties dealing with the evacuation of the German minorities from Italy (Oct. 21, 1939), Lithuania (Oct. 15, 1939), Estonia (Oct. 30, 1939), Rumania (Oct. 22, 1940), and the USSR (Nov. 3, 1939, Oct. 5, 1940, and Jan. 10, 1941).
6. *Ibid.*, pp. 214–15.
7. Schechtman, pp. 455–56, lists the sponsors of the transfer: Bernard Lavergne, William C. Bullitt, Leopold C. Klausner, Harold Butler, Warren S. Thompson, Nicolas Politis, Bernard Newman, Jacob Robinson, Herbert Hoover, Hugh Gibson, Nansen, and Venizelos.
8. Stephen P. Ladas, Stellio Seferiades, David Thomson, and Erich Hula (*ibid.,*

could not conceal the grave character of such a measure, which was bound to bring with it human sufferings, hardships, and individual injustices. Transfer presented an extreme solution which was to be applied where all other means had failed. Its desirability in each case could be best determined by its results. There is common agreement, for example, on the success of the Greco-Turkish exchange of populations.[9] The American author Joseph B. Schechtman appeared to grasp the complexity of the whole problem in his final assessment:

> In view of all the evidence provided by past experience it cannot be denied that the redistribution of ethnic groups is a painful operation for the persons concerned, or that it may cause, at least for a time, serious difficulties in the economic life of the country of departure and the country of resettlement. The disruptive incidence of the operation cannot be overlooked and should not be underestimated. Nevertheless, there may be situations when the alternatives are even less desirable, and where this is the case, transfer remains as the only solution. As one observer has said, 'to cut out the cancer from a sick body is not cruel, it is necessary.' . . . Fortunately, most diseases do not require surgical treatment. Any serious and responsible physician considers every other possible means of effecting a cure, and has recourse to the scalpel only as a last resort. And so it is with the drastic method of population transfer. It is by no means a universal method of solving all minority problems, and should not be applied until all other agencies have been explored. . . . The transfer of populations should be decided on only in the last instance, not as an ideal solution, but as a necessary evil.[10]

The demand for the transfer of the Germans from Czechoslovakia was in full accordance with this balanced assessment.

---

pp. 459–60). Quite recently G. C. Paikert opposed "all forcible population transfers" (*The German Exodus. A Selective Study on the Post-World War II Expulsion of German Populations and Its Effects*, The Hague, 1962, p. 76).

9. Schechtman, pp. 462–64.
10. *Ibid.*, pp. 467–68.

The End of the War

Under the double impact of the plan of transfer and the opposition of the Jaksch group to the Beneš conception of the Republic, the German exiles from Czechoslovakia split into two camps. The majority of those living in Great Britain met at their first national conference in London on Oct. 16–17, 1943.[1] The representatives of the main German parties at this meeting courageously recognized the fact that the majority of their countrymen were supporting the Nazi regime;[2] and they realized that the fate of the Germans in the Republic depended upon their stand in the present fight. They felt that only open resistance against the Nazis could restrict the full measure of the steps to be taken. Minister Ripka reiterated the official policy, declaring that the German democrats who stood by the Czechoslovak fight for freedom "will continue to be regarded . . . as citizens with full civic rights."[3] The conference elected the Sudeten German Committee as the highest body representing those German refugees who were willing to recognize the fact that the Sudeten Germans at home actively participated in the suppression of the Czech people.[4]

1. *Sudeten Germans and Czechs. Condensed Report of the First National Conference of German Anti-Fascists from Czechoslovakia, passim.*
2. For example, the Social Democratic leader Josef Zinner made the following confession: "Our people stand—except for the active anti-Fascist minority—on the side of the forces of darkness" (*ibid.*, pp. 25, 30).
3. *Sudeten Germans and Czechs*, p. 30.
4. The committee included 49 members of various political parties.

During 1944 it became clear even to the most optimistic German democrat that most of the Sudeten people were fighting Hitler's war as their own. The anti-Jaksch group became reconciled to the idea of transfer,[5] and the group around Jaksch remained isolated[6] with its plan for "an interim solution under Allied auspices" favoring a provisory autonomous administration of the "Sudeten territory" during the period between the armistice and the peace conference.[7] Even the Labor Party favored the idea of organized transfer,[8] and the Sudeten Social Democrats and Communists publicly exposed the reckless attitude of the majority of the Sudeten people. At their joint conference in January 1945, they espoused the necessity of the removal and punishment of all pro-Nazi Germans from the Republic.[9]

The subscription to the Czechoslovak view by the majority of the German exiles was of considerable assistance to the general effort in which the Czechoslovak government was engaged. Their adherence to the Czechoslovak approach to the German problem helped to create a more favorable general understanding of the Czechoslovak desire to deal efficiently with this fundamental problem and not to be satisfied with mere stopgaps.

There was a general agreement among Czechoslovak exiles with the idea of transfer. The political leaders were deeply committed to

5. See the Communist-biased German biweekly *Einheit,* July 1 and Oct. 7, 21, 1944.
6. Jacksch constituted his Democratic Sudeten Committee on Aug. 1, 1944. It consisted of 11 members of the Social Democratic group which had remained faithful to Jaksch and of two Catholics, one of whom resigned on Dec. 16, 1944. Only three Socialist deputies—out of eight who escaped after Munich—became members (*Einheit,* Aug. 12, 1944).
7. *Einheit,* Aug. 12, 1944; Jan. 13, 1945. In its declaration of Aug. 1, 1944, the Committee called for the establishment of the Czechoslovak Republic along federal lines.
8. The report of the executive committee of the Labor Party to the annual Congress (*Einheit,* May 20, 1944).
9. The joint declaration affirmed that the Sudeten Germans "haben so nicht nur in ihrer grossen Mehrheit diesen räuberischen Krieg herausgefordert, sie haben ihn auch nach Kräften unterstützt." It demanded "die Bestrafung der deutschen Kriegsverbrecher und Hochverräter, und die Aussiedlung jener deutschen Elemente, die den inneren und äusseren Frieden der Republik neuerlich gefährden werden." It asserted that the Sudeten working class "hat in ihrer Mehrheit ebenso wie die Arbeiterschaft des Reiches in diesem Kriege am internationalen Proletariat Verrat geübt" (G. Beuer—Fanny Blatny—J. Zinner, *Gemeinsamer Weg—Gemeinsames Ziel! Reden auf der gemeinsamen Konferenz der deutschen Sozialdemokraten und Kommunisten aus der ČSR am 27. und 28. Jänner 1945,* pp. 44–45). J. Zinner declared openly: "Lassen Sie mich die Frage anwerfen, was wir mit den Henleinnazis im Jahre 1938 getan hätten, falls wir die Macht gehabt hätten, sie aus dem Lande zu treiben. . . . Wir hätten sie alle hinausgejagt. Alle!" (*ibid.,* p. 17).

search for a practical solution of the whole problem, although they realized that the final settlement depended primarily on the people at home. Some among them did not possess a clear view of the real impact of the Nazi occupation on Czech-German relations, and still lived under the impression that a part of the Sudeten working class sympathized with the Czech struggle for freedom. Thus, as late as 1944, there were divergences within the Czechoslovak Social Democratic Party. The original draft of the declaration of principles failed to include any mention of the German problem. The final text, issued on April 16, 1944, called for the establishment of a Slav state but still made a distinction between the bourgeois and nonbourgeois elements of the German population.

> The reactionary strata of the German and Magyar people that were the recruiting ground of the present oppressors of the Czechoslovak people . . . will be expelled. The position of those Germans and Magyars who remained loyal to the Republic will be determined on the basis of full civil, political, economic and social equality.[10]

The party leaders discussed mutual relations with the German Social Democratic group headed by Zinner on June 8, 1944. A majority opposed the establishment of a united party with the Germans. It was agreed that contacts between the party and the Zinner group would be maintained in private discussions between individual leaders.[11]

On April 8, 1944, the Red Army reached the Czechoslovak border. Its rapid advance confirmed the correctness of the Beneš policy in concluding agreements which would recognize Soviet strategic requirements while guaranteeing the independence of the Republic. To have one more Soviet engagement, Beneš concluded with Moscow the agreement on the establishment of the Czechoslovak administration in the Czechoslovak territory liberated by the Red Army.[12] However, when the Soviet troops did occupy Sub-Carpathian Ruthenia, they refused to hand it over to the Czechoslovak authorities, and Beneš had to bow to superior force, although he kept trying to save the independence of the Republic by pinning Moscow down to its promises.[13]

As the Soviet Army continued to occupy a larger part of the

10. Papers of Němec.
11. The minutes of the meeting of the executive committee of the Czechoslovak Social Democratic Party, June 8, 1944 (*ibid*).
12. On May 8, 1944 (Holborn, ed., *War and Peace*, II, 767–79).
13. Táborský, "Beneš and Stalin," p. 172.

Republic, Beneš found it necessary to come to terms with the Czechoslovak Communist Party. He arrived in Moscow on March 17, 1945, and conferred with Stalin and Molotov and was again assured by Stalin that the Soviet Union was anxious to preserve Czechoslovak independence and would not interfere in her internal affairs.[14] Even more important were the negotiations on the program of the new cabinet and its composition between the Communists and representatives of the other political groups. In 1943, it was agreed by Beneš in Moscow that the Communist Party would enter the new government to be formed at the end of the war. The impossibility of forming a cabinet without the Communists was an almost inevitable consequence of the chain of events set in motion by the Nazi attack on the Soviet Union. In 1943–44, it became obvious that the Communist Party was destined to play a dominant role in the new cabinet unless Czechoslovakia was willing to follow the example of Poland. Hence the Communists were in a strong position in the Moscow negotiations. The democratic parties, represented mostly by personalities of less than average abilities who came unprepared to challenge the Communists with an imaginative and popular democratic program of their own, accepted the Communist draft of the governmental program with only small changes. They complied with most of the Communist demands concerning the composition of the new coalition government which would consist of six Czech and Slovak parties—there was to be no opposition party. The Communists exercised a dominating influence and their leaders assumed vital positions in the renovated cabinet.[15]

Contrary to the promises voiced by Beneš and other exile leaders, representatives of the Czech Resistance—unlike in Slovakia—did not become members of the new cabinet, whose program was elaborated in Moscow by the exiles. The new coalition government of the National Front under the premiership of the leftist Social Democrat Zdeněk Fierlinger was promulgated on Czechoslovak territory at Košice on April 4, 1945. Its program, enunciated the following day, called for radical economic, political, and social reforms. Its eighth chapter, dealing with the German question, practically took over the principles set forth by Klement Gottwald in December 1943.

> The Republic has no wish to persecute its loyal German . . . citizens and they, and above all those who proved their faithfulness

14. *Ibid.*, p. 179.
15. *Ibid.*, p. 180. The Stalinist version is given by Václav Kopecký, *Gottwald v Moskvě*, pp. 40–41; Laštovička, pp. 496 ff. Two of the six parties were the Czech and Slovak Communist parties.

even in times of great difficulty, will be unaffected. The culprits however will be severely and pitilessly punished.

The Germans were to be divided into three categories, and the government's policy was enunciated as based on the following principles:

> Czechoslovak citizenship for Germans . . . who held it before Munich 1938 will be confirmed and the possibility of their return to the Republic will be assured only if they were anti-Nazis and anti-Fascists, if they fought against Henlein . . . for the Czechoslovak Republic in the period before Munich and if, after 15 March, they were persecuted for their resistance, their struggle against the regime then in power and their loyalty to the Republic by the German . . . official authorities, were thrown into prisons and concentration camps or had to flee abroad from the German . . . terror, where they actively participated in the struggle for the restoration of Czechoslovakia.
>
> Czechoslovak citizenship of other Czechoslovak citizens of German . . . nationality will be cancelled. Although they may again opt for Czechoslovakia, public authorities will retain the right of individual decision in the case of each application.

Finally, those Germans who were condemned for crimes committed against the Republic and those who moved into the territory of the Republic after Munich in 1938 would be expelled forever.[16] All war criminals, traitors, and active helpers of the Nazis would be punished. The program was regarded as relatively moderate, since it offered the right of option. The Communists in exile apparently had not yet sensed the radical mood of the country.[17] It was only after the liberation that they set off their nationalistic propaganda to win over the masses.

Following Stalingrad, the Reich moved from defeat to defeat. Because of the traumatic experiences of the Nazi occupation, the Czechs were shocked into the realization that their whole fate was now at stake. The reorganized Resistance movement aided by small groups of Czechoslovak and Soviet parachutists entered into an active guerrilla campaign during the last part of 1944, with the central role played by the Council of the Three,[18] the largest underground

16. For the text of the Košice program, see *Dokumentation*, IV/1, 184–203. I quote from the abridged English translation (IV, 183).

17. In the first phase of the war the Communists were cautious in their opinions on the German question. For example, see Gottwald, *Spisy*, XI, 245; Jan Šverma, *Vybrané spisy (Selected Works)*, Prague, 1955, p. 395.

18. Veselý-Stainer, p. 151; Rudolf Hrdlička, ed., *Sborník. Památce divisního generála Vojtěcha Luži, passim.* The articles are of unequal value.

organization of the last stage of the war, and the partisan groups headed by Soviet parachutists. The program of the council called for sweeping internal reforms on a democratic and socialist basis, close alliance with Soviet Russia—highly popular with almost the entire nation—and expulsion of the Germans. From April 1944 the council was in steady radio contact with Beneš who enjoyed its full confidence. There was even a strong undercurrent in favor of the temporary dictatorship of Beneš whose popularity was then at its peak.[19] The situation in the Protectorate deteriorated rapidly with the outbreak on Aug. 29, 1944, of armed insurrection in Slovakia.[20] Some 2,000 Czechs clandestinely crossed the frontiers to participate in the Slovak uprising,[21] despite the fact that anyone seeking to escape to Slovakia was liable to the death penalty.[22] During the fall of 1944, centers of armed resistance emerged in many parts of the country. In the winter months of 1944–45, some 40 acts of sabotage and partisan raids occurred daily.[23] In an effort to crush the partisans, the Germans formed a special Bandenbekämpfungsstab which set up specially trained groups, the so-called Jagdkommandos.[24] By April 1945, the partisan battle raged in all wooded and hilly sections of the country. The struggle pitting the partisans[25] against the Germans and home traitors increased in intensity in the last weeks of the war. Many sections of the countryside were controlled by the partisans.

K. H. Frank, recognizing the desperate situation, attempted to contact the Anglo-American armies in order to prevent the occupation of the Protectorate by the Soviet Army. However, all his attempts to

19. Veselý-Štainer, pp. 131, 153–159.
20. The revolt in Slovakia was prepared by the members of the Slovak Resistance movement in close cooperation with President Beneš. A part of the Slovak Army took part in the uprising which was finally crushed by the Germans on Oct. 28, 1944. The partisan war went on, however, until the liberation of Slovakia by the Red Army. After the war 3,131 victims were found in more than 35 mass graves. The German Special Commandos had arrested 18,937 persons by Dec. 9, 1944 (Lettrich, pp. 308–11).
21. According to the German report of Sept. 3, some 1,000 Czechs had already crossed the border (J. Doležal, Slovenské národní povstání, pp. 179–80.)
22. Zpověď, p. 156. Frank reported to Himmler on September 3: "The response is great among the Czech population. I am convinced that the events would develop into a dangerous and serious situation unless the revolt in Slovakia is quickly put down. . . . One cannot lose one minute" (Zločiny nacistů, p. 107).
23. For the partisan activities, see the strongly biased and Stalinist volume by Benčík et al., Partyzánské hnutí v Československu, passim. Also see Zločiny nacistů, pp. 113 ff.; Hrdlička, Sborník, pp. 19 ff., 45 ff.; Veselý-Štainer, pp. 142 ff.; Zpověď, p. 155.
24. Ibid., pp. 154–55. The Jagdkommandos were notorious for their brutality.
25. The Soviet prisoners who had escaped from the frightful conditions of the German prisoner camps formed an elite part of the Czech partisan movement. Their role was often of decisive importance.

conclude an arrangement with the West failed. The new German head of state, Adm. Karl Dönitz, ordered Frank to Flensburg on May 3, and agreed to declare Prague an open city, abolish the Protectorate, and transfer power to the conservative Czech elements.[26]

At the beginning of 1945, the Council of the Three, the illegal trade unions, and the underground Communist Party formed a Czech National Council as the supreme center of the Resistance and prepared to set off the revolt in Prague at an appropriate moment. The advance of the American[27] and the Soviet armies caused a tremendous stir. In the first days of May, national committees took over the administration in many communities; German inscriptions were removed, and Czechoslovak flags appeared. Signs of revolt spread around the country. The German Army conducted a fighting retreat through Slovakia and the eastern part of Moravia, and the German Army Group (Mitte) under the command of Marshal Ferdinand Schörner concentrated in the Bohemian basin for a last ditch battle. The Protectorate became a vast German military camp.

In the midst of rumors of the approaching American Army, shortly before noon on May 5 groups of Czech patriots occupied public buildings in Prague and hoisted national flags. Scattered fighting broke out throughout the city. The Prague uprising started as a spontaneous and popular movement undertaken against the advice of the underground leaders.[28] The patriots seized the radio station and

26. *Ibid.*, p. 178; Juergen Thorwald, *Flight in the Winter*, p. 225. Thorwald gave a description of Frank's intentions. Frank wanted to form an independent Czech government so that the Allies would be faced with a fait accompli. He intended to leave the country taking with him the German officials and the newly arrived Germans "as well as the old settlers who wanted to leave." Frank even tried to explain this plan to Hitler in April but was turned down (*ibid.*, pp. 223–24). See also Král, *Pravda*, pp. 333 ff.
27. The American 90th Infantry Division entered west Bohemia on April 18 (Ivo Ducháček, "Czechoslovakia," as cited in Stephen D. Kertesz, ed., *The Fate of East Central Europe, Hopes and Failures of American Foreign Policy*, p. 201). The American Sixteenth Armored Division arrived in Pilsen on May 6. According to an officer of the division, "the exultation, excitement and happiness of the Czech population of the city was beyond my powers to adequately describe" (Dana Adams Schmidt, *Anatomy of a Satellite*, p. 86).
28. The illegal Communist Party and the Czech National Council—on May 4 and 5, respectively—decided against any immediate uprising (Karel Bartošek, *Pražské povstání 1945*). The volume of Bartošek gives a biased but good description. See also the article by Prof. Otakar Machotka in *Svobodné slovo*, May 5, 7, 9, 1946. The German version is in Thorwald, pp. 226–40; *Dokumentation*, IV/1, 55–63. Thornwald took over the false affirmation that the Communists set off the revolt. *Dokumentation* (p. 54) contains an imaginary description of the Czech Resistance movement and does not accept the spontaneous character of this truly popular uprising.

broadcast urgent appeals for assistance. The moment of surprise enabled them to break the German communication system and slow down the main German counterattack, which had been launched on May 7. On the afternoon of May 5, the National Council assumed leadership of the revolt. Prague was now in Czech hands except for a few places held by the German Army. Overnight, from May 5 to May 6, some 1,600 barricades were erected throughout Prague.[29] The fight between the almost unarmed Czechs and about 37,000 to 40,000 heavily equipped Germans, who used over 250 tanks at one moment, was more than unequal. Appeals from insurgent Prague for aid and arms remained unheeded, although American troops were waiting less than 50 miles from Prague.[30] The unexpected intervention of a part of the General Vlasov Army on the Czech side cushioned the impact of the German assault and helped the insurgents over the critical period.[31]

The battle raged for three days. After protracted negotiations General Toussaint, commander of the German Prague garrison, signed the capitulation of his troops at 4 P.M. on May 8. A few SS units opposed the surrender, however, and opened fire, and some of

29. Bartošek, p. 145. On the Czech side about 30,000 men participated in the fighting (*ibid.*, p. 246).
30. It seems to be fairly well established that the American Army was prevented from advancing toward Prague beyond the line Carlsbad-Pilsen-Budějovice on the direct order of General Eisenhower, anxious to maintain coordination between the Allied and Soviet fronts. Eisenhower complied with the request of General Antonov to refrain from advancing beyond the designated line, May 6, 1945 (*The Department of State Bulletin*, May 22, 1949, pp. 665–67). The press release of the State Department stated that "decisions and actions of the Allied Command in this connection were purely operational without any political implications" (*ibid.*, p. 665). Churchill advocated the advance to Prague, clearly realizing its political impact. President Harry S. Truman appeared to leave the decision to General Eisenhower (Winston S. Churchill, *The Second World War*, VI, 506–507; Herbert Feis, *Churchill—Roosevelt—Stalin. The War They Waged and the Peace They Sought*, pp. 610–11). Hubert Ripka described how the Allies prevented the Czechoslovak airmen from helping embattled Prague. "The crews were already aboard their planes" when the flights were forbidden by the Inter-Allied Command (*Czechoslovakia Enslaved: The Story of the Communist Coup d'Etat*, p. 37). The reconnaissance detachments of the American Army entered Prague on May 7 (Ducháček in Kertesz, ed., p. 202). Ducháček reprinted the unfair article in *Rudé právo* of Jan. 18, 1948: "The 3rd Army . . . stood in Czechoslovakia . . . armed to the teeth . . . while the uprising was drowned in blood. All Prague saw the Soviet tanks but there was no one who had seen American and English tanks near Prague. Why? Those who consider it their duty to rehabilitate their overseas protectors explain it by the existence of a 'demarcation line.' When one wants to help people in danger 'demarcation lines' do not exist" (*ibid.*, p. 203).
31. The Vlasov Army—a part of the German war machine—was composed of Russian war prisoners taken by the Germans. Some of its detachments fought brutally against the Czech partisans in the winter and spring of 1945.

the fiercest and cruelest fighting followed. At 4 A.M. on May 9, 1945, the first tanks of the Koniev Army Group reached the outskirts of Prague, followed by other units enthusiastically welcomed by the Prague population.

During the uprising some of the worst brutalities of the occupation occurred. Units of the SS murdered Czech children and women; Germans shot at Czechs from roofs and basements; and Czech women and children were shot in front of German assault tanks. To quote only one Czech police report:

> In Pankrác and Krč members of the S.S. began maltreating the Czech population as early as May 6th, when they succeeded in penetrating into this quarter of the city from the south, supported by armed German civilians. Their violence reached its height on May 8th at 6:30 P.M., when a mass advance was begun on Krč. . . . The worst acts of violence were committed by young men between 17 and 20 years of age. The doors of houses and flats were burst in, houses and shops were plundered, dwellings were demolished, furniture shot to pieces and set fire to. The inhabitants were driven from their homes, forced to form a living wall with their bodies to protect the German patrols, and constantly threatened with automatic pistols. Many Czechs lay dead in the streets. . . . A great many dead bodies of Czech civilians were later found in a little church. They included men, women and even children from one to three years of age, all killed in a terrible way. Their heads and ears had been cut off, their eyes gouged out and their bodies run through and through with bayonets. There were some pregnant women among them whose bodies had been ripped open. Twenty-three men from an estate were shot in the courtyard after being tortured for a long time. The state of affairs in Krč is best shown by the fates of the inhabitants of two of the many houses broken into. In house No. 295 alone, 37 persons were murdered, ten of them being children between the ages of 6 and 15, 13 women, two of them pregnant, and 14 men.[32]

Almost 2,000 Czechs were killed during the Prague uprising.[33] The six years of the Nazi regime had created an immense reservoir of anger and fear. The Germans were beaten whenever found, forced to remove the barricades, and in the first moments of the postwar

32. V. Urban, pp. 43–44. For a description of the brutalities by the SS in Prague, see Buben, ed., Šest let, pp. 255–64.

33. Bartošek, p. 246. The *Central European Observer* (XXIII, Oct. 5, 1945) took over the list of the casualties in the Prague uprising from *Rudé právo:* 2,216 Czechs and 935 Germans dead.

agitation a few of them were set on fire in the streets of Prague by the violent crowds. This explosion of hatred and revenge was touched off by the very existence of the Nazi shadow of death menacing the whole nation. The last weeks of the occupation also brought many acts of Nazi savagery.

On April 19, 1945, the village of Ploštiny was burned down and 28 inhabitants slain. On May 1, the city of Přerov was the stage of Nazi brutalities. On May 5, the community of Javoříčko was also razed and 38 men were killed; on May 6, 34 Czechs were murdered in the prison courtyard in the city of Třešt.[34] On May 7, all the members of the national committee were publicly hanged in Velké Meziříčí. From the end of January 1945, long transports of political prisoners passed across the country, leaving behind hundreds of dead.[35] The uprising in Prague was preceded or accompanied by similar actions in many other cities in the Protectorate. The countryside became one vast battlefield.[36] Any SS men found were mercilessly shot down. The last fights took place as late as May 11.[37] The cruelties committed by the SS on the unarmed population in the very last days of Nazi occupation intensified the refusal of the Czechs to show compassion toward anything German.

With the liberation of Prague the last chapter of the Czechoslovak Resistance movement, starting with the Slovakian national uprising in August 1944 and ending with the insurrection in Prague and guerrilla fighting all over the country, was brought to a victorious end in an outburst of popular feeling calling for the expulsion of all Germans.[38]

34. *IMT*, XXXVI, 91–93. The Czechoslovak report on crimes committed by the SS described other cases of mass murder. See also Konopka, ed., *Živé tradice*, pp. 196 ff.
35. *IMT*, XXVI, 88 ff.; *Živé tradice*, pp. 197–202. For example, the SS transported 828 political prisoners from the camp near Carlsbad on April 26, 1945. During the march some 800 prisoners died and the road was lined with 22 mass graves (Hanušová, *Co s nimi?*, p. 137). *Rudé právo* (July 5, 1945) wrote about the victims of this death march.
36. For example, in the region of Kladno 157 patriots were killed in action during the May days (Pěnička, *Kladensko*, p. 197). In the cities of Nymburk, Poděbrady, Nový Bydžov, Nová Paka, and Mělník, and the region of Turnov, Mladá Boleslav, etc., the population rose against the Germans during the period of May 2–9, 1945 (*Svobodné slovo*, May 4, 1947).
37. Amort, *Partyzáni*, pp. 244–45.
38. Ygael Gluckstein stated: "A week before the occupation of Prague by the Russian Army there was no armed resistance among the Czechs . . . to the German occupation. . . . All the evidence shows that the expulsion was imposed by the organized pressure of the Czech Communist Party and the bourgeoisie on a disoriented people" (*Stalin's Satellites in Europe*, p. 194). It is perhaps best to leave this part of the book unread. The present Sudeten German propaganda keeps repeating the thesis that the expulsion "was not a spontaneous reaction of the Czech people against the German occupation of their country,

In May 1945, Czechoslovakia drew up the balance sheet of her losses: 250,000 persons had reportedly died,[39] and more than 100,000 people suffered permanent injury as the result of the occupation.[40] Many large and smaller cities had been damaged by air attacks or military operations in the winter of 1944–45 and the spring 1945.[41] Almost all the large industrial plants had suffered heavy damage.[42] Eastern Slovakia[43] and the eastern part of Silesia[44] were the most badly hit. In Bohemia and Moravia 690 railroad bridges and 7 tunnels were destroyed or heavily damaged. In the entire country, 52.6 percent of steam locomotives, 68.3 percent of passenger cars, and 74.5 percent of freight cars were destroyed, damaged, or carried off. Of the prewar total, 49 percent of passenger motor cars, 47.9 percent of buses, and 63.5 percent of trucks were lost. The road network was dislocated; and 29.2 percent of all roads were seriously damaged or destroyed.[45] According to the official assessment the material damage

---

but an act planned by Czech politicians in exile" (B. Carroll Reece, "The Expulsion of the Sudeten Germans," *Sudeten Bulletin*, V, September 1958, 186).

39. [Czechoslovak Ministry of Information], *Czechoslovakia, Old Culture and New Life*, p. 17; *Statistický zpravodaj* (Statistical Bulletin), XI (1948), 6. Chmela (*Economic Aspect*, p. 135) put the losses at 245,000 people. Ivan Kochanovskov's estimate was 220,000 persons (*Demografie*, April 1960, 108–23). *Facts about Czechoslovakia* (Prague, 1958, p. 10) stated, however, that "75,000 people were put to death" during the occupation.

40. Chmela, *Economic Aspect*, p. 135. He gave a different estimate of the number of permanently or seriously disabled persons: 127,816 (*ibid.*, p. 5). The booklet *Czechoslovakia* ([Czechoslovak Ministry of Information], p. 14) gave another figure: 114,000.

41. For example, Lanžhot, České Budějovice, Kolín, Kralupy, Beroun, Most, Ústí nad Labem, Karlovy Vary, Děčín, Olomouc, Pilsen (the Škoda Works were 70 percent destroyed), Opava, Vyškov, Cheb, Znojmo, Brno, etc. In Moravia 11,862 buildings were destroyed and over 19,000 heavily damaged. In Bohemia the respective figures were 3,014 and more than 10,000. In Prague 149 buildings were destroyed and 633 badly damaged (*Svobodné slovo* and *Rudé právo*, 1945–46, *passim*).

42. The mining district of Ostrava, the Škoda Works, Brno Small Arms Works, and large Prague and Brno industrial plants, among others.

43. Report by Deputy Dr. Ing. Kácl, in the National Assembly, Jan. 16, 1946 (*Stenographic Reports on the Meetings of the Provisional National Assembly*, 22nd Session). (This document will hereafter be cited as *Stenographic Reports*. I am using the English translation of the Czech title.) In all, 169 villages were destroyed and 300 damaged; 200,000 persons lost all possessions; and 24,000 homes were destroyed or heavily damaged (UNRRA European Regional Office, *Agriculture and Food in Czechoslovakia*, p. 13).

44. Report by Deputy Svoboda of April 12, 1946. The capital of Silesia, Opava, was 60 percent destroyed. Out of 90,000 buildings in Silesia 34,986 were destroyed (*Stenographic Reports*, 48th Session).

45. Chmela, *Economic Aspect*, pp. 128–29. See also Eduard Vyškovský, ed., *Deset let lidově demokratického Československa* (*Ten Years of Popular Democracy in Czechoslovakia*), Prague, 1955, p. 35. For some slightly different figures, see UNRRA European Regional Office, *Transport Rehabilitation in Czechoslovakia*, pp. 7–11.

caused by the Nazi occupation amounted to 1,289.5 milliard crowns.[46] Industry was still working at about 50 percent of its capacity at the beginning of 1946.[47]

In 1947 the Association for the Protection of Sudeten German Interests prepared an estimate of the national property of the Sudeten Germans confiscated in 1945. As a basis for its enumeration, two dates were selected, namely Sept. 30, 1938, and May 8, 1945. Property was calculated for both dates in Reichsmarks and dollars at the 1938 value. The figures were as follows: Sept. 30, 1938: 33,616,370,000 RM, or $13,440,000,000; May 8, 1945: 48,587,230,000 RM, or $19,440,000,000.[48] Hence, according to the representatives of the Sudeten Germans themselves, their war gains amounted to 6 billion dollars.

46. At the 1948 value (Chmela, pp. 4–7). The claim, in Protectorate and Pre-Munich crowns, amounted to 611.8 milliard. The figure transmitted to the Paris reparation conference—361 milliard Protectorate crowns—was incomplete as it was prepared on the basis of the estimates from September 1945 (*ibid.*, p. 7).
47. UNRRA European Regional Office, *Industrial Rehabilitation in Czechoslovakia*, p. 11. However, the Germans left vast war stocks in the country in areas which were relatively remote from the war fronts.
48. Turnwald, ed., *Dokumente zur Austreibung*, p. 557. (See also *Atlas*, p. 53.) When one examines the breakdown of 13.44 and 19.44 billion dollars more closely, one finds with surprise that these final figures should have been the result of the total addition of the following items:

	Values in millions of dollars	
	Sept. 30, 1938	May 8, 1945
Agriculture and forestry	3,220.73	4,822.00
Industry	2,393.38	3,824.10
Commerce	308.58	308.58
Handicraft	600.00	600.00
Hotels, inns, health resorts, spas	642.84	734.00
Banks	640.00	3,600.00
Insurance companies	297.64	3,323.00
Cinemas	16.00	16.00
Free professions	6.76	8.80
Personal and landed property	3,956.00	3,956.00
Property of the Provincial government and the state	3,363.60	1,243.20
	15,445.53	22,435.68

The breakdown of 13.44 and 19.44 billion dollars gives 15.45 and 22.43 billion dollars, according to the calculation of the Sudeten German leaders. Although this document was compiled by "experts on the Sudeten German economic situation over a period of several months," these experts have not even been able to carry out a simple addition (Turnwald, ed., p. 557).

Part IV

THE TRANSFER

THE TRANSFER

CHAPTER II

From Chaos to Order

During the final series of Soviet offensives, many German inhabitants of eastern Sudetenland (Sudetengau) and Moravia either were removed or fled before the approaching Red Army. In February 1945 the authorities of the Sudetenland prepared for the evacuation of its eastern section.[1] The measures were concerned mostly with women, children, and the aged, since most of the men were either serving in the army or the SS, or mobilized into the Volkssturm. The districts of Krnov, Nový Jičín, and Rýmařov, and such cities as Opava and Těšín had been abandoned by most of their German inhabitants in April. The cities of Moravská Ostrava, Olomouc, Brno, and Jihlava were deserted by most Germans.[2] Everywhere the exponents of the Nazi regime fled to the Reich, where many other Germans also sought refuge. Numbers of the evacuees and refugees from Moravia were overtaken by the Red Army and found themselves in the midst of Czech insurrectionists and the remnants of the German Army attempting to reach the American lines. The major part of the Germans caught by the end of war near their homes, returned there.[3] The leaders of the Sudetenland followed Hitler's orders up to the very last days. On Jan. 31, 1945, Henlein called from Opava for a last effort.

1. *Dokumentation*, IV/1, 21. Some 30,000 Germans were evacuated during February.
2. *Ibid.*, pp. 22–25.
3. *Ibid.*, pp. 26–27.

Neue deutsche Formationen kommen nun Tag um Tag heran und sie werden nicht zu spät kommen . . . Wenn aber doch einer schwachherzig werden sollte, erinnert ihn, dass der Allmächtige uns einen Adolf Hitler gegeben hat, der allein diesen Kampf zu einem siegreichen Abschluss bringen kann.[4]

As late as the beginning of May, Henlein still intended to defend Liberec with 7,000 members of the Volkssturm "bis zum letzten Mann."[5] The defeat was accepted with deep disappointment by the majority of the Sudeten people. The Sudetens seemed to be surprised at the amount of Czech animosity they had generated. They gave no evidence of an awareness of guilt and did not expect their coming expulsion. All they apparently realized was that their dream of a Greater Germany was demolished. In May 1945 Czechoslovak troops took possession of the entire borderland, encountering no resistance.[6]

The collapse of Nazi Germany, the presence of the Red and American armies, and the complete overhaul of the Czechoslovak administrative apparatus[7] created an executive vacuum within the first few weeks after the cabinet's return to Prague on May 10. Gradually, however, new administrative commissions composed exclusively of Czechs took over the government of the former Sudetenland.[8] Their improvised character and lack of experience made for chaotic conditions in the borderland. A number of doubtful Czech elements set out from the Czech interior to the frontier sections where, under varying pretexts, they plundered and looted German homes and ill-treated the German inhabitants.[9] Some summary execu-

4. Jaksch, *Europas Weg*, p. 415.
5. *Ibid.*
6. Alfred Bohmann, *Die Ausweisung der Sudetendeutschen dargestellt am Beispiel des Stadt- und Landkreises Aussig*, pp. 45–46. Although biased, the book is a fairly good monograph.
7. The old Czechoslovak bureaucratic system of local, district, and provincial administration was replaced by a system of popularly elected national committees which supervised the bureaucratic apparatus.
8. The district administrative commissions were nominated by the Ministry of the Interior. They nominated, in turn, the local administrative commissions. Since in many places some of their members were recruited from among newcomers, it happened that a number of doubtful elements became members of the commissions. It took some time before they were arrested and punished. Up to the beginning of July 1945, there was a total of 45 district commissions in Bohemia and Moravia. Out of the total of 450 members, 76 were dismissed because of incompetence or criminal behavior. See the report by the minister of the Interior, Václav Nosek, for Jan. 31, 1946, in *Stenographic Reports*, 27th Session.
9. The Ministry of the Interior, June 7, 1945, and the national security headquarters (June 6, 1945) warned in unusually strong terms of any looting, robbery, and plunder of the confiscated German property. There were

tions and maltreatment of the Germans—particularly of SS and SA members—occurred, since the people were stirred by fresh memories of Nazi cruelties. These deplorable transgressions were an almost inevitable phenomenon accompanying the Nazi defeat in most of the occupied countries.[10]

Disciplinary measures ordered by the Czechoslovak authorities for Germans were extremely harsh. On May 17 the Germans were given smaller food rations.[11] They had to wear special white armbands and

---

large-scale thefts of German property (*Úřední list* [Official Bulletin], Prague, June 6, 7, 1945). Minister Nosek declared on April 26, 1946, that 7,136 cases of plunder and looting were reported to the security organs, with damage amounting to 429,028,690 Kčs. In 2,549 cases, 3,173 culprits were jailed and property amounting to 160,730,541 Kčs was confiscated (*Printed Matter Appended to the Stenographic Reports on the Meetings of the Provisional National Assembly*, No. 412).

10. Molestations, beatings, and killings occurred between May and July 1945. According to information supplied by a reliable Czech source, there were no more than 3,000 German victims. The officials responsible for brutal treatment of the prisoners in the internment camps at Terezín, Česká Kamenice, Most, Bílina, and Kolín were punished (*Stenographic Reports on the Meetings of the Constituent Assembly*, 68th Session, July 11, 1947; this document will hereafter be cited as *Stenographic Reports*). A total of 104 cases of maltreatment of prisoners was reported to the Ministry of Justice (minister of Justice, Prokop Drtina, July 2, 1947. *Ibid.*, 63rd Session). In the first quarter of 1947, the National Assembly appointed a special investigation committee to inquire into reports of cruelties committed against the German population. A resolution was adopted calling for punishment of the culprits. "The Investigation Committee carried out its explorations on the spot. . . . A number of witnesses were interrogated and culprits were detected" and turned over to the authorities. "It was decided to wait for the outcome of the judicial proceedings before submitting a final report to the plenary body of the National Assembly. The results of the investigation showed that assertions claiming extensive mass killing of German population during the transfer were not based on fact. All the detected incidents took place in the aftermath of military and revolutionary actions against the Germans motivated by recollections of recent atrocities committed by the German administration. The investigated cases had all occurred in May and June 1945" ("A Concise Memorandum on the Sudeten German Question" by the Council of Free Czechoslovakia, July 25, 1951, Washington, D.C.).

11. According to the government order of May 17, 1945, the Germans were given the same basic food rations as the Jews had received during the occupation. This restriction was abolished in April 1947. Those Germans who were actively fighting Nazism and remained faithful to the Republic were exempted. Special rations were given to children and heavy workers (*Stenographic Reports*, May 7, 1947). In September 1946 German specialists and their families became entitled to the same rations as the Czechs. The food situation of the Germans was relatively good, however, because the country was fairly well stocked and there was no food shortage. Moreover, food was also distributed outside the ration system. There were no complaints on the quantity of food. One has to take into consideration that rationing was introduced in the Soviet Zone only in the late fall of 1945 (Peter-Heinz Seraphim, *Die Heimatvertriebenen in der Sowjetzone,*

were not allowed to use public means of communication. They could shop only at certain hours and were forbidden to change their residence or visit places of public amusement.[12] In June all German schools were closed.[13] Compulsory labor conscription was introduced for them to clear up war damages and to help to restore the economy.[14] Thus, some Germans were assigned to farms, to mines, or to industrial plants, not infrequently in a predominantly Czech area. In their own cities they had to clear the ruins or mend the pavements.

New Czechoslovakia was playing from strength and a new sense of accomplishment. From May 1945 she went through a national and social revolution. Remembering the former state of national emergency and the proximity of national death, the majority of the Czechs demanded an end, once and forever, to the German threat. The Košice government program was regarded as too moderate and was not adhered to. In this radical spirit the new Republic drafted a series of harsh decrees, justified only by the past extraordinary peril.

The Republic was established as a national state of Czechs and Slovaks. As part of the international agreement on the punishment of Nazi criminals and denazification, all officials of the Nazi Party or SdP and all members of the SS and FS were declared criminals. Whoever had supported the Nazi regime, or consented to or defended the Nazi government, was to be prosecuted. Extraordinary People's Courts were created to try these crimes.[15] All German nationals who had

---

p. 13). The total intake in the ration for the Sudetens in the period of Nov. 11–Dec. 9, 1946 (with Czech rations in parentheses) was as follows: Normal consumers, 1,443 (1,757) calories; light workers, 1,831 (2,173); heavy workers, 2,102 (2,452); very heavy workers, 2,508 (2,749) calories (UNRRA European Regional Office, *Agriculture and Food in Czechoslovakia*, pp. 39, 41–42).

12. *Dokumentation*, IV/1, 79–80.

13. *Ibid.*, p. 95.

14. Decree of the president of the Republic of Sept. 19, 1945. In some cases special camps were set up for the assembled Germans.

15. Decree of the president of the Republic of June 19, 1945. The court was composed of a five-member senate. One of them had to be a professional judge, who took the chair. During their existence—up to May 4, 1947—the courts sentenced 713 persons (475 Germans) to death, 741 (443 Germans) to life imprisonment, and 19,888 persons to imprisonment (report by Minister Dr. Drtina, May 29, 1947: *Stenographic Reports*, 55th Session). The Czechoslovak retribution decree, prepared in London during the war, followed the spirit of the Potsdam agreement on the punishment of Nazi criminals. It was directed against Czech Fascists as well as Sudeten Nazis. The American policy in Germany followed the same lines. In the United States Zone the arrests numbered more than 120,000 Germans, and 125,738 persons were tried by the end of 1946 (The Department of State, *Occupation of Germany. Policy and Progress 1945–46*, pp. 20, 113–117).

acquired Reich citizenship lost their Czechoslovak citizenship. Only those Germans who were able to prove that they had remained loyal to the Czechoslovak Republic, that they had never committed any offense against the Czech or Slovak people, and that they had either participated actively in the struggle against Nazism or suffered under Nazi terror could apply for Czechoslovak citizenship.[16]

All German property was confiscated without compensation;[17] only those Germans were exempted who had already qualified under the former decree. Practically all movable and immovable property belonging to the German Reich, to German legal persons, and to persons of natural German citizenship was taken away. Czech and Slovak traitors shared the fate of the Germans. Their confiscated property was either directly allotted to individuals or placed under temporary national management. Complete liquidation of German farm properties was to be the last decisive step of the liberation movement in restoring Czechoslovak soil to its former proprietors — the Czech people.[18] Confiscated German holdings were allotted among Czech and Slovak farmer families who were to resettle the frontier zones.[19] German industrial and financial property was nationalized.[20]

During this national readjustment in the years 1945–47, some 1,460,000 persons moved to the Czech borderland.[21] The entire economic structure of the region passed through profound changes.

16. Constitutional decree of the president of the Republic of Aug. 2, 1945; order of the Ministry of the Interior of Aug. 24, 1945. All Czechoslovak citizens of German nationality had automatically become Reich German citizens at the time of the German occupation. The Košice program giving the right of option to the Germans was considered too lenient.

17. Presidential decrees of May 19, 1945, June 21, 1945, and Oct. 25, 1945.

18. This was the main theme of the government thesis. The confiscation would make good wrongs committed on the Czech nation since the end of its independence in 1620. The Communist Party in particular strongly emphasized the national moment and became the most nationalist party in the Republic (Gottwald, Spisy, XII, 1945–1946, passim, and Rudé právo, 1945–47, passim).

19. In the Czech borderland 1,955,076 ha were confiscated and 937,745 ha were given to 157,495 applicants. The rest remained in the hands of the state. In the Czech interior 445,373 ha were taken away; 99,535 ha were allotted to 65,909 persons. The property of the Czech traitors was included (Imrich Rubík in Historický ústav ČAV, ed., Otázky národní a demokratické revoluce v ČSR [Prague, 1955], p. 276).

20. Eduard Beneš, "Postwar Czechoslovakia," Foreign Affairs, XXIV (April 1946), 408; Miriam E. Oatman, "The Nationalizations Program in Czechoslovakia," The Department of State Bulletin, XV (Dec. 8, 1946), 1027–31. The major part of industry, banks, and insurance companies was nationalized on Oct. 24, 1945.

21. Miroslav Blažek, Hospodářská geografie Československa, p. 70.

Vast fertile farming areas were split into smaller parcels, large units of the land were turned to meadow, and the mountainous and largely uninhabitable land was allotted to new pasturing cooperatives.[22] Handicraft and household industries were liquidated in most cases, and some of the plants were transferred to Slovakia or concentrated in order to be economically viable.[23] The Sudeten German property was regarded by the Paris Conference on Reparations as Czechoslovak property and was not charged to the Czechoslovak reparation account.[24] Thus the right of the Republic to retain the property of its former German inhabitants was internationally recognized.

The radical mood of the country called for immediate removal of the disloyal majority of the German population. During May, June, and July 1945, some local commanders of the Czechoslovak Army[25] or local revolutionary committees issued instructions ordering the expulsion either of some elements of the Germans or of the entire population of a town or village. The evacuations were often carried out under excessively harsh conditions, the Germans being transported in trains or forced to march to the border.[26] Frequently the

22. Gordon Shepherd, *Russia's Danubian Empire*, p. 158; William Diamond, *Czechoslovakia between East and West*, pp. 99–101.

23. Up to May 1947, more than 2,000 industrial enterprises (38 percent) were liquidated in the frontier zone. Household industries disappeared, and handicraft dropped by 50 percent. Up to the end of 1947, some 26,000 opportunities for work were transferred to Slovakia (Blažek, pp. 83–84). Bruno Kiesewetter stated that 2,620 enterprises with 286,000 workers remained in the borderland and 1,010 enterprises were closed down (*Die Wirtschaft der Tschechoslowakei seit 1945*, p. 73). The book is instructive.

24. Article 6, paragraphs A and D of the final act of the Paris Conference signed on Dec. 21, 1945 (*The Department of State Bulletin*, XIV, Jan. 27, 1946, 114–24; *Stenographic Reports*, Jan. 30, 1946, 26th Session). Article 6, paragraph D, runs as follows: "In applying the provisions of paragraph A (Each Signatory Government shall . . . hold or dispose of German enemy assets within its jurisdiction in manners designed to preclude their return to German ownership or control and shall charge against its reparation share such assets . . .) above assets which were the property of a country which is a member of the United Nations or its nationals who were not nationally of Germany at the time of occupation or annexation of its country by Germany, . . . shall not be charged to its reparation account. It is understood that this provision in no way prejudges any questions which may arise as regards assets which were not the property of a national of the country concerned at the time of the latter's occupation . . . by Germany."

25. The core of the army was composed of units that went through hard fighting on the Eastern Front (Jan Fiala in *Historie a vojenství*, IX, August 1962, 499).

26. Bohmann (*Ausweisung*, pp. 48 ff.) gave a good description of these sporadic expulsions in the region of Ústí. The most striking case was that of the German inhabitants of Brno who, on May 30, were ordered to leave the city precipitately for Austria.

Germans were notified only several hours prior to their departure. This first wave of sporadic and disorderly removals, carried out without any central planning, was concentrated in the regions bordering on the Soviet Zones in Germany and Austria and directed toward those parts of the Reich occupied by the Red Army.[27] They did not occur in the regions occupied by the American Army,[28] as the American authorities in Germany refused to receive such transports.

This exodus of Germans, often taking place without any pretense of fair treatment by local Czech authorities, aroused criticism and protests in the Western press.[29] It was brought to an end toward the end of July when the official transfer of the Germans was negotiated at Potsdam. It was only during this unorganized phase of the transfer that cases of ruthless and precipitous evacuation occurred, however; and the excesses were frankly confessed and all the authorities called to order by President Beneš in a speech at Pilsen on June 15, 1945. He emphasized that the transfer could be effected only in full agreement with the Great Powers; recognized that the state organs had not behaved correctly in some cases; and appealed to the Czechs to exercise reason and patience until the Sudeten question was solved. The address by Beneš presented an official reply, particularly to British reactions to reports of Czech atrocities during the unorganized stage of the transfer.[30]

Beneš remained inflexible in his demand[31] for the transfer. He had

27. The border sections concerned reached from Carlsbad to Silesia and comprised southern Moravia and the German enclaves of Jihlava and Brno.
28. The American sector comprised the line Cheb—Pilsen—Český Krumlov.
29. See Victor Gollancz, *Our Threatened Values*, pp. 43–45, 97; American Friends of Democratic Sudetens, *Tragedy of a People. Racialism in Czecho-Slovakia*, pp. 3–4. Sidney Hook stated: "The spirit of Hitlerism has flown . . . to the governmental offices of Prague. The Czech government . . . has adopted. . . . the Hitlerian techniques of persecution and mass expulsion" (*New Leader*, Oct. 6, 1945). A wave of German suicides accompanied this initial phase of the transfer.
30. Göttinger Arbeitskreis, *Deutschlands Ostproblem*, p. 133. The volume is biased.
31. Beneš declared in Tábor, on June 16, 1945: "In my speech of May 2, 1938, I called for tolerance, forgiveness. . . . The world today knows the German answer to this appeal of mine; their answer spelt terror, treason, concentration camps for us Czechs. . . . Can it therefore surprise anybody in the whole world when we say that we are determined to get rid of these Germans forever?" (Hanušová, *Co s nimi?*, p. 47). At Lidice (June 10), Beneš stated: "It will not be long . . . before we hear various apologies for the German fury and madness displayed in this second great war. And here let us remember that we owe it to ourselves, to our children and to our future generations to do everything to prevent these terrible bestialities from ever happening again" (Šedivý, *Why We Want*, p. 77).

always realized that he needed Allied sanction, and that the Western Powers would give their assent only under the assurance that the transfer would be carried out in a humane and orderly fashion. The Czechoslovak legislation clearly distinguished between loyal and disloyal German and Czech elements. Those Germans who had remained loyal and had actively participated in the fight against Hitler were given the same civil rights as the Czechs. They were permitted to stay and their property was exempted from the wholesale confiscations. The Communist and Social Democratic parties were allowed to set up a list of those Germans who had remained faithful to the Republic. The Social Democrats also set up a special office in their central secretariat entrusted with the care and protection of the German Social Democrats, and made recommendations for the issuance of special identity cards[32] to Germans considered worthy of becoming Czechoslovak citizens,[33] who in some cities formed special anti-Fascist committees. Many democratic Germans, however, voluntarily elected to emigrate because no German education was provided for their children and no national cultural rights were recognized. These were allowed to take with them their movable belongings and were allotted special transport facilities, and their abandoned property was administered by representatives nominated by them.[34] Another special category was the specialists—workers and experts regarded as indispensable for the normal performance of industry. They enjoyed many personal and material advantages.[35] Germans and Czechs falling under the retribution decree were brought into internment camps. Conditions in many of these camps left much to be desired. By the fall of 1945, however, the situation improved as the revolutionary guards were replaced by regular security forces. However, one must take into consideration the fact that the inmates were mostly members of the SS or officials of the NSDAP and other Nazi organizations, who bore the burden of guilt for the outrages of the occupation.[36] The Czech press sharply criticized conditions in some camps and helped to

32. The interview with the former secretary general of the Social Democratic Party, Blažej Vilím, London, Sept. 13, 1958. All the party district secretaries were invited to assist the local German Social Democrats.
33. For Czechoslovak legislation including special exemptions for the German anti-Fascists, see Wiskemann, *Germany's Eastern Neighbours*, pp. 105–106; *Dokumentation*, IV/1, 97 ff.; Ralph Parker, "Czechs and Sudetens," *Nation*, CLXI (Sept. 29, 1945), 307–309.
34. Otto Friedman, *The Break-up of Czech Democracy*, p. 47; *Central European Observer*, XXIII (Feb. 1, 1946).
35. They were given special green cards by the respective ministries.
36. *Dokumentation*, IV/1, 80–83. In some cities, particularly inland, many German civilians were confined. In a few camps typhus broke out (Bohmann,

remedy the treatment of the inmates.[37] President Beneš also devoted his public address at Mělník on Oct. 14, 1945, to the past period of unorganized expulsions and unsettled conditions.

> But lately we have been criticised in the international press, which writes about an undignified transfer. We are said to be doing the same as the Nazis did to us. We are said to be acting against our national tradition and moral reputation. We are finally said to be imitating the Nazis in their uncivilised methods. Even if in individual cases reproaches are justified I proclaim categorically: our Germans must and will leave for the Reich. They will leave because of their immense guilt and their work and policy before the war against our State and our people. Those who have been proved to be anti-Fascists and have been faithful to our Republic can remain with us. All our proceedings connected with the transfer must be carried out in a humane, fair and correct way and on a moral basis. . . . All minor officials who act otherwise will be held responsible. The Government will under no circumstances allow the good reputation of the Republic to be soiled by irresponsible individuals.[38]

Czech resentment was kept inflamed by rumors of German sabotage against trains, tracks, and bridges,[39] and of acts of arson. This mood subsided in the latter part of 1945, when order was brought into the chaotic conditions prevailing in the borderland.

Die Ausweisung, pp. 69–70). For Sudeten reports, see *Dokumentation* IV/2 and the moving diary by Margarete Schell (*Ein Tagebuch aus Prag 1945–46*), published as a supplement to the *Dokumentation.*

37. See note 10, above. There were three kinds of camps: internment camps, labor camps, and assembly camps. The last category served as transit stations for those destined for transfer. There were no serious complaints on the situation from this last group, and the conditions and food were often adequate (Bohmann, *passim;* the report by Minister Nosek, Jan. 31, 1946, *Stenographic Reports,* 27th Session; Wiskemann, pp. 122–23). But compare the critical report by British Deputy R. Stokes, Oct. 10, 1946 (*Dokumentation,* IV/1, 63–64).

38. Beuer, *New Czechoslovakia,* pp. 185–87. Gustav Beuer, a former Sudeten German Communist deputy, made a pointed comparison: Imagine British feelings if the things the Germans committed against the Czechs had happened in Great Britain. Let us assume a compact group of British citizens had lent themselves to Nazi Germany. Suppose that three million British citizens had taken up arms in order to fight side by side with the Germans against the British people. Would the British have shrunk from taking the sternest possible measures to prevent the recurrence of such an open insurrection (*ibid.,* p. 190)?

39. *Rudé právo* reported frequently on acts of sabotage in the spring and summer of 1945 (Aug. 2, 3, 30, 1945). See also Jan Fiala in *Historie a vojenství,* IX, August 1962, 500. The explosion at Krásné Březno near Ústí on July 30, reportedly caused by sabotage, gave rise to deplorable incidents in which innocent Sudeten Germans were beaten up and thrown into the Elbe.

On Oct. 28, 1945, the Provisional National Assembly met in Prague and confirmed Beneš as president.[40] The return to the normal parliamentary regime, combined with the withdrawal of the American and Red armies from the country,[41] was hailed as a triumph for President Beneš and the Republic. The new Czechoslovakia, a loyal ally of Soviet Russia as well as a friend of the Western democracies, could play an important role in European affairs provided the West-East balance remained steady. The growing economic consolidation, the demographic upsurge, the final settlement of the Czech-German struggle, the series of advanced democratic, economic, and social reforms, and the remarkable demonstration of national unity seemed to give promise that the Republic was on the threshold of a bright future, despite certain difficulties and tensions springing from Communist attempts to enlarge their already considerable sphere of power.

40. The Assembly was composed of 300 members—200 Czechs and 100 Slovaks—and consisted of one chamber. Elections for a Constituent Assembly were held on May 26, 1946. The real power rested in the caucus of the party leaders, the National Front. The Communists and the leaders of the existing parties succeeded in blocking the suggestion of Beneš and the Resistance leaders for a complete overhaul of the party system. As a result, four Czech parties remained from the first Republic while the others—particularly the Agrarian Party—were forbidden.

41. The United States forces were withdrawn from Czechoslovakia by Dec. 1, 1945 (*The Department of State Bulletin*, XIII, 766). The same date was set for withdrawal of the Soviet troops.

CHAPTER 12

Potsdam and the Organized Transfer

In 1945 the overwhelming nature of the Nazi collapse proclaimed to the world that the time had come for a profound change in the conditions of Germans living outside Germany. No shadow of doubt could detract from the clear meaning spelled out by the Allied victory. Certainly the most impressive feature for Czechoslovakia was the decision to remove the majority of disloyal Germans from its lands.

Except for the first few angry weeks of reprisal, the measure was taken not as an act of revenge but as an act of obligation in order to maintain the national existence and safeguard the independence of the state, since Czechoslovakia was determined that her experiences of the past should never happen again. The idea of transfer evoked a great popular response because it satisfied the yearning for a more effective protection.

During the war Czechoslovakia had won general approval for the removal of her German minority. After the liberation of the country, Prague emphasized again to London, Washington, and Paris the great weight it placed on the settlement of its German problem. Soviet Russia agreed to the new Czechoslovak measures.[1] However, the first hasty improvised measures, resulting in the eviction and rough handling of the Sudeten Germans, brought a note from the British

1. The state secretary in the Czechoslovak Foreign Ministry, Dr. Vladimír Clementis, in a Prague broadcast on June 13 (*Central European Observer*, XXII, June 29, 1945).

government registering its disagreement with the Czechoslovak policy of mass evacuation and declaring that the measure of transfer concerned not only the Republic but all the Great Powers.[2] Prague answered on June 18 that the transfer would be conducted according to plan, and in full agreement with the Allies as soon as the material and technical conditions were available.[3] The United States, too, urged that any such action be taken only on the basis of the agreement of the Great Powers on the orderly procedure for the whole problem of German minorities.[4] It was the view of the United States and Great Britain that "the determination of the method and timing of the repatriation of the Reich Germans now in Czechoslovakia and the transfer of the German minority in Czechoslovakia must be left to the Allied Control Council in Germany."[5] Moscow fully supported the Czechoslovak proposal to expel unreliable Germans.[6] The Soviet and Communist eagerness to espouse the transfer contrasted with their original half-heartedness during the early phase of the war.

On July 3 the Czechoslovak government asked Great Britain, the United States, and the Soviet Union that the question of transfer be put on the agenda of the Three-Power Conference.[7] In its answer, the United States government reiterated its views (stated in its note of Jan. 31, 1945), welcomed the preparation of a Czechoslovak plan for transfer, and requested Prague to bring its plan to the attention of the Control Council of Germany.[8] The Czechoslovak officials communicated their plan for an orderly removal of Germans to the Three Powers on July 22.[9] The heads of government of the Three Powers met at Potsdam from July 17 to August 2,[10] and the question of the transfer arose at the conference in connection with a discussion of

2. Institut National de la Statistique, *Les transferts internationaux de populations*, p. 19; Fred K. Hoehler, *Europe's Homeless Millions* (New York, 1945), p. 44.
3. *Les transferts*, pp. 19–20. On June 18, the Prague government proclaimed its intention of removing the Sudetens (*Central European Observer*, June 29, 1945).
4. House Committee on the Judiciary, *Report No. 1841*, 81st Congress, 2nd Session. The report disclaims any American responsibility for the transfer.
5. *FRUS 1945*, I, 648.
6. Prime Minister Fierlinger went to Moscow and broadcast a report on his visit on July 2 (*War and Peace Aims*, p. 1045).
7. For the text of the note, see *FRUS 1945*, I, 646–47.
8. *Ibid.*, pp. 648–50.
9. *Dokumentation*, IV/1, 114; Federal Statistical Office, *Statistical Pocket-Book on Expellees in the Federal Republic of Germany and Western Berlin*, p. 109.
10. G. Bernard Noble, chief of the historical division of the Department of State, stated to this writer in a letter of March 28, 1958: "The question of transferring German minorities did not appear in the agenda proposed by the United States

Polish borders. On July 25 Marshal Josef Stalin emphasized the existence of a fait accompli, as the Polish and Czechoslovak governments were powerless to prevent the expulsion which was already occurring because of national feelings against the Germans. President Harry S. Truman and Prime Minister Winston Churchill held that an unorganized transfer of German populations would confront the Allies with a mass of starving people. On the proposal of Churchill it was agreed that the foreign ministers would examine the question.

On the same day the ministers agreed to direct the Control Council to secure an orderly transfer and appointed a subcommittee to draw up a draft on the question. The subcommittee subsequently drafted Article XII of the Potsdam agreement, and on July 31 the article was the subject of a brief discussion. Stalin objected to its adoption because he felt that Poland and Czechoslovakia would continue removing Germans without regard for any agreement. U.S. Secretary of State James F. Byrnes stated that such a document would help to slow the expulsions as the governments concerned would be requested to suspend their actions pending preparations of an orderly transfer. Stalin finally approved the text of Article XII; the French government raised no objections.[11]

Orderly Transfer of German Populations.

The Three Governments having considered the question in all its aspects, recognize that the transfer to Germany of German populations, or elements thereof, remaining in Poland, Czechoslovakia and Hungary, will have to be undertaken. They agree that any transfers that take place should be effected in an orderly and humane manner.

Since the influx of a large number of Germans into Germany would increase the burden already resting on the occupying authorities, they consider that the Allied Control Council in Germany should in

---

for the Potsdam Conference as communicated to the British and Soviet Governments in early June 1945. In the United States preparatory papers this was recognized as a topic likely to be raised by others, but it was not felt by the President's advisers to be desirable for him to raise it."

11. The description of the Potsdam discussion of the transfer is based upon *FRUS 1945*, II, 383, 387, 398, 523, 536, 1545, 1551; a letter by G. Bernard Noble; and *Report No. 1841*. See also William D. Leahy, *I Was There*, p. 424; Herbert Feis, *Between War and Peace. The Potsdam Conference*, pp. 269–70; J. W. Brügel, "Die sudetendeutsche Frage auf der Potsdamer Konferenz," *Vierteljahrshefte für Zeitgeschichte*, X, January 1962, 56–61. At Yalta the United States supported the principle of transfer. The official publication of the Department of State (*Occupation of Germany*, p. 25) stated that "the United States, although not viewing with favor the unilateral or indiscriminate expulsion of Germans from the East, has approved the transfer to Germany of German population . . . in order to avoid the rise of dangerous minority problems in the states concerned."

the first instance examine the problem with special regard to the question of the equitable distribution of these Germans among the several zones of occupation. They are accordingly instructing their representatives on the Control Council to report to their Governments as soon as possible the extent to which such persons have already entered Germany from Poland, Czechoslovakia and Hungary, and to submit an estimate of the time and rate at which further transfers could be carried out, having regard to the present situation in Germany.

The Czechoslovak Government . . . are at the same time being informed of the above, and are being requested meanwhile to suspend further expulsions pending the examination by the Governments concerned of the report from their representatives on the Control Council.[12]

The transfer was merely part of a vast redistribution of population which took place at the end of the war. Almost 20 million people fled from their homes, were removed, transferred, or exchanged in Europe during 1944–45.[13] The death toll in the countries occupied by Hitler amounted to almost 10 million.[14] The Soviet Union alone lost seven million.[15] In all, about 15 million people were killed during the war.[16] There were also some six million displaced persons in Germany who had been dragged off to forced labor during the war.[17] All German enclaves in Europe—except for South Tyrol—were liquidated.[18] Potsdam was only the last act of the European tragedy which resulted from the Nazi dream of a Third Reich.[19]

12. The transfer was the subject of Article XII of the "Protocol of Proceedings," and Section XIII of the "Report on the Tripartite Conference of Berlin" (FRUS 1945, II, 1495, 1511).
13. Joseph B. Schechtman, "Postwar Population Transfers in Europe: A Study," Review of Politics, XV (April 1953), 151.
14. Gregory Frumkin, Population Changes in Europe since 1939, p. 182. Frumkin put the figure at 9,982,000 dead, the USSR excluded.
15. Marshal Stalin in March 1946 (Eugene Kulischer, Europe on the Move. War and Population Changes, 1917–47, p. 276).
16. Frumkin, p. 181. He set the military deaths at 5,824,000.
17. As of Sept. 30, 1945, some 5,261,000 deportees were repatriated from Germany; 1,045,000 remained (Military Governor of Germany, Monthly Report of the Military Governor U. S. Zone, Oct. 20, 1945; hereafter cited as Monthly Report. In October 1946 it changed to Bimonthly Review). There were 34,439 Czechoslovaks repatriated.
18. In September 1950 the German refugees numbered 12,448,000 (Proudfoot, European Refugees, p. 377). Hungary and Yugoslavia each expelled over 200,000 Germans; Rumania ejected more than 110,000 (Stephen Kertesz, "The Expulsion of the Germans from Hungary: A Study in Postwar Diplomacy," Review of Politics, XV (April 1953), 205; Vernant, The Refugee, p. 95). The countries of Western Europe also removed their Germans.
19. Schechtman considered the cases of Poland and Czechoslovakia as solid.

The Czechoslovak government replied to the agreement of Potsdam by sending a note to the governments of the Soviet Union, the United States, and Great Britain on August 16 giving assurances that the Czechoslovak government had always intended to carry out the transfer in an orderly and humane way and informing them that it postponed its actual implementation. The note suggested that the transfer should be carried out as soon as possible and be finished within one year.

The Allied Control Council in Berlin was sent a Czechoslovak report on its German minority. It estimated that there were 3,320,000 German inhabitants in the Republic before Munich. After taking into consideration the Germans who had fled from their homes shortly before the end of the war or thereafter, became prisoners, or were killed, the Czechoslovak authorities considered 2,500,000 as the most probable estimate of the Germans to be removed. The report broke down the total number according to age, sex, and employment.

Boys up to 12 years	322,000
Girls up to 12 years	314,500
Men from 13 to 60 years	541,000
Women from 13 to 60 years	1,010,000
Men over 60 years	140,500
Women over 60 years	172,000
Total	2,500,000 persons

Employment, in Percentages

Agriculture	22.0	550,000
Forestry	1.6	40,000
Mining and foundry	1.2	30,000
Industry	43.0	1,075,000
Commerce and finance	8.5	212,500
Transportation	4.0	100,000
Public service and free professions	4.5	112,500
Domestic and personal services	2.9	72,500
Other	12.3	307,500
Total	100.0	2,500,000[20]

Because of the utter impossibility of a peaceful cohabitation of the Germans and Czechs within one state, "the only conceivable alternatives were thus Munich or transfer" ("Postwar Population," p. 177).

20. The author had at his disposal a confidential memorandum of the Czechoslovak Foreign Ministry on the transfer compiled in 1949; hereafter cited as the *Memorandum*. It gives an excellent survey based on official statistical data.

Prague did not remove any German of Czech origin. Female members of mixed Czech-German marriages were permitted to remain in the Republic.[21] The transfer also bypassed those 300,000 Czechs or Slovaks who were forced to register as Germans or Magyars during the war.[22] The German anti-Fascists were also excluded and were free either to stay or to emigrate.[23]

In August 1945 the Czechoslovak authorities formulated the main lines for the administrative and technical implementation of the transfer. A special department of the Ministry of the Interior was created to carry out the details.[24] It supervised regional delegates[25] who, in turn, exercised control over special transfer branches set up under district national committees or district administrative committees and many local national committees. The district committees compiled registers of Germans designed for removal, and set up the proper order in which the transfer would be carried out. Reich Germans[26] came first, followed by officials of various Nazi organizations. Next came unemployed Germans, public servants, and teachers, and finally artisans, workers, and farmers. Close cooperation was assured with the Ministry of Health and its epidemic center, the Ministry of National Defense, and the Ministries of Transportation and Finance. A network of 107 assembly camps was prepared,[27] and the army became responsible for transport of the evacuees from the assembly camps and their delivery to the Allied authorities. Each transport by train included 1,200 people.[28]

21. Minister Nosek reported that there were about 15,000 Czech or Slovak women in mixed German or Magyar marriages (Jan. 31, 1946, *Stenographic Reports*).
22. *Ibid.* For example, in the districts of Těšín, Fryštát, and Frýdek, 110,000 Czechs were forced to register as Germans.
23. *Dokumentation*, IV/1, 97–99, 245–58.
24. It was established by the order of the cabinet of Jan. 4, 1946. Dr. Kučera became its head (Minister Nosek, Oct. 24, 1946, *Stenographic Reports*).
25. There were nine regional delegates in Bohemia and four in Moravia-Silesia. They were assisted by the officers of the army and security forces (*ibid.; Memorandum*, p. 8).
26. It was estimated that some 400,000 Reich Germans came to the Sudetengau or were evacuated there during the war, and 200,000 went to the Protectorate and other parts of the former Czechoslovak territory. The estimate of German refugees fleeing from the East and being caught in Czech countries in May 1945 amounted to more than one million. The figures are approximate, and it appears impossible to find out the exact number of German refugees and evacuees remaining in Czechoslovakia in May 1945 (*Dokumentation*, IV/1, 17).
27. There were 75 camps in Bohemia, 29 in Moravia-Silesia, and 3 in Slovakia. Each of them had a capacity of 1,200 people. The reserve transfer centers were established close to the border stations where the Germans were taken over by the Allies. Two quarantine centers were readied (*Memorandum*, p. 8).
28. The description of the technical plan is taken from *Memorandum*, p. 8, and from the report by Minister Nosek to the National Assembly, Oct. 24, 1946

In application of the Potsdam agreement the Allied Control Council set up a "Combined Repatriation Executive" (CRX) on October 10 and made it responsible for the direction of the transfer and allocation of German minorities.[29] At its twelfth meeting, held in Berlin on November 20, the Control Council authorized the removal of the German minorities from Austria, Czechoslovakia, Hungary, and Poland into the four occupied zones of Germany. It approved the Czechoslovak plan to remove two and a half million Germans and decided that 1,750,000 of them were to be moved into the American Zone and the remaining 750,000 to the Soviet Zone. It pledged to do everything to effect the transfers in accordance with the Potsdam agreement in an orderly and humane manner. The move was to start in December 1945, and be completed by Aug. 1, 1946.[30] The schedule, however, was not maintained and the transfers began as late as January 1946.[31]

The care of the transferees became the responsibility of the German authorities. In November 1945, the German Länderrat (Council of States) allocated the expellees among Bavaria (50 percent), Greater Hessen (27 percent), and Wuerttemberg-Baden (23 percent). A special committee was set up to coordinate transportation and resettlement. It directed the creation of 13 reception or redistribution centers along the frontier or inside the United States Zone. In early December steps were taken to prepare the points of entry into the zone and provide for adequate distribution of the expellees. At the border reception stations the trains were directed to the three provinces.

Upon arrival at a reception center of the respective Land (province), the transferees underwent medical inspection, screening, and classification as to their skills and professions. Five such centers were

---

(*Stenographic Reports*). The 7th Section of the General Staff was entrusted with all matters pertaining to the transfer (interview with its former head, Gen. František Dastich, June 14, 1956).

29. It was composed of repatriation officers of all Four Powers and helped to facilitate the movement of German refugees primarily through bilateral agreements between the zonal authorities (Proudfoot, pp. 279, 374). See also Joseph B. Schechtman, "Resettlement of Transferred Volksdeutsche in Germany," *Journal of Central European Affairs*, VII (October 1947), 262.

30. *The Department of State Bulletin*, XIII, 937; *Documents on Germany under Occupation 1945–54*, pp. 89–90.

31. The postponement was due to transport difficulties encountered by Czechoslovakia, the necessity of providing heated rolling stock, and the food shortage in Germany. The Soviet authorities stopped the transfer at the end of November on account of the poor food conditions in their zone. However, small transports of anti-Fascists continued. The Soviet Zone received 21,015 Germans in the period of Jan. 25–April 30, 1946 (*Svobodné slovo*, Jan. 4, 6, May 19, 1946).

established near the Bavarian-Czechoslovak borders. For the majority the next destination was the transit camp and the base camp where the expellees remained until they were integrated into the German economy. Some of them moved directly to the local communities.[32]

The Czechoslovak authorities suspended further transfers in August 1945. However, even after Potsdam, 373,000 Germans arrived at the Soviet and American Zones by either regular transports, unorganized local transfers, or flight.[33] On Jan. 8–9, 1946, a series of meetings was held between American and Czechoslovak officials in Prague. It was agreed that one trainload would include 1,200 persons in 40 heated cars. The Czechs were to provide sufficient food for the journey and three additional days. Families should not be divided; clothing should be adequate; and every German should be allowed to take personal belongings weighing between 30 and 50 kg. They were each allowed 1,000 RM.[34] Beginning with January 25,[35] one train arrived

32. *Monthly Report,* Jan. 20, April 20, June 20, Sept. 20, 1946; Schechtman, "Resettlement," pp. 267–68. In December a quadripartite agreement was reached setting the conditions for the transfer. It required the use of heated rolling stock and set up clothing, health, and food requirements (*Monthly Report,* Jan. 20, 1946).

33. *Memorandum,* p. 11. A total of 223,000 Germans went into the American Zone and 150,000 into the Soviet Zone. According to the *Bimonthly Review* (Nov. 23, 1947), 356,094 Sudetens had arrived in the U.S. Zone prior to the organized transfer or had infiltrated thereafter. More than 200,000 Sudetens had fled prior to Nov. 20, 1945, and more than 100,000 had entered the zone between Nov. 20, 1945, and the beginning of the organized transfer on Jan. 25, 1946. According to Kulischer (p. 282), some 300,000 Sudetens had fled before and after the end of the war. However, according to an official American report, the American authorities had received only 132,472 Germans prior to the beginning of the regular transfer (*Svobodné slovo,* May 19, 1946). The German sources estimate that prior to Potsdam some 750,000 Germans were expelled to the Soviet Zones of Germany and Austria (*Dokumentation,* IV/1, 134). The American estimate was closer to reality, with 250,000 persons (*Report No. 1841,* p. 11). Many among the fleeing Germans who continued their flight after the end of the war were regarded as Sudeten Germans only because they came via Czechoslovakia. Some 250,000 Sudetens were prisoners of war and almost all of them returned directly to the Reich (Frumkin, p. 51). The various and strikingly different figures show the high degree of arbitrariness and inaccuracy and provide only a very general picture. They have to be considered as highly conjectural, rough estimates with a wide margin of error. This author has attempted to use the most reliable figures, but the dearth of statistical data and the unreliability of material have made his task extremely difficult. For instance, some 75,000 Germans, transferred in an organized way to the Soviet Zone from after Potsdam until the end of 1945 and regarded by German sources as Sudeten Germans, were listed by the Czechs as German refugees from the East (*Svobodné slovo,* May 19, 1946; *Dokumentation,* IV/1, 112, 332).

34. *Ibid.,* pp. 328–33.

35. See the description of the first organized transfer on January 25, from Mariánské Lázně. About 300 journalists were present (Jean Danès in the *Central European Observer,* XXIII, March 15, 1946).

in Germany daily. On February 25 the number was increased to two trains per day. On April 1 the daily movement was increased to four trains with 4,800 Germans.

On April 9–10 American and Czechoslovak officials met in Prague again to discuss further technical arrangements. The daily rate of movement was increased to six trains, and the Czechs agreed to provide each expellee with 500 RM. It was stated by both sides that the transfer was running in an orderly and humane manner.[36] The critical housing shortage and dilatoriness in granting transferees economic and social opportunities forced the American authorities to demand a reduction from six to four in the number of trains, at a meeting held on June 19 at Prague. In addition, new provisions safeguarding a humane transfer were agreed upon. The transferees were to be moved as a family unit, and the Czechoslovaks consented to permit up to 100 kg of personal effects, food, and hand tools to be taken out. Persons without financial means were provided with adequate clothing and monetary allowance by the Czechoslovak authorities. They were also free to take their watches, wedding rings, alarm clocks, and bankbooks for accounts on German banks.[37] The American survey of the redistribution centers was prepared during the latter part of July. It stated that the expellees from Czechoslovakia

> were in reasonably good physical condition, fairly well clothed and in possession of the 500 RM which are to be furnished them under agreement. Many of the expellees brought household goods and working tools. The food they received and messing facilities en route were satisfactory. The former complaints that working males were being separated from their families have almost entirely ceased.[38]

36. *Dokumentation*, IV/1, 334–36; *Memorandum*, p. 7.
37. *Monthly Report*, Aug. 20, Sept. 20, 1946. This specification indicated an alleviation of the original rigid Czechoslovak stand. The Americans complained that the Czechs were withholding young, able workers while sending chiefly women, children, and the aged. Some difficulties were also experienced in the withdrawal of personal belongings of the transferees (Lucius D. Clay, *Decision in Germany*, p. 314). Jane Perry Clark Carey (*The Role of Uprooted People in European Recovery*, p. 37) disproved this contention of General Clay and indicated that in the census figure of Oct. 29, 1946, the proportion of men in the age group between 14 and 48 years was higher than among the Reich Germans. It seems that the prisoners and former soldiers coming directly to the Reich made up for the better age proportion.
38. *Monthly Report*, Aug. 20, 1946. The contention of *Report No. 1841* (p. 8), that "the provisions of Article XIII of the Potsdam agreement have never been adhered to by Soviet Russia and by the countries under its control or domination" is false as far as the Czechoslovak Republic was concerned.

The reduction to four trains daily after July 15 decreased the monthly influx from 220,000 to 147,000 Germans. In November there was another drop in the number of trains, to three per week. The American Zone was unable to absorb all the expellees and there was a backlog of more than 100,000 Germans in the distributing centers. On October 31 the American authorities asked Prague either to speed up the movement or to suspend it during the winter, completing it in the spring of 1947. As the bulk of the Germans had already been evacuated, the Czechoslovaks chose the second alternative, and on November 12 an agreement was signed providing for the suspension of the transfer from December 1 until April 1947.[39] From Jan. 25 to Nov. 30, 1946, 1,334,856 Germans were removed from Czechoslovakia in an organized movement to the American Zone.[40]

The Soviet military authorities suspended the transfer to their zone toward the end of 1945 because of an unfavorable food situation. Only small transports of German anti-Fascists continued to be moved there.[41] In Berlin Marshal Sokolovsky refused to implement the Control Council decision. It was due finally to a direct Czechoslovak appeal to Marshal Stalin that the necessary negotiations took place between Soviet and Czechoslovak representatives in Berlin on May 3-4, and were continued in Prague on June 1. As a result, an agreement on the transfer of the Germans to the Soviet Zone was concluded, similar to that agreed upon by the Americans.[42] Regular transfer commenced on June 10, 1946.

At the outset two trains were dispatched daily; from June 21, three

39. *Memorandum*, p. 9.
40. The monthly tabulation of the organized movement was as follows in 1946:

January	11,012	July	167,595
February	44,659	August	146,156
March	105,639	September	128,720
April	172,035	October	113,000
May	211,900	November	31,840
June	202,300		

Small numbers of Germans continued to arrive even after the suspension. As of July 31, 1947, there were 1,336,065 Sudeten transferees evacuated in an organized way into the United States Zone of Germany (*Monthly Report*, Sept. 20, 1946; *Bimonthly Review*, Nos. 16, 17, 25). Compare Bohmann, *Sudetendeutschtum*, pp. 253-72.
41. *Svobodné slovo*, Jan. 4, 6, 1946. The trains with the anti-Fascists, including 250-300 Germans in each train, went three times weekly (*ibid.*, May 19, 1946).
42. *Memorandum*, pp. 9-10. See also a letter to the author by Dr. František Ševčík, Nov. 25, 1956. Dr. Ševčík was the official of the Foreign Ministry entrusted with transfer affairs (see also *Svobodné slovo*, May 19, 1946). The Germans were allowed to take 50 kg of personal belongings to the Soviet Zone.

trains were available. In the period July 1 to October 18, the daily rate was set at six trains with 7,200 Germans, Sundays excepted. Some were transported by trucks or ships. On Nov. 13, 1946, a final agreement stated that the removal had been completed under the provisions of Potsdam.[43] In all, 636,482 persons were moved to the Soviet Zone of Germany from the beginning of the organized transfer.[44]

The final result was impressive. According to official Czechoslovak figures, 1,859,541 Germans were transferred by the end of 1946.[45] Further transfers were effected only in order to unite family members,[46] although some 30,000 Germans emigrated individually to Germany or abroad during 1947–48.[47] The Czechoslovak Social Democratic and Communist parties set up special offices to provide for the voluntary emigration of members of their former German sister parties, directed and administered by the Germans themselves.[48] Transfers into the American Zone started in May 1946, and over

43. *Memorandum*, pp. 9–10.
44. The cabinet gave its consent to the inclusion of 150,000 Germans who had come to the Soviet Zone after the Potsdam agreement within the quota of 750,000 Germans. Hence the Soviets took over 786,482 Germans from Czechoslovakia (*Memorandum*, p. 11).
45. According to official Czechoslovak figures, 1,223,059 Germans were transferred to the American Zone and 636,482 to the Soviet Zone during the organized removal. Prague agreed to include in the official Potsdam quota 223,000 and 150,000 Germans, respectively, who had left the Republic after Potsdam. As a result, out of the Potsdam quota of 2.5 million Germans, the Americans received 1,446,059 Germans, including 53,187 anti-Fascists, and the Soviet share was 786,482, including 42,989 anti-Fascists. The total was 2,232,541 Germans (*ibid.*). These figures differ from those published by the American authorities. According to another official Czechoslovak report, 2,170,598 Germans were transferred—1,420,598 to the American and 750,000 to the Soviet Zone—as of Nov. 1, 1946 (*Svobodné slovo*, Dec. 19, 1946). State Secretary Dr. Clementis used different figures on Dec. 2, 1947 (as quoted by Fritz Peter Habel, ed., *Dokumentensammlung zur Sudetenfrage*, p. 122. The collection will hereafter be cited as *Dokumentensammlung*.)
46. During 1947 the total figure was 2,339 Germans in the United States Zone and 2,539 in the Soviet Zone; the corresponding figures for 1948 were 2,951 and 4,995, a total of 12,824 Germans. Up to June 15, 1949, a further 5,303 Germans were removed (*Memorandum*, p. 13).
47. *Ibid.*, p. 11. It seems that these were mostly anti-Fascists. A group of 200–300 persons was entitled to one train with 40 cars. Some of the transports used trucks or ships. (See also Bohmann, *Ausweisung*, passim.)
48. Only these two German parties did not join the Henlein Party in 1938. A few of the German Christian Democrats were also given assistance. The Social Democratic Party set up a special bureau under the guidance of Alois Ullmann in September 1945. Some 6,000 Social Democrats left for the Soviet Zone in 1945 (*Dokumentation*, IV/1, 128, 343–45). Local German trustees and anti-Fascist committees were set up to register the anti-Fascists. The Ministry of the Interior issued two orders setting up the main lines for the transfer of the anti-Fascists on Nov. 26, 1945, and Jan. 17, 1946. Through the intervention of the Social Democratic Party, the cabinet issued a decree in favor of the anti-Fascists on Feb. 15, 1946 (*ibid.*, pp. 128–31, 346–55).

100,000 anti-Fascists were transported to the Soviet and American zones in 1945–46.[49]

Genuine efforts were made to provide the most suitable conditions for the transfer. Transports were dispatched from assembly camps (over which the Czech authorities exercised only a general control) which served as collection centers for those who were to be removed. The stay in the camps was made as short as possible. There the Germans underwent final registration formalities and general health examinations by a German medical staff. Baggage and physical inspections followed. Then the camp leader distributed financial allowances. Transport to the railroad station was usually effected by truck. The trains were accompanied by German Red Cross sisters and taken over by Allied officers at the border stations. Efforts to improve the conditions of the transfer continued unabated.[50]

The humane policies which had been enunciated were not permitted to be ignored and local shortcomings were quickly remedied. At the beginning some confusion might have existed, since in such a large and complex operation no one could have asked for perfect results in so short a time unless he had expected miracles. The technical problems faced were tremendous. A total of 1,646 trains with 67,748 cars and 6,580 locomotives were used, as were 4 lazaret trains, 60 trucks, and 12 boats. During the peak period in the first half of July 1946, 12 trains with 14,400 persons arrived daily at the border centers. This figure was gradually reduced to 10 trains with 12,000 persons.[51] The National Bank put one milliard RM at the disposal of the transferees up to the end of October 1946. The transfer itself cost over one half milliard Kčs.[52]

Czechoslovak authorities took all possible care to carry out the transfer according to the principles of the Potsdam agreement. Foreign correspondents, observers, and diplomatic representatives

49. The Czechoslovak official figures gave the total of 96,176 anti-Fascists. Schechtman ("Postwar Populations," p. 157) stated that 55,017 anti-Nazis desired to stay while 86,176 asked for transfer. The official German study (Dokumentation, IV/1, 131) put the number of the transferees to West Germany under Social Democrat guidance at 82,600 persons. It estimated that 30,000 Communists left for East Germany.

50. Letter by Dr. Ševčík; Bohmann, Ausweisung, passim. Dr. Ševčík stated that the Foreign Ministry made a proposition to the effect that the immovable property of the transferees should be paid for in German marks to be deposited at the Allied Control Council. There were milliards of practically worthless marks in Czechoslovakia. However, strong objections were lodged, particularly by the Ministry of Finance, because of the huge damages incurred during the occupation.

51. Memorandum, p. 10; Svobodné slovo, Dec. 19, 1946.

52. The Minister of Finance, Dr. J. Dolanský, Nov. 20, 1946 (Stenographic Reports, 23rd Session).

were provided with every facility to follow the progress of the transfer in their own way. They were free to visit any assembly camp, to talk with the transferees, and to inspect any place they desired. Among others, Gen. Lucius Clay, the American delegate to the Control Council in Berlin, declared on receiving the Czechoslovak delegation after the completion of the main movement, that the transfer was organized and carried out so efficiently and humanely that he wished to express his thanks to the Czechoslovak government.[53] Soviet General Leljushenko also voiced his appreciation of the perfect organization of the transfer.[54] The American, British, and French ambassadors, Steinhardt, Nichols, and Dejean, respectively, frequently used the opportunity provided by the authorities to make inspections through the borderland. For example, United States Ambassador Lawrence A. Steinhardt asked for a Czechoslovak officer as his escort as he visited various cities, transports, and assembly and internment camps where he inquired personally as to prevailing conditions. An American liaison officer was attached permanently to the Czechoslovak General Staff, where he was in charge of problems pertaining to the transfer to the United States Zone. The American authorities took over the transports only after they had inspected the trains and had found that all the provisions of the transfer agreement had been met adequately.[55] There is no doubt that the organized transfer was effected in an efficient and humane way.[56] There is,

53. See the letter by Dr. Ševčík; *Memorandum.*
54. Schechtman, "Resettlement," p. 278. Col. Gen. Kurochkin decorated the Czechoslovak organizers of the transfer on Nov. 15, 1946 (*Svobodné slovo,* Nov. 16, 1946).
55. Interview with Col. Ferdinand Monzer, who was the successor of General Dastich (Paris, Dec. 20, 1952). President Beneš received and decorated the American and Soviet military delegations who were responsible for the carrying out of the transfer. The American delegation led by Maj. Gen. Frank K. Keating was introduced by Ambassador Steinhardt on Dec. 16, 1946 (*Rudé právo,* Dec. 17, 1946).
56. Schechtman ("Postwar Population," p. 156) stated that the transfer was "on the whole carried out in the orderly and humane manner stipulated by Potsdam." Only the pre-Potsdam expulsions were neither orderly nor in some instances humane (*ibid.,* p. 155). The statement of *Report No. 1841* (p. 11) that the organized expulsion could not be termed humane and orderly was inaccurate. The Sudeten German postwar literature attempted to prove that hundreds of thousands died of cruel treatment during the expulsion. It grossly exaggerated some real individual hardships and deliberately mixed up local violences occurring during the first postwar months with the organized move of population in 1946 (*Deutschlands Ostproblem,* p. 131; *Das andere Lidice, passim; Die Vertriebenen,* p. 176; Preidel, ed., p. 102; *Dokumente zur Austreibung, passim*). Some misinformed authors adopted the Sudeten figures. For example, Charles R. Joy ("Four Lidices and Christian Conscience," *Catholic World,* CLXXII, September 1951, 406-11) stated that from 1945 to 1949 "800,000 Sudeten Germans were shot, hanged or killed in some other manner by the Czechs."

however, every reason to demur at the useless hardship of the property requirements which legally stripped the transferees of all their property except for 500–1,000 RM and 50–100 kg of their personal belongings. The original plan of Beneš to compensate for the confiscated individual property in Reichsmarks was rejected. Extremists on both sides were the final beneficiaries of this senseless measure of expropriation. The relative haste of the transfer, effected in an intranquil atmosphere, made also for some improvisations.[57]

At the end of 1946, when the principal part of the population removal was completed, the total number of registered German inhabitants of the Czech part of the Republic was as follows:

Region	Number of Germans in Nov. 1946	Before transfer in 1930[58]
Č. Budějovice	14,446	(171,162)
Liberec	43,889	(457,719)
Litoměřice	40,294	(547,197)
Carlsbad	50,609	(461,674)
Pardubice	3,900	(55,167)
Pilsen	14,674	(201,187)
Prague	4,696	(50,616)
Trutnov	17,049	(184,516)
Žatec	11,426	(141,806)
Brno	10,231	(259,468)
Olomouc	10,186	(223,630)
Opava	11,023	(229,744)
Ostrava	7,488	(82,222)
Bohemia	200,983	
Moravia-Silesia	38,928	
Total	239,911	(3,066,108)

57. See the critical remarks by J. Smutný, pp. 78–80. President Beneš viewed a five-year period as necessary to carry out the transfer, although he expected that the majority of the Germans would be evicted within two years (*ibid.*). American policy toward the German population and particularly the Nazis was also hard, and many harsh acts occurred during the initial period. For instance, President Truman complained to General Eisenhower (Aug. 31, 1945) that "we appear to be treating the Jews as the Nazis treated them except that we do not exterminate them" (*Documents on American Foreign Relations*, VIII, 252). This volume presents some examples of the policy that expressed neither sympathy nor pity for the German people. Arrests, requisitions, confiscations, and the collecting of Germans into special assembly centers were among the many means used by the occupation forces in Germany in 1945. The Czechoslovak measures are to be viewed against the background of postwar Allied anti-Nazi policy.

The total can be broken down as follows (exclusive of some unspecified groups):

Experts working in industry with special protection cards	33,537
Members of their families	53,103
Germans with provisory certificate of state citizenship	13,045
Germans in mixed marriages	33,055
Germans of Jewish origin and confession	1,876
Germans permitted to stay because they received a pardon	4,351
Germans with a postponement of their transfer	6,500
German anti-Fascists asking for transfer	24,899
Germans subjected to transfer	66,936

Some 10,000 German wives of Czech nationals were not included in the number of the Germans listed as partners in mixed marriages. In the final months of 1946, about 19,000 Germans were transferred and about 6,000 anti-Fascists emigrated. On Dec. 31, 1946, the number of registered Germans in the Czech provinces amounted to some 225,000. Up to June 15, 1949, 18,127 Germans were removed to Germany and 30,000 Germans emigrated abroad. After this date some 177,000 registered Germans still remained in the Czech part of the Republic.[59]

58. The figures in parentheses indicate the result of the census of 1930.
59. The figures are taken from *Memorandum*, p. 12, which also indicated that there were about 14,000 to 15,000 German wives of Czech nationals. Only 10,-000 declared themselves as Germans. See the chart below. Waller Wynne, Jr. (*The Population*, p. 9) estimated the number of Germans in Czechoslovakia at 250,000 in May 1947. He included the Carpathian Germans living in Slovakia. More than half of them were evacuated toward the end of the war. According to Czechoslovak official figures, 62,653 Germans were listed as inhabiting Slovakia at the beginning of the transfer. Their first transport left on April 30, 1946. Up to Oct. 31, 1946, 32,450 Germans were removed. The number of exempted Germans was 15,496 (*Svobodné slovo*, May 3, 1947). For the Carpathian Germans, see *Dokumentation*, IV/1, 137–78. The nationality of the Czechoslovak population was ascertained in the census of March 1, 1950, for the first time. There were 165,117 Germans. Their number increased to 165,167 at the next census on Dec. 31, 1955 (*Statistický obzor* [*Statistical Review*], XXXVII, 384. In the period 1950–56, 18,307 Germans moved from Czechoslovakia to West Germany (Bohmann, *Sudetendeutschtum*, p. 244). On Oct. 31, 1948, 2,599,169 persons inhabited the Czech borderland (*Memorandum*, p. 56).

Thus, the German minority left the Republic in three main stages: (1) Up to the end of the war; (2) to the Potsdam agreement with some movement thereafter;[60] (3) in the regular organized removal in 1946.

60. Wiskemann (*Germany's Eastern Neighbours,* p. 106) put the number of Germans living in Czechoslovakia at the time of Potsdam at 2,359,906, which was the number of German ration cards issued for the period Aug. 20–Sept. 16, 1945. This figure, however, included Reich Germans.

CHAPTER 13

The Final Balance Sheet

German sources have indicated that between 200,000 and 500,000 Sudeten Germans lost their lives during the transfer.[1] On June 14, 1952, Dr. Walter Becher[2] published a statistical article in the two leading Sudeten weeklies[3] wherein he attempted to prove that 304,000 Sudeten Germans were "victims of the unchained hatred." The gravity of the accusation and the fact that it represented the official opinion of the Sudeten German leadership[4] necessitate its close scrutiny, taking into consideration the more recent statistical estimates published in the *Sudetendeutscher Atlas*,[5] the official

1. For example, Prof. Rudolf Schreiber, as quoted in Preidel, ed., p. 102; *Deutschlands Ostproblem*, p. 132; *Die Vertriebenen*, p. 176; *Dokumentation*, IV/1, 135.
2. Former Bavarian provincial deputy for the German Refugee Party and now secretary general of the central organization of the Sudeten Germans, the Sudeten German Council.
3. *Der Sudetendeutsche* and *Die Sudetendeutsche Zeitung*. The Sudeten leaders, Dr. Lodgman and deputies R. Reitzner and H. Schütz, addressed a special memorandum to the Katyn committee of the American Congress in which they accused the Czechs of murdering 300,000 Sudeten Germans (*Der Sudetendeutsche*, Dec. 19, 1952).
4. *Atlas* (p. 54) estimated the losses at 302,445 Germans. See also the introduction by Turnwald in *Documents on the Expulsion; ibid., Renascence or Decline of Central Europe. The Sudeten-German-Czech Problem*, p. 67. Mr. Becher's figures were inserted by Rep. Usher L. Burdick into the *Congressional Record*, 84th Congress, 1st Session, April 25, 1955, p. A2709. Rep. B. Carroll Reece used them on April 22, 1958 (*ibid.*, 85th Congress, 2nd Session, p. A3628).
5. *Atlas*, p. 54.

Dokumentation, the compilation by the Federal Statistical Office, and studies by Alfred Bohmann.[6]

Dr. Becher based his findings on the figure of the last Czechoslovak census of 1930, in which Germans numbered 3,318,445 persons.[7] He evaluated German natural increase at 10,000 persons per year and arrived at the figure of 80,000 persons for the period 1930–38. The natural increase began to rise after 1938 and reached its peak in 1941. Becher selected May 8, 1943, as the date when the increased war losses started to exercise an influence and offset the increase.

1930–1938	80,000
1939–1943	70,000*
	150,000

*This figure was given without any evidence.

By adding the total natural increase to the original number of 3.3 million persons, Dr. Becher arrived at 3,468,445 Germans alive on May 8, 1943. By deducting the number of Germans from Czechoslovakia supposedly alive at the time of the West German census of Sept. 13, 1950 — their war losses included — he came to a final estimate of the number lost during the expulsion. In 1950, 1,912,000 Sudetens lived in West Germany, 140,000 in Austria, 150,000 in Czechoslovakia, 800,000 in East Germany, 10,000 in Europe and overseas, and 4,000 in Sweden. Hence the total number was 3,004,000 Germans from Czechoslovakia alive in 1950. War losses were estimated at 160,000 persons. Dr. Becher deducted the war losses from the number of Germans alive in 1943 (3,468,445), and after comparing the result (3,308,445) with his estimate for 1950 (3,004,000) he concluded that 304,000 persons were killed by the Czechs during the expulsion.[8]

An examination and review of the data given by Dr. Becher will indicate their real value.

6. German estimates of the number of German victims during the expulsion from Czechoslovakia differ. *Dokumentation,* IV/1, 13 ff., 134–35, put the number at 225,600 German inhabitants of the Republic. The estimate by Statistisches Bundesamt, ed., *Die deutschen Vertreibungsverluste,* pp. 322–26, was 237,900 Germans (224,900 Sudeten and 13,000 Carpathian). Dr. Bohmann prepared the section dealing with Czechoslovakia. This work will hereafter be cited as *Vertreibungsverluste.* See also Bohmann, *Sudetendeutschtum,* pp. 245–52. Bohmann estimated the Sudeten losses at 241,000. He did not include Carpathian Germans.

7. The same figure was used by Wynne, Jr., pp. 9, 65.

8. The attentive reader would find out easily that the sum of 3,004,000 was wrong, as Dr. Becher was unable to add correctly and managed to "annihilate" 12,000 persons by a single stroke of his pen. *Atlas* (p. 54) used the same figures except that it put the natural increase at 160,000 persons for the period 1930–45.

1) The German minority group numbered 3,231,688 persons on Dec. 1, 1930.[9] (Dr. Becher included 86,757 foreigners in his figure.)[10]

2) Dr. Becher estimated the German natural increase at 150,000 persons. The facts do not warrant his assumption. The war of 1914 brought about a decline of births among the Sudeten Germans. Only lower death rates balanced the gradual drop in the rate of natural increase. One may follow the rate of natural increase of the Czechoslovak Germans according to the data compiled by the Czechoslovak State Statistical Office for the period 1931–37.[11]

	Live births	Deaths	Excess of births over deaths
1931	57,790	46,271	11,519
1932	55,640	45,645	9,995
1933	51,066	45,106	5,960
1934	49,768	42,727	7,041
1935	46,904	44,853	2,051
1936	46,003	43,515	2,488
1937	45,000	44,349	651

As a result, during this period the number of Germans increased by 39,705 (the yearly average being 5,672). On Jan. 1, 1938, the total number was estimated at 3,271,000. Emigration and immigration had no practical bearing on the figures. A. Bohmann estimated the Sudeten rate of increase from 1939 till May 1, 1945, and arrived at the figure of 123,974, which, however, included the natural increase of Czechs, foreigners, and non-Sudeten Reich Germans living in the German occupied territories of former Czechoslovakia.[12] The official German survey estimated the natural increase of all German inhabit-

9. *Annuaire statistique de la république tchécoslovaque*, p. 8.

10. *Dokumentation* (IV/1, 14–15) based its estimates on the number of Sudetens in the Reich census of May 1939. Its figure amounted to 3,305,000 Germans in Bohemia and Moravia-Silesia. *Vertreibungsverluste* (p. 322) arrived at the figure of 3,323,000 Sudeten and 154,000 Carpathian Germans (in May 1939). However, both studies included a number of Czechs who registered as Germans at the census.

11. *Annuaire statistique*, 1932–38.

12. Bohmann, *Sudetendeutschtum*, pp. 140, 143, 247–48. A. Bohmann disregarded the Czechs living in the Sudeten territories and counted their natural increase as the German one. The natural increase of the Protectorate Germans (Sudeten and non-Sudeten) was an estimated 9,000 (*ibid.*, pp. 248, 252). Bohmann used material published by the Statistical Office of the Reichsgau Sudetenland. The figures included Czechs and Reich Germans and appear exaggerated. *Dokumentation* (IV/1, 18) estimated the natural incease from 1939 to May 1945 at a rate of 3.65 percent and reached a total of 121,000 Sudeten Germans. The war losses were not considered, however.

ants of Czechoslovakia at 126,000 during the period. This figure still included some Czechs registered as Germans, foreigners, and other Germans than Sudetens. The natural increase in 1938 was estimated at 5,000.[13] Hence by May 1, 1945, the number of the Czechoslovak Germans was less than 3,402,000. No reliable figures on the migration of the Sudetens to the Reich and their return during the war are available.[14]

3) *Die Sudetendeutsche Zeitung* (June 7, 1952) put the number of Germans from Czechoslovakia living in Austria at 147,000. The German estimate was 142,000 in 1950.[15]

4) There were 165,117 persons registered as Germans in the Republic on March 1, 1950. Toward Nov. 1, 1946, there were 33,055 German husbands of Czech partners and 14,000 to 15,000 German wives of Czech nationals.[16] I estimate that some 50,000 formerly registered Germans were listed as Czechs in 1945–50. They included a large part of the German partners in mixed marriages and a number of Czechs who were registered as Germans in 1938–44.

5) According to the census of Oct. 29, 1946, the number of Germans from Czechoslovakia living in the Soviet Zone of Germany amounted to 840,843.[17] Some 10,000 Germans were removed from the Republic to the Soviet Zone[18] in the period from 1947 to June 15, 1949,[19] and about 30,000 Germans emigrated there. An official Czechoslovak document surmised that some 914,000 former members of the German minority in Czechoslovakia inhabited the Zone in 1949.[20]

6) In Sub-Carpathian Ruthenia, first annexed by Hungary and later taken by the Soviet Union, there were 13,240 Germans in 1930. Some

13. In view of the decreasing rate of German natural increase this figure seems exaggerated (*Vertreibungsverluste*, pp. 322 ff.; Bohmann, *Sudetendeutschtum*, p. 140). War losses and the overall consequences of the war seem to have offset the natural increase from 1943.
14. The German estimate is some 30,000 Sudetens returning home. No evidence is given for the figure (*Vertreibungsverluste*, p. 338; Bohmann, *Sudetendeuschtum*, p. 248). On the other hand, Kulischer gives some information on the recruitment of Sudeten labor for the Reich and the heavy losses due to migration to Reich territory (pp. 202–203).
15. *Vertreibungsverluste*, p. 349. See also Luža, *Odsun*, p. 33.
16. *Memorandum*, p. 12. For the figures of the census in 1950, see *Statististický obzor*, XXXVII, 1957, 384.
17. Seraphim, p. 184. There were 345,316 males and 495,527 females. See also Federal Statistical Office, *Statistical Pocket-Book*, p. 3.
18. For the Sudeten move from the Soviet Zone to the United States Zone, see *Bimonthly Review*, June 15, July 1947.
19. In 1947, 2,539 Germans; and in 1948, 4,995 Germans. During the period Jan. 1–June 15, 1949, 5,303 Germans left for both zones (*Memorandum*, p. 13).
20. *Memorandum*, p. 17. The estimate can be broken down as follows: Saxony-Anhalt, 357,000; Thuringia, 222,000; Mecklenburg, 160,000; Saxony, 127,000; Brandenburg, 48,000 (*ibid.*).

returned to Germany; the fate of the remainder is unknown. An estimated 4,000 Germans were supposed to be still alive in 1950. It is surmised that 8,700 Czechoslovak Germans (civil and war prisoners, missing persons) still lived outside Czechoslovakia in September 1950.[21]

7) The census of Sept. 13, 1950, listed 1,912,000 Germans from Czechoslovakia living in West Germany.[22] Some 5,800 lived in West Berlin, 2,000 in East Berlin, and 600 in Saarland.[23]

8) The war losses of Czechoslovak Germans amounted to 215,000.[24]

9) The loss by emigration totaled about 25,000.[25]

10) Finally, Dr. Becher included the murdered German Jews among the victims of the Czechs. In 1930, 356,830 Czechoslovak citizens were of the Jewish faith. This figure included 76,301 Jews in Bohemia, 41,250 in Moravia-Silesia, 136,737 in Slovakia, and 102,542 in Ruthenia.[26] Their real number was higher because some ethnic Jews were Christians or belonged to no denomination. Some Jews declared themselves of German nationality, namely 35,657 in the Czech provinces and 10,075 in Slovakia and Ruthenia.[27] In the territory annexed by Hitler in 1938 there were 30,000 Jews, the greatest number of whom fled to Czechoslovakia. On May 17, 1939, only 2,649 Jews remained in the Sudetengau.[28] On March 15, 1939, the Protectorate had an estimated Jewish population of 118,310. On Jan. 1, 1943, there remained only 15,550 Jews. During the period from March 16, 1939, to Dec. 31, 1942, 25,699 Jews emigrated; the excess of deaths over births was 7,074; and 69,677 Jews were "evacuated" to the East.[29]

---

21. *Vertreibungsverluste,* pp. 353–55. The figure includes 4,000 Germans from Ruthenia.

22. However, only 1,822,679 Germans possessed a special refugee certificate (*Wirtschaft und Statistik,* December 1952, No. 12). The census figure includes the natural increase in 1945–50, which was an estimated 70,000. This increase amounted to 9,000 for the Germans outside of West Germany. See *Vertreibungsverluste,* pp. 350–51.

23. *Ibid.,* pp. 349–50.

24. *Ibid.,* pp. 340–42.

25. *Ibid.,* pp. 349–50; *Dokumentation,* IV/1, 135.

26. Winkler, *Die Tschechoslowakei im Spiegel,* pp. 12, 58.

27. *Ibid.* There were 45,732 Jews declaring themselves as Germans and 87,489 as Czechoslovaks.

28. Report on "Die Endlösung der europäischen Judenfrage," No. 5194, elaborated by Dr. Korherr, the inspector for statistics, for presentation to Himmler on March 27, 1943. The abridged version for presentation to Hitler was prepared on April 19, 1943 (Centre de documentation juive contemporaine, Paris, CXXXVIIIa-72, 74). This is a document of great value, containing the official German figures.

29. *Ibid.* Hitler ordered the extermination of the Jews on Nov. 11, 1941. Reinhard Heydrich decided on the final solution of the Jewish question through mass

The "evacuations" continued during 1943, particularly in the first months of the year. The Czechoslovak census of 1947 did not ascertain the religion of the groups, and therefore it is very difficult to arrive at an estimate of the number of Czechoslovak Jews who remained alive. In 1946 some 22,000 Czechoslovak Jews who had survived the Nazi regime lived in Czech lands.[30] Against this background one can reach an approximate estimate of the Jewish death toll in the Historic Provinces (the pre-Munich territory). To the number of deported Jews up to Jan. 1, 1943 (69,677), one adds 15,550 Jews deported thereafter and includes the Jews inhabiting the Sudetengau (2,649) and the former Czechoslovak territory attached to Ober- and Unterdonau. As a result, about 90,000 Jews were deported. Taking into account the fact that about 22,000 Jews survived the war, one can surmise that at least some 68,000 were exterminated.[31] Since in the Czech countries 30.3 percent of the Jews declared themselves to be Germans,[32] it may be estimated that about 20,500 German Jews were murdered by the Nazis. This fact has not prevented Dr. Becher from counting these gassed Jews as "victims of the unchained Czech hatred." The same could be said about 7,800 German Jews who were able to emigrate.[33] It was not the Czechs who chased them out of their homes.

So-called Free Slovakia belonged, with Croatia, to the few states which took the initiative in the Jewish question.[34] The number of its Jews amounted to 89,000.[35] Some 46,000 Jews remained in the

deportations to the East on Jan. 20, 1942 (K. G. Adler, *Theresienstadt 1941–1945. Das Antlitz einer Zwangsgemeinschaft*, p. 22). A good description of the German Jewish policy in the Protectorate was given by Gerhard Jacoby in *Racial State. The German Nationalities Policy in the Protectorate of Bohemia-Moravia*.

30. They included 15,000 Jews who managed to survive or reemigrated and 6,850 Jews who returned from the Terezín ghetto (Adler, p. 741; Léon Poliakov, *Bréviaire de la haine, passim;* Gerald Reitlinger, *The Final Solution*, pp. 492–93.

31. Reemigrants were included in the figure of 22,000. Reitlinger (p. 493) put his estimate at 63,000 Protectorate Jews. *The Black Book* (New York, 1946, p. 136), spoke of 77,000 murdered Jews in the Protectorate.

32. Winkler, p. 58.

33. The figure represents 30 percent of the number of emigrant Jews. From Feb. 15, 1939 to Dec. 31, 1942, there were 26,009 Jewish emigrants. (See the Korherr report.) Jewish emigration was banned on Oct. 1, 1941 (Reitlinger, p. 29).

34. The Korherr report stated: "Die Evakuierungen aus der Slowakei und aus Kroatien wurden von diesen Staaten selbst in Angriff genommen." For Slovakian anti-Jewish legislation, see Reitlinger, pp. 386 ff.

35. The Korherr report.

Slovakian territory annexed by Hungary.[36] During 1942 there were 57,000 Slovakian Jews deported to the East.[37] The deportations resumed after the end of the Slovakian uprising in the fall of 1944, with 9,000 Jews being sent to the East.[38] About 28,000 to 35,000 Jews lived in Slovakia in 1945,[39] but the number also included some Ruthenian Jews and others from the formerly annexed part of Slovakia. In the territory of the Fascist Slovakian state alone, there were more than 66,000 Jews exterminated.[40]

The fate of the Jews in the territory annexed by Hungary was more favorable, only 30,000 Slovakian Jews having been deported.[41] One may surmise that at least 20,000 deported Jews were subsequently killed.[42] The total death toll of the Slovakian Jews would then amount at least to some 86,000 persons. As 7.3 percent of the Slovakian Jews were of German nationality,[43] more than 6,000 German Jews may be considered Nazi victims.

In all, the Nazis killed more than 26,500 German Jews in Czechoslovakia. It is to be noticed that German authors neglect to mention this rather staggering fact, although they have always been very careful to count the German Jews among the members of the German group. In this case, the German Jews were murdered notwithstanding Czech resistance and opposition. This did not prevent Dr. Becher from registering them as slain during the transfer.

36. *Les juifs en Europe 1939–45* (Paris, 1949), p. 217.
37. The Korherr report put the number at 56,691. The verdict of Dieter Wisliceny, the German councilor for the Jewish question in the Slovakian government, put the number of deported Jews at 57,037 in 1942 (*Centre de documentation juive contemporaine*, Paris). Almost all of them perished (Reitlinger, p. 493).
38. *Ibid.*, pp. 392, 493. Others set the number higher. For example, Henri Monneray (*La persécution des juifs dans les pays de l'Est présentée à Nuremberg*, p. 214) put the number at 25,000 Jews.
39. Reitlinger, *Final Solution*, p. 385.
40. I have added together the numbers of deported Jews.
41. *Ibid.*, p. 493. It was estimated that from the 1942 deportations 284 Jews finally returned.
42. Reitlinger estimated the death toll of the Slovakian Jews at 85,000–95,000 (*ibid.*).
43. Winkler, p. 58. Only 130 Ruthenian Jews were of German nationality.

As a result, the final figure would be rather different from that reached by Dr. Becher:

	Germans from Czechoslovakia
West Germany	1,912,000
West Berlin	5,800
East Germany	914,000
East Berlin	2,000
Saarland	600
Austria	147,000
Czechoslovakia	215,000
Europe and overseas	25,000
Living outside Czecho-slovakia	8,700
War losses	215,000
German Jews killed	26,500
German Jews emigrated	7,800
Total	3,479,400

To arrive at the final estimate one has to subtract the natural increase of the Czechoslovak Germans in the years 1945–50 (79,000) from the above-mentioned total. The final figure (3,400,400) is indicative only and cannot be considered precise. It gives an overall picture based on approximate data as far as these are available for a population which was subject to sudden and abrupt movements. This assessment, however, puts to the test the allegations of Dr. Becher and other German sources using misleading data. In comparing the final figure with the estimated figure of less than 3,402,000 Czechoslovak Germans by May 1, 1945, one arrives at the conclusion that many of the alleged 300,000 victims never existed, a further number is still alive, and the remainder was gassed by the Nazis.

CHAPTER 14

Present Prospects and Perils

After their victory in 1945 the Allied Powers divided defeated Germany and gradually encouraged the formation of two German states. The result was a split into two hostile parts: the Federal Republic, which was granted sovereignty in 1954, and the German Democratic Republic, which became sovereign in September 1955. Meanwhile, the East-West struggle set forces in motion that led to the Communist take-over of Czechoslovakia in February 1948. The technological development of atomic weapons helped to freeze the German split and established a delicate power balance in Europe. Concomitantly, the Kremlin sought to draw Central Europe into its orbit, making the region a focus of the Cold War.

Strategic location and recent history combined to make Central Europe a problem area caught and pulled by the rival forces of the Communist and democratic blocs. Where national conflicts had spread their impact among peoples, the Communist pressures presented a major challenge of a different character. Although national fervor still simmered in Germany and Czechoslovakia, the immediate problems of the East-West struggle overshadowed any possible upsurge of nationalist feelings. To be sure, the average Czech in the Communist-dominated Republic seemed to be aware of the lessons of recent history and vaguely uneasy about the future development of Germany. Apprehension of a potential German threat seemed to have played a definitive role in Beneš' reluctance to resort to force during the Communist take-over.

Czechoslovak suspicions of a future powerful Germany may have caused some Czechs to become more amenable to Communism. Yet in 1948 those sinister familiars of propaganda known as the "revanchists" seemed far off as the weight of Stalinism pressed more and more heavily on the population. Simultaneously the Communist national enthusiasm was on the wane and anti-German clamors were kept down as Prague made preparations to embark on the Stalinist path of intensive industrialization.

After its take-over of Czechoslovakia in 1948, the Communist Party inaugurated a more moderate policy toward Hungarian and German groups. In 1948–49, the Prague cabinet issued two decrees enabling Germans to become Czechoslovak citizens if they applied individually for restitution of their citizenship. As these measures achieved only meager results, the new law of April 24, 1953, automatically granted citizenship to all persons of German nationality.[1] Clearly Prague sought to normalize its minority policy.

The cabinet issued instructions on April 12, 1951, encouraging Germans to apply for the return of their house properties, provided ownership had not been transferred to some other person. The tendency toward national moderation also found expression in the publication of a new German paper, *Aufbau und Frieden,* in September 1951. In 1954 a German theater group was set up and eventually some 60 cultural groups were established. A special fifteen-minute broadcast in German was introduced on Feb. 4, 1957. The special commissions for work among the citizens of German nationality, established under the various national committees in the regions with German inhabitants, took charge of German cultural activities. In 1953 German school circles for teaching the German language were introduced for German children at elementary schools. The Ministry of Education began to publish a German monthly, *Freundschaft,* for German schoolchildren.

With the grant of citizenship the Germans won back active and passive voting rights. Three Germans became members of the National Assembly at the election of 1954. Despite all these improvements, however, many German children lost their national consciousness. In later years, the process of "voluntary assimilation" was

1. There were 163,067 Germans in Czechoslovakia on Jan. 1, 1958. The bulk of the German population—157,908—lived in the Historic Provinces (State Statistical Office, *Statistická ročenka Republiky československé,* 1959, p. 59). For the texts of the decrees of May 6, 1948 and Nov. 29, 1949, and the new law, see *Dokumentation,* IV/1, 308 ff. According to the census of March 1, 1961, the number of German inhabitants dropped to 140,402 (*Demografie,* Jan. 1964, p. 83).

endorsed by the regime which used it as the explanation of its clearly discriminatory anti-German measures. While recognizing the existence of Hungarian, Polish, and Ukrainian groups, the new Constitution of 1960 failed to consider the Germans as an ethnic group. Stalinist leaders affirmed that there was no German minority in the Republic and that the German nationals enjoyed the same rights as all the other citizens.[2] No doubt the sharpening of the Berlin crisis made Communist policy increasingly harsh. The danger for Stalinist Prague lay in the fact that deplorable national oppression of the German group clearly played into the hands of the frustrated Sudeten leaders in the Federal Republic, who were provided with a telling political argument.

The mobilization of manpower brought about by forced industrialization shaped the lines for a resettlement of the former predominantly German borderland in a manner which had been quite successful in the larger cities and industrial areas. Because of the needs of industrialization, higher wages in industry, and the relative comforts of city life, the repopulation of the cities had proceeded at a quick pace. The move of labor from the countryside to the cities had been a logical result of the industrialization policies, which had left agriculture dangerously understaffed.[3] A shortage of agricultural labor and a general lack of interest in collectivized agriculture were the main causes of the depressed state of some agricultural areas in the borderland. As the resettlement problems reflected all the shortcomings of the slackening tempo of agricultural development, they pressed on the government with mounting intensity. The regime was committed by temperament, policy, and the imperatives of the Stalinist-type of industrialization to disregard agriculture.

It was the inauguration of the so-called New Course in 1953 that marked a turning point for the Prague resettlement policy. The party resolved to give more than lip service to the promotion of agriculture; hence farm resettlement enjoyed greater encouragement as part of a grand design to put agriculture into better shape. The new policy of resettlement in the depressed agricultural areas of the borderland was designed to bring the hitherto untilled lands to cultivation.

2. I have used the excellent article by Pavel Korbel, "Národnostní menšiny v Československu," *Československý přehled*, V (February 1958), 20–27. For the Communist point of view, see *Život strany (Party Life)*, 1960, pp. 770–71, 985–88; for the Sudeten German view, see Sudetendeutscher Rat, *Menschen vor dem Volkstod, passim.*

3. In the period 1949–55, some 222,000 persons left agriculture for better paid jobs in industry (Alois Rozehnal in *Československý přehled*, III, June 1956, 21).

At its meeting on Dec. 16, 1953, the Central Committee of the Communist Party of Czechoslovakia set up a special governmental commission aimed at coordinating and supervising problems connected with the situation in the borderland. The cabinet launched a campaign to win new labor forces for the area.[4] Although the measures brought about some degree of improvement, the regime was still unable—within the framework of its ill-advised agricultural policy—to grapple with the real problem: to crack the hard core of the shortage of agricultural labor. The young people were not offered enough incentives and failed to respond to party declamations. However, from 1953 Prague, being unable to afford the waste of tens of thousands of uncultivated hectares, moved toward a planned resettlement. Increased aid to employees working in agriculture, who were provided with newly renovated family houses and better public services, tended to spur the economic growth of the frontier areas.

The emphasis on the priority of the construction of heavy industry, the collectivization of agriculture, the currency reform of 1953, and other economic and social measures left the individual Czechoslovak citizen, with regard to immovable property, in substantially the same position as were the transferred Germans. Had the Germans not already been expelled, the economic orientation of the Communist policy would have disintegrated and wrecked their economic basis.[5]

Since the completion of the transfer, the Czechoslovak government, conditioned for so long to reactions to German challenges, had been expressing alarm over new Sudeten German efforts to inveigh against the integrity of the Republic and to form political organizations in the Western zones of Germany. The Czechoslovak will to forestall the repetition of the war events and to eliminate the potential centers of revanchism among the transferred Germans was made evident in a series of notes exchanged between the Prague Foreign Office and the United States Department of State dealing with propaganda efforts of the Sudeten Germans in the American Zone of Germany.[6] With the

4. In 1954 some 4,000 persons and in 1955 more than 6,000 persons moved to the 27 border districts (*ibid.*, p. 22). In the period 1954–63, 43,897 persons settled in the borderland and 13,123 persons left the border districts (*Rudé právo,* Jan. 12, 1964).

5. This is also the view of Miss Wiskemann (*Eastern Neighbours,* pp. 252, 256) and of P. Korbel (p. 21).

6. For the Czechoslovak notes of Oct. 6, Oct. 23, Dec. 6, Dec. 17, 1947, and the American replies—some of them by the American Military government in Germany—of Oct. 21, Nov. 8, Dec. 17, Dec. 22, 1947, see *Memorandum,* pp. 48–50; Ústav pro mezinárodní politiku a ekonomii, *Dokumenty československé zahraniční politiky 1945–1959,* pp. 375 ff.; hereafter cited as *Dokumenty.*

creation of the two German states in 1949, Prague started to echo more strongly the Soviet anti-Western line and to condemn the new West German state as the center of German militarism and Sudeten revanchism. The unchanged policy of the United States government was stated in its reply of Sept. 29, 1951, to the Czechoslovak note of Aug. 7, 1951. Washington reiterated its declaration of Nov. 8, 1947, which stated that the aim of the American authorities in Germany had been to achieve assimilation of the transferred Germans.[7]

Communist Prague marched side by side with the Ulbricht regime, which it recognized on Oct. 18, 1949. The provisional government of East Germany in its turn recognized "the transfer of the Germans from the Czechoslovak Republic as unchangeable, just and definitively settled" in the joint Prague declaration on June 23, 1950.[8] Prague went to great lengths to rationalize its new friendship by emphasizing that the East Germans were good democrats. This line of propaganda—accompanying a gradual improvement in the status of the remaining Germans—did not seem to make much impression on the Czech people, who were suspicious of any German rearmament, irrespective of whether the Germans were Communists or not.

The increasingly strident tones of the anti West German propaganda concealed a growing restless desire on the part of Prague to enter into commercial contacts with Bonn. To bolster its straining economy Czechoslovakia needed to keep up commercial contacts with the West, and by 1958 the Federal Republic was already her largest commercial partner outside of the Communist bloc.[9] While keeping alive the stern tone of its propaganda, Prague sought to accommodate Bonn with a series of unspectacular but not unimportant steps.

The removal of the Sudeten Germans to the United States Zone was made difficult by the demand voiced in the letter by Maj. Gen. G. P. Hays, on Nov. 3, 1948, that any transferred German had to be provided with a military entry permit. The Czechoslovak authorities

7. *Ibid.;* Voice of America, Sept. 29, 1951.
8. *Dokumenty*, p. 500. In its session of July 14, 1950, the German Federal Assembly declared the Prague agreement "invalid" and stated that "the Prague agreement is incompatible with the inalienable right of people to live in their own country. The German Federal Assembly solemnly protests against the resignation of the rights to their homeland of the Germans from Czechoslovakia who live under the protection of the Federal Republic" (Bundesministerium für Vertriebene, Flüchtlinge und Kriegsgeschädigte, *Vertriebenenproblem, Recht auf die Heimat und Selbstbestimmung im Deutschen Parlament* [*von 1949 bis Mitte 1960*], II, 33; hereafter cited as *Vertriebenenproblem*).
9. The Communist German Democratic Republic was the second largest commercial partner of Czechoslovakia.

reacted by allowing the Germans to cross the border illegally, without any immigration permit, and even by pushing them over the border into Bavaria.[10] On Oct. 26, 1949, the Bonn government applied to the Allied High Commission for the transfer of 20,000 Germans from Czechoslovakia in order "to reunite the persons . . . with their relatives who had become domiciled in West Germany as a result of the transfer." The agreement of Jan. 31, 1950, concluded between the Prague cabinet and the United States High Commission called for "the emigration from Czechoslovakia . . . of 20,000 persons of German ethnic origin."[11] A total of 16,832 Germans were removed up to April 28, 1951.[12] Particularly after the establishment of diplomatic relations between the Soviet Union and the Federal Republic in September 1955, many of the Germans sentenced after 1945 were released and most of them were permitted to move to West Germany. The most prominent among them was former Reich Protector Konstantin von Neurath[13] who had been released in 1954.

The embittered Sudeten leaders found themselves isolated in the middle of a postwar Germany saddled with her own urgent problems. The transfer no doubt generated a deep process of dislocation in the masses of the Sudeten Germans concentrated in West Germany. In view of the enormity of the tasks of resettlement in their new homeland, credit has to be given them for the courage and discipline with which they set about creating better living conditions. The economic boom of the Federal Republic played a large part in restoring confidence among the Sudeten Germans by removing economic and social strains and mitigating existing hardships. Simultaneously it accustomed many members of the rising generations to a new kind of life divorced from traditional settings and borderland psychology. The new prosperous environment tended to remove the traditional control mechanisms of nationalism.

The long-term implications for the Sudeten transferees have to be

10. *Dokumentation*, IV/2, 540–44; *Memorandum*, p. 14. After the German capitulation, there were 7,568 German war prisoners in charge of the Czechoslovak Army. On June 30, 1948, there still remained 4,655 prisoners, all of whom were reported to be released by Jan. 1, 1949 (*ibid.*).
11. *Dokumentation*, IV/1, 356–57.
12. *Ibid.*, p. 127. This stage of the transfer started on March 17, 1950.
13. The release of von Neurath was hailed by the highest political organ of the Sudeten expellees in a congratulatory cable. The cable called Neurath an "innocent victim." The official paper called him "a moderate element" and continued: "In the history of German-Czech relations there will not be forgotten the name of von Neurath as one of the men who have endeavored to achieve tolerance and final settlement" (*Sudetendeutsche Zeitung*, 1954; hereafter cited as SZ). Some 1,500 political prisoners were released and left for the Federal Republic (Sudetendeutscher Rat, *Justiz im Dienste der Vergeltung*, p. 7).

viewed in the context of the transformations which surrounded them. The texture of post-1948 West German society brought a change in the economic and social manners of the Sudeten Germans, a weakening of the traditional political pressures, a loosening of the old community ties, and a slackening of the pressures of economic necessity. For many Sudeten Germans the prospects of a return to Czechoslovakia entailed the abandonment of what they considered to be their true homeland, the Federal Republic. For all practical purposes, many Sudetens based their political and economic prospects on the existence of the West German state and weighed carefully all the advantages and benefits that accrued to them. In the final resort, there is no doubt that they would allow these considerations to outweigh and offset the prospects of a life in a now almost completely strange country, as was the Czechoslovak Republic.

However, notwithstanding the slow-moving social and psychological tendencies, the grinding persistence of the traditional outlook was brought to bear upon the average Sudeten German. The Sudeten leaders nursed the unhappy memory of their defeat, and the remembrances of the happenings of 1945-46 left a residue of personal bitterness. They sought to reconcile immediate needs with their long-range aims and to devise a program of action accordingly.

The first Sudeten German organizations on West German territory, which sprang up as early as the summer of 1945, were concerned with the realities of the urgent human situation of the refugees and expellees. As the bulk of the Germans from Czechoslovakia moved to the American Zone of Germany in 1946, it was evident that certain political grievances hitherto submerged would now be articulated. The traditional leaders moved again into positions of influence and power within the Sudeten group. Organizational media through which various political aims and grievances could find expression were created in 1947-49. Despite many personal and political divergences, the various groups voiced surprisingly similar interpretations of the past, blaming Czechoslovakia for almost all the post-1918 tragedies and crimes and crediting the Sudeten Germans with statesmanlike contributions toward securing peace and security in Central Europe up to 1945.[14]

The most important factions expressing discontent felt by broad

14. For surveys of the Sudeten German activities, see the thorough treatment by Eugen Lemberg—Friedrich Edding, ed., *Die Vertriebenen in Deutschland*, hereafter cited as *Die Vertriebenen;* Boris Čelovský, "The Transferred Sudeten Germans and Their Political Activity," *Journal of Central European Affairs,* XVII (July 1957), 127–49; Antonín Šnejdárek, "Počátky revanšistického 'Sudetoněmeckého krajanstva' v západním Německu," *Příspěvky k dějinám KSČ* (April 1962), pp. 192–206.

sections of the Sudeten Germans reflected Social Democratic, Catholic, and national tendencies. They formed three ideologically different groups: The Catholic Ackermann-Gemeinde, founded in 1946, united the Christian Democrats. (Although some of its members took an exceptionally moderate stand, the leaders around Hans Schütz gave indications of their hostility toward the Czechoslovak state.)[15] The Social Democratic Seliger-Gemeinde—established in 1951—was built upon the various organizations of Sudeten German Social Democrats created since 1946.[16] The national-minded Witiko Bund (WB) drew together the former members of the Kameradschaftsbund (KB), the Aufbruch Circle, and the Bereitschaft group. Most of the former prominent members of the Henlein Party became members of the WB.[17]

The Sudeten leaders realized that in order to become influential politically they had to unite all Sudeten Germans living in West Germany in one organization. In their minds, only such an organization would be able to draw the necessary attention to their political aims. It was against this background that the Association for the Protection of Sudeten German Interests (AG) was formed by Dr. Walter Becher, Hans Schütz, and Richard Reitzner in the summer of 1947. The goal of the AG was to represent the Sudeten interests in their efforts to establish their right to the Sudeten homeland and reparation. It claimed to be the highest Sudeten organ, as it was composed of representatives of all the political parties and the Sudeten German National Union; and it felt itself called into action to gain support at the international level. It published documentary materials and sought to cast itself in the role of spokesman for the whole group.

Because of friction between Dr. Rudolf Lodgman von Auen, who became a member in 1948 and aspired to almost dictatorial powers, and the other political representatives, the AG ceased functioning by

15. *Die Vertriebenen*, I, 526. The articles of the *Volksbote*, the organ of the Christian Democratic expellees, were indicative of the existing mood. For example, on Nov. 12, 1955: "The Czech attempt to form their own state was out of place in the twentieth century. . . . The small, talented and hard-working Czech nation found a better safeguard in the old Habsburg Empire than in the deceitful national state."

16. *Die Vertriebenen*, I, 563–64.

17. Georg Herde and Hans Maier, . . . *bis alles in Scherben fällt* . . . , pp. 5–33. Dr. W. Becher, Dr. W. Sebekowsky, Dr. F. Köllner, Ing. F. Karmasin, R. Sandner, K. Höss, F. Höller, F. Seiboth, Ing. R. Staffen, and other prominent Sudeten National Socialists belonged to the leadership of the WB. The WB claimed to have initiated the declaration of the Federal Assembly of July 14, 1950. The membership of the elite WB was reported to amount to 634 in 1959 (*ibid.*, p. 32).

November 1952. It was reorganized as the Sudeten German Council on April 3, 1955, which has remained the supreme body of the Sudeten German group on the international scene. Its task has consisted in the defense of the Sudeten right to their homeland on the basis of the principle of self-determination. The council is composed of three curiae with ten members each. One curia is appointed by the Sudeten German National Union, one by the representatives of the political parties, and one by cooptation. The council consists of a bureau, general assembly, chairman, secretariat, and financial committee. The real responsibility lies in a four-member bureau whose members rotate as chairman every six months.[18]

However, the real fulcrum of power has been the Sudeten German National Union (Sudetendeutsche Landsmannschaft; SL) representing Sudeten Germans around the world and claiming to have 350,000 members. The gradual easing of the American decree forbidding the formation of political groups and the appearance of a dynamic leader in the person of Dr. Rudolf Lodgman[19] broke the ground for the creation of the SL, harnessed together by national frustrations and by a leader who was able to bridge the divergences and thus enjoy political power far beyond anything he would have had by virtue of any party following.

Dr. Lodgman's bid for power was well prepared. In June 1948, 256 delegates of the various Sudeten groups met at Heppenheim. Dr. Lodgman delivered the main address, in which he reaffirmed the validity of the Munich agreement of 1938. He called for a revision of the status of 1945 and a new territorial settlement in Central Europe that would remove Czechoslovakia from the map. Under the impetus of the Heppenheim conference, concrete steps were taken toward the formation of the SL in 1950.

Elected speaker of the SL, Dr. Lodgman possessed enough authority to give the organization an authentic sense of purpose. A man of strong convictions, Dr. Lodgman clung to the old Central Europe of traditional attitudes and fierce nationalism exacerbated by pan-German dreams. His authoritarian manners and propensity for personal decisions aroused the ire of many Sudeten politicians. Yet it was Dr. Lodgman who devised and directed policies and inspired a wide range of projects. On May 1–2, 1954, he, as its undisputed head,

18. *Der Sudetendeutsche*, April 16, 1955; *Sudetendeutscher Artikeldienst*, April 16, 1955. Dr. R. Lodgman, R. Reitzner, H. Schütz, and Dr. J. Strosche became members of the bureau. Dr. Becher was elected its general secretary.

19. Dr. Lodgman was an old nationalist leader. (See above, pp. 37–38.) After 1945 he was transferred to the Soviet Zone of Germany. He moved to Bavaria in 1947 and died in December 1962 (*Die Vertriebenen*, I, 565).

presided over a reorganization of the SL which gave it a more democratic character. Its provincial unions elected 71 members of the assembly of the SL. Federal Minister Dr. Ing. Hans-Christian Seebohm[20] became its chairman. As its executive organ, a federal council was formed with Frank Seiboth[21] at its head. Dr. Lodgman was reelected speaker of the Sudeten Germans. In September 1959, when Dr. Lodgman withdrew from politics, Minister Seebohm became his successor.[22]

Once again, the defeat of 1945 and the ensuing events revealed the gulf between the reality and the dream. In 1945, many Sudeten German leaders were thoroughly disenchanted over their defeat. In their querulous and uneasy mood, most of them were less pained by the charges made by democratic public opinion than consumed by the frustrations that they felt.

The Sudeten masses were bound to respond to a program that promoted their hopes and restored their confidence. It might be that at that time new solutions could have been explored which might have involved scrapping some of the nationalist slogans. However, with their persistent insensitivity to past experiences, the Sudeten leaders adopted an almost absurd nationalist panacea by exhibiting disdain for the recent terrible occurrences. They took the measure of the forces at work and articulated their ideology and program in the worn-out terms of the Henlein provenience.

The tone of the Sudeten German leaders has grown tougher with the rising international prestige of the Federal Republic. Their first two program declarations displayed a careful modulation of the usual chorus of national exhortations. The more moderate Eichstätt declaration of Nov. 27, 1949, signed by prominent Christian Democratic, Social Democratic, and national leaders, asked for a return to the homeland "within the framework of an overall federal organization of Europe." The Detmold declaration of Jan. 24, 1950, represented a

20. Dr. Ing. Seebohm has been minister of Transport in all the federal cabinets since Sept. 20, 1949. Although he is not a Sudeten German (he was born in Upper Silesia on Aug. 4, 1903), his family owned lignite mines in Bohemia. He entered the Federal Assembly in Bonn as a representative of the right-wing German Party in 1949. Later, he joined the CDU. Seebohm's numerous pan-German utterances have aroused indignation in many countries. He advocated the recovery of the German frontiers of 1914 with the Sudetenland included (*The New York Times*, June 24, 1954).

21. Seiboth was head of NSDAP educational activities in the Sudetengau. A prominent member of the WB, he became head of the German Refugee Party and was a member of the Bonn Federal Assembly up to 1957.

22. There were many other organizations around the SL, such as the Sudeten German Youth, the Gymnastics Association, the Association of Sudeten German Educators, the Adalbert Stifter Association, and so on.

more radical claim by Dr. Lodgman and the SL. The Sudeten German national group as a "part of the German nation" was "aware of the common destiny with Germany" and stated that it

considers as its task preserving itself to the German nation . . . and the legal claim to its homeland, and bearing for the German nation its frontier experiences. . . . At any moment propitious to the regaining of its homeland, it wants to stand prepared to decide its future on its own responsibility.[23]

B. Čelovský rightly cites a telling observation: "As Professor Lehmann has pointed out, the moderate . . . Eichstätt declaration could be considered the program intended for consumption abroad, while the more abrupt nationalistic declaration from Detmold supplied the domestic program. The implication is clearly that Lodgman's openly worded program is not fully *salonfähig* abroad."[24]

The Sudeten declarations coincided with official German statements heralding a return to the Stresemann policy for the East. Although the West German cabinet claimed the frontiers of Dec. 31, 1937 (as they were defined by the Four Power declaration of June 5, 1945), and therefore gave its recognition to the Czechoslovak borders,[25] the preamble to the Federal Constitution of May 23, 1949, urged the entire German nation "to achieve the unity and freedom of Germany on the basis of self-determination." The right of self-determination was connected with the newly developed claim of a right to homeland expressed by the Charter of German Expellees, signed by the German expellee organizations in Stuttgart on Aug. 5, 1950.

The Federal government endorsed the right to homeland on the basis of the right of self-determination as its political principle (politisches Ordnungsprinzip).[26] Bonn thus devised a potential argument for its future East European policy.[27] The official policy of Bonn, however, has been sensible and remote from the radical declamations of the Sudeten leaders. It has been assumed by responsible Sudeten

23. Čelovský, "The Transferred," p. 135. For texts of the declarations, see *Dokumentensammlung*, pp. 127–29.
24. Čelovský, "The Transferred," p. 136.
25. *The New York Times*, May 5, June 11, 1951.
26. For the declaration by State Secretary Prof. Dr. Hallstein on May 28, 1956, see *Vertriebenenproblem*, p. 115. For the Charter, see *Dokumentensammlung*, pp. 15, 16. For the declaration of the Federal Assembly on Dec. 2, 1952, see *ibid.*, pp. 42–43.
27. Mention is nowhere found of the possible application of these principles to the western neighbors of Germany, such as Holland, France, Luxemburg, etc. These countries expelled their Germans without any international agreement in 1945.

politicians, however, that a future strong German state would endorse their aspirations. Their time schedule implied the existence of a definite plan to be carried out in three stages: First, the unification of West and East Germany; then, the recovery of the borders of 1937; and finally, a unified Germany which would solve the Sudeten German problem either by annexation or by the creation of a new Czech-Sudeten German federation. Slovakia would become an independent state.[28]

The Sudeten attitude displayed a tendency to revert to inflated statements and pompous clichés combined with a taste for saccharine pathos which blurred the facts and glossed over real issues while using the outward trappings of democracy. According to them, the Czechoslovak Republic remained the real culprit, in that it persecuted the Germans up to their liberation by Hitler in 1938. It was not Hitler who destroyed Czechoslovak democracy (which was described by Dr. Lodgman as an artificial product tending to disturb peace up to 1938).[29] "The first Czechoslovak Republic perished because of its contradictions."[30] The espousal of Nazism by the Sudeten Germans was explained away.

> Henleins Sammlung der Volksgruppe, seit 1935 Partei, war weder offensiv noch antidemokratisch—höchstens erstrebte sie Erweiterung der individuellen Menschenrechte durch demokratische Kollektivrechte. . . . Die breite Bewegung war so volkstreu wie menschheitsgläubig, so universell national wie reell sozial und konstruktiv europäisch—Europa sollte ein starkes Herz haben.[31]

The Nazi terror of the years 1938–45 was persistently passed over in silence, while the names of K. H. Frank and other prominent Nazis were published with full titles.[32] The Nazi occupation was depicted as

28. For the speeches at the Federal Assembly on Feb. 2, 1955, see *Vertriebenenproblem*, pp. 85–88. See also SZ, June 8, 1962; Wenzel Jaksch in *Die Brücke*, Sept. 19, 1959. Almost 100 Sudeten members of the Federal Assembly and provincial Diets affirmed on June 8, 1957: "Es besteht keine zwingende Veranlassung, die sudetendeutsche Frage ausschliesslich in dem Sinn zu erörtern, welches die rechtmässige Staatsgrenze zwischen der Tschechoslowakei und Deutschland heute ist. Diese Frage ist zumindest offen" (*Dokumentensammlung*, p. 137).
29. SZ, March 8, 1952.
30. Statement of the Sudeten members of the Federal Assembly in Bonn on June 7, 1952.
31. Prof. Herbert Cysarz (SZ, Nov. 10, 1951).
32. "Wohl nie hat eine in die Oberhand gelangte Volksgruppe die unterlegenen Nachbarn rechtlicher behandelt, man darf wohl sagen, anständiger behandelt, als die Sudetendeutschen ihre Anrainer seit 1938" (*ibid.*).

offering to the Czechs a "quiet life, all material awards" and providing "more favorable conditions for the biological development of the whole Czech nation."[33]

Through such distortions the Sudeten leadership sought the obfuscation of German understanding of the real situation in Czechoslovakia in the years 1933–45. This propaganda provided the framework for its major thematic emphasis, i.e., the Sudeten Germans were endowed with a right to return to their territories in the borders designated by Hitler in Munich and to obtain the restitution of their properties. They would resolve the future of the Sudetenland at a plebiscite.[34]

As for the final solution, there were essentially two main currents of opinion. One group advocated the fusion of the Sudetenland with the Federal Republic; another pleaded for federation between what amounted to the former Protectorate and the Sudetenland of 1938–39. The remainder of the Czech territory would be annexed by Germany and Austria.[35] On the whole, both groups espoused the Henleinist policy of 1938.[36]

The annual Sudeten rallies present solemn background for announcements of the objectives. On May 29, 1955, at the Nuremberg rally, Dr. Lodgman stated:

Almost all the Sudeten Germans welcomed the Munich Pact and today we refuse unequivocally to be ashamed of it. We salute, therefore, our liberation in 1938. Another question is whether it is possible for a state situated in the heart of Europe [Germany] to give up the implementation of the tasks which happened to have been those of the Holy Empire [of the German nation].[37]

At its meeting on Nov. 26–27, 1955, the Sudeten German council issued the policy lines for its future activities: (1) The nations and national groups in the area of Bohemia-Moravia-Silesia should accept

33. Alfred Bohmann in *Der Sudetendeutsche*, April 2, 1955.
34. This aim has been stated in numerous official declarations by the SL and the Sudeten Council (*Volksbote*, Dec. 5, 1955; *SZ*, April 27, 1957, May 13, 1961; *The New York Times*, May 18, 1959).
35. *SZ*, April 27, 1957; May 13, 1961. Dr. Franz Böhm in *SZ*, June 8, 1962. (See also *Der Sudetendeutsche*, Aug. 25, 1952.)
36. Dr. Lodgman declared in 1955: "Neither the West nor the East indicated any direct interest in the Sudeten Germans. At best, Moscow would agree upon their return to Czechoslovakia under the condition of the maintenance of the integrity of this state. The Sudeten Germans cannot display any interest in such a settlement" (*SZ*, Feb. 5, 1955). See also W. Jaksch, *Die Brücke*, May 30, 1959.
37. *SZ*, June 4, 1955. See also the article by Dr. R. Hilf, a former aide to Dr. Lodgman (*SZ*, Sept. 20, 1952).

a new federalist solution; (2) the Sudeten German council considered the Sudeten German problem as a German problem. A new settlement of the future of this vital area was urgently needed because of its importance for Europe.[38]

Gradually, however, it became evident to some of the leaders that at least for reasons of international propaganda the group had to renounce its Nazi past. Yet, when on May 7, 1961, the SL assembly discussed the draft of its Twenty-Point Program, a majority reaffirmed their espousal of the Munich pact. It was due only to the strong pressure of the SL Bureau that a slight majority vote was recorded in favor of the rejection of Munich.[39] The meeting reemphasized "the right of the Sudeten German ethnic group to return to its homeland." The Germans would determine the fate of their territory at a plebiscite in which they would decide whether they wanted fusion with the Federal Republic, independence, or autonomy within federalized Czechoslovakia. The speaker of the SL, Dr. Ing. Seebohm, called autonomy an "unsatisfactory solution" and articulated some details of the plebiscite. Not only those Sudeten Germans who were born or lived in the borderland but also their close relatives—even if these latter were born and lived in the Federal Republic—would be entitled to a vote. Those Czechs or Slovaks who had moved to the borderland after 1945 would be expressly denied the right to vote.[40] The official Sudeten German policy thus plainly evidenced an unwillingness to forget past tragedies and evoked serious misgivings among the Czechs.[41]

Since the end of the war, the Sudeten leaders have been determined to implement their plans. They have entered into alliances with former Fascist groups who actively supported Hitler. They have

38. *Volksbote*, Dec. 3, 1955.
39. SZ, May 13, 1961. For the text, see *Dokumentensammlung*, pp. 141–42.
40. SZ, March 31, 1961. According to the statutes of the SL from May 2, 1954, persons are also considered Sudeten Germans if they had one Sudeten parent or grandparent, married a Sudeten German partner, or lived a longer time in Czechoslovakia (*Dokumentensammlung*, p. 134). The Federal Expellees Law of May 19, 1953, classified children of expellees as expellees themselves (*ibid.*, p. 17). These claims were destined to keep alive the East German problem even after the death of all the expellees.
41. Dr. Franz Böhm, chairman of the SL Bureau, dispensed with the usual verbiage in his frank article in the SZ (June 8, 1962). He called for "the destruction of the fraudulent picture of Germany in the borders of 1937, because such a picture presented an inadequate basis for the conception of the German eastern policy, which had to be based on the pan-German program. . . . Not Hitler but the Treaty of Versailles was at the origin of the Second World War. . . . Because one could not be satisfied with the dangerous and unimaginative cliché of a Germany within the borders of 1937, it was necessary to find an all-German program as the basis of the new Eastern policy."

recognized the former leaders of the Slovak Fascist puppet regime as the spokesmen of Slovakia.[42] The Fascist Hungarian Arrow Cross, the Rumanian Iron Guard, the Croatian supporters of the Pavelić regime have all been greeted by the Sudeten leaders as their allies.[43]

All of these obscure groups have been selected to play a leading role in the Sudeten program of a new East Central Europe. The alliances have been regarded as a part of the "pioneering activity" of the Sudeten Germans in West Germany.[44] Although the Charter of the German Expellees of 1950 solemnly renounced all thoughts of revenge and retaliation, the Sudeten leaders have stated in the name of the AG that the Sudeten Germans "have a right, also, to reparation and to the punishment of the culprits."[45]

The experienced Sudeten politicians also played a prominent part in the West German expellee movement, which originally split into two main groups. One group, the Zentralverband der vertriebenen Deutschen (ZvD), led by Dr. Linus Kather, was mainly concerned with the improvement of the social and economic conditions of the refugees, while the second group, the Verband der Landsmann-schaften (VdL), engendered the support of nationalist elements and sought to articulate a program in terms of the right to homeland.[46] The Sudeten leaders lent their support to the VdL, which gradually gained preeminence. In 1958, both associations formed the Bund der Vertriebenen (BdV)[47] and thus overcame mutual tensions arising out of the differences of their tasks. The radical SL met some opposition among the national unions representing the expellees from within the German borders of 1937. The Sudeten leaders complained against the ensuing "split within the BdV into two camps."[48] As the spokesmen of

42. See Edo Friš in Historický ústav SAV, Nemecká otázka, pp. 180 ff.

43. The New York Times, Dec. 13, 1954; SZ, March 12, 1955. On Aug. 4, 1950, Dr. Lodgman, R. Reitzner, and H. Schütz signed with former Czech General Lev Prchala an agreement recognizing the return of the Germans to their homes. The agreement remained a dead letter. L. Prchala died in 1963.

44. Dr. Lodgman in Der Sudetendeutsche, May 21, 1955.

45. Turnwald, Documents, p. V; see also SZ, Aug. 20, 1955. The official program of May 7, 1961, expressly states: "We shall not forfeit our legitimate title to restoration of our rights violated by the expulsion, and of reparation for the damage sustained" (SZ, May 13, 1961). The sweeping changes of Czechoslovak society shifted the balance of social forces and made the idea of any restoration irrelevant and meaningless.

46. For more information, see Die Vertriebenen, I, 532–605. Franz Thedieck, state secretary in the Federal Ministry for All-German Affairs, described the aim of the SL and other national unions as "den Willen zu wecken und zu pflegen, jene heute von Fremden besetzten Gebiete für die deutsche Gemeinschaft zurückzugewinnen" (Der Sudetendeutsche, Aug. 23, 1952).

47. The expellees from Western Europe are not represented in the BdV.

48. Dr. F. Böhm in SZ, June 8, 1962.

the so-called foreign Germans (Auslandsdeutsche), the Sudeten Germans displayed in the BdV a discipline and experience which they had gained in their long struggle in the middle of a foreign territory.[49]

The rigidity of the Sudeten German policy did not meet with unanimous approval. There were a few Catholic and Social Democratic groups and many individuals who were ready to effect a real reconciliation and to explore new solutions. However, the framework of circumstances and the truly negative quality of the old nationalist conception have not allowed much opportunity for the formation of a Sudeten German democratic alternative. No evidence can be adduced to this effect, and even those very rare Czechoslovak exiles who have ventured to enter into contacts with the Sudeten leaders have been compelled to abandon their efforts. The Sudeten leadership, at once so immobile and so insensitive to all past defeats, followed the nationalist tradition.[50] Only the weight of time and the framework of a prosperous, self-asserting, dynamic, and forward-looking Europe may be able to soothe the old fears and create a new democratic consciousness and thus liberate the vast reservoir of Sudeten German abilities for more constructive tasks.

49. Sometimes the Sudeten Germans even tended to regard the inhabitants of the Federal Republic with suspicion (*Die Vertriebenen*, I, 598).
50. The strivings of the expellees have been supported by the so-called Ostforschung (Studies of East Europe). In 1961 there were some 65 institutions doing research in this area. For a Communist-biased but interesting survey, see Milan Myška, "Věda ve službách agrese," *Příspěvky k dějinám KSČ* (June 1962), pp. 391–409.

Conclusion

The observer who tries to understand German-Czech relations apart from their historical and geographical context often finds them unintelligible. For behind recent political crises lie many decades of Czech and German history which helped to shape their modern form. Central Europe has been a traditional ground of national conflicts. Despite the many human, economic, cultural, and geographical bonds between peoples who inhabit the same country, the struggle between the Czechs who lived in the Bohemian salient (thrust deep into the German territory) and the Germans, who came into Bohemia as colonists, has been a permanent feature of the history of this area.

The fall of Austria-Hungary and the foundation of the Czechoslovak Republic weighed heavily on the minds of the Germans when they suddenly lost their dominant position. The lack of a democratic political conception, the attrition of their younger generation, the lost war, and the existence of the new Republic under Czech leadership, helped to account for their frustrations and bitterness and their determination not to efface the idea of Greater Germany. They became part of the new state merely because of the outcome of the war and geopolitical and economic circumstances, since the independence of Czechoslovakia required the inclusion of predominantly German sections in her borders. The paradox was that the presence of the German minority was a condition of the existence of the independent Republic.

The Czechoslovak democratic system, built on a liberal and humanitarian tradition which prided itself on being able to settle national disputes, presented a unique chance for bringing about a more permanent solution of German-Czech strife. The framework of democracy made it certain that neither side could impose its will, and the working of the democratic process enhanced the chances of a peaceful settlement. The Locarno period provided an opportunity to launch a political and economic offensive among the Germans, since it imposed upon the Prague cabinet a cautious policy of compromise. It originated a psychological momentum which could have been used with maximum efficiency toward negotiating a German-Czech settlement. The Prague government, though it included three German members, had no long-range program to serve as a guide in its day-to-day policy. As a consequence, official activities vacillated between tempting the German Activists with offers of cooperation and taunting the Germans with petty annoyances.

The failure to set up and carry out adequate plans did not improve relations with the Germans, who were traditionally respectful of firm authority. By 1933 all the elements of the later fateful events were already present. Added to this, the economic crisis hit the state with devastating results. It became the immediate background for the rise of National Socialism in Germany. The crisis made the Western Powers more fearful of Communism, whose presence hung like a red shadow over all the vicissitudes of pre-Munich Europe. Again, the coming of the crisis coupled with the rise of Nazism transformed the situation in Czechoslovakia and awoke the latent forces of German nationalism. It gave impetus to the Henlein Party as embitterment seized the majority of the Sudeten Germans, who imputed their own distress to the democratic regime and to the mere existence of the Republic. Still living under the aegis of classical economic theory, the Prague cabinet was reluctant to envision a "New Deal" for the Germans. In view of their Great German past it was doubtful whether most Germans would have been reconciled to the Republic even by a far-reaching program of economic aid. Prague, however, could have strengthened enormously the democratic forces still in existence among the Germans.

National Socialism elicited a popular response among the Germans in Czechoslovakia. In a democratic election more than 85 percent of the Germans deliberately chose Nazism as represented by the Henlein Party, which finally emerged as an instrument of a regime predicated on the destruction of the democratic Republic. Pretending to act on behalf of the right of self-determination, the party, in cooperation with Berlin, secretly fomented civil strife. It attested the entire future of the Sudeten Germans and opened doors to Munich and the Nazi occupation. In voluntarily handing the decision over their destiny to Henlein and Hitler, the Germans of Czechoslovakia inevitably paved the road toward their own bitter end.

Through the intervention of Hitler, what was an internal problem, which could have been solved on its own merits, became a pretext for the Nazi Great German plans. Munich was a result of the transcendent character of the Sudeten German-Czech issue, which was deliberately woven into the expansionist objectives of Henlein and Hitler. Thus Munich became a question of war or peace. As such it was a matter of international concern for the Great Powers who gave little thought to the actual protagonists, the Czechs and Sudeten Germans. At this juncture only extraordinary courage could have met the extraordinary peril. But Prague let the initiative slip out of its hands when it failed to take energetic measures and to institute sweeping reforms in 1937. Its procrastination and lack of audacious leadership played into the hands of Chamberlain, whose policy of seeking to conclude the British-German agreement designed to bar Communism overlooked the real issue of power politics—the removal of the Czechoslovak barrier to the Nazi drive to the East. By taking the issue of the Sudeten German right of self-determination as the sole question, London made Hitler stronger and brought the outbreak of war closer.

An air of unreality rippled over the surface of Europe following the capitulation of the Prague cabinet and the Munich appeasement. Between the Czechs and the Sudeten Germans, however, the battle lines were drawn with greater clarity. What for the one was a struggle for a greater living space and a hegemonic position, was for the other a matter of life or death. The opposition of their aspirations coincided with the opposition of programs and ideologies. The dismemberment of the Republic in 1939 stripped bare the true issue of power politics. The Czechs, however, learned their lesson. Their rivals had used the democratic regime—which was a model of democracy and tolerance in Central and East Europe—to destroy the Republic and to wreck its democratic system. This abuse of democratic freedoms annihilated what remained of the possibilities of German-Czech cooperation, and left unbridged a no-man's-land between the two peoples. Henceforward a reconciliation became almost impossible.

With the outbreak of war, the Czech position hardened, supported as it was by powerful allies. Poignant reflections on Munich burdened the spirit of President Beneš and his followers at home and abroad when they scanned the war horizon. The principle "never again Munich" became the guiding light of the Czechoslovak foreign policy. It led directly to the alliance with Soviet Russia in 1943 and to the final settlement of the Sudeten question by transfer in 1945–46. What had so often been for the Czechs a struggle for their national existence reached its climax as the Nazis, under the prompting of the Sudeten leaders, prepared to exterminate the Czech nation.

No nation could erase from its memory the threat of its own physical destruction. The psychology of the Czech people was conditioned by a series of physical and spiritual shocks suffered during the Nazi rule. The staggering terror and the imminent danger of Germanization made the Czechs determined not to risk a repetition of the attempt to disrupt their state and to menace their national existence. In the acute circumstances of the struggle for survival, the heart of the Sudeten German question was no longer a problem of momentarily restraining a hostile party, but of dispossessing it forever. The Czechoslovak Resistance movement at home and the exile government formulated and proposed the idea of a transfer of the disloyal majority of the German group to Germany as a necessary measure of protection, not of punishment. President Beneš was firmly resolved on the removal of the Germans even at the price of the cession of some fragments of the Czechoslovak territory. The horror, savagery, and brutality of the Nazi regime which had held the country in bondage during the war helped to create a favorable terrain for the acceptance of the principle of the transfer by the Great Powers. But the real impetus toward the transfer was supplied by the Czech people at home. The comprehensive reappraisal of the minority policy to tackle the Sudeten problem at its roots was endorsed by all the Czechoslovak political leaders. The transfer presented a new approach toward its definitive settlement. It was felt that it was the price to be paid as a guarantee of the independent existence of the Czechoslovak state.

As the last act of the long German-Czech dispute, the transfer was a response to circumstances created by the Sudeten Germans themselves and implicit in the Nazi war regime. It was an immensely popular move carried forward by the Czech masses and at the outset accompanied by the deplorable irregularities which are part of all similar revolutionary outbursts. Despite some initial uneasiness in the Western world over its moral character, it was finally agreed upon by all the Great Powers. Its alternative seemed to be far worse: civil war, political chaos, and chronic insecurity in Central Europe. Being neither Communist nor Soviet inspired, the transfer was a corollary of the Allied anti-Nazi policy and the war population movements. On the whole, however, the organized transfer was carried out decently, in a humane way. The German anti-Fascists were exempted and enjoyed full individual rights with other citizens.

In the final historical analysis, the issue between two contending groups cannot be reduced to a simple question of moral values, for in every issue there are also innumerable other forces involved, forming an inseparable part of the complex problem. There are no perfect solutions for the great problems of today. The existence of the Czech people and the independence of their state were considered important enough to Europe and to the peace structure of the world to be protected even at the expense of such a hard measure as the evacuation of the German minority.

The ultimate settlement laid a foundation for reconciliation, close cooperation, and lasting friendship between democratic Germany and a Czechoslovakia freed from the nightmare of the internal peril. The Czechoslovak people would not need to feel menaced any more by the Sudeten fifth column and the German extremists would find no encouragement for their pan-German plans in the existence of the German minority in the Republic. The powerful element which by its sheer presence had barred any regeneration of the relations between the German and Czechoslovak states was removed and the path toward mutual amity and friendly association was laid wide open. The words of Sudeten German Deputy Hans Krebs before the People's Court on Jan. 15, 1947, indicated a way for the future cooperation of Czechs and Germans.

In this moment a full thousand years of a common, hard, but also great, historic period are closing. The Czech Nation will now, at the last, live alone in its national State, which not only in name, but also in fact is really becoming a national State. Three million Germans have been transferred. This is the greatest transfer since the migration of nations. . . . Nearly one-third of the population of Bohemia, Moravia and Silesia have left or are leaving their old homes. They are leaving behind their homes, what they once called their property, their past and their dead. They are leaving the work of millions and the work of many centuries, never to return. It is hard for anybody who has not gone through it to measure the moral and spiritual burden we are bearing now. . . . From this time you will have no more nationality disputes in your country. I only wish that the great sacrifices we are making may not be without profit, but that from them there may at last be born a peaceful fellowship between us—which, alas, we did not succeed in establishing in one State—namely, the fellowship of the German State and the Czech State which will again be neighbours in the future. . . .

May the separation of Germans and Czechs finally bring peace to both! May the sufferings of our time end our sufferings for all time! Only so will all these immeasurable sacrifices have any meaning which we Sudeten Germans must now make and which the Czechs also have had to make in so great a measure. They will have served the highest ideal of mankind—a lasting and honourable peace.[1]

It is up to the rising generations of both nations to implement this profession of faith.

1. Beneš, *Memoirs*, pp. 223–24.

APPENDIX

GERMAN AREAS OF SETTLEMENT WITHIN BOHEMIA AND MORAVIA - SILESIA[1]

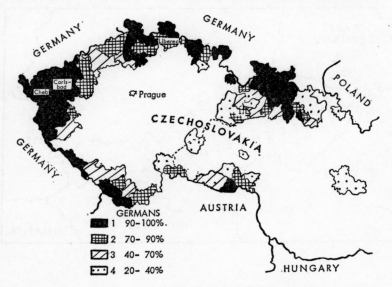

GERMANS
1 90-100%.
2 70- 90%
3 40- 70%
4 20- 40%

[1]The map is based on census of 1930. J. Chmelař, Le problème allemand en Tchécoslovaquie.

TERRITORIES SEPARATED FROM THE CZECHOSLOVAK REPUBLIC AFTER THE PACT OF MUNICH IN 1938[1]

territory ceded to the Reich
territory ceded to Hungary
territory ceded to Poland

[1]German-Czechoslovak border of November 20, 1938.

TERRITORY OF CZECHOSLOVAKIA IN 1945

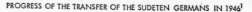

PROGRESS OF THE TRANSFER OF THE SUDETEN GERMANS IN 1946[1]

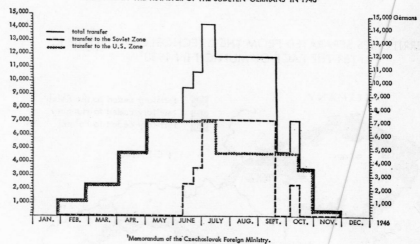

[1]Memorandum of the Czechoslovak Foreign Ministry.

NUMBER OF GERMAN INHABITANTS of the HISTORIC PROVINCES of CZECHOSLOVAKIA (December 31, 1946)*

REGION	1 Number of Germans in 1930	2 Number of Germans on Nov. 1, 1946	3 German experts with special protection card	4 Members of their families	Breakdown of the Total of Column 2						
					5 Germans with provisory certificate of citizenship	6 Germans in mixed marriages	7 Germans of Jewish origin	8 Germans permitted to stay	9 Germans with a postponement of their transfer	10 German Anti-Fascists asking for transfer	11 Germans subjected to transfer
Č. Budějovice	171,162	14,446	1,009	1,611	985	2,179	59	292	1,038	2,234	5,085
Liberec	457,719	43,889	9,066	12,612	2,168	6,448	227	320	626	3,162	9,260
Litoměřice	547,197	40,294	5,582	7,983	1,245	7,474	435	827	877	4,184	9,808
Carlsbad	461,674	50,609	11,188	18,399	2,503	1,469	117	142	1,551	7,298	7,092
Pardubice	55,167	3,900	15	26	213	916	1	270	312	320	1,827
Pilsen	201,187	14,674	906	2,169	588	1,807	32	259	343	949	7,608
Prague	50,616	4,696	30	28	645	944	621	121	75	3	2,385
Trutnov	184,516	17,049	2,592	4,456	1,183	1,580	23	424	210	4,357	2,226
Žatec	141,806	11,426	718	1,005	586	1,572	21	243	138	1,264	5,779
Brno	259,468	10,231	147	230	1,031	2,873	115	619	49	130	5,037
Olomouc	223,630	10,186	867	1,565	1,146	2,652	50	407	621	332	2,546
Opava	229,744	11,023	881	1,977	553	1,675	97	249	600	374	4,646
Ostrava	82,222	7,488	536	1,042	199	1,466	78	178	60	292	3,637
Bohemia		200,983	31,106	48,289	10,116	24,389	1,536	2,898	5,170	23,771	51,070
Moravia-Silesia		38,928	2,431	4,814	2,929	8,666	340	1,453	1,330	1,128	15,866
TOTAL	3,066,108	239,911 -15,000ª	33,537	53,103	13,045	33,055	1,876	4,351	6,500	24,899 -6,000ª	66,936 -19,000ª
TOTAL	3,066,108	224,911	33,537	53,103	13,045	33,055	1,876	4,351	6,500	18,899	47,936

*Memorandum of the Czechoslovak Foreign Ministry, p. 12. ª Some 10,000 German wives of Czech nationals (out of the total number of 14,000 to 15,000) were not included in the number of Germans listed as partners in mixed marriages. In November 1946, about 19,000 Germans were transferred and about 6,000 anti-Fascists emigrated.

NUMBER OF TRANSFERRED GERMANS AFTER THE
END OF THE MAIN STAGE OF THE TRANSFER*

	1947		1948		1949
	American Zone	Soviet Zone	American Zone	Soviet Zone	
January	59	1	223	543	
February	80	–	201	88	
March	74	1149	301	15	
April	123	1223	215	61	
May	187	9	208	55	
June	220	38	102	55	
July	402	79	382	73	
August	318	–	263	58	
September	185	–	185	147	
October	272	22	259	1506	
November	184	18	212	1045	
December	235	–	400	1349	
TOTAL	2339	2539	2951	4995	

Provisional number of Germans
who either were transferred or
moved voluntarily to Germany
in the period Jan. 1 -- June 15, 1949   5303

*Memorandum of the Czechoslovak Foreign Ministry, p. 13.

Bibliography[1]

Manuscripts and Unpublished Documents

Centre de documentation juive contemporaine, Paris. "Die Endlösung der europäischen Judenfrage" (CXXXVIIIa–72, 74).

[Czechoslovak Ministry of Foreign Affairs]. "Memorandum on the transfer of the Sudeten Germans." (In possession of this writer.)

The Library of Congress. Manuscript Division. "The Deutsches Auslandsinstitut Collection" (Containers nos. 3, 93, 94, 131, 137).

———. "The Rehse Collection" (Containers nos. 463–68).

———. "The Anton Schäfer Papers" (Containers nos. 686–87).

———. "The Fritz Wiedemann Papers" (Containers nos. 578, 604).

———. "The Reich Government Items" (Container no. 468).

National Archives of the United States. *Records of the German Foreign Ministry*. Captured German Documents (Containers nos. 2443–44).

———. "The Himmler Files." In the Custody of the Military Records Branch, Federal Records Center, Region 3, General Services Administration, Alexandria, Va. Record Group 1010.

———. "Records of the NSDAP." Record Group 1035.

Němec, František. "Private Papers." Montreal, Canada.

1. The following bibliography does not claim to be complete, as I have hesitated to list all the material I have explored on the subjects discussed in this book. This would have made a much longer list which seems already, as it is, too long. I have, however, tried to list most of the sources which the reader will find in the text.

YIVO Institute for Jewish Research. New York. "The Reichssicher-heitshauptamt Files" (Occ. E7, a-5).
———. "The Collection of Documents of the Reich Ministry for Propaganda" (Occ. E7, a-4.

Published Documents

Anklageschrift gegen die Abgeordneten und Senatoren der Sudeten-deutschen Partei (SdP). Munich, 1962.
Berber, Friedrich, ed. *Europäische Politik 1933–1938 im Spiegel der Prager Akten.* Essen, 1942.
Bundesministerium für Vertriebene, Flüchtlinge und Kriegsgeschä-digte. *Vertriebenenproblem, Recht auf die Heimat und Selbst-bestimmung im Deutschen Parlament (von 1949 bis Mitte 1960).* Bonn, 1960.
Carnegie Endowment for International Peace. *International Concilia-tion. The Crisis in Czechoslovakia, April 24–October 13, 1938.* New York, 1938.
Congressional Record, 83d Congress, 1st Sess., pp. A2284 ff., A5796 ff.
———. 84th Congress, 1st. Sess., pp. A2702 ff.
———. 85th Congress, 2d Sess., pp. A3627 ff.
[Czechoslovak] Ministry of Information. *Československo a norim-berský proces. Hlavní dokumenty norimberského procesu o zločinech nacistů proti Československu* (Czechoslovakia and the Nuremberg Trial. Principal Documents of the Nuremberg Trial for Nazi Crimes against Czechoslovakia). Prague, 1946.
———. *Český národ soudí K. H. Franka* (K. H. Frank on Trial be-fore the Czech Nation). Prague, 1946.
———. *Zpověď K. H. Franka. Podle vlastních výpovědí v době vazby u krajského soudu trestního na Pankráci* (Confession of K. H. Frank. According to His Own Depositions at the Regional Criminal Court at Pankrác). Prague, 1946.
[Czechoslovak] Ministry of the Interior. *Lidice. Čin krvavého teroru i porušení zákonů a základních lidských práv* (Lidice. Act of Terror and Violation of Laws and Basic Human Rights). Prague, 1946.
———. *Persekuce českého studentstva za okupace* (Persecution of Czech Students during the Occupation). Prague, 1946.
Documents on American Foreign Relations. VII: July 1944–June 1945. Ed. by Leland M. Goodrich, and Marie J. Carroll; VIII: July 1, 1945–December 31, 1946. Ed. by Raymond Dennett and Rob-ert K. Turner. Boston, 1947–48.
Documents on British Foreign Policy, 1919–1939. Ed. by E. L. Wood-

ward and Rohan Butler. Third Series, vols. I–III: 1938–1939. London, 1949–1950.

Documents on the Expulsion of the Sudeten Germans. Ed. by Wilhelm K. Turnwald. Munich, 1953.

Documents on German Foreign Policy, 1918–1945, from the Archives of the German Foreign Ministry. Series C (1933–1937). *The Third Reich: First Phase.* Vol. I: Jan. 30–Oct. 14, 1933; vol. II: Oct. 15, 1933–June 13, 1934; vol. III: June 14, 1934–March 31, 1935; Vol. IV: April 1, 1935–March 4, 1936. London, 1957–63.

———. Series D (1937–1945). Vol. I: *From Neurath to Ribbentrop* (September, 1937–September, 1938); vol. II: *Germany and Czechoslovakia* (1937–1938); vol. IV: *The Aftermath of Munich* (October, 1938–March, 1939). Washington, 1949–51.

Documents on Germany under Occupation 1945–1954. Ed. by Beate Ruhm von Oppen. London, 1955.

Documents on International Affairs for 1934–50. London, 1935–54.

Dokumente der deutschen Politik. Ed. by Paul Meier-Benneckenstein. Vol. V: *Von der Grossmacht zur Weltmacht, 1937.* By Hans Volz; vol. VI: *Grossdeutschland 1938.* By Hans Volz; vol. VII: *Das Werden des Reiches 1939.* By Hans Volz. Berlin, 1938–40.

Dokumentensammlung zur Sudetenfrage. Ed. by Fritz Peter Habel. Munich, 1962.

Dokumenty o protilidové a protinárodní politice T. G. Masaryka (Documents on Anti-People and Anti-National Policy of T. G. Masaryk). Ed. by František Nečásek, Jan Pachta, Eva Raisová. Prague, 1953.

Les événements survenus en France de 1933 à 1945. Témoignages et documents recueillis par la Commission d'enquête parlementaire. 9 vols.—*Rapport de M. Charles Serre, député, au nom de la Commission d'enquête parlementaire.* 2 vols. Paris, 1947 ff.

Foreign Relations of the United States. Diplomatic Papers. 1938. Vol. I: *General.* Washington, 1955.

———. *The Conference at Malta and Yalta 1945.* Washington, 1955.

———. *The Conference of Berlin 1945.* 2 vols. Washington, 1960.

Holborn, Louise W. ed. *War and Peace Aims of the United Nations* Vol. I: Sept. 1, 1939–Dec. 31, 1942; vol. II: Jan. 1, 1943–Sept. 1, 1945. Boston, 1943, 1948.

House Committee on the Judiciary. *Report no. 1841,* 81st Congress, 2d Session.

House Report, 83d Congress, 2d Sess., no. 2684.

Hungarian Ministry for Foreign Affairs. *Hungary and the Conference of Peace.* Vol. II: *Hungary's International Relations before the*

Conference of Paris; vol. IV: *Hungary at the Conference of Paris.* Budapest, 1947.

Institut für Internationale Politik und Oekonomie—Historisches Institut der Tschechoslowakischen Akademie der Wissenschaften. *Die Vergangenheit warnt. Dokumente über die Germanisierungs- und Austilgungspolitik der Naziokkupanten in der Tschechoslowakei.* Ed. by Dr. Václav Král. Prague, 1960.

International Military Tribunal. *Trial of the Major War Criminals before the International Military Tribunal, Nuremberg, 1945–46.* 42 vols. Nuremberg, 1947–49.

Král, Václav, ed. *Politické strany a Mnichov* (Political Parties and Munich). Prague, 1961.

Military Governor of Germany. *Monthly Report of the Military Governor U. S. Zone* (In October, 1946, changed to *Bimonthly Review*). U. S. Zone, 1945–47.

The Ministry for Foreign Affairs of the Czechoslovak Republic and the Ministry for Foreign Affairs of the Union of Soviet Socialist Republics. *New Documents on the History of Munich.* Prague, 1958.

Ministry of Foreign Affairs of the USSR. *Documents and Materials Relating to the Eve of the Second World War.* 2 vols. Moscow, 1948.

Mnichov v dokumentech (Munich in Documents). 2 vols. Prague, 1958.

Nazi Conspiracy and Aggression. 8 vols. Washington, 1946–47.

Německý imperialismus proti ČSR (1918–1939) (German Imperialism against the Czechoslovak Republic). Prague, 1962.

Orlík Josef ed. *Opavsko a severní Morava za okupace* (The Region of Opava and Northern Moravia during the Occupation). Ostrava, 1961.

Senate Document, 81st Congress, 1st Sess., no. 123.

Štěpán, František, ed. "Nové dokumenty o protičeskoslovenských plánech dnešních revanšistů z let 1938–1939" (New Documents on Anti-Czechoslovak Plans of Today's Revanchists from 1938–1939), *Příspěvky k dějinám KSČ* (December, 1961), pp. 326–39.

Těsnopisecké zprávy o schůzích poslanecké sněmovny Národního shromáždění republiky Československé, IV. volební období (Stenographic Reports on Meetings of the Chamber of Deputies of the Czechoslovak National Assembly. IV. Electoral Period). Prague, 1935–38.

Těsnopisecké zprávy o schůzích Prozatímního Národního

shromáždění republiky Československé (Stenographic Reports on Meetings of the Provisional National Assembly of the Czechoslovak Republic). Prague, 1946.

Těsnopisecké zprávy o schůzích Ústavodárného Národního shromáždění republiky Československé (Stenographic Reports on Meetings of the Constituent Assembly). Prague, 1947.

Tisky k těsnopiseckým zprávám o schůzích Prozatímního Národního shromáždění republiky Československé (Printed Matters Appended to the Stenographic Reports on Meetings of the Provisional National Assembly of the Czechoslovak Republic). Prague, 1946.

Tisky k těsnopiseckým zprávám o schůzích Ústavodárného Národního shromáždění republiky Československé (Printed Matters Appended to the Stenographic Reports on Meetings of the Constituent National Assembly). Prague, 1946–47.

Trials of War Criminals before the Nuremberg Military Tribunal under Control Council Law No. 10. 15 vols. Nuremberg, 1946–49.

Ústav pro mezinárodní politiku a ekonomii. *Dokumenty československé zahraniční politiky 1945–1960* (Documents on the Czechoslovak Foreign Affairs, 1945–1960). Prague, 1960.

Zločiny nacistů za okupace a osvobozenecký boj našeho lidu (Nazi Crimes during the Occupation and the Struggle of Liberation of Our People). Prague, 1961.

Books

Adler, H. G. *Theresienstadt 1941–1945. Das Antlitz einer Zwangsgemeinschaft. Geschichte, Soziologie, Psychologie.* Tübingen, 1955.

American Friends of Democratic Sudetens. *Tragedy of a People. Racialism in Czecho-Slovakia.* New York, 1946.

American Jewish Committee. *American Jewish Year Book, 1946–47.* Philadelphia, 1946.

Amort, Čeněk. *Partyzáni na Podbrdsku* (Partisans in the Region below Brdy). Prague, 1958.

[Anon.] *Endlich Befreit! Sudetendeutsche Jugend erzählt von der Befreiung ihrer Heimat.* Reichenberg, 1939.

App, J. Austin. *History's Most Terrifying Peace.* San Ambrosio, Texas, 1946.

Avon, The Earl of. *The Eden Memoirs. Facing the Dictators.* London, 1962.

Bareš, Gustav. *Klement Gottwald—muž proti Mnichovu* (Klement Gottwald—Man against Munich). Prague, 1946.

Barton, Betty. *The Problem of 12 Million German Refugees in To-day's Germany.* Philadelphia, 1949.

Bartošek, Karel. *Pražské povstání 1945* (Uprising in Prague, 1945). Prague, 1960.

Basch, Antonín. *Germany's Economic Conquest of Czechoslovakia.* Chicago, 1941.

———. *The Danube Basin and the German Economic Sphere.* New York, 1943.

Battaglia, Otto Forst de. *Zwischeneuropa. Von der Ostsee bis zur Adria.* Part 1. Frankfurt a. Main, 1953.

Beckmann, Rudolf. *K diplomatickému pozadí Mnichova. Kapitoly o britské mnichovské politice* (On the Diplomatic Background of Munich. Chapters about the British Policy of Munich). Prague, 1954.

Bednář, F. *The Transfer of Germans.* Prague, 1948.

Beloff, Max. *The Foreign Policy of Soviet Russia 1929–1941.* 2 vols. London, 1952.

Benčík Antonín et al. *Partyzánské hnutí v Československu za druhé světové války* (Partisan Movement in Czechoslovakia during World War II). Prague, 1961.

Beneš, Eduard [An Active and Responsible Czechoslovak Statesman]. *Germany and Czechoslovakia.* 2 vols. Prague, 1937.

———. *Memoirs of Dr. Eduard Beneš. From Munich to New War and New Victory.* Boston, 1954.

———. *Mnichovské dny* (Days of Munich). London, 1955.

———. *Projev presidenta republiky na staroměstském náměstí v Praze dne 16. května 1945* (Address of the President of the Republic at the Old Town Square in Prague). Prague, 1945.

———. *Šest let exilu a druhé světové války. Řeči, projevy a dokumenty z r. 1938–45* (Six Years of Exile and World War II. Speeches, Addresses and Documents). Prague, 1946.

———. *The Struggle for the Liberation of the Republic and the Rehabilitation of the State. Message . . . Delivered to the Provisional National Assembly, October 28, 1945.* Prague, 1945.

———. *The Way to Victory.* London, 1942.

———. *What Would Be a Good Peace.* London, 1943.

Beneš, Vojta. *The Vanguard of the "Drang nach Osten."* Chicago, 1943.

Betts, R. R., ed. *Central and South East Europe 1945–48.* London, 1950.

Beuer, Gustav–Blatny, Fanny–Zinner, Josef. *Gemeinsamer Weg— Gemeinsames Ziel! Reden auf der gemeinsamen Konferenz der deutschen Sozialdemokraten und Kommunisten aus der Tsche-choslowakei am 27. und 28. Jänner 1945.* London, 1945.

Beuer, Gustav. *New Czechoslovakia and Her Historical Background.* London, 1947.

Bílek, B. *Fifth Column at Work.* London, 1945.

Bischoff, Ralph F. *Nazi Conquest Through German Culture.* Cambridge, Mass., 1942.

Black, C. E., ed. *Challenge in Eastern Europe.* New Brunswick, N. J., 1954.

Blažek, Miroslav. *Hospodářská geografie Československa* (Economic Geography of Czechoslovakia). Prague, 1954.

Bohemicus. *Czechoslovakia and the Sudete Germans.* Prague, 1938.

Bohmann, Alfred. *Die Ausweisung der Sudetendeutschen dargestellt am Beispiel des Stadt- und Landkreises Aussig.* Marburg, 1955.

———. *Die Entvölkerung der Sudetenländer als Folge der Auswei-sung der sudetendeutschen Volksgruppe.* Troisdorf bei Köln, 1951.

———. *Das Sudetendeutschtum in Zahlen.* Munich, 1959.

Bolton, Glorney. *Czech Tragedy.* London, 1955.

Bonnet, Georges. *Défense de la paix.* vol. 1: *De Washington au Quai d'Orsay.* Geneva, 1946.

Borovička, J. *Ten Years of Czechoslovak Politics.* Prague, 1929.

Brand, Walter. *Die sudetendeutsche Tragödie.* Lauf near Nürnberg, 1949.

———. *Von der inneren Struktur der sudetendeutschen Volksgruppe.* Frankfurt a. Main, 1953.

Brown, MacAlister. "Expulsion of German Minorities from Eastern Europe: The Decision at Potsdam and Its Background." Unpublished Ph.D. thesis, Harvard University, Cambridge, Mass., 1953.

Brügel, J. W. *Ludwig Czech. Arbeiterführer und Staatsmann.* Vienna, 1960.

Buben, Václav, ed. *Šest let okupace Prahy* (Six Years of the Occupation of Prague). Prague, 1946.

Buk, Pierre [Weisskopf, F. C.]. *La tragédie tchécoslovaque. De sep-tembre 1938 à mars 1939. Avec des documents inédits du Livre blanc tchécoslovaque.* Paris, 1939.

Bullock, Alan. *Hitler. A Study in Tyranny.* New York, 1952.

Bundesministerium für gesamtdeutsche Fragen. *Die Bevölkerungs-bilanz der sowjetischen Besatzungszone 1939 bis 1949.* Bonn, 1951.

Byrnes, James F. *Speaking Frankly.* New York, 1947.

Campbell, John C., ed. *The United States in World Affairs 1945–1947.* New York, 1947.

Cannac, R. *La Tchécoslovaquie.* Paris, 1938.

Čapek, Karel. *Hovory s T. G. Masarykem* (President Masaryk Tells His Story). New York, 1951.

Carey, Jane Perry Clark. *The Role of Uprooted People in European Recovery.* Washington, 1948.

Celovsky, Boris. *Das Münchener Abkommen 1938.* Stuttgart, 1958.

César, Jaroslav–Černý, Bohumil. *Od sudetoněmeckého separatismu k plánům odvety* (From Sudeten German Separatism to the Plans of Revenge). Liberec, 1960.

——. *Politika německých buržoazních stran v Československu v letech 1918–1938* (Policy of German Bourgeois Parties in Czechoslovakia in the Years 1918–1938). 2 vols. Prague, 1962.

Československý studijní ústav. *Hospodářské následky Mnichova* (Economic Consequences of Munich). 2 vols. London, 1942.

Charléty, S. *Tchécoslovaquie.* Paris, 1940.

Chmela, Leopold. *The Economic Aspect of the German Occupation of Czechoslovakia.* Prague, 1948.

——. *Hospodářská okupace Československa. Její metody a důsledky* (Economic Occupation of Czechoslovakia. Its Methods and Consequences). Prague, 1946.

Chmelař, Josef. *The German Problem in Czechoslovakia.* Prague, 1936.

Ciller, A. *Deutscher Sozialismus in den Sudetenländern und der Ostmark.* Hamburg, 1943.

Císař, Jaroslav. *The Role of Czechoslovakia.* London, 1944.

Clay, Lucius D. *Decision in Germany.* Garden City, N. Y., 1950.

Cobban, Alfred. *National Self-Determination.* London, 1945.

Collegium Carolinum. *Bohemia. Jahrbuch des Collegium Carolinum.* 2 vols. Munich, 1960, 1961.

——. *Dr. Walter Brands Aufzeichnungen vom 21. Juni 1958.* Archiv, No. 203.

——. *Walter Schmidts Aufzeichnungen vom 3. Juni 1958.* Archiv, No. 202.

——, ed. *Die Sudetenfrage in europäischer Sicht.* Munich, 1962.

Columbia Broadcasting System. *Crisis—A Report from the Columbia Broadcasting System.* New York, 1938.

Craig, Gordon A.–Gilbert, Felix, ed. *The Diplomats 1919–1939.* Princeton, N. J., 1953.

Czechoslovak Consulate General at New York. *Agreement between the Czechoslovak Government and the Germans Concerning Minority Policy.* New York, 1937.

————. *The Proposals of the Sudeten German Party in Czechoslovakia. Why They Are Put Forward.* New York, 1937.

Czechoslovak Documents and Sources. *German Imperialism and Czechoslovakia. Analysis of a Speech by K. H. Frank.* London, 1943.

————. *German Minorities—Spearhead of Nazism. Henlein's Deceit.* London, 1943.

Czechoslovak Information Service. *Speeches of Jan Masaryk in America.* New York, 1942.

————. *President Beneš on War and Peace. Statements by Beneš during His Visit to the United States and Canada in May and June 1943.* New York, 1943.

Czechoslovak Ministry of Foreign Affairs. *Czechoslovakia in Postwar Europe. Problems of Reconstruction.* London, 1943.

————. *On the Reign of Terror in Bohemia and Moravia under the Regime of Reinhard Heydrich.* London, 1942.

————. *Four Fighting Years.* London, 1943.

————. *Czechoslovakia Fights Back.* Washington, 1943.

[Czechoslovak Ministry of Information]. *Czechoslovakia, Old Culture and New Life.* Prague, 1947.

————. *Czechoslovakia.* Prague, 1947.

————. *Czechoslovakia.* Prague, 1953.

Czechoslovak Sources and Documents. *The Problems of Czechoslovakia. Speeches of the President of the Republic, Dr. Edvard Beneš, in Northern Bohemia.* Prague, 1936.

————. *Czechoslovak Cabinet Ministers on the Complaints of the Sudete German Party in the Czechoslovak Parliament.* Prague, 1937.

[Czechoslovak State Statistical Office]. *Annuaire statistique de la république tchécoslovaque.* Prague, 1932–38.

————. *Statistická ročenka Republiky československé 1959* (Statistical Yearbook of the Czechoslovak Republic). Prague, 1959.

The Department of State. *Occupation of Germany. Policy and Progress 1945–46.* Washington, 1947.

Deubner, Karl August. *Der Politiker Konrad Henlein. Schöpfer der sudetendeutschen Einheit.* Bad Fürth bei München, 1938.

Deutsche Bank. *Das Sudetenland im deutschen Wirtschaftsraum.* Berlin, 1938.

Deutscher Turnverband in der Tschechoslowakei. *Die völkische Turnbewegung.* [193-?] Jablonec n. Nison, [193-?].

Diamond, William. *Czechoslovakia between East and West.* London, 1947.

Dobrý, Anatol. *Hospodářská krize československého průmyslu ve vztahu k Mnichovu* (Economic Crisis of the Czechoslovak Industry with Regard to Munich). Prague, 1959.

——. *Materiály ke studiu dějin československého hospodářství v letech 1918–1945* (Materials for the Study of the History of the Czechoslovak Economy during the Years 1918–1945). Prague, 1955.

Doležal, Jiří. *Slovenské národní povstání. Příspěvek k jeho vzniku a průběhu* (Slovak Uprising. Contribution toward Its Origin and Development). Prague, 1954.

Dresdner Bank. *Volk und Wirtschaft im Reichsprotektorat Böhmen und Mähren und in der Slowakei.* Berlin, 1938.

Duff, Shiela Grant. *A German Protectorate. The Czechs under Nazi Rule.* London, 1942.

Edding, Friedrich. *The Refugees as a Burden, a Stimulus, and a Challenge to the West German Economy.* The Hague, 1951.

Essler, F. W. *Twenty Years of Sudeten German Losses 1918–1938.* Vienna-Leipzig, 1938.

Feder, Richard. *Židovská tragedie* (Jewish Tragedy). Kolín, 1947.

Federal Statistical Office. *Statistical Pocket-Book on Expellees in the Federal Republic of Germany and West Berlin.* Wiesbaden, 1953.

Feierabend, Ladislav. Paměti (Memoirs). Unpublished manuscript. Washington, 1956–.

——. *Ve vládách Druhé republiky* (In the Cabinets of the Second Republic). New York, 1961.

——. *Ve vládě Protektorátu* (In the Protectorate Government). New York, 1962.

Feiling, Keith. *The Life of Neville Chamberlain.* London, 1946.

Feis, Herbert. *Between War and Peace. The Potsdam Conference.* Princeton, N. J., 1960.

——. *Churchill–Roosevelt–Stalin. The War They Waged and the Peace They Sought.* Princeton, N. J., 1957.

Fetter, Joseph. *The Sudetens—a Moral Question.* New York, 1947.

Fierlinger, Zdeněk. *Ve službách ČSR: Paměti z druhého zahraničního odboje* (In Service of the Czechoslovak Republic. Memoirs on the Second Resistance Movement Abroad). 2 vols. Prague, 1947–48.

Fischer, Fritz. *Griff nach der Weltmacht. Die Kriegszielpolitik des kaiserlichen Deutschland 1914–1918.* Düsseldorf, 1961.

Fischer, Josef–Patzak, Václav–Perth, Vincenc. *Ihr Kampf. Die wahren Ziele der Sudetendeutschen Partei.* Carlsbad, 1937.

Foerster, F. W. *Europe and the German Question.* New York, 1940.

Foerster, Wolfgang. *Generaloberst Ludwig Beck. Sein Kampf gegen den Krieg. Aus nachgelassenen Papieren des Generalstabschefs.* Munich, 1953.

Frank, Ernst. *Sudetenland—Deutsches Land. Erzählte Geschichte des sudetendeutschen Freiheitskampfes.* Görlitz, 1944.

Frank, Karl Hermann. *Sudetendeutschtum in Kampf und Not. Ein Bildbericht.* Kassel-Wilhelmshöhe, 1936.

Franzel, Emil. *Sudetendeutsche Geschichte—eine volkstümliche Darstellung.* Augsburg, 1958.

Freund, Richard. *Watch Czechoslovakia!* London, 1938.

Friedman, Otto. *The Break-up of Czech Democracy.* London, 1950.

Frumkin, Gregory. *Population Changes in Europe since 1939.* New York, 1951.

Fuchik, Julius. *Notes from the Gallows.* New York, 1948.

Gajan, Koloman. *Německý imperialismus a československo-německé vztahy v letech 1918–1921* (German Imperialism and Czecho-slovak-German Relations in the Years 1918–1921). Prague, 1962.

Gajanová, Alena. *Dvojí tvář* (Double Face). Prague, 1962.

Galéra, Karl Siegmar Baron von. *Sudetendeutschlands Heimkehr ins Deutsche Reich.* Leipzig, 1939.

Gamelin, General. *Servir.* 3 vols. Paris, 1946–47.

Gedye, G. E. R. *Betrayal in Central Europe.* New York, 1939.

Glaser, Kurt. *The Iron Curtain and American Policy.* Washington, 1953.

Gluckstein, Ygael. *Stalin's Satellites in Europe.* London, 1952.

Gollancz, Victor. *Our Threatened Values.* London, 1946.

Görlitz, Walter. *Der Zweite Weltkrieg 1939–1945.* 2 vols. Stuttgart, 1951–52.

Göttingen Research Committee, ed. *Documents of Humanity during the Mass Expulsions.* New York, 1954.

Göttinger Arbeitskreis. *Deutschlands Ostproblem. Eine Untersuchung der Beziehungen des deutschen Volkes zu seinen östlichen Nachbarn.* Würzburg, 1957.

———. *Sudetenland. Ein Hand—und Nachschlagebuch über die Siedlungsgebiete der Sudetendeutschen.* Kitzingen, 1954.

Gottwald, Klement. *Spisy* (Works). 15 vols. Prague, 1950–61.

Griffin, Joan and Jonathan. *Lost Liberty. The Ordeal of the Czechs and the Future of Freedom.* New York, 1939.

Guderian, Heinz. *Panzer Leader.* London, 1952.

Gus, M. *Američtí imperialisté—inspirátoři mnichovské politiky* (American Imperialists—Initiators of the Policy of Munich). Prague, 1953.

George, Pierre. *Le problème allemand en Tchécoslovaquie* (*1919–1946*). Paris, 1947.

Glänzel, G. *Die Wirtschaft der Tschechoslowakei*. Hamburg, 1936.

Habřina, Rajmund, ed. *Žalm Moravy* (Psalm of Moravia). Brno, 1948.

Hajda, Jan, ed. *A Study of Contemporary Czechoslovakia*. Chicago, 1955.

Hájek, J. S. *Německá otázka a československá politika* (The German Question and Czechoslovak Policy). Prague, 1954.

———. *Mnichov* (Munich). Prague, 1958.

Hájek, Miloš. *Od Mnichova k 15. březnu* (From Munich to March 15). Prague, 1959.

Hanušová, Libuše. *Co s nimi? Dokumentární svědectví nacistické propagandy o velezrádné činnosti pohraničních Němců v Československu* (What to Do with Them? Documentary Evidence of the Nazi Propaganda on the Treasonable Activities of the Border Germans in the Czechoslovak Republic). Prague, 1946.

Hassell, Ulrich von. *Diaries 1938–1944*. Garden City, N. Y., 1947.

Hassinger, Hugo. *Die Tschechoslowakei. Ein geographisches und wirtschaftliches Handbuch*. Vienna, Leipzig, Munich, 1925.

Hauptmann, Karl. *Sudetendeutsche Presse im Befreiungskampf. "Die Zeit" 1935–1938*. Würzburg, Aumühle, 1941.

Heiss, Friedrich, ed. *Das Böhmen und Mähren-Buch. Volkskampf und Reichsraum*. Prague, 1943.

Henderson, Alexander. *Eyewitness in Czecho-Slovakia*. London, 1939.

Henderson, Nevile. *Failure of a Mission: Berlin 1937–1939*. New York, 1940.

Henlein, Konrad. *Heim ins Reich. Reden aus den Jahren 1937 und 1938*. Ernst Tscherne ed. Reichenberg, 1939.

———. *Sudetendeutschtum und gesamtdeutsche Kultur*. Prague, 1936.

Herde, Georg und Maier, Hans. . . . *Bis alles in Scherben fällt*. . . . *Beiträge zur Zeitgeschichte*. Band 1. Munich, 1960.

Historický ústav ČSAV. *Přehled československých dějin* (Survey of Czechoslovak History). 3 vols. Prague, 1958–60.

Historický ústav SAV. *Německá otázka a Československo* (*1938–1961*) (The German Question and Czechoslovakia (1938–1961). Bratislava, 1962.

The History of the Times. The 150th Anniversary and Beyond. 1912–1948. 4 vols. London, 1952.

Hitchcock, Edward B. *"I Built a Temple for Peace." The Life of Eduard Beneš*. New York, 1940.

Hitler's Secret Conversations, 1941–1944. New York, 1953.

Hoch, Charles. *The Political Parties in Czechoslovakia.* Prague, 1936.

Hoch, Karel. *Pangermanismus.* Prague, 1946.

Höller, Franz. *Von der SdP zur NSDAP. Ein dokumentarischer Bild-bericht.* Reichenberg, 1939.

Hořec, Jaromír, *Cesty, ktoré viedli k Mníchovu. Niekolko kapitol o protisovietskej a protinárodnej politike českej buržoázie a svetových imperialistov* (Ways Leading toward Munich. Several Chapters on Anti-Soviet and Anti-National Policy of the Czech Bourgeoisie and World Imperialists). Bratislava, 1955.

Höss, Konstantin, ed. *Die SdP im Parlament. Ein Jahresbericht 1935–36.* Karlsbad-Leipzig, 1937.

Hossbach, Friedrich. *Zwischen Wehrmacht und Hitler 1934–1938.* Wolfenbüttel and Hanover, 1949.

Hrdlička, Rudolf, ed. *Sborník. Památce divisního generála Vojtěcha Luži* (A Collection of Articles to the Memory of General Vojtěch Luža). Brno, 1945.

Hronek, Jiří. *Od porážky k vítězství* (From Defeat to Victory). Prague, 1947.

Hulička, Karel. "The Politics of Czechoslovakia 1938–1951." Unpublished Ph.D. thesis, University of California, 1952.

Hull, Cordell. *The Memoirs of Cordell Hull.* 2 vols. New York, 1948.

Hummel, Hans. *Südosteuropa und das Erbe der Donaumonarchie.* Leipzig and Berlin, 1937.

Hutak, J. B. *With Blood and with Iron. The Lidice Story.* London, 1957.

Hysko, Miroslav. *Slovenské národné povstanie* (Slovak National Uprising). Bratislava, 1954.

Institut National de la Statistique et des études économiques. *Les minorités ethniques en Europe centrale et balkanique.* Paris, 1946.

———. *Les transferts internationaux de populations.* Paris, 1946.

Jacoby, Gerhard. *Racial State. The German Nationalities Policy in the Protectorate of Bohemia-Moravia.* New York, 1944.

Jaenicke, Wolfgang. *Vier Jahre Betreuung der Vertriebenen in Bayern 1945–49.* Munich, 1950.

Jahn, Rudolf. *Konrad Henlein. Leben und Werk des Turnführers.* Carlsbad-Drahowitz, 1938.

Jaksch, Wenzel. *Benesch war gewarnt!* Munich, 1949.

———. *Europas Weg nach Potsdam. Schuld und Schicksal im Donauraum.* Stuttgart, 1958.

———. *Sudeten Labour and the Sudeten Problem.* London, 1945.

Janowsky, Oscar I. *Nationalities and National Minorities (With*

Special Reference to East-Central Europe). New York, 1945.

Jelínek, Jaroslav. *PÚ. Politické ústředí domácího odboje* (PC. Political Center of the Home Resistance Movement). Prague, 1947.

Jong, Louis de. *The German Fifth Column in the Second World War*. Chicago, 1956.

Les juifs en Europe 1939–45. (Centre de documentation juive contemporaine). Paris, 1949.

Jung, Rudolf. *Die Tschechen. Tausend Jahre deutsch-tschechischer Kampf*. Berlin, 1937.

Kallina, Othmar. *Von grossdeutschen Gedanken in Böhmen*. Breslau, 1940.

Karlgren, Anton. *Henlein–Hitler a československá tragedie* (Henlein–Hitler and the Czechoslovak Tragedy). Prague, 1945.

Kašpar, M. F. *Why without the "Sudeten" Germans?* London, 1952.

Kern, Erich. *Das andere Lidice. Die Tragödie der Sudetendeutschen*. Klagenfurt, 1950.

Kerner, Robert J., ed. *Czechoslovakia: Twenty Years of Independence*. Berkeley, Calif., 1949.

Kertesz, Stephen D., ed. *The Fate of East Central Europe, Hopes and Failures of American Foreign Policy*. Notre Dame, Ind, 1956.

Kiesewetter, Bruno. *Die Wirtschaft der Tschechoslowakei seit 1945*. Berlin, 1954.

Klement, Anton. *The German Settlement Area in Czecho-Slovakia*. Vienna and Leipzig, 1938.

Klepetář, Harry. *Seit 1918 . . . Eine Geschichte der tschechoslowakischen Republik*. Moravská-Ostrava, 1937.

Koegler, Franz. *Oppressed Minority?* London, 1943.

Koehl, Robert L. *RKFDV: German Resettlement and Population Policy 1939–1945. A History of the Reich Commission for the Strengthening of Germandom*. Cambridge, Mass., 1957.

Konopka, Vladimír, ed. *Živé tradice. Kapitoly z národně osvobozeneckého a protifašistického boje našeho lidu* (Living Traditions. Chapters from Our Liberation and Anti-Fascist Struggle). Prague, 1959.

Kopecký, Rudolf. *Československý odboj v Polsku v r. 1939* (Czechoslovak Resistance Movement in Poland in 1939). Rotterdam, 1958.

Kopecký, Václav. *ČSR a KSČ* (The Czechoslovak Republic and the Communist Party of Czechoslovakia). Prague, 1960.

———. *Gottwald v Moskvě* (Gottwald in Moscow). Bratislava, 1949.

Kordt, Erich. *Nicht aus den Akten* . . . Stuttgart, 1950.

Král, Václav. *Otázky hospodářského a sociálního vývoje v českých zemích v letech 1938–1945* (Questions of the Economic and Social Development in the Czech Territories in 1938–1945). 3 vols. Prague, 1957–59.

———. *Pravda o okupaci* (Truth about the Occupation). Prague, 1962.

Krebs, Hans. *Kampf in Böhmen.* Berlin, 1936.

Krebs, Hans–Lehmann, Emil. *Wir Sudetendeutsche!* Berlin, 1937.

Křen, Jan. *Do emigrace* (Into Emigration). Prague, 1963.

Krofta, Kamil. *The Germans in the Czechoslovak Republic.* Prague, 1937.

———. *Les nouveaux états dans l'Europe centrale.* Prague, 1930.

———. *Z dob naší první republiky* (From the Times of Our First Republic). Prague, 1939.

Kučera, Eduard–Kučerová, Zdeňka. *O agrárnický stát* (For the Agrarian State). Prague, 1955.

Kühne, Erich, ed. *Sudetendeutscher Schicksalskampf.* Leipzig, 1938.

Kulischer, Eugene M. *Europe on the Move. War and Population Changes 1917–1947.* New York, 1948.

Kvaček, Robert. *Osudná mise* (Fatal Mission). Prague, 1958.

Labour Party. *Hitler's Threat to Czech Democracy. The Facts.* London, 1938.

Laffan, R. G. D. *Survey of International Affairs 1938. The Crisis over Czechoslovakia. January to September 1938.* London, 1951.

Laštovička, Bohuslav. *V Londýně za války. Zápasy o novou ČSR 1939–1945* (During the War in London. Struggles for a New Czechoslovak Republic in 1939–45). Prague, 1960.

Laun, Rudolf-Lange, I. *Czecho-Slovak Claims on German Territory.* The Hague, 1919.

Leahy, William D. *I Was There.* New York, 1950.

Lemberg, Eugen. *Osteuropa und die Sowjetunion. Geschichte und Probleme.* Salzburg, 1956.

Lemberg, Eugen–Edding, Friedrich, ed. *Die Vertriebenen in Deutschland. Ihre Eingliederung und ihr Einfluss auf Gesellschaft, Wirtschaft, Politik und Geistesleben.* 3 vols. Kiel, 1959.

Lemkin, Raphael. *Axis Rule in Occupied Europe. Laws of Occupation—Analysis of Government—Proposals for Redress.* Washington, 1944.

Lestschinsky, Jacob. *Crisis, Catastrophe and Survival.* New York, 1948.

Lettrich, Jozef. *History of Modern Slovakia.* New York, 1955.

Lewis, Bracket. *Democracy in Czechoslovakia.* New York, 1943.

Lisický, Karel. *Československá cesta do Mnichova* (Czechoslovak Road to Munich). London, 1954.

Lockhart, R. H. Bruce. *Comes the Reckoning.* London, 1947.

————. *My Europe.* London, 1952.

Louda, Vlastimil. *Politika soustavné zrady. Studie o německé politice na území ČSR* (Policy of Permanent Treason. A Study of the German Policy on the Czechoslovak Territory). Prague, 1948.

Luža, Radomír. *Odsun. Příspěvek k historii česko-německých vztahů v letech 1918–1952* (Transfer. Contribution Toward the History of Czech-German Relations in 1918–1952). Vienna, 1953.

Mackenzie, Compton. *Dr. Beneš.* London, 1946.

Masaryk, Jan. *Statement on the Foreign Policy of Czechoslovakia— Made before the Provisional National Assembly on March 6th, 1946.* Prague, 1946.

————. *Statement on the Foreign Policy of Czechoslovakia—Made before the Constituent National Assembly on March 20, 1947.* Prague, 1947.

Memorandum du Comité National Tchécoslovaque relatif aux persécutions de l'enseignement et à la suppression de l'activité scientifique en Bohême et en Moravie. Paris, 1940.

Meyer, Henry Cord. *Mitteleuropa in German Thought and Action 1815–1945.* The Hague, 1955.

Meynen, E., ed. *Sudetendeutscher Atlas.* Munich, 1954.

Mercier, M. *La formation de l'état tchécoslovaque.* Paris, 1923.

Mikuš, Joseph A. *La Slovaquie dans le drame de l'Europe. Histoire politique de 1918–1950.* Paris, 1955.

Monneray, Henri. *La persécution des juifs dans les pays de l'Est presentée à Nuremberg.* Paris, 1949.

Morrell, Sydney. *I Saw the Crucifixion.* London, 1939.

Múdrý, Michal. *Milan Hodža v Amerike. Medzi americkými Slovákmi. Články, reči, studie. Hodža a stredná Europa* (Hodža in America. Among American Slovaks. Articles, Lectures, Studies. Hodža and Central Europe). Chicago, 1949.

Murphy, Raymond E., ed. *National Socialism. Basic Principles. Their Application by the Nazi Party's Foreign Organization, and the Use of Germans Abroad for the Nazi Aims.* Washington, 1943.

Namier, L. B. *Diplomatic Prelude 1938–1939.* London, 1948.

————. *Europe in Decay. A Study in Disintegration, 1936–1940.* London, 1950.

————. *In the Nazi Era.* New York, 1952.

Nationality Policy in Czechoslovakia. Speeches by Dr. Hodža,

Franke, Nečas and Dérer in the Czechoslovak Parliament. Prague, 1938.

Neumann, Franz. *Behemoth. The Structure and Practice of National Socialism.* New York, 1942.

Nicholson, Harold. *Peacemaking 1919.* Boston, 1933.

Notter, Harley A. *Postwar Foreign Policy Preparation 1939–1945.* Washington, 1949.

Nováček, Silvestr. *Mikulovsko a Pohořelicko od nástupu nacismu k osudnému Mnichovu* (The Region of Mikulov and Pohořelice from the Rise of Nazism to Fateful Munich). Brno, 1960.

Oberkommando des Heeres. *Denkschrift über die tschechoslowakische Landesbefestigung.* Berlin, 1941.

Oberschall, Albin. *Berufliche Gliederung und soziale Schichtung der Deutschen in \der Tschechoslowakei.* Teplitz-Schönau, 1935.

Office of Strategic Services. *Transfers of Population in Europe since 1920.* Washington, 1945.

Olšovský, Rudolf, ed. *Přehled hospodářského vývoje Československa v letech 1918–1945* (Survey of the Economic Development of Czechoslovakia in the Years 1918–1945). Prague, 1961.

Opočenský, Jan. *The Collapse of the Austro-Hungarian Monarchy and the Rise of the Czechoslovak State.* Prague, 1928.

———. ed. *Edward Beneš. Essays and Reflections Presented on the Occasion of His Sixtieth Birthday.* London, 1945.

Papánek, Ján. *Czechoslovakia.* New York, 1945.

Pátá kolona v severních Čechách. Fakta a dokumenty (The Fifth Column in Northern Bohemia. Facts and Documents). Liberec, 1960.

Pěnička, Alois. *Kladensko v boji za svobodu* (The Region of Kladno in Struggle for Freedom). Prague, 1953.

Peters, Gustav. *Der neue Herr von Böhmen. Eine Untersuchung der politischen Zukunft der Tschechoslowakei.* Berlin, 1927.

Pfitzner, Josef. *Sudetendeutsche Einheitsbewegung, Werden und Erfüllung.* Carlsbad-Leipzig, 1937.

———. *Das Sudetendeutschtum.* Cologne, 1938.

Pleyer, Wilhelm, ed. *Wir Sudetendeutschen.* Salzburg, 1949.

Poliakov, Léon. *Bréviaire de la haine.* Paris, 1951.

Polzer, Robert. *Die sudetendeutsche Wirtschaft in der Tschechoslowakei.* Kitzingen, Main, 1952.

Preidel, Helmut, ed. *Die Deutschen in Böhmen und Mähren. Ein historischer Rückblick.* Gräfelfing near Munich, 1952.

Procházka, Theodor. "La Tchécoslovaquie de Munich à mars 1939." Unpublished doctoral dissertation, Université de Paris, 1954.

Proudfoot, Malcolm J. *European Refugees 1939–52. A Study in Forced Population Movement*. Evanston, Ill., 1956.

Rabl, Kurt. *Das Ringen um das sudetendeutsche Selbstbestimmungsrecht 1918–19*. Munich, 1958.

Raschhofer, Hermann. *Die Sudetenfrage. Ihre völkerrechtliche Entwicklung vom ersten Weltkrieg bis zur Gegenwart*. Munich, 1953.

———. ed. *Die tschechoslowakischen Denkschriften für die Friedenskonferenz von Paris 1919–1920*. Berlin, 1937.

The Rectors of the Czechoslovak Universities, Technological Institutes and Other Schools of Superior Education. *Czech School Facilities under the Austrian Government and on German School Facilities under Czechoslovak Government*. Prague, 1938.

Reichenberger, E. J. *Ostdeutsche Passion*. Düsseldorf, 1948.

Reitlinger, Gerald. *The Final Solution. The Attempt to Exterminate the Jews of Europe 1939–45*. London, 1953.

———. *The SS. Alibi of a Nation 1922–1945*. New York, 1957.

Reynaud, Paul. *In the Thick of the Fight*. New York, 1955.

Richter, Hans. *No Oppression of the Sudeten Germans in Czechoslovakia?* Vienna-Leipzig, 1937.

Ripka, Hubert. *Československo v nové Evropě* (Czechoslovakia in New Europe). London, 1945.

———. *Czechoslovakia Enslaved: The Story of the Communist Coup d'Etat*. London, 1950.

———. *The Future of the Czechoslovak Germans*. London, 1944.

———. *Likvidace Mnichova* (The Repudiation of Munich). London, 1943.

———. *Munich: Before and After*. London, 1939.

Ritter, Gerhard. *Carl Goerdeler und die deutsche Widerstandsbewegung*. Stuttgart, 1954.

Robinson, Jacob et al. *Were the Minorities Treaties a Failure?* New York, 1943.

Rönnefarth, Helmuth K. G. *Die Sudetenkrise in der internationalen Politik. Entstehung–Verlauf–Auswirkung*. 2 vols. Wiesbaden, 1961.

Rosenberg, Alfred, ed. *Das Parteiprogramm. Wesen, Grundsätze und Ziele der NSDAP*. Munich, 1941.

Rossipaul, Lothar. *Die Presse der Sudetendeutschen Partei und der Deutschen christlich-sozialen Volkspartei bis zur Heimkehr Sudetendeutschlands 1938*. Würzburg, 1942.

Roucek, Joseph S., ed. *Contemporary Europe. A Study of National*,

International, Economic and Cultural Trends. New York, 1947.

Royal Institute of International Affairs. *Survey of International Affairs, 1933–46.* London, 1934 ff.

Schechtman, Joseph B. *European Population Transfers 1939–1945.* New York, 1946.

Schlesinger, Rudolf. *Federalism in Central and Eastern Europe.* London, 1945.

Schieder, Theodor, ed. *Dokumentation der Vertreibung der Deutschen aus Ost-Mitteleuropa. IV/1–2: Die Vertreibung der deutschen Bevölkerung aus der Tschechoslowakei. 2.* Beiheft: *Ein Tagebuch aus Prag 1945–46* by Margarete Schell. Bonn, 1957.

Schmidt, Dana Adams. *Anatomy of a Satellite.* London, 1953.

Schmidt, Paul. *Hitler's Interpreter.* Ed. by R. H. C. Steed. New York, 1951.

Schreiber, Ludwig. *Die Vertriebenen. Die Tragödie einer Heimat.* Sinsheim, Elsenz, Baden, 1949.

Sebekowsky, Wilhelm. *The Expansion of the Czechs—Its Psychology, History, Methods, and Results.* Carlsbad-Leipzig, 1938.

Section historique de l'Académie tchécoslovaque des sciences. *Historica I–IV. Historical Sciences in Czechoslovakia.* Prague, 1959–62.

Šedivý, Karel. *Why We Want to Transfer the Germans?* Prague, 1946.

Seraphim, Peter-Heinz. *Die Heimatvertriebenen in der Sowjetzone.* Berlin, 1954.

Seton-Watson, Hugh. *The East European Revolution.* London, 1950.

———. *Eastern Europe between the Wars 1918–1941.* Cambridge, 1945.

Seton-Watson, R. W. *A History of the Czechs and Slovaks.* London, 1943.

———. *Munich and the Dictators.* London, 1939.

Shepherd, Gordon. *Russia's Danubian Empire.* New York, 1954.

Sigl, Christian. *Quellen und Dokumente. Ein Tatsachenbericht über die Lage im sudetendeutschen Gebiet und über die Entwicklung der tschechoslowakischen Innenpolitik.* Vienna, 1938.

Sigl, Franz. *Die soziale Struktur des Sudetendeutschtums, ihre Entwicklung und volkspolitische Bedeutung.* Leipzig, 1938.

Smutný, Jaromír. *Němci v Československu a jich odsun z republiky* (Germans in Czechoslovakia and Their Transfer from the Republic). London, 1956.

Sobota, Emil. *Das tschechoslowakische Nationalitätenrecht.* Prague, 1931.

Soják, Vladimír, ed. *O československé zahraniční politice 1918–1939* (On the Czechoslovak Foreign Policy 1918–1939). Prague, 1956.

Statistisches Bundesamt. *Statistisches Jahrbuch für die Bundesrepublik Deutschland.* Wiesbaden, 1957.

———, ed. *Die deutschen Vertreibungsverluste. Bevölkerungsbilanzen für die deutschen Vertreibungsgebiete 1939–50.* Wiesbaden, 1958.

Statistisches Reichsamt. *Statistisches Jahrbuch für das Deutsche Reich.* Berlin, 1942.

Strang, Lord. *Home and Abroad.* London, 1956.

Stránský, Jaroslav. *Odsun Němců z ČSR z hlediska národního i mezinárodního* (Transfer of the Germans from the Czechoslovak Republic from Both National and International Point of Views). London, 1953.

———. *K otázce česko-německé* (On the Czech-German Question). London, 1956.

Stresemann, Gustav. *His Diaries, Letters and Papers.* 3 vols. New York, 1935–40.

Sudetendeutsche Partei. *Der Lebenswille des Sudetendeutschtums. Bericht über die Haupttagung der Sudetendeutschen Partei am 23. und 24. April 1938 in Karlsbad mit der Rede Konrad Henleins.* Carlsbad-Leipzig, 1938.

———. *Sudetendeutschtum im Kampf. Ein Bericht von Arbeit und Not.* Carlsbad, 1936.

Sudetendeutscher Rat. *Justiz im Dienste der Vergeltung.* Munich, 1962.

———. *Menschen vor dem Volkstod. 200,000 Deutsche in der ČSSR.* Munich, 1961.

Sudeten Germans and Czechs. *Condensed Report of the First National Conference of German Anti-Fascists from Czechoslovakia. At the Beaver Hall, London, October 16–17, 1943.* London, 1944.

Svaz československých důstojníků v exilu. *Generál Ingr.* Washington, 1957.

Táborský, Eduard. *The Czechoslovak Cause. An Account of the Problems of International Law in Relation to Czechoslovakia.* London, 1944.

———. *Czechoslovak Democracy at Work.* London, 1945.

Thomson, Harrison, S. *Czechoslovakia in European History.* Princeton, 1953.

Thorwald, Jürgen. *Flight in the Winter.* London, 1953.

Tscherne, Ernst, ed. *Das ist Konrad Henlein.* Carlsbad, 1938.

Turnwald, Wilhelm K. *Renascence or Decline of Central Europe. The Sudeten-German-Czech Problem.* Munich, 1954.

Uhlíř, František. *Prague and Berlin.* London, 1944.

Ullrich, Oskar. *Der grosse Irrweg der Tschechen.* Prague, 1943.

———. *Sie kamen aus aller Herren Länder. Aus dem Tagebuch des SdP-Dolmetschers.* Carlsbad-Leipzig, 1940.

United Nations Relief and Rehabilitation Administration, European Regional Office. *Agriculture and Food in Czechoslovakia.* London, 1946.

———. *The Foreign Trade in Czechoslovakia.* London, 1947.

———. *Industrial Rehabilitation in Czechoslovakia.* London, 1947.

———. *Transport Rehabilitation in Czechoslovakia.* London, 1947.

United Nations War Crimes Commission. *History of the United Nations War Crimes Commission and the Development of the Laws of War.* London, 1948.

Urban, Rudolf. *Tajné fondy III. sekce. Z archivu ministerstva zahraničí republiky česko-slovenské* (Secret Funds of the Third Section. From the Archives of the Czecho-Slovak Republic). Prague, 1943.

Urban, Vincent. *Hitler's Spearhead.* London, [1945].

Ústav dějin Komunistické strany Československa. *Na obranu republiky, proti fašizmu a vojně. Sborník dokumentov k dějinám KSČ v rokoch 1934–1938 a k VI., VII. a VIII. sväzku spisov Klementa Gottwalda* (For Defense of the Republic Against Fascism and War. Collection of the Documents to the History of the Czechoslovak Communist Party in 1934–38 and to Volumes VI–VIII. of the Collected Works of Klement Gottwald). Bratislava, 1955.

———. *Za svobodu českého a slovenského národa. Sborník dokumentů k dějinám KSČ v letech 1938–1945 a k IX., X. a XI. svazku spisů Klementa Gottwalda* (For Freedom of the Czech and Slovak Nations. Collection of the Documents to the History of the Czechoslovak Communist Party in 1938–1945 and to Volumes IX–XI of the Collected Works of Klement Gottwald). Prague, 1956.

Ústav pro mezinárodní politiku a ekonomii. *Německý revanšismus—hrozba míru* (German Revanchism—A Threat to Peace). Prague, 1959.

Vernant, Jacques. *The Refugee in the Post-War World.* London, 1953.

Veselý-Štainer, Karel. *Cestou národního odboje. Bojový vývoj domácího odbojového hnutí v letech 1938–45* (With the National Resistance, A Development of the Struggle of the Resistance Movement in 1938–45). Prague, 1947.

Viererbl, Karl, ed. *Sudetenland im Reich. Ein Querschnitt durch die Aufbauarbeit und Leistung des Reichsgaues Sudetenland.* Reichenberg, 1943.

Vondráček, Felix J. *The Foreign Policy of Czechoslovakia 1918–1935.* New York, 1937.

Vorbach, Kurt. *200,000 Sudetendeutsche zuviel! Der tschechische Vernichtungskampf gegen 3.5 Millionen Sudetendeutschen und seine volkspolitischen Auswirkungen.* Munich, 1936.

Vozka, Jaroslav. *Hrdinové domácího odboje* (Heroes of the Home Resistance). Prague, 1946.

Wagner, Georg. *Sudeten-SA in Polen. Ein Bildbericht.* Carlsbad-Leipzig, 1940.

Wandycz, Piotr S. *France and Her Eastern Allies, 1919–1925. French-Czechoslovak-Polish Relations from the Paris Peace Conference to Locarno.* Minneapolis, 1962.

Wanklyn, Harriet. *Czechoslovakia.* New York, 1954.

Wannemacher, Walter. *Sudetendeutscher Schicksalskampf.* Leipzig, 1938.

Warriner, Doreen. *Revolution in Eastern Europe.* London, 1950.

Weizsäcker, Ernst von. *Erinnerungen.* Munich, Leipzig, Freiburg/B., 1950.

Weizsäcker, Wilhelm. *Geschichte der Deutschen in Böhmen und Mähren.* Hamburg, 1950.

Wheeler-Bennett, John W. *Munich. Prologue to Tragedy.* New York, 1948.

Winkler, Erwin. *Die Tschechoslowakei im Spiegel der Statistik.* Carlsbad-Leipzig, 1937.

Wiskemann, Elizabeth. *Czechs and Germans. A Study of the Struggle in the Historic Provinces of Bohemia and Moravia.* London, New York, Toronto, 1938.

———. *Germany's Eastern Neighbours. Problems Relating to the Oder-Neisse Line and the Czech Frontier Regions.* London, New York, Toronto, 1956.

Woodbridge, George. *UNRRA. The History of the United Nations Relief and Rehabilitation Administration.* 3 vols. New York, 1950.

Wynne, Waller, Jr. *The Population of Czechoslovakia.* Washington, 1953.

Young, Edgar P. *Czechoslovakia: Keystone of Peace and Democracy.* London, 1938.

Za svobodu do nové Československé republiky. Ideový program domácího odbojového hnutí vypracovaný v letech 1939–41 (For

Freedom toward the New Czechoslovak Republic. Ideological Program of the Home Resistance Movement Elaborated in the Years 1939–41). Prague, 1945.

Zeman, Z.A.B. *The Break-up of the Habsburg Empire 1914–1918.* London, 1961.

Articles

Amort, Čestmír. "Die Sowjetunion und die Verteidigung der Tschechoslowakei gegen die faschistische Aggression im Jahre 1938," *Zeitschrift für Geschichtswissenschaft,* IX (no. 5, 1961), 1055–71.

Armengaud, Général. "La Tchécoslovaquie devant l'Allemagne," *Revue des deux mondes,* CVIII année, tome 44e (15 avril 1938), 766–79.

Armstrong, Hamilton Fish. "Armistice at Munich," *Foreign Affairs,* XVII (January, 1939), 197–290.

Beneš, Eduard. "The New Order in Europe," The *Nineteenth Century and After,* CXXX (September, 1941), 150–55.

———. "The Organization of Postwar Europe," *Foreign Affairs,* XX (January, 1942), 226–42.

———. "Czechoslovak Plans for Peace," *Foreign Affairs,* XXIII (October, 1944), 26–37.

———. "Postwar Czechoslovakia," *Foreign Affairs,* XXIV (April, 1946), 397–410.

Bodensieck, Heinrich. "Der Plan eines "Freundschaftsvertrages" zwischen dem Reich und der Tschecho-Slowakei im Jahre 1938," *Zeitschrift für Ostforschung,* X (September, 1961), 462–76.

——— "Die Politik der zweiten Tschechoslowakischen Republik," *Zeitschrift für Ostforschung,* VI (April, 1957), 54–71.

———. "Das Dritte Reich und die Lage der Juden in der Tschecho-Slowakei nach München," *Vierteljahrshefte für Zeitgeschichte,* IX (July, 1961), 249–61.

Bohmann, Alfred. "Die landschaftliche Herkunft der in der Bundesrepublik lebenden Sudeten-und Karpatendeutschen," *Zeitschrift für Ostforschung,* X (No. 2, 1961), 245–61.

Broszat, Martin. "Das Sudetendeutsche Freikorps," *Vierteljahrshefte für Zeitgeschichte,* IX (January, 1961), 30–49.

Brown, MacAlister. "The Third Reich's Mobilization of the German Fifth Column in Eastern Europe," *Journal of Central European Affairs,* XIX (July, 1959), 128–48.

Brügel, Johann Wolfgang. "Die Aussiedlung der Deutschen aus der

Tschechoslowakei," *Vierteljahrshefte für Zeitgeschichte,* VIII (April, 1960), 134–64.

———. "Die sudetendeutsche Frage auf der Potsdamer Konferenz," *Vierteljahrshefte für Zeitgeschichte,* X (January, 1962), 56–61.

———. "Henlein a češsti agrárnici" (Henlein and the Czech Agrarians). *Tribuna,* XII (No. 2, 1960), 5–6.

Čelovský, Boris. "The Transferred Sudeten-Germans and Their Political Activity," *Journal of Central European Affairs,* VI (April, 1957), 127–49.

César, Jaroslav–Černý, Bohumil. "The Nazi Fifth Column in Czechoslovakia," *Historica,* IV (1962), 191–255.

Haight, John McVickar, Jr. "France, the United States, and the Munich Crisis," The *Journal of Modern History,* XXXII (December 1960), 340–58.

Hanč, Josef. "Czechs and Slovaks since Munich," *Foreign Affairs,* XVIII (October, 1939), 102–15.

Heiber, Helmut. "Zur Justiz im Dritten Reich. Der Fall Eliáš," *Vierteljahrshefte für Zeitgeschichte,* III (July, 1955), 275–96.

Joy, Charles R. "Four Lidices and Christian Conscience," The *Catholic World,* CLXXIII (September, 1951), 406–11.

Kořalka, Jiří. "Jak se stal německý lid v Československu kořistí fašismu" (How the German People Became Prey to Fascism in Czechoslovakia), *Československý časopis historický,* III (No. 1, 1955), 52–81.

Korbel, Pavel. "Národnostní menšiny v Československu" (National Minorities in Czechoslovakia), *Československý přehled,* V (February, 1958), 20–27.

Krajina, Vladimír. "La résistance tchécoslovaque," *Cahiers d'histoire de la guerre,* No. 3 (February, 1950), pp. 55–76.

Král, Václav. "The Policy of Germanization Enforced in Bohemia and Moravia by the Fascist Invaders during the Second World War," *Historica,* II 1960), 273–303.

Křen, Jan. "Revanšisté s protinacistickou minulostí" (Revanchists with an Anti-Nazi Past), *Československý časopis historický,* IX (No. 1, 1961), 42–59.

Křížek, Jurij. "Příspěvek k dějinám rozpadu Rakouska-Uherska a vzniku Československa (Contribution toward the History of the Breakdown of Austria-Hungary and the Formation of Czechoslovakia), *Příspěvky k dějinám KSČ* (September, 1958), 13–120.

Lockhart, R. H. Bruce. "The Second Exile of Eduard Beneš," The *Slavonic and East European Review,* XXVII (November, 1949), 39–59.

Myška, Milan. "Věda ve službách agrese" (Science in the Service of Aggression), *Příspěvky k dějinám KSČ* (June, 1962), pp. 391–409.

Odložilík, Otakar. "Concerning Munich and the Ides of March," *Journal of Central European Affairs,* IX (January, 1950), 419–28.

————. "Edvard Beneš on Munich Days," *Journal of Central European Affairs,* XVI (January, 1957), 384–93.

Pachta, Jan and Reiman, Pavel. "O nových dokumentech k otázce Mnichova" (About New Documents toward the Question of Munich), *Příspěvky k dějinám KSČ,* I (No. 1, 1957), 104–133.

Procházka, Theodor. "The Delimitation of Czechoslovak-German Frontiers after Munich," *Journal of Central European Affairs,* XXI (July, 1961), 200–18.

Rimscha, Hans von. "Zur Gleichschaltung der deutschen Volksgruppen durch das Dritte Reich," *Historische Zeitschrift,* CLXXXII (1956), 29–63.

Roucek, Joseph S., ed. "Moscow's European Satellites," The *Annals of the American Academy of Political and Social Sciences,* CCLXXI (September, 1950).

Rozehnal, Alois. "Osídlení pohraničí" (Settlement of the Borderland), *Československý přehled,* III (June, 1956), 19–26.

Schechtman, Joseph B. "Postwar Population Transfers in Europe: A Study," The *Review of Politics,* XV (April, 1953), 151–78.

————. "Resettlement of Transferred Volksdeutsche in Germany," *Journal of Central European Affairs,* VII (October, 1947), 262–84.

Schiefer, Hans. "Deutschland und die Tschechoslowakei von September 1938 bis März 1939," *Zeitschrift für Ostforschung,* IV (No. 1, 1955), 48–66.

Seton-Watson, R. W. "The German Minority in Czechoslovakia," *Foreign Affairs,* XVI (July, 1938), 651–66.

Šnejdárek, Antonín. "Počátky revanšistického 'Sudetoněmeckého krajanstva' v západním Německu" (Origins of the Revanchist "Sudeten German National Union" in West Germany), *Příspěvky k dějinám KSČ* (April, 1962), 192–206.

Táborský, Eduard. "Beneš and the Soviets," *Foreign Affairs,* XXVII (January, 1949), 302–14.

————. "Beneš and Stalin—Moscow, 1943 and 1945," *Journal of Central European Affairs,* XIII (July, 1953), 154–81.

————. "The Triumph and Disaster of Eduard Beneš," *Foreign Affairs,* XXXVI (July, 1958), 669–84.

Tapié, Victor-L. "Les Mémoires (Paměti) sur la seconde guerre mondiale du président Eduard Beneš," *Revue historique,* 76 année, CCVII (January–March, 1952), 25–48.

Vnuk, F. "Munich and the Soviet Union," *Journal of Central European Affairs,* XXI (October, 1961), 285–304.

Weinberg, Gerhard L. "The May Crisis, 1938," The *Journal of Modern History,* XXIX (September, 1957), 213–25.

———. "Secret Hitler-Beneš Negotiations in 1936–37," *Journal of Central European Affairs,* XIX (January, 1960), 366–74.

Whiteside, André C. "Industrial Transformation, Population Movement and German Nationalism in Bohemia," *Zeitschrift für Ostforschung,* X (No. 2, 1961), 261–71.

———. "Nationaler Sozialismus in Oesterreich vor 1918," *Vierteljahrshefte für Zeitgeschichte,* IX (October, 1961), 333–59.

Wiskemann, Elizabeth. "Czechs and Germans after Munich," *Foreign Affairs,* XVII (January, 1939), 291–304.

Wolfgramm, Eberhard. "'Grenzlandkämpfer.' Zur Ideologie, den historischen Wurzeln und den Hintergründen des sudetendeutschen Revanchismus," *Jahrbuch für Geschichte der UdSSR und der volksdemokratischen Länder Europas,* Vol. IV (Berlin, 1960), 9–39.

Newspapers and Periodicals

Newspapers

Die Brücke, 1951–63. Munich.

Čechoslovák, 1940–44. London.

Dnešek, I–II, 1946–47. Prague.

Einheit, I–VI, 1940–45. London.

Lidové noviny, 1938. Brno.

Národní politika, 1941. Prague.

Der neue Tag, I–VI. 1939–44. Prague.

Prager Presse, 1938. Prague.

Právo lidu, 1945, 1947. Prague.

Rudé právo, 1945–63. Prague.

Der *Sozialdemokrat,* 1942, 1946. London.

Svobodné slovo, 1945–48. Prague.

Die *Sudetendeutsche Zeitung,* 1951–63. Munich.

Der *Sudetendeutsche,* 1951–57. Hamburg.

Úřední list Republiky československé, 1945–46. Prague.

Volksbote, 1952–61. Munich.

Die Zeit, 1939. Liberec.

Periodicals

The *American Slavic and East European Review*, I–XX, 1941–60.
Aussenpolitik, I–VIII, 1950–58.
Böhmen und Mähren, I–V, 1939–44.
The *Central European Observer*, X–XXIII, 1933–46.
Československý časopis historický, I–X, 1952–62.
Československý přehled, I–VI, 1953–58.
The *Department of State Bulletin*, XIII–XX, 1945–49.
Der *Donauraum*, I–VI, 1956–61.
Der *europäische Osten*, I–IX, 1954–62.
Europa Archiv, I–X, 1946–55.
Historický časopis, I–VIII, 1954–61.
Historie a vojenství, VIII–IX, 1961–62.
The *Journal of Central European Affairs*, I–XXI, 1940–61.
The *Journal of Modern History*, XX–XXXIII, 1948–61
Národnostní obzor, I–VIII, 1930–38.
Naše cesta, 1951–55.
Naše doba, XXXXI–LIV, 1933–48.
Nation Europa, I–VII, 1951–58.
Nová mysl, VIII–XVI, 1954–62.
Osteuropa, I–XII, 1951–62.
Příspěvky k dějinám KSČ, 1957–62.
Revue d'histoire de la deuxième guerre mondiale, I–XIII, 1950–63.
Svědectví, I–V, 1957–62.
Statistický obzor, X–XXXX, 1930–60.
Statistický zpravodaj, VIII–XII, 1945–49.
Sudeten Bulletin, I–IX, 1951–62.
Sudetendeutscher Artikeldienst, I–VII, 1951–58.
Sudetendeutsche Monatshefte, 1943–44.
Tribuna, I–XII, 1948–60.
Válka a revoluce, I–II, 1947–48.
Vierteljahrshefte für Zeitgeschichte, I–X, 1953–62.
Volk und Reich, XVI–XIX, 1940–44.
Wirtschaft und Statistik, II, IV, 1950, 1952.
Zahraniční politika, 1934–37.
Zeitschrift für Ostforschung, I–XI, 1951–62.

Other Sources

Interview with Dr. Walter Brand, former member of the central political committee of the Sudeten German Party, June 10, 1963.

Interview with Gen. František Dastich, former head of the 7th Section of the Czechoslovak General Staff, June 14, 1956.

Interview with Gen. Antonín Hasal, former Czechoslovak minister, May 1, 1958.

Interview with Arnošt Heidrich, former secretary general of the Czechoslovak Ministry of Foreign Affairs, June 26, 1956.

Interview with Col. Ferdinand Monzer, successor of General Dastich as head of the 7th Section, Dec. 20, 1952.

Interview with Dr. Hans Neuwirth, former member of the central political committee of the Sudeten German Party, June 14, 1963.

Interview with Blažej Vilím, former secretary general of the Czechoslovak Social Democratic Party, Sept. 13, 1958.

Interview with Dr. Petr Zenkl, former deputy premier of the Czechoslovak cabinet, April, 28, 1958.

Letter to author from Dr. Walter Brand, former member of the central political committee of the Sudeten German Party, July 31, 1963.

Letters to author from Gen. František Dastich, June 14 and Aug. 4, 1952.

Letter to author from Herman Kahn, director of Franklin D. Roosevelt Library at Hyde Park, New York, Feb. 10, 1958.

Letter to author from Prof. Vladimír Krajina, former member of the ÚVOD and former secretary general of the Czech Socialist Party, May 26, 1958.

Letter to author from G. Bernard Noble, chief of the Historical Division of the U. S. Department of State, March 27, 1958.

Letter to author from Dr. František Ševčík, former delegate of the Czechoslovak Foreign Ministry for the transfer, Nov. 25, 1956.

Letter to author from Prof. Eduard Táborský, former secretary to President Eduard Beneš, Jan. 13, 1958.

INDEX

Abwehr, 216, 217 n.
Abyssinia, 85
Accident Insurance Institute, 201
Activists and activism, 39, 96, 115, 318
Adalbert Stifter Association, 310 n.
Adolf, Bernard, 196 n.
Agrarian Party (BdL), 12, 37 n., 38, 73, 75, 76, 80, 81, 96 n., 111, 115, 119 n., 154, 165, 276 n.
Aircraft industry, Czech, 196 n.
Allied Control Council, 278, 279, 280, 283, 286, 288 n.
Allied High Commission, 306
Altenburg, Günther, 99–100
American Army, 258, 259 n., 268, 273, 276
American Zone of occupation, 283, 284, 285, 287, 289, 304, 305, 307
Amman, 92
Anschluss, 112, 113, 126
Anti-Czech ideology, 48, 49, 59, 79, 95, 116, 130, 142, 159–60, 175
Anti-Jewish ideology, 48, 71 n., 76, 87, 95, 130, 142, 159, 171, 172 n., 173, 175, 195, 209, 290 n., 297–99
Antonov, General, 259 n.
Arbeitsblock (Working Bloc), 37
Armament industry, Czech, 88 n.
Aryanization, 195
Aš, 144, 154, 230
Ashton-Gwatkin, F., 135 n., 136 n.
Assembly camps, 275 n., 282, 289
Association for the Protection of Sudeten German Interests (AG), 263, 308–09

Association of Sudeten German Educators, 310 n.
Atlantic Charter, 231
Attlee, Clement, 247 n.
Auersperg, Pavel, 85 n.
Aufbau und Frieden, 302
Aufbruch Circle, 98, 308
Auslandsorganisation (AO), 102 n.
Austria, 158, 198, 294, 296, 313; annexation of, 106, 110, 111, 112, 126, 128
Austria-Hungary, 24, 29, 317
Avenol, Joseph, 183

Badeni, Count Kasimir Felix, 24
Balfour, Arthur, 247 n.
Banking system, Czech, 9–10
Bavaria, 127, 158, 306
Becher, Walter, 293, 294, 295, 297, 298, 299, 300, 308
Bechyně, Rudolf, 77 n.
Beck, General, 107 n., 153
Bečko, Ján, 229
Behrends, Hermann, 102 n.
Beneš, Eduard, xvi, xvii, xviii, 26, 27 n., 33 n., 36 n., 78, 82–86, 88, 89–91, 103, 108 n., 112, 120, 124, 133 n., 135, 137, 138–39, 140, 141 n., 145, 146, 149, 151 n., 153, 154, 165, 166, 182, 184, 214, 216, 218–19, 223, 224, 225–29, 230–34, 235–36, 237, 238–46, 248, 254–55, 257, 273–74, 275, 276, 289 n., 290 n., 310, 319
Beneš, Vojta, 3 n.

DUE

PRINTED IN U.S.A.